THE COMPLETE GUIDE TO
GAME CARE
& COOKERY

3rd Edition

by
Sam & Nancy Fadala

DBI BOOKS, INC.

Editorial Staff

Editors
John L. Duoba
Jamie L. Puffpaff

Production Manager
John L. Duoba

Editorial/Production Assistant
Holly J. Porter

Assistant to the Editors
Katherine B. Roane

Electronic Publishing Manager
Nancy J. Mellem

Electronic Publishing Associate
Robert M. Fuentes

Electronic Publishing Assistant
Edward B. Hartigan

Cover Photography
John Hanusin

Managing Editor
Pamela J. Johnson

Publisher
Sheldon L. Factor

ISBN 0-87349-155-6   **Library of Congress Catalog Card #81-68258**

Table of Contents

Table of Contents

Preface

WARNING: Hunting is a serious activity that requires concentration and common sense. Anything that cuts or shoots can inflict damage on its user. Follow the Ten Commandments of Arms Safety as outlined by the National Rifle Association. Use all cutting instruments with great care, especially when field-dressing a big game animal with a sharp knife. Cut away from your body at all times, and be especially watchful of your partner, who may be in line should your knife slip. A deep cut is extremely serious, that seriousness escalated when the injured person is far away from medical attention, as big game hunters usually are. Stop and think. Before handling gun, bow or knife, remember the rules of safety and follow them. Also, if tackling high elevations or any physically demanding outing, have a physical beforehand. Do not exert yourself to the point of exhaustion or hunt in unfamiliar country without a map, compass or a global positioning device. Know your First Aid. Take a class, or at least check out a video on First Aid methods. Statistically, hunting and the use of knives are safe. However, this fact is of no comfort to the person who gets hurt. Don't get hurt or harm anyone else. Know and follow the rules of safety.

The Third Edition of *Complete Guide to Game Care and Cookery* is newly designed and written to make the book easier to use. Game care techniques are in the first several chapters of the book, with recipes gathered under one canopy in the latter portion of the text. The separation of game care and cookery into two distinct sections facilitates recipe location, while paying special tribute to important game care tips. The goal of this book is wise, prudent, and economical use of game meat through proper field care and excellent recipes.

What is a good hunter? Many things. He's a true outdoorsman, knowing the ways of the wild. He enjoys the total experience. He loves animals, from hunting dogs to the buck that broke cover and got away. Just being there is fantastic, but it's not enough. The real hunter is a harvester. He takes part in cropping a renewable resource. He loves hunting for its own sake, but he likes to put game on the table, too. After all, that's why hunting licenses and tags are issued: for an opportunity to leave the field with edibles. Today's game laws reflect the modern hunter's attitude—wise use. After all, the rules were made by hunters for hunters to guarantee the continuation of all species.

Some hunters believe the apex of an outing is stalking a harvestable animal, taking aim on it, then backing off without firing a shot. That sounds sporting, but to those elitists I say, "Buy a camera and take photographs." I have found no way to cook film or memories, so I hunt for meat. You can, too—in good conscience. Rabbits, for example, live a year or two at best. They are a "replacement species," cycling up and down. Hunted or not, rabbits continue to cycle. Deer and other big game are no different. The mature buck or bull a hunter passes up will not be there several years later just because it wasn't tagged. The most important aspect of game welfare is habitat, not the reduction of hunting.

Overhunting is wrong, but a hunter should never be ashamed of harvesting an animal or bird taken fairly and lawfully. But every hunter who takes game is obligated to get it from field to table with the best care and cooking. That's why this book was written, to help hunters do that. Hunting is an honorable adventure: exciting, enjoyable, healthful, relaxing, rewarding in many ways. But it's also an obligation to use what is harvested.

Game care means wise field tactics: Dressing and transporting the edible portion of the harvest from the outdoors to the dinner table.

This book is dedicated to shortcut gourmet cooking. If the dish tastes like it took an afternoon to prepare, but the chef "slaved" behind a hot stove for a fraction of that time, the goal is realized. The First Edition contained many tested recipes; the Second Edition offered the reader more of the same; this Third Edition is even more replete with top-notch recipes.

"This doesn't taste like my venison," a staunch woodsman remarked at a special game dinner one evening. "I want my venison to taste wild, as it should."

"Yes, so nobody but you will eat it," his wife replied. Is it right to disguise wild game as something else? Absolutely! But don't think of it as a disguise. Think of it as familiar-tasting meat that people enjoy. In many instances, wisely prepared game tastes even better than the same dish with domestic meat. The recipes in this book were tested by a multitude of eaters before earning inclusion.

Each chapter of the Third Edition is designed to help an outdoorsman become self-sufficient in the wise use of wild meat. But a great many people won't eat wild meat. Why not? Here are five reasons.

First, everyone in the world harbors food prejudice. It's a matter of culture and family upbringing. I'm prejudiced, and so are you. You won't get me to happily pop a grub into my mouth, although I ate caterpillars in Africa just to say I did it. And it may come as a surprise, but an African Bushman might turn his nose up at your favorite meal. A general movement to packaged food has escalated prejudice against wild game. A thick juicy beefsteak resting in a white styrofoam flat covered with cellophane is far removed from the moo cow that provided that hunk of meat. It's understandable that consumers who spend a lifetime eating prepared or packaged food have a naturally difficult time thinking of it as something that used to be alive. By definition, prejudice is without reason. So think it over. If you hunt, discover how you can make harvested game great tasting. Overcome your own prejudices.

A second reason for disliking game meat is poor field care. The best beef would taste "gamey," too, if the carcass got a two-day ride on top of a car before it reached the butcher shop.

Third, the finest meat in the world can be ruined—beef, lamb, pork or venison—through improper cooking. A tender filet can be turned into a piece of shoe leather. An incorrectly spiced dinner can spoil anyone's appetite. Meat, wild or tame, is only as good as the recipe.

Fourth, a great many people won't eat wild meat because they think hunting is wrong. At the same time, these folks will consume a slice of bologna made from various meats that once roamed on the hoof, or eat an apple without thinking about where the apple came from, a piece of earth that used to be habitat for wild animals. Anti-hunting is another form of prejudice. However, a significant number of *non-hunters* condone hunting for food.

A fifth reason many people don't like wild meat is the fact that they have never tried any. They just don't like it anyway.

Of the five reasons, numbers two and three are valid. No one should be asked to enjoy wild meat badly handled in the field or ill-cooked in the kitchen.

Enjoy your wild harvest. Game is good food, when it's handled and cooked the right way.

Man has always been a hunter, as this Siggy Fuchta sculpture displays with a Native American and his bow, not in warfare, but in the field procuring food.

Chapter 1...

Hunting for Food
Game Care & Cookery

IN SEPTEMBER of 1991 the most important find in recent archaeology was made by two mountain climbers in the Italian Alps. They found a body frozen in the ice of a glacier. Another hapless mountain climber, authorities assumed, but soon that theory was shattered. Thought to be 2,000 years old, the Iceman, as he was called, turned out to be over 5,000 years old, a traveler who lived before Columbus landed on the shores of America, before Christ preached to the multitudes, before Plato or Socrates taught in Greece.

Experts speculated on what brought this man to the high regions of the mountains. Was he a sheepherder or shaman? Found with him but ignored by the experts were the tools alongside his body—an axe with a copper head, an ash-handled flint knife, a grass cape, head covering, footgear, and most interesting of all to a great many of us, a bow made of yew, a wood still used today by bowyers who build selfbows (bows made of a single material). Again the experts leapt at a conclusion, stating the bow was unfinished, because it had no nocks or grooves for stringing. However, bows can be designed for stringing without nocks or grooves, so we cannot be certain of the bow's status.

The Iceman carried arrows in a quiver. His equipment was nearly identical in principle to the tackle used by modern bowhunters, especially current archery traditionalists. Fourteen arrows were found with the Iceman, only two completed. The shafts were made of dogwood and laburnum, and fletched with feathers. The Iceman understood arrow stabilization, for the feathers of his arrows were offset to promote a spiral effect in flight. His arrows were tipped with efficient stone heads—flint and obsidian can be sharper than a modern razor blade. The man from prehistory was, of course, a hunter.

Man has hunted for eons, as evidenced by the bones of mastodons found with embedded spear points. Man is now, and probably always was, omnivorous, eating both plant life and meat. He has always sought protein for his diet. Tons of wild meat are brought to the table annually from five categories of wild game: small game, big game, upland birds, waterfowl, and exotics. Dividing edible wildlife into these categories gives the outdoorsman an opportunity to see what is available when he hunts for food. No attempt is made to include all edibles in the listing, because that would fill a large portion of this book. But here is a look at some of the renewable resource that can be harvested.

Small Game

The number one small game animal is the rabbit with the tree squirrel number two in popularity. Hares, represented by snowshoes and jackrabbits, are also edible, but jackrabbits are usually labeled non-game. Where I live, jacks are classified as predators, due to the damage they wreak upon the habitat, while snowshoes are small game animals. Categorizing edible wildlife is important for game laws, but state game departments do not always agree in which category an animal belongs. For example, the fox is a small game animal in one state, but a furbearer in another. For this book, only rabbits, hares, and tree squirrels are small game.

The Cottontail Rabbit

"Rabbit" loosely refers to both cottontails and hares, but the two differ. Cottontails are altricial; they are born blind, naked, and helpless, usually in a fur-lined den. Hares are precocious. They're often born above ground, furred, with eyes open, nearly ready to run. All cottontails are of the genus *Sylvilagus*, but there are eight major species. Just as an example of how different cottontail species can inhabit one state, four thrive where I hunt: the desert cottontail, most common, found among shrubs and rocky outcroppings; Nuttall's cottontail, smaller than his desert cousin, living in aspens, juniper and foothill shrub communities at higher elevations; the eastern cottontail, located only in the southeast corner of my state; and the pygmy rabbit, smallest of the four, living only in the southwest corner of Wyoming among dense sagebrush stands.

Rabbits live in all 50 states and Canada, surviving in many different ecological niches. Georgia, for example, has a marsh rabbit, sometimes called a pontoon. Swimming is very much a part of this cottontail's life. Meanwhile, the little cottontail of the Sonoran desert may seldom get rained on, let alone swim. How many cottontails are there in North America? Nobody really knows. Michigan alone has an estimated 34,000 in the upper northern third of the state, another 600,000 centrally, and as many as 1,600,000 in the southern third. It's

The cottontail rabbit is number one in the land, the most popular small game animal of all. This short-lived mammal provides tons of delicious food annually to thousands of hunters.

Although there are far fewer antelope than deer in America, the pronghorn provides hunters with excellent food in several western states.

Bowhunters enjoy numerous hours afield every year. Their success rate is relatively low; however, the bow and arrow accounts for considerable edible game on American and Canadian tables every year.

The tree squirrel is the number two small game animal in North America. These were taken along creekbottom country, where badlands and brushy waterways meet. As with all game, the secret to taste is in the care and cooking. These squirrels will be delicious, because they're going to receive both good field care, and good cooking.

Food is in the eye of the beholder. Food prejudice decides for all of us what is good to eat, and what is not. Bear meat is good food, if you know how to cook the meat.

easy to see why cottontails are number one, and why seasons are long with generous bag limits.

The Tree Squirrel

The six different types of tree squirrels include the red squirrel of spruce and pine habitat. The red squirrel is the smallest of the clan. He lives mostly in coniferous forestlands. Chickarees, also called Douglas squirrels, like tall pines and spruce trees. They inhabit the Northwest off the coast. Gray squirrels make a home in both the East and far West in two varieties. The Western gray is bigger than the Eastern gray. Tassle-eared squirrels, or Abert's, are larger than grays. They live in pine forests, especially in the Southwest, and are especially prominent in forests above the Grand Canyon of Arizona. Fox squirrels are larger yet. They call eastern America home and can grow to a couple feet in total length. Finally, there are flying squirrels, living in parts of northern and eastern North America. These six varieties are all tree dwellers, as opposed to ground squirrels. Ground squirrels are not normally considered tablefare, although they are edible in a pinch. Chipmunks are non-game species.

Hares

The varying hare or "snowshoe rabbit," as it is popularly called, is scientifically *Lepus americanus*. He belongs to a special order known as *Lagomorpha*, and is therefore not considered a rodent. Rodents have only two incisor teeth. Hares have four. Also, the snowshoe has a "hare-lip," split longitudinally. Snowshoes are found over forested Canada, the New England states, New York, Pennsylvania, Tennessee, Michigan, into North Dakota, Idaho, Wyoming, Colorado, and so forth. The jackrabbit is also a hare, though generally not considered small game, as the snowshoe is. Jacks live over much of the West. Young ones are edible. While snowshoes love timberlands, jacks are often found in Sahara-like territory, as well as badlands.

Big Game

The white-tailed deer is number one in the land among edible big game species. Mule deer are also highly popular, as are blacktails in their

more limited ranges of Alaska, California, Washington, and the Oregon Coast. Elk supply thousands of pounds of meat each year for game consumers. Black bear are also palatable big game. Although considered inedible by many hunters, blackies are good food. Grizzly and polar bears were standard fare for American natives, but today are hunted on a very limited basis. Moose are an extremely important protein source in specific niches, especially Alaska and Canada. The pronghorn antelope supplies tons of good meat year in and year out. Javelina are "little pigs" that live in the Southwest. They are not important on a large scale, but they do supply meat for Texas, Arizona, and New Mexico hunters.

Bighorn sheep and Rocky Mountain goats are on the big game list, but receive scant attention in our book because they are hunted only by special permit. Even in Canada and Alaska, these animals do not represent nearly the harvest that other big game animals provide. However, many recipes good for venison also work for sheep, while slow-cooking roasts are useful for the oftentimes less than delectable mountain

Those fortunate enough to have moose on their menu enjoy one fine-tasting wild meat. And when you get one, there's plenty of him, too.

Food from the sky, waterfowl provide some of the finest eating of all. A Christmas goose is especially delicious, and it doesn't have to be Christmas to enjoy it.

goat. There are also a number of foreign species huntable in the United States. Some of these, such as the Barbary sheep, are established in the wild. Others are confined to game farms. Most foreign species can be field-handled and cooked like similar species of American big game.

Wild boar are also fantastic big game animals worthy of the table, and their range is increasing steadily. Caribou are not hunted over much of North America, but where they are, they often constitute an important big game meat source. Then we have bison, the largest four-footed wild animal on the continent. Bison, or "buffalo," are not harvested widely, but there are a few wild herds that receive some attention, and private herds must also be cropped to keep numbers stable. Wild goats (not the Rocky Mountain goat, but the type that live in Hawaii and California) are also good food, but as with many other species, these animals are not widespread, and therefore do not have recipes in our book. Many venison recipes, however, do serve for wild goat.

Nicole Fadala with her first wild turkey. She helped cook it, too. Young hunters should be taught that hunting is more than a great outdoor experience; it's also a way to obtain some great food.

Upland Birds

Although considered big game by law in many regions, the wild turkey is the largest of the upland game birds and is an important and wide-spread meat source. Dove and quail are extremely important, too, as are pheasants, one of the most harvested birds in North America. Grouse of all kinds, as well as partridges, make dishes fit for kings, while ptarmigan are less known, but only because of smaller distribution. The woodcock is another upland bird worth consideration on the table. Wild pigeons are another huntable upland bird, as are rails.

Waterfowl

Edible waterfowl include ducks and geese. Ducks have fared poorly over the past decade, especially with reference to wetland nesting grounds and, in short, a place to breed. Geese are doing great. There are reportedly forty-three different species of ducks, and fifteen of geese. For our purposes—waterfowl for food—these different species are hunted in strict accord with the law, which varies from locale to locale. Each hunter must know what waterfowl he can hunt, and how to identify individual types. Some waterfowl hunting is very limited. For example, sandhill cranes are huntable, but only in very specific zones, with special permits required.

The whitetail deer is the number one big game animal in North America. While there is nothing wrong with hunting deer for their great trophy status, the meat is delicous.

Gathered around for a meal in the outdoors, friends share a bounty from the land—wild game, well-prepared.

Exotics

Perhaps this is a misnomer, but the title serves as a heading for a number of animals not normally used for food, yet each is a good source of protein. The rattlesnake comes to mind immediately. Porcupines fit the exotic list, too. So do bullfrogs, prairie dogs, turtles, woodchucks, rockchucks, beaver, mountain lion, and muskrat. Limited recipes are offered for exotics because they are, by comparison with small game, big game, upland bird, and waterfowl species, taken less frequently by fewer hunters. Opossum and raccoon are two more animals that probably fit best in the exotic lineup, although both are quite common in specific regions, and both can be turned into good food. Attitude always plays a tremendous role in hunting for food. An armadillo is a pest to some, food to others. While coyotes and foxes are not listed as food, not even in this text, you can bet these canines fed people in the past. They are edible protein, although out of vogue as tablefare. Then there's the bobcat and lynx. I tried bobcat meat on two occasions, and while mountain lion proved a taste treat I'll never forget, bobcat did not tickle my palate.

How Many Can We Take?

Bag limit laws were created many years ago, the concept spearheaded by hunters who realized wildlife is a crop, and as a crop, you take some, but not too many. For example, in many regions, one deer per year is the rule, although deer are in such great numbers in other regions hunters may take several annually. In Alabama, it is legal to harvest a number of deer per hunter each year. Bag limits vary season to season. For example, following a particularly hard winter, numbers of permits may be curtailed significantly. This condition existed in 1994 in Wyoming, for example, when antelope permits were cut dramatically following two hard winters.

As a crop, wild animals and birds are a renewable resource. Some species, like antelope, can double or triple their numbers in only one or two breeding seasons. Antelope does normally have two young, one male, one female. So a buck and doe can become four after one breeding season considering two fawns born to the female. Cottontail rabbits have an amazing potential to multiply. One pair can produce four young per litter, four times a year. That's sixteen young, plus the parents, totaling eighteen rabbits. In the second year, theorizing that of the eighteen nine are males and nine are females, and they all breed, the potential number of cottontails is 162. In only six years, the original grandpa and grandma rabbits could potentially have over a million grandkids. Of course, no such thing happens.

Consider antelope. In many areas, coyotes make great inroads on fawn numbers. On the Anderson Mesa of Arizona a study revealed extremely heavy fawn loss to coyotes. A baby antelope is no match for a "prairie wolf." Golden eagles take a toll, too, and harsh winters can reduce herd numbers faster than all the predators in the area put together. Our fast-breeding cottontails also lose most of their numbers annually to predators and the environment. Nonetheless, deer, antelope, rabbits, elk—all game has the potential to increase numbers every year. That's why man, the hunter, can take an annual harvest. But, as noted, that harvest must be in accord with game law limitations. Wildlife biologists must also consider habitat as a key to species continuance. Millions of acres of wildlife habitat have become farmlands for vegetables and fruit, as well as wheat and other crops. Development also takes up wildlife habitat. All the same, we have managed to preserve a great deal of habitat in North America with an abundance of wildlife that can be hunted annually.

Some areas are actually underharvested. Texas wildlife expert Mike Reagan of the Texas Parks and Wildlife Department pointed

Hunting is much more than filling the freezer with meat. It's often a challenge in itself, requiring a multitude of skills and many aspects of knowledge. Striking out into roadless areas like this one calls upon some of those skills and pieces of knowlege.

What About Trophy Hunting?

This book is dedicated to eating the good game meat provided by gun and bow. Is trophy hunting compatible with that concept? In fact, yes. Trophy hunting is worthwhile because in order for an animal to gain trophy status, it must have the proper genetics, plus four things: enough food, sufficient water, reasonable cover, and maturity. Starve an animal, deny it water or cover, and it fails. At the same time, if an animal carries poor genetics, it's highly unlikely that any amount of food, water, or cover conditions will cause it to grow huge. Do not believe the rhetoric about two-year old bucks and bulls with immense antlers. It's highly unlikely.

Hunting is much more than shooting game with gun or bow. It's learning the ways of the wild. In the off-season, scouting treks provide long healthy walks, plus a great opportunity to learn more about wildlife and the outdoors.

out back in 1985 that although the state showed a harvest of 373,000 deer a year, 500,000 was a more reasonable goal considering overall herd numbers. That harvest number was reached in the 1987-1988 season with 504,953 deer tagged in Texas. Other states also have excellent deer numbers. Pennsylvania boasts a million whitetails. Deer harvests have improved in recent times in that state, because herd sizes have escalated. Only 1300 Pennsylvania whitetails were taken in 1915. By 1950, about 23,000 were tagged. That number reached 45,000 in 1955, 65,000 in 1965, 72,000 in 1975, and over 75,000 in 1985.

A healthy deer herd can be cropped by about 40 percent annually without the herd falling in overall numbers, because a doe can drop one, and often two or more fawns per season. But this does not mean hunters can take 40 percent of a deer herd every year, because wild animals cycle within the laws of nature. The so-called balance of nature is a myth. This "balance" is not a straight line, where numbers remain constant. Hunted or not, animal numbers rise and fall. The cycle of the rabbit is a perfect example. In some seasons there is hardly a cottontail to be found, where earlier the area was loaded with bunnies. Where did they go? Not to hunters. The rabbits cycled, as they have for centuries. Mule deer are down in numbers "out West" currently, but elk numbers are up. The norm for nature is a jagged line of peaks and valleys.

This is why we need wildlife biologists to tell us what we can hunt, when we can hunt, and how many we can take of any wildlife species. That is what game laws and bag limits are all about. Bag limit rules are made so that wildlife is neither overhunted nor underharvested. It's impossible for game departments to hit it exactly right every time, but setting prudent seasons and limits is their goal, and overall they do a good job of achieving that goal.

Having aged dozens of big bucks and bulls over the years, all but a rare few were fully mature animals. So there is nothing wrong with trophy hunting. But at the same time, the trophy hunter should maintain the proper perspective. No matter how much the antlers or horns score, the carcass remains highly valuable and of primary importance. It is wrong to do anything less than take excellent care of the meat in the field, followed by careful packaging and good cooking at home.

We no longer hunt for survival, but that does not mean wild meat is unimportant in modern times. The exact dollar figure in consumed wild protein is impossible to calculate, but it begins with a "b" for billions. A significant amount of wild meat can be brought home every year, legally, prudently, and with no damage to the resource. All over America, edible game in huntable numbers thrives, some of it not far from big cities. Putting this good food on your table is a matter of finding out what you have to hunt in your region, where it lives, and how you can gain legal access to the habitat. You must also know seasons and bag limits. You have to buy the correct hunting licenses and tags, as well. And you will need the right equipment for the harvest, not only for securing the game, but for taking care of it. Finally, you'll have to nurture a desire to take good care of what you harvest from the moment it comes into your possession until you cook and serve it to your family and friends. That's what modern hunting is all about.

MY MATERNAL GRANDFATHER ate six eggs every day, rain or shine. He consumed them soft boiled, sometimes fried. An Old Country gentleman, his theory was "Eggs, they are good for you because they gotta lot of the sulfur in them." I didn't buy Grandpa's sulfur theory then, nor do I now. But if the eggs harmed the fellow, we should all be so lucky. He retired at sixty-five, got bored, went back to work full-time for ten more years, retired, was bored again, and put in another five-plus years part-time. But cholesterol finally got him. At ninety, he went to sleep and didn't wake up.

Our family, and a number of friends, knew about Grandpa's egg routine. We told him it was terrible. But a lesson came out of it. Genetics. The old man simply didn't have a problem with high-cholesterol foods. I have a friend who is, on the other hand, bothered by them. They cause plaque build-up in his blood vessels. I think consuming any single food in excess is unwise. Conversely, eating grains, vegetables, fruit, fish and meat, with a semblance of balance, is probably good for us—proof lacking. Also, from what we know today, it's smart to watch fat intake. A lot of saturated (animal) fat is considered dangerous to our health.

Game meat is lean. Yes, a fall buck or bull can be loaded with thick layers of fat under its hide—subcutaneous fat—but this can be literally stripped away and discarded. Game meat, all in all, is not marbled. High quantities of fat are not found laced within the muscle tissue. If avoiding fat is smart, then eating game meat is good for us because it is lean. Currently, it's socially correct to avoid red meat. Of course, not one of a thousand persons really worries about it, but it

Chapter 2...
Wild Game Is Nutritious Food
Game Care & Cookery

sounds good, so people talk about eating fish and avocado dip, while preaching against a hunk of red meat broiling on the coals.

But meat does not carry a lot of saturated fat just because it's red. Lean red meat is good food, and game is lean. Therefore, game is good food. If I'm slightly suspicious of "tests" showing red meat, across the board, bringing on heart attacks, then I must also cast a suspicious eye on tests concluding the opposite—that lean red meat helps to prevent heart attacks. I don't know if it does or not. I do know that dairy products are accused of containing more "bad cholesterol" than the fattiest hunk of beef in Christiandom. I have friends who won't go near red meat these days, but who eat enough palm oil, coconut oil and saturated fats to float the battleship *Bismarck*. They bought into the rhetoric without studying the facts.

Kathy Etling, in her always excellent writing style, penned a piece called "The Wild Diet," *Outdoor Life*, August, 1992, issue. Packed into a small space, Etling provided a multitude of facts pertaining to wild meat and its value as human food. Her research included conclusions from Professor Marty Marchello of North Dakota State University. Marchello, professor of range and animal sciences, has studied the nutritional value of meats for several years and to great depth. His work with antelope and deer meat has been particularly valuable, with some of his conclusions to follow.

All the evidence shows people have been eating red meat from the days of the Ice Man and long before. Scientists analyzing ancient human bone find about a third of early man's diet consisted of meat.

Venison steak, fast fried in minimal hot fat, provides a meal of lean meat, along with superb taste.

Just being there is great—in the outdoors. Cooking a fine meal outdoors is an additional treat, especially if part of it consists of good game meat.

Plants made up the rest of his food intake. At this point, it doesn't really matter what the Ice Man and his amigos ate. What matters is that we, especially as Americans and Canadians, put an awful lot of refined foods into our systems: tons of sugar and plenty of grease. As one of my friends says, "I believe in the four basic food groups: salt, sugar, grease and beer."

Maybe our ancestors could get away with eating more "bad stuff" than we can because they were more physically active than we are. Machines do a lot of our work. We are transported all over town with our backsides planted on a car seat instead of walking. Plus, our food may be more fun to eat than ever before, but as noted above, it's also loaded with fat and sugar. As for salt, the latest documentation following a long study shows salt does not harden anybody's arteries and never did, although overdoing salt is no doubt unwise all the same, based on the theory that overdoing anything we consume isn't smart.

The latest information from the medical community, as this is written, states that eating red meat is OK. The cholesterol level in red meat is not considered the problem. But researchers do believe that animal fat, in and of itself, is a problem. So lean red meat, in sensible amounts, is no longer considered dangerous to our health. Wild meat is roughly seven times less fatty than a nice hunk of marbled (U.S.D.A. Choice) beef. Even the American Heart Association has gone on record in favor of wild meat as part of a healthy diet.

Oddly enough, wild meat is generally higher in cholesterol than beef. That's due, Professor Marchello points out, to the anatomical makeup of game meat. All meat is composed of what are called red

13

Wild meat is lean. These tree squirrels demonstrate that fact very well.

Game meat is good food, and that means wild turkeys like this one as well as four-footed fare. Taken with a recurve bow, this bird will provide a memorable feast for hunter and family.

NUTRIENT CONTENT: TALE OF THE TAPE

Species	Protein %	Fat %	Cholesterol (mg/100g*)	Calories (Kcal/100g*)
Beef (USDA Choice)	22.0	6.5	72	180
Beef (USDA Standard)	22.7	2.0	69	152
Lamb	20.8	5.7	66	167
Pork	22.3	4.9	71	165
Wild Boar**	28.3	4.38	109	160
Buffalo	21.7	1.9	62	138
Whitetail Deer	23.6	1.4	116	149
Mule Deer	23.7	1.3	107	145
Elk	22.8	.9	67	137
Moose	22.1	.5	71	130
Antelope	22.5	.9	112	144
Squirrel	21.4	3.2	83	149
Cottontail	21.8	2.4	77	144
Jackrabbit	21.9	2.4	131	153
Chicken	23.6	.7	62	135
Turkey (Domestic)	23.5	1.5	60	146
Wild Turkey	25.7	1.1	55	163
Pheasant (Domestic)	23.9	.8	71	144
Wild Pheasant	25.7	.6	52	148
Gray Partridge	25.6	.7	85	151
Sharptail Grouse	23.8	.7	105	142
Sage Grouse	23.7	1.1	101	140
Dove	22.9	1.8	94	145
Sandhill Crane	21.7	2.4	123	153
Snow Goose	22.7	3.6	142	121
Duck (Domestic)**	19.9	4.25	89	180
Mallard	23.1	2.0	140	152
Widgeon	22.6	2.1	131	153

*100 grams equals about 3½ ounces. **Not trimmed of fat before analysis. In the above chart, all visible fat was trimmed before analysis. However, surveys show that carcasses of domesticated animals have 25 to 30 percent fat while the average fat content of wild game animals is only 4.3 percent. Not only is the quantity of fat lower in game, but the quality is also healthier. Fat from wild game contains a much higher proportion of polyunsaturated fatty acids—good fat—and is lower in saturated fat—bad fat. Source: North Dakota State University

and white muscle fiber. Wild animal red muscle fibers are dense. Cholesterol is found in red muscle fiber more than white. Therefore, wild meat shows up higher in cholesterol content than domestic meat. Sounds bad, but it's not, due to a little gem called EPA (eicosapentaenoic acid) which lowers blood cholesterol. Wild meat has a lot more EPA than domestic meat. This is not a diatribe against beef. I eat beef because I like it. Leaner cuts are probably the intelligent choice, and many ranchers are now working to raise cattle that lean toward lean. But wild meat is also excellent. Cottontail rabbit, for example, contains 25.4 percent polyunsaturated fatty acids, which are known to *lower* blood cholesterol. Other game meats with high polyunsaturated fatty acid content include antelope at 31.6 percent, squirrel at 37.6 percent, and moose at a surprising 39.1 percent.

Then there is the calorie question. Game meats are generally lower in calories than domestic meats. One study shows whitetailed deer meat at 149 calories per 100 grams, while U.S.D.A. Choice beef has 180 calories per 100 grams. In all fairness, we must point out that the "new beef," raised to be leaner, has 152 calories of fat per 100 grams (see the nearby charts). I think more important than calorie content is the fact that wild meat contains a multitude of important vitamins such as iron, which humans absorb into the system more readily from

Game provides a renewable resource. A mature whitetail buck will survive only so many winters, and then he'll fall. An attrition rate of about 40 percent of the herd annually will not deplete the overall population. Taken with one of Fadala's favorite bows, a custom Herb Meland Pronghorn longbow, this buck, though small of rack, proved to be several years old. Its meat was delicious. Venison can be cooked in a multitude of ways, and this one was.

GOOD FAT, BAD FAT

Species	Saturated	—%Fatty Acids— Monounsaturated	Polyunsaturated
Beef	46.3	45.5	8.2
Buffalo	43.2	45.0	11.8
Mule Deer	48.0	31.8	20.2
Whitetail Deer	45.6	30.6	23.9
Elk	48.4	26.6	24.9
Antelope	41.2	27.1	31.6
Moose	36.6	24.3	39.1
Boar	35.7	47.0	17.3
Caribou	46.6	36.4	17.0
Rabbit	39.0	35.6	25.4
Squirrel	15.2	47.2	37.6

Some game meat is higher in dietary cholesterol than domestic meats, but the combination of more lean body tissue, generally fewer calories, less saturated fat and a significantly higher percentage of cholesterol-reducing polyunsaturated fatty acids makes game a heart-healthy choice. Game meat also has a significantly higher content of EPA than domestic meat. EPA is thought to reduce the risk of developing atherosclerosis, one of the major causes of heart attack and stroke. Sources: North Dakota State University and U.S. Department of Agriculture

meat than vegetable matter. What wild meat does not seem to have is equally important—saturated pesticides and herbicides. Domestic animal meats contain a bit more of these because animals raised for food are often fed from crops treated with pesticides and herbicides. Furthermore, wild meat is not treated with growth hormones. In a word, we might say wild meat is "organic."

All of this is very important to those of us who enjoy hunting for meat. It's good to know that what we harvest is healthy food. Furthermore, the very act of taking game includes exercise—sometimes mild, sometimes heavy. Slow pacing in the act of still-hunting provides good, steady exercise, especially in relatively flat terrain. High-altitude mountain hunting can mean rigorous exercise. Some hunting—standing at the edge of a field waiting for doves to fly overhead—offers very little physical exertion, but this type of game-taking is not the rule. Most outings require at least modest hiking. Being outdoors is good for us in its own right, too, and there is no way to measure how healthy a day in the woods really is. Most hunters relax and, in general, feel good when they are "on the trail."

All game is good food. However, some might be harder to prepare than others. Javelina can be delicious, but special field care is paramount to success in the kitchen.

GAME IS GOOD food, so let's partake of the harvest. Required are a hunting license and, if you're hunting big game, many regions also require a big game tag. In some instances, the license and big game tag are one. In spite of negative bombardment from the press, Hollywood, politicians, teachers and members of the public at large, hunting is immensely popular today. Getting a license for small game is not a problem and deer are so abundant that a big game tag for that species is usually assured for general hunts, although deer tags for special seasons may be exceedingly difficult to draw. And draw you must for a lot of big game species. A lottery system is necessary because there are more hunters than resources in certain regions for specific big game animals.

For example, if everyone in Maine or Wyoming wanted a moose—both states have huntable moose populations—within a few years, the resource would be damaged. In Wyoming, in spite of an abundance of antelope, there are no wide open seasons on prong-horns. A drawing is held for all buck tags, with additional non-buck tags available on a first-come/first-served basis. Because hunting is currently so popular, the first step a meat hunter must take is finding out what species of small game, big game, upland birds, waterfowl and exotics are open season in his state, when hunts are held, and what licenses and tags are required. Fortunately, this is a simple matter of contacting the local game and fish department. Licenses and hunting information are also available at many sport shops.

How Much Per Pound?

People talk about elk meat costing $100 per pound. In many instances, it's true: Wild meat can cost a lot. A guided trophy hunt out of state may run into thousands of dollars. On the other hand,

Chapter 3...
Methods for Meat Hunters
Game Care & Cookery

it's possible to secure wild meat at an entirely reasonable cost. Hunt close to home for a bargain. If you plan to go out of state, go with friends and share costs. Four hunters dividing gasoline, lodging and guiding fees drives costs down in a hurry. And remember, wild meat is special. It's good and good for you. It's worth paying for, especially considering the health value that hunting provides in the first place.

Know the Lay of the Land

Know your area. It's paramount to hunting for meat. There are many ways to learn where game lives. One way is searching on your own, but before striking out, buy a land status map if there is any doubt about property ownership. Trespassing is unsportsmanlike, as well as illegal. Trespassing through ignorance is not immoral, but can be a problem all the same. So find out who owns what before crossing that fence. Tell the owner you want to harvest game for the table. Oftentimes, legal entry to private hunting lands is granted gratis. Sometimes a fee is charged. There are also lease lands, where one or more hunters pay for access to a plot of private hunting ground. Maps of land status show public as well as private property. Learn where you can hunt in your region, then study the lay of the land until every hill, valley, waterway and thicket become entirely familiar.

Scouting

The previous sentence also describes scouting: Studying the lay of the land and getting a look at a place first-hand. Scouting is more than

river bottoms, but not in the hills that surround these brushy and treed waterways. Their niche is specific and rather small compared to the entire range of the area.

Habitat is that specific area within the niche that provides life for any given game animal or bird. Water, cover and food are essential elements of a piece of habitat. A hunter needs to study the niche to specifically locate the best habitat for a given species within that territory.

The niche is that one special area that specific game animals call home. These whitetail bucks have a certain area they thrive in. The smart hunter knows where to look for what game because he understands the concept of the niche.

(Left) Scouting is one way to learn an area, and what is in it. Scouting during small game season is one way to go; it allows a hunter an opportunity to go home with good game meat, while learning a habitat.

this, however. On a scouting trip, a hunter learns a great deal about how game lives in a specific locale. He can also test all kinds of gear, from clothing, backpacks, camping outfits, down to guns and archery tackle. When I scout before bow season, I carry the bow I plan to use on big game. If small game and birds are open, I might gather some meat as I scout out big game. If the small game/bird season is closed, I "rove." Roving, also known as stump-shooting, is the process of shooting arrows at inanimate objects, such as pine cones, leaves, sticks on the ground, even tree stumps. It's a way of practicing. I use blunts on my arrows. Blunts do not penetrate stumps, dead tree limbs, old hunks of fallen fenceposts, and other objects that target points deeply stick in, often making them impossible to remove. Scouting pinpoints game populations. How many deer live where you plan to hunt this coming season? Scout to find out.

The Niche

Finding out where to go, in general, is vital. Then the wise hunter learns the niche, that specific habitat enjoyed by game. Animals and birds uniquely live in the land, and good hunters understand how wild animals and birds use this land. Migratory game does not seem to have a niche, and perhaps the term is wrongfully applied to these four-legged or winged creatures. But even the migrating goose follows a pattern. Mule deer and elk may leave the high mountains when winter snows fall, but they don't go to Florida. They stay in some part of their niche. Certain animals are extremely niche-specific. In parts of the West, for example, whitetails live along creek and

Know your area. When you know your area, you know where to look for game.

Networking means cooperation. This camp of hunters is comprised of outfitter, wife, and daughter, plus guides, all working together for hunters.

Still-hunting means covering ground, but with a purpose. Sometimes it is all right to simply hike, too, in order to see a lot of territory.

The Network

We are not alone in finding good game ranges. Every hunter needs a network to help him. Comprised of game department personnel and information officers, the United States Forest Service with its maps and rangers, the Bureau of Land Management (BLM), as well as ranchers, farmers and fellow hunter-friends, hunter networks are more popular than ever. The North American Hunting Club prints a hunter trade section every issue. Hunts are often traded. You hunt antelope with me in Wyoming, and I'll hunt whitetails with you in Alabama. Local networks are even more workable for meat hunters. I may know a great spot for mule deer; you know one for geese. Let's share our knowledge. That's networking.

Hunting Methods

The art of hunting is astonishingly broad in scope. Meat hunters have a special goal: To find and cleanly harvest game for the table, while ruining an absolute minimum of edibles. Also, as alluded to above, it's nice to keep the cost per pound reasonable if you're on a budget, as most of us are. Here is a brief overview of a few hunting methods.

Walk 'em Out

About as basic as dry toast, the walk 'em out method of hunting is how many of us got started. The idea is to cover ground. Mathematically, the more ground covered, the better the odds of running into something. We all use this basic hunting procedure at one time or another throughout our careers. I've hunted mountain grouse and partridges, for example, by simply walking as far as possible through good habitat. Even then, I tried to find watering or dusting sites to help narrow the chase. Power hunting, as it's sometimes called, is a useful means of locating wild animals for the table, but it's not an advanced style.

Still-Hunting

There is a lot more purpose involved in still-hunting, and this does not mean staying still. It means moving quietly, with the direction of the wind coming into the hunter, and in a specific and meaningful direction at all times. It also means noting "field position" carefully, which means maintaining a location in the field where seeing game and getting a shot is always possible. When a hunter jumps game, mammal or bird, and cannot get a shot, he was out of field position. Sometimes this can't be helped, of course. A full treatise on the subject is contained in the old classic book, *The Still-Hunter* by Theodore Strong Van Dyke. First printed in 1882, the book went through numerous editions, plus a 1987 reprint. Copies can still be located through book dealers, local libraries and interlibrary loans.

Still-hunting is a highly involved process that cannot be covered here. Suffice it to say that it is a rewarding and interesting way to put meat on the table. Read what T.S. Van Dyke had to say about the sport. Then, let me add one little tip about still-hunting. Carry wind detection powder every step of the way and use it often. Deer and other big game do not always detect an incoming hunter by scenting the outdoorsman, but when the wind eddies capriciously here and there, or swaps ends like a jackrabbit chased by a coyote, the still-hunter is often whipped. Wind detection powder shows just what the wind is doing—not mere direction, but currents as well. Archery glove powder is excellent for this purpose. A little puff of this white, odorless powder in the air is all it takes to "read" the wind like a novel. Wind detection powder is also useful on ground stands, because a hunter can change locations when he knows his scent is wafting right toward a watched trail.

Using a Deer Creek 36-caliber muzzleloader, Fadala got this wild turkey by waiting for it on stand. When the birds came down mountain via a creek bottom, he was able to mount a stalk in the snow for a close shot.

Sometimes a ground blind is perfect for getting a good close shot. These bucks were lured close with a Burnham Brothers deer call. The caller, concealed by a ground blind, was not seen.

Scouting is half the fun of hunting, because it's an adventure in discovery. Learn a habitat by scouting it. It's a fine method for meat hunters.

The Stand

Stand-hunting has been elevated to an art—and elevated is the right word because tree stands are more popular than ever. At first glance, climbing into a tree stand seems a boring way to harvest game, but it's not. Erect a tree stand just any old place, and you can wait until moss grows on your boots and you won't get a shot at game, while another tree stand placed on the basis of animal behavior within the niche provides its occupant with a look at game every day. Mainly, deer are hunted from tree stands. However, turkeys can also be taken from tree stands as well as elk and other big game in some areas.

Ground stands are also valuable. My own form of ground stand is a portable folding seat with attached packsack. I use it only for bowhunting and have had some good luck waiting in extremely specific locations, wearing camouflage. Also, to keep the animal's nose from detecting my presence, a small plastic spray bottle is put into play. The bottle contains about 80 percent water along with 20 percent lure. A mist of water/lure in the air acts as a cover to confuse incoming game. The ground stand plan is a great way to hunt, especially combined with still-hunting; the still-hunter covers ground, then takes a ground stand for a while in a particularly ideal spot to await the game.

The Drive

In some locales, drives are absolutely the best way to fill a deer tag. Along creek bottoms, and in fields and brushy areas that have well-defined trails, "pushing deer" is a sure-fire way to harvest venison. Drives require careful planning and total knowledge of the landscape. There are "many-drives and mini-drives." The many-drive is where several hunters—three, four or more—push in the direction of one or more waiting hunters. The mini-drive may employ as few as two hunters. While the many-drive is a real push, the mini-drive is different. The moving hunter tries to get deer to sneak away from him, rather than bursting from cover and disappearing in the thicket, or wheeling around and retreating to the rear, where the waiting hunter will never get a chance. It's best to have the waiting hunter with the wind in his face, while the moving hunter allows deer to catch his scent so the deer can sneak off, hopefully right into the partner quietly and secretly located up ahead.

Spot and Stalk

In the West, the spot and stalk method of hunting is highly popular. It's a bit like still-hunting, but generally calls upon a high level of skill with optics. I find the vast majority of my own big game with good optics where I live in the West. Last season, my 10x42 B&L

19

A good method for meathunters is to sweep an area clear of all tracks, going back later to see what came by a specific area. It's one way to find out what game animals are using a specific trail or waterhole.

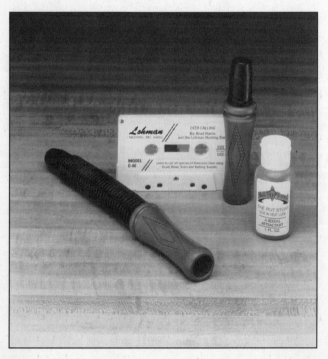

Lohman's Model 3100 is a deer calling kit that includes scent as well as grunt call and doe bleat.

Elites picked up several big game animals, as well as birds and small game. Spot and stalk is just that: Spot with the glass or naked eye, then stalk for a clean shot. Every hunter is obligated to make the perfect, humane shot. The outdoorsman who covets the meat also wants to make the shot that will bring the animal down cleanly and quickly, without undue loss of edibles.

Packing In

I began packing in many years ago. My friend, the late Ted Walter, and I had homemade pack frames of wood and rope that carried water bottles, sleeping bags and tarps that turned into a tent. Our annual treks took us far into the back country. Once we stayed a full month—the longest tour we ever made together. We carried bows and arrows to supply our daily meat and never went hungry. Today's backpack equipment is the best the world has ever seen. A hunter can hike off the main trail, harvest game, large and small, and backpack it out again. And with global positioning units, getting lost is less likely than ever.

Tracking

Tracking on dry ground is for those few blessed with the ability. I watched a tracker in Africa follow a specific game animal across dry ground, and I was amazed. I did not know it could be done and would never have believed the man's skill without seeing it for myself. The rest of us can forget tracking a buck overland on dry ground. But snow tracking is another story. The trick to successful snow tracking is following a snow trail without staying right on it. Dog a deer directly on its back trail and chances are you will never see the animal. The wise snow tracker follows directly only for a short distance, circling ahead to catch sight of the deer.

Calling

Today's calls are nothing short of remarkable. I had a bull elk "in my lap" last season using a call developed by Dr. Ed Sceery. I didn't get a clear view of the bull and did not turn an arrow loose, but that wasn't Dr. Ed's fault. His call brought the bull right in. I also called several antelope bucks in close using a Lohman antelope call. And everyone knows that wild turkeys come when called, if the hunter knows what he's doing. I listened to two lads from the South doing their magic on turkey calls and will never feel good about my own turkey-tooting again. These fellows sounded better than the real thing. They could call a turkey in a rainstorm. Calls are made for everything from dove to deer, moose to quail. Videos and audio tapes showing how to use calls are invaluable and superb teaching devices.

Scents

While I use scents more for cover than luring game in close, by the same token, I would not try to call game without a plastic spray bottle loaded with water/scent to send a mist out now and then between calling. A particularly fine javelina call is made by the Hayden company. I had a couple peccaries coming right to me using that call, but suddenly the bristly pigs beat a hasty retreat. The wind had switched on me. Had I been spraying water/scent in the air, maybe the hogs would have continued to come my way.

Waiting in the right place is sometimes quite effective. Using ears as well as eyes is also a good move for meat hunters. Listening for wild turkeys with the Silencio Super Ear is a good way to pick up sounds the unaided ear cannot detect.

Silencio's Super Ear picks up sounds from the distance, an aid to hunters.

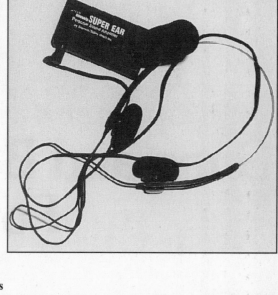

The spot and stalk method remains highly viable, especially in the West. Good binoculars like these Bausch & Lombs are an asset in this type of hunting.

Decoys

One afternoon, I set up a decoy of a bedded doe whitetail. I decided to still-hunt a while, then climb a ridge where I could get a look at my decoy. I reached the ridge in late afternoon, peered down below, but did not immediately spot my decoy. "There it is," I finally said. It was lying on its side. Later, when I reached the decoy, the ground told me what happened. Hoof prints said a deer kicked my decoy. The Feather Light decoy said so, too. It was trampled. A friend uses an antelope decoy, coupled with a call, to bring bucks in close during rut. So decoys represent another way to bag game. Decoys worked for American Natives centuries ago, and they still do.

The serious meat hunter knows his game animals and birds, and the unique traits of each species he hunts. Antelope, for example, tend to lose caution in late afternoon. All antelope all the time? No, but how many times I've gotten close in late afternoon to bucks I could not approach at midday, I cannot recall. Antelope drink water as a habit, often twice daily. So I check waterholes where I hunt to see who has come in for a drink. Pronghorns sometimes have trouble with fences, although they can, and often do, leap tall fences in a single bound, as witnessed by many hunters. However, pronghorns are also likely to follow a sheep fence for a long distance, rather than jumping it. The smart hunter gets ahead and waits for his chance. The meat hunter must decide on where he wants to go for all types of game and how to hunt that game. There are many different species to hunt and numerous ways to hunt them. You don't hunt frogs the same way you hunt deer, so why hunt elk the same way you hunt wild pigs? Know your quarry, and how to specifically hunt that game.

A **HUNTER MUST** decide what tools of the harvest are for him, because there are many. The goal in selecting any one of them, however, is bifold. First, since hunting is a sport, the bow, air rifle or firearm must suit the hunter's sense of sportsmanship. The trend backwards to bows and arrows and blackpowder firearms satisfies that sense of sportsmanship in some outdoorsmen, while others prefer the most modern high-tech harvesting tools available. Second, no matter the choice, the bow or gun must be capable of a clean harvest.

The Air Rifle and Its Ammo

The modern air rifle is no toy. I am most familiar with RWS air rifles because I own that brand, but there are many other good makes on the market. An example of the modern *hunting* air rifle is my own RWS Diana Model 48, side-lever. It shoots a 17-caliber pellet at over 1000 feet per second. Another fine RWS air rifle is the Model 34, also a spring-piston type, requiring but one cocking for full power. The Model 34 in carbine or rifle style, 17- or 22-caliber, is a barrel-break rifle also capable of 1000 fps. The All-Weather version of the Model 34 comes with nickel plating and black epoxy-coated stock. A truly high-tech modern air rifle is the RWS Model 54, which offers 1100 fps pellet velocity with recoilless performance. Opposing pistons offset any jarring effect in this excellent spring-piston air rifle.

Many years ago, I had a Diana 17-caliber precision German air rifle brought back from Berlin after the conflict. With that pellet rifle, I took home cottontail rabbits and bullfrogs, also dispatching other

Chapter 4...

Guns and Bows For Meat Hunters

Game Care & Cookery

small animals with correctly placed, one-pellet head shots. Today's air rifles shoot faster pellets, so they are entirely capable of cleanly harvesting rabbits and squirrels at close range. The shooter who is uncomfortable with iron sights should scope the modern air rifle. A tip: Buy a scope made for spring-piston air rifles. Scopes intended for 22 rimfire rifles may become internally scrambled from the recoil of the spring-piston design. The Model 54, which is recoilless, does not have this problem, of course. There are true airgun scopes available that withstand the recoil of the spring-piston rifle.

Pellets

The 17-caliber pellet is entirely satisfactory for close-range harvesting of rabbits and squirrels with head shots. Caliber 20 is another excellent pellet, offering a little more weight, while the 22-caliber pellet is heavier yet. And there is now a selection of good 25-caliber pellets on the market. My small game hunting with a pellet rifle is limited to rabbits (sometimes tree squirrels) at a normal range of about 20 yards. If I hunt small varmints with a pellet rifle, I still hold to 20 or 25 yards as maximum range. Therefore, the 17-caliber pellet size is my choice. I like the higher velocity and flatter trajectory. Pellet styles are numerous. All are good for small game, but the newer hunting types are the best.

The advantage of the air rifle for small game hunting is extreme quietness. But on the other hand, pellets will ricochet and I treat the modern air rifle just as I treat the 22 rimfire, with a great deal of

The modern air rifle is a viable hunting tool for small game at close range. A high level of accuracy allows for good pellet placement. This brace of cottontails was taken with an RWS scoped 17-caliber air rifle.

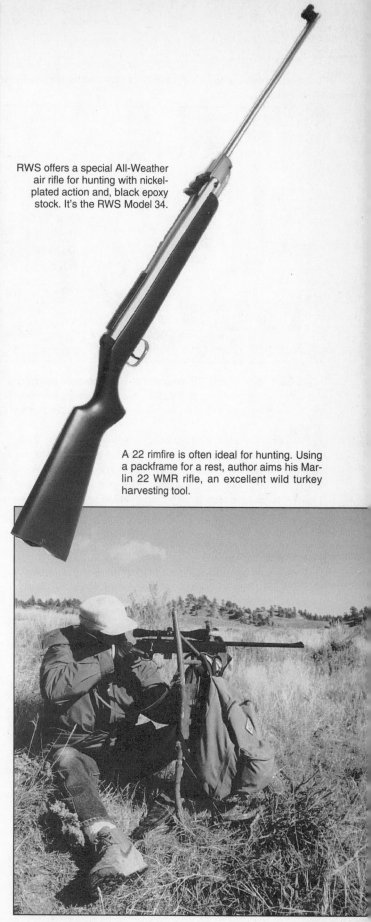

RWS offers a special All-Weather air rifle for hunting with nickel-plated action and, black epoxy stock. It's the RWS Model 34.

A 22 rimfire is often ideal for hunting. Using a packframe for a rest, author aims his Marlin 22 WMR rifle, an excellent wild turkey harvesting tool.

respect. However, the extreme range of the pellet is relatively short, making airguns ideal for farm and ranch small game hunting.

22 Rimfire Rifles

I never met a 22 rimfire rifle I didn't like. For small game, every 22 rimfire style is perfectly fine, from single shot to semi-automatic. Currently, I hunt small game with one of two rimfire rifles: Kimber Model 82 or H&R Targeteer, the latter a bolt-action model from long ago. Both are scoped. Head shots on rabbits and squirrels up to 50 yards, sometimes a bit farther, are no problem with either of these accurate bolt-action repeating rifles.

22 Rimfire Ammo

Short, Long and Long Rifle ammunition work well on small game with head shots. The 22 Short hollowpoint remains a quiet and potent close-range round. The Long, despised by gun writers, but holding its own anyway, functions admirably in rifles that will not handle Shorts, giving Short-plus performance. All Long Rifle rounds are good for small game. I'm partial to target-quality ammo because of its high level of accuracy when head shots only are the rule. Another worthwhile close-range 22 rimfire round is the CB (conical ball). Today, these are available in Longs, which means they run through a cham-

A 22 rimfire rifle firing 22 Short
hollowpoints accounted for these
cottontail rabbits.

Twenty-two rimfire ammunition comes in many brands and loads. Here are just a few.

ber suited to the 22 Long Rifle round. The CB is not very powerful, but with head shots, it is acceptable for close-range small game hunting. One advantage: CB ammo is very quiet, not much louder than an air rifle.

The 22 rimfire rifle is king for small game work. With head shots, meat is obviously safeguarded entirely, yet, the effectiveness of the 22 rimfire on small mammals is superb. In the mountains of the West, the 22 rimfire is also legal and prudent for grouse and partridges. Head shots are again ideal when possible, but low-velocity 22 rimfire ammo does not destroy a grouse or partridge should body shots be taken.

Larger Rimfire Ammo

In days gone by, there were dozens of different rimfire cartridges on the market. *Rimfire Cartridges in the United States and Canada* by John L. Barber lists well over a hundred rimfire rounds. There has been some call for the return of a few of these, especially the 32 rimfire, as well as 25- and 30-caliber rimfires. Why? Because some wild turkey hunters would like to have a rimfire round of modest velocity and minimal meat disruption. The 32 rimfire, for example, with a 90- or 100-grain bullet, would do well on wild turkeys. The return of the larger rimfire round is doubtful, however, because ammo would cost much more than 22 rimfire fodder, and sales would probably be quite low. But it is a round worth noting for its historical significance and meat-hunting efficacy.

22 Rimfire Magnum Rifles and Ammo

All 22 rimfire magnum rifles are excellent, so let's talk about the round. The 22 WMR (Winchester Magnum Rimfire) stands alone in its own little world. There is nothing else like it. Where legal and prudent to shoot full metal jacket ammo, the 22 rimfire magnum is super for mountain birds and small game. It's also a fine wild turkey cartridge, but hollowpoint ammo is preferred on these large avians. The hottest 22 WMR turkey fodder I've tested is from RWS, with a 40-grain softnose hollowpoint bullet at over 2100 fps muzzle velocity. All other hollowpoint ammo is excellent, too. Federal's 50-grain hollowpoint bullet penetrates well on wild turkeys.

Fadala sometimes carries a 22 semi-auto pistol on big game hunts. Here, a cottontail has been taken with a Ruger pistol.

Centerfire Rifle Ammunition

Also in their own small world are the venerable 25-20 Winchester and 32-20 Winchester rounds. Marlin makes a lever-action rifle for both, and several companies offered rifles in the past for these rounds, many of these firearms still functional. The two cartridges make good wild turkey rounds, especially using all-lead bullets at modest velocity, with close-range shooting the rule. They take turkeys positively, but without a lot of meat loss.

Good shots with 243 Winchester, 6mm Remington or other 24-caliber cartridges take deer-sized game neatly and with minimal meat loss. Many different rifles are available.

The 30-30 and 30 Remington are mid-range cartridges. Either takes deer-sized game cleanly. A lever-action 30-30 rifle in the hands of an expert is worthy of any big game. The 35 Remington falls into this class, too, only it's more powerful.

The 30-06, and a bushel of rounds offering similar ballistics such as the 270 Winchester and 280 Remington, are highly regarded in the U.S.A. Everything from single shot to semi-auto rifles are available in 30-06 and similar chamberings. The 30-06 is the number one round west of the Mississippi, used on antelope to moose by thousands of hunters.

Lumping all the cartridges larger than the 30-06 together, from 338 Winchester to 375 Magnum, and larger, there are numerous powerful cartridges that meat hunters employ with terrific success. Using well-made bullets, these big rounds don't "blow up" a lot of meat.

Nancy Fadala has taken many fine game animals with her Frank Wells custom 6mm/222, among them this antelope buck. The little cartridge is a giant-killer.

A specialized plains rifle harvested this antelope buck for the author. Built by Dale Storey of Casper, Wyoming, the rifle is capable of great long-range accuracy and power.

The old-time 30-30 Winchester continues to bring home the bacon—the venison, in this case. The rifle is a custom by Dale Storey.

Served by modern shotgun slug ammunition that is the best ever, the slug-shooting shotgun has come of age. Top is Remington's Model 11-87 with rifled barrel; bottom shotgun is Remington Model 870 pump.

Shotguns

Without question, the shotgun is our most versatile meat-taker. All shotguns do the job, so discussing shotguns at length is not necessary. However, here are a few points worth considering.

Gauge

Apply gauge accordingly. For medium-range work on smaller fare, the 410 shotgun is fine. I've taken plenty of edibles with my Hatfield 28-gauge, too. The 16-gauge is not that popular today, but it's still a great one for putting meat on the table. The 12 is simply king, with tremendous versatility, and the 10-gauge is for heavy-duty work.

Shot

Steel shot is the law on waterfowl. Remember, however, that steel shot can ruin a barrel not intended to handle such hard pellets, and this goes for muzzleloaders as well as modern guns. Also note that steel shot does not demand as tight a choke as lead shot. A Modified choke normally gives lead pellet Full choke results with steel shot.

Buckshot

I'm not a fan of buckshot on big game, and I'll stand by that opinion. If someone suggested hunting deer and other big game with a muzzle-loading squirrel rifle, the comment would raise eyebrows, yet the smallbore frontloader has more power per pellet than a 12-gauge shotgun using buckshot. For example, a 32-caliber muzzleloader shoots a 45-grain round ball at about 2000 fps. Buckshot, even 00 and 000, is similar in size, yet muzzle velocity is a lot closer to 1400 fps. If many pellets hit from very close range, that's different, but when one or two pellets land on target, buckshot is not big game worthy.

Slugs

The modern shotgun slug is a powerful choice for shotgunners going for big game. More accurate than ever, the new slug from today's special shotguns delivers a big punch out to 100 yards, and maybe a tad farther.

Blackpowder Shotguns

The blackpowder shotgun is close to its modern brother in potential, although nothing quite catches up to Winchester, Remington and Federal shotgun shells loaded the way they are nowadays. A 12-gauge muzzle-loading shotgun can, however, put out a strong shot column at well over the speed of sound. Buy your blackpowder shotgun already choked to give best patterns.

These Remington 12-gauge slugs are a good and often the only legal choice of ammo for taking deer.

Muzzleloaders are extremely popular for hunting. Loaded correctly, blackpowder rifles like this CVA model do a great job of harvesting big game. Nick Fadala poses with a whitetail buck he took with a Buffalo Bullet.

Today, there are dozens of different bullet styles for muzzleloaders. Shown here are Black Belt bullets from Big Bore Express. The hollowpoint promotes bullet expansion.

Most popular bow today is the compound, although the past five years have seen quite a rush to longbows and recurves.

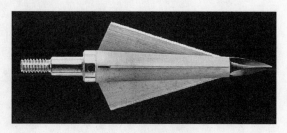

The Razorbak broadhead is of modern materials and design. This three-blade model uses surgical steel and Space Age synthetics.

Handguns

Pistols and revolvers, from airguns to magnums, are used for taking game. The handgun hunter is a specialist. He knows his sidearm inside and out, and its ammo. I've taken small game and mountain birds with an RWS target pellet pistol shooting a 17-caliber pellet at about 450 fps, but only from close range, normally not farther than about 10 yards. My Smith & Wesson 44 Magnum has also accounted for game, especially with super-power ammo from Garrett Cartridge Company. Modern handguns are powerful, including blackpowder models. For example, the Thompson/Center Scout Pistol is a single shot muzzleloader that carries more potency than a 30-30 rifle. All the same, handgun hunters should get close for absolutely certain bullet placement. While a few experts, such as Elmer Keith, could get away with handgun hunting at longer ranges, the rest of us cannot.

Bows and Arrows

A good hunter can pack the meat home with any bow type. It happens all the time. For the archer who does not plan to practice often, the compound is probably the best choice. Many features—sights, the relaxation factor, also known as letoff—make compounds easier to master than stick bows shot off the shelf (without sights). For the archer who intends to shoot a great deal, stick bows are excellent and entirely capable of delivering arrows to the mark with sufficient power to drive through the chest cavity of a bull elk, or a bull moose for that matter.

Compounds

The compound bow shoots the fastest arrow. Compounds also have a relaxation (letoff) factor, so that the bowman holds only a percentage of the draw weight of the bow. This means 70- and even 80-pound bows can be mastered, provided the archer has the strength to draw these bows to the break-over point. Also, the compound bow has a "valley." That is, the archer does not have to pull an absolutely perfect draw length each and every time for top bow performance. The arrow takes off at the same speed even with slightly inconsistent draw lengths. Finally, compounds generally have sights, and those familiar with guns get used to sighted compounds quickly.

Recurve Bows

The composite (made of more than one material) modern recurve bow is capable of taking any game on earth. Although some say otherwise, the truth is, today's recurves are better designed than ever. They shoot arrows as fast as some "round wheel" compounds, although nothing shoots faster than a high-tech compound, as a chronograph proves. Stick bows (recurves and longbows) have made a remarkable comeback within the past several years. Thousands of archers have turned away from compounds and gone back to stick bows, desiring to return to old-time bowhunting.

Longbows and Self-Bows

Modern longbows are also a far cry from longbows of the past. Made with cores of excellent woods, plus fiberglass, some of these longbows rival modern recurves for arrow speed.

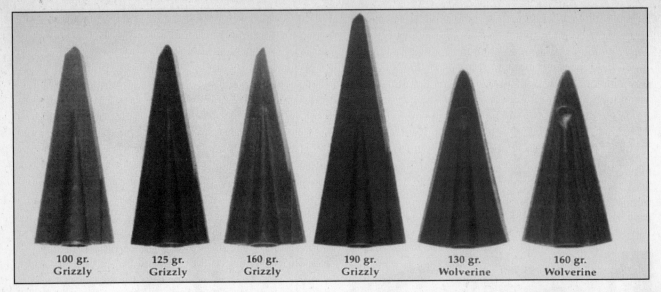

| 100 gr. Grizzly | 125 gr. Grizzly | 160 gr. Grizzly | 190 gr. Grizzly | 130 gr. Wolverine | 160 gr. Wolverine |

Following an ancient style, these modern Abel Grizzly broadheads are extremely strong and fully capable of harvesting the largest game on earth.

One of Fadala's favorite bows is this Herb Meland creation, a three-piece takedown longbow from Pronghorn Custom Bows of Casper, Wyoming. Close-up shows riser of bow with quiver.

Also growing in popularity are bows that go beyond traditional almost to primitive. These are self-bows, bows made of one type of material. For example, a longbow made of osage orange alone is a self-bow.

The return to traditional and even primitive bow types has brought with it a new wave of instinctive shooting. Some argue with the term. I don't. It simply means shooting without the aid of sights, using hand-eye coordination to deliver the arrow on target. The vast majority of recurves, longbows and self-bows are shot "off the shelf" without sights.

Arrows and Broadheads

The modern aluminum arrow is more precise than ever before, which is saying a great deal, since aluminum arrows have always been good. Easton Aluminum provided shafts to test for this book. They proved extremely uniform. Other materials also serve for arrows, and very well at that, including carbon and similar synthetics. Wood has made a big comeback along with the stick bow. Cedar remains the most popular arrow wood, but other woods, such as slow-growth pine, make superb arrow shafts.

As a guest of Bear Archery Company, I enjoyed an Alabama deer hunt in which several deer were taken with bow and arrow. Broadheads of many different types were used. Not one failed in any manner. Broadhead selection should be based, however, on how an individual head shoots from a specific bow. Basically, there are two types of broadheads: modular and one-piece. Modular heads use razor-like blades attached to a common body. One-piece heads are just that, made of one piece of steel. The latter may be two-bladed, three-bladed, or two-bladed with small razor-edges called "bleeder blades" attached. There are many options. The advantage of the modular head is its pre-sharpened state. The advantage of the one-piece head is shear ruggedness. Both, when properly sharp, cleanly harvest all manner of game.

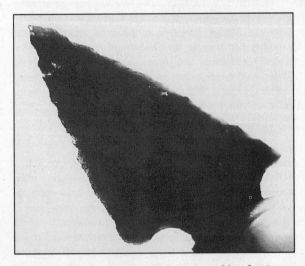

The ancient "stone" arrowhead was capable of extreme sharpness for a quick and humane harvest of game.

Saving the Meat

The Broadhead

Arrows impart very little energy, yet anyone who has studied a number of carcasses stands in awe of the tissue damage done by a broadhead. Nonetheless, arrows work by creating a "leak" in the system, whereby body fluids depart and the animal loses consciousness, as in medical shock. I have gone to broadheads for all game, finding blunts and other head types less desirable. Even on rabbits, broadheads are more certain.

Amazingly, broadheads can "bloodshoot" a large area on a deer-sized game animal. Fortunately, most hits are in the chest region, and little edible meat is lost. There isn't much we can do about broadhead authority, nor would we want to reduce such effectiveness, because the ability of the broadhead to disrupt tissue causes a quick dispatch.

Bullets, on the other hand, impart great energy to the target, disrupt tissue, and promote a loss of body fluids. The meat hunter can do quite well for himself with just about any "mushrooming type" bullet, provided he places that bullet in the chest cavity of a big game animal, where little edible meat is located. Bullets with super-hard jackets are not recommended for thin-skinned game. They do not disrupt readily. Instead, they form long, narrow wound channels, and they also deliver a great deal of their energy to the hill or tree behind the game, rather than in the game itself. The best way to save meat is through good bullet placement, rather than super-hard bullets.

Full metal jacket bullets (FMJ) drive through, break bone, and disrupt tissue. They are used for the heaviest game in Africa, but are of no practical value on big game in North America. They are generally illegal, with the exception of the 22 WMR full metal jacket bullet on some game in some regions. The expanding bullet is the choice of big game hunters.

Think about it. Can a 30-caliber bullet, less than one-third of an

The modern big game bullet is superb for big game hunting. Hornady's big game bullets are designed for big game hunting.

Nancy Fadala often carries a Sako rifle in 7mm-08 for big game hunting. She has taken elk and other big game with the round, including this mule deer buck.

The 7mm-08 Remington is an excellent medium-sized cartridge for big game hunting. It offers mild recoil with effectiveness. It's a good cartridge for the meat hunter.

Designed for penetration without bullet blow-up, these RWS bullets have been around for many decades and used on hundreds of different species. They're excellent for meat hunters who want results without undue meat loss.

inch in diameter, expand in a deer to the breadth of a teacup? The answer is no. Yet, teacup-size exit holes are not rare in game from bullets of 30-caliber and even smaller. What made the exit hole if the bullet, itself, did not? The best bet is the shock wave in front of the projectile created by the bullet changing shape, or mushrooming, if you will. Ideally, the big game bullet holds together well enough to create a long wound channel, with a good exit hole. However, bullets that disrupt and impart full energy within the chest cavity also do well.

Bullets are made in various ways. Solid copper is nothing new. I have German-made solid copper bullets that were produced decades ago. Solid copper makes a fine big game bullet, however, with decent upset and good wound channel. All-lead bullets, either of "pure lead" or an alloy of lead plus tin, zinc or other metal, also work well, but do not stand up to velocities much over 2000 fps. Lead bullets from muzzleloaders, especially heavy, big-bore missiles, make long wound channels. All-lead bullets tend to stay together, rather than fragment, due to high molecular cohesion. The jacketed big game bullet is most popular today, a lead core surrounded by a copper, copper/nickel or other metals. All of these bullet types are useful for meat hunting.

Energy

The only energy formula used by modern ammo factories today is Newton's. Because velocity is squared in this formula, that factor increases energy more than bullet weight. Obviously, the most powerful bullet is the largest one at the highest speed. The big bullet vs. high velocity argument will live forever. It's a moot point, really. High velocity medium-weight bullets work fine. So do slower big bullets. The meat hunter should assess energies according to the game hunted. No deer demands 4000 foot-pounds of energy, for example, but the elk/moose hunter who wants that sort of authority has a right to choose it, as with a 300 Weatherby Magnum or similar cartridge.

Shock

Medical shock is a specific condition tied to loss of body fluids, low blood pressure, rapid pulse, increased respiration rate and unconsciousness. Hunters consider shock the disruption of tissue caused by the "shock wave" in front of a mushrooming high-speed bullet.

All hunters gravitate to the guns and bows they like best. This happens, most often, through trial and error, and also with information from magazines, books, videos, audios and knowledgeable fellow hunters. The one thing a meat hunter cannot abide is wasted meat. The best way to avoid that is correct bullet placement, followed by a choice of projectiles that open up to impart energy, but are not overly powerful for the animal hunted. Hit a tender cottontail with a high-speed thin-jacketed varmint bullet, and the result is undue meat loss. Wrong gun for the job. Use a 22 rimfire, however, or a shotgun, and you have a prize in hand. Place the 22 bullet in the head, and all of the meat is left to eat, or use #5 shot instead of a heavy dose of #8s, and the same result is enjoyed. It's a matter of matching gun to game.

Fadala took this desert mule deer buck with his favorite all-around modern cartridge, the 7mm Remington Magnum. There's a lot of good food represented here.

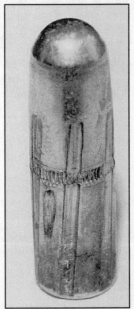

Sometimes penetration is called for. This RWS 300-grain bullet was taken from a Cape buffalo. Called a "solid," a bullet like this is designed for zero deformation.

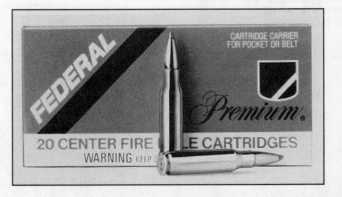

Author has found the 308 Winchester round ideal for meathunting big game. Results are fast and positive without undue loss of meat. The 180-grain bullet, as shown here, is for larger-than-deer game, and may not open up on smaller animals. Always match the bullet to the game for best results.

FIELD CARE OF small game, big game, upland birds, waterfowl and exotics requires, at the very least, a knife. A good bladesman can do it all with one knife, from field-dressing small game and birds, to boning a big game carcass for carry-back to vehicle or camp. Of course, be watchful of the laws of wildlife management when boning big game. Sometimes proof of the animal's gender is required by law. Along with knives, some sort of field sharpener is nice to have, plus a saw and, for very large game—elk and moose—a hand axe for quartering. The latter is entirely optional. The largest North American game can be quartered with a knife by understanding anatomy. Here are a few sportsman's blades to consider for field work. *For the reader's convenience, there is a mini-glossary of knife terms on page 35 of this chapter.*

Knives

Jackknives and Pocketknives

On May 2, 1991, an astronaut used a pocketknife to repair a broken wire aboard the space shuttle *Discovery*. You can bet that on the same day, a businessman in New York peeled an apple with his pocketknife, trying to remove the skin in one long continuous piece; a rancher in Wyoming drilled holes in a piece of leather with the punch tool of his pocketknife; and a housewife in Seattle used a pocketknife to open a package. We've been using jackknives and pocketknives for hundreds of years, to sculpt a stick into meaningful form, cut a steak in camp, peel a potato, even play a game called mumbley-peg.

Besides being pocket-sized, the pocketknife has one or more blades that fold into its handle. It differs from a folding knife in size.

Chapter 5...

Tools for Field Care

Game Care & Cookery

Not all folders will fit in a pocket, while all pocketknives will. First cousin to the pocketknife is the jackknife, described in the dictionary as "a large pocketknife." Knives that fit into pockets have been around almost as long as pockets themselves. The Romans had a pocketknife of sorts, but not until the 17th century did the style come into its own, supposedly invented by one Jaque De Liege, who also named the knife. In that time frame, knives for pockets gained considerable popularity. The pocket or jackknife became a household item following World War I.

There are numerous pocketknife designs. Knowing the different styles is not important to this chapter. Function of the jackknife or pocketknife in the field is what's important, and that function is multiple. The pocketknife or jackknife can be used for any field task from cleaning a quail to dressing a moose. In camp, the same knife serves dozens of purposes from mending a pack to cutting rope. The jackknife, however, is like any tool that performs many functions. It is suitable for multiple tasks, but not perfect for any one specific field function, with the exception of small game and bird preparation. There, the pocketknife shines. Nothing more than a pocketknife is necessary for field-working these edibles.

A few good examples of fine pocketknives are the following: Remington Limited Edition "Camp" Bullet Knife with two 440 stainless steel blades and two utility blades. Another interesting pocketknife is the Remington Sportsman Series Upland Knife (R1) with

2³/₈-inch clip-blade, gut hook, and 12/20-gauge choke tool screwdriver. Aptly named, the Upland is for bird hunters. Buck Ultrablade pocketknives in various forms, two-blade, three-blade and other combinations, are typically well-constructed and utilitarian. This is but a tiny sample from the world of pocketknives. See DBI's annual edition of *Knives*, edited by Ken Warner, as well as *The Gun Digest Book of Knives*, edited by Jack Lewis, for a look at the many different kinds of knives for sporting use.

Swiss Knives and Multi-Tool Knives

The Swiss Knife is very much like a multi-tool, but instead of carrying this knife in a sheath, it's normally packed in a pocket. The Swiss knife, and its many counterparts, is a pocketknife with many integral tools.

The multi-tool is just that—many tools incorporated into one unit, generally worn in a compact holster on the belt. There is a joke about an inventor who created a multi-tool model with thirty-one functions. A friend studied the invention carefully. "Charley," he said, "this is a fantastic knife, but where's the blade?" I have owned but one multi-tool knife, the Coast Cutlery Company Pocket Mechanic. And yes, Coast did not forget the blade, which is a large spear-point. The Pocket Mechanic also has a wood saw, wire cutters, pliers, pry bar, screwdrivers and other tools. A small game hunter could get by quite nicely with a multi-tool knife like this one.

Folding Knives (Clasp Knives)

Eventually, we synthesize our hardware to suit our needs. My current cutlery set is tri-part: knives, saw, sharpener. Most of the time, the knife, or knives, is a folder. Folding knives, also called folders, are important field blades. They're hard-working and compact. Folders often differ from pocketknives in blade style, and the fact that the folder generally has a single blade. They also differ in application. Where the pocketknife is a jack-of-all-trades, the folder is more for field-dressing, especially larger game animals. For the sake of classification, I've broken folders down into three categories by size: small, medium and large. Most used by me is the medium folding knife. I often carry two medium folders on my belt, or one medium and one

No visible knife. That's because this wild turkey, taken with a Black Widow recurve bow, is easily field-dressed with a small pocketknife.

A pocketknife is useful not only for small game care, but also for general cooking chores, as shown here with a Guttmann model.

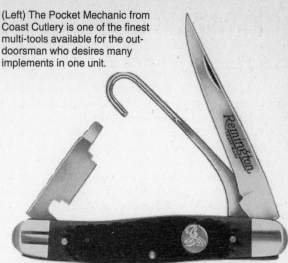

(Left) The Pocket Mechanic from Coast Cutlery is one of the finest multi-tools available for the out-doorsman who desires many implements in one unit.

Remington's special Upland Knife is ideal for bird hunting. It has a gut hook for assistance in removing entrails, and a shotgun choke tool with screwdriver, plus a long, slender blade, ideal for field-dressing birds.

small. These knives are completely out of the way until I need to field-dress game.

The small folder is ideal for cottontails, squirrels and similar small game. Of course, it serves to dress deer, too, but larger knives do the job better, easier and generally faster. The small folder is also useful for birds of all kinds, including the wild turkey. Compactness is the small folder's strong suit. Lack of blade length and, in some cases, insufficient overall strength are the small folder's weak points when big game is handled in the field. An example of an excellent small folding knife is the Puma Protec from Coast Cutlery. Another Puma, the Hobbytec, is even smaller, but the Protec is, in my opinion, more ideal for the field because of its versatility. I prefer the clip-point Protec, while others want the drop-point Protec. Each has a $3^1/_8$-inch hollow-ground blade and an overall length of $4^1/_2$ inches, closed. It's a strong, well-made knife. The fine, but smaller, Hobbytec has a $2^3/_4$-inch blade, with an overall closed length of 4 inches.

The medium folder is nearly ideal for all hunting because it is workable for small game and birds, yet entirely adequate for big game. If there is one knife that can do it all, it's the medium folder, although this knife is not necessarily ideal for truly large game, such as elk. A medium folder that works hard for me is the Buck Titanium XLTi model. This is a sturdy knife with $3^3/_4$-inch clip-blade. It's a flat knife, very easy to carry on a belt. Length of the XLTi is 5 inches closed. On many hunts, I'll carry the Protec, mentioned above, plus the XLTi. It's a tough combination to beat, and I don't even know either knife is there until I need to field-work something.

The large folder is not as handy as the medium model, but it works harder. For big game only, large folders are excellent. On small game, they are oversized and unnecessarily large, but will do the job if called upon. Some large folders shine because of their ruggedness, however, and hunters prefer them on long treks into far-away places. Well-made large folders do not break under normal field use, even when big game animals are worked on daily, as I saw in Africa where one camp skinner used a large folding knife on big game carcasses day in and day out for three weeks. He had no complaints about the knife. A good example of a sturdy large folder is the Katz K-900CL with Kraton handle and $3^3/_4$-inch clip-point blade.

These three Puma folding knives offer two different sizes, smaller one on left, plus different knife blade designs. The one on the far right is a drop-point. The one in the middle is a clip-point.

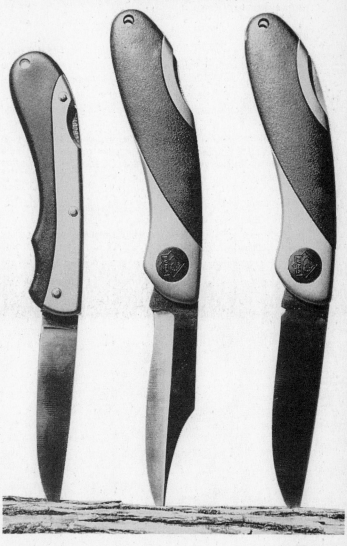

It's easy to see why the hunting folder became popular. A folding knife is compact, outworks its size, and can be built to work hard in the field. It's sparrow small when you don't need it, and eagle big when you do. That's why folders have been around so long. Archaeologists found folding knives that, they think, date back to the first century A.D. Carl P. Russell, author of *Firearms, Traps & Tools of the Mountain Men*, notes that folders were on American soil in the 18th century. An expense sheet for the French Fox War, 1715 and 1716, shows "horn handled clasp knives, 6 livres a dozen."

Before leaving folding knives, perhaps it's worthwhile to look at a few characteristics that mark these models. Early folding knives shared certain common traits, according to Russell. They had a single folding blade controlled by a spring. These knives were not "switchblades." Blades were generally secured in the open position so they would not fold back on the hand of the user. Folding knife, jackknife, pocketknife, clasp knife, switchblade—would the true folding hunter please stand up? Webster says it is "a large one-bladed folding knife having a catch [a clasp, in other words] to hold the blade open rigidly." Perhaps we can add that a folder normally rides in a scabbard on the belt, because that's the way I carry mine, and I'll bet you do, too, rather than in a pocket like a pocketknife.

Finally, there are many custom folders available. Ken Warner thinks the trends in custom knives are changing. "There will come the day," says Warner, "when folder makers will outnumber straight knifemakers." And why not? The folder is a great knife, especially for the hunter who wants a rugged unit that doesn't run from belt half-way to knee in length.

Fixed-Blade Knives

Fixed-blade knives start with petite models, such as my Katz Caper's Pal, which is as thin as a starved grass snake and lighter than a dry leaf. This little knife has a skeletonized handle, and while it's designed to cape big game trophies (prepare trophies in the field for taxidermy), it's also useful for small game and general camp duty,

(Top right) Appropriateness is the key to choosing a knife. A large Guttmann hunting knife is shown with a pocketknife from the same company. Size difference is obvious. Application differences are also obvious.

(Below) Folder or fixed blade? It's obvious that the two knives are extremely different in design, and final choice is usually a personal one.

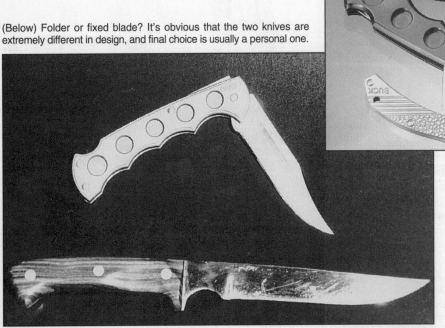

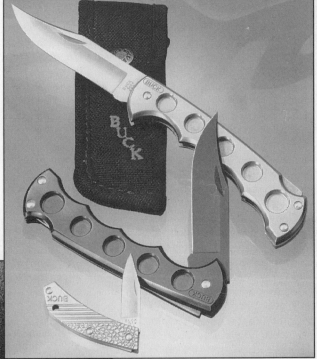

(Above) Buck's folding knives are many and high-grade. The upper two knives shown here have titanium handles. Author once left a Buck titanium handled knife at the site of harvest. The knife was picked up again after a Wyoming winter. It showed no sign of rust or damage.

Mini-Glossary of Knife Terms

Back of Blade: Opposite side of the cutting edge of a knife blade.

Bolster: The metal end of the folding knife.

Boning Knife: Knife with thin, narrow blade for removing meat from bones.

Camp Knife: Large hunting knife, capable of chopping as well as cutting.

Clip-Point: Blade shape where top front of point is a concave cutout, making a very sharp point.

Drop-Point: Forward part of blade falls below the level of the handle.

False Edge: Back of blade is sharpened part-way.

Fixed Blade: Blade does not fold into handle, but always remains rigid.

Folding Knife: Generally with one blade that folds into handle.

Gut Hook: There are at least two kinds of gut hooks incorporated into knives. One is shaped like a wire with a sharply and tightly curved end. The hooked end is used on small game and birds to withdraw viscera. The other type of gut hook is integral to a knife blade. It is used mainly to cut the incision on the underside of big game for the evacuation of viscera.

Guard of the Knife: A projection that stops the hand from going forward of the handle.

Handle Scales: The side panels on a jackknife or pocketknife.

Lockback Knife: A folding knife whose blade locks in place.

Pommel: A metal (usually) protective cover on the end of a knife handle.

Sheepsfoot Blade: Short blade with straight edge and a rounded blade back.

Spear-Point: Both top and bottom of the blade are rounded to the point.

Spey Blade: Thin, sharp blade with rounded point.

Tang: The portion of the knife blade that runs back through the handle, all or part-way.

Tanto: Short Japanese sword, but now a popular knife blade style with a squared front portion of the blade.

(Below) Countless blade styles exist. This fine Schrade knife shows a sweeping style with sharp point, good for field dressing, but also useful for skinning.

(Above) These two fixed blade knives from Buck epitomize the sheath knife style. Both Vanguards have hollow ground drop-point blades. One has a woodgrained handle, the other a rubberized handle.

(Top left) This Buck fish filet knife is called the FishLocker. Intended for filleting fish, it's also ideal for boning meat, especially on the trail where its folding quality allows for compactness. It weighs 3.2 ounces, and folds to 7¼ inches.

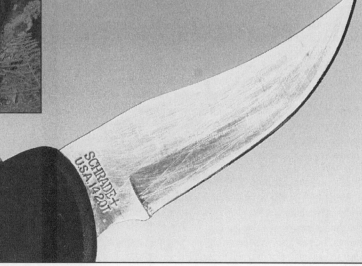

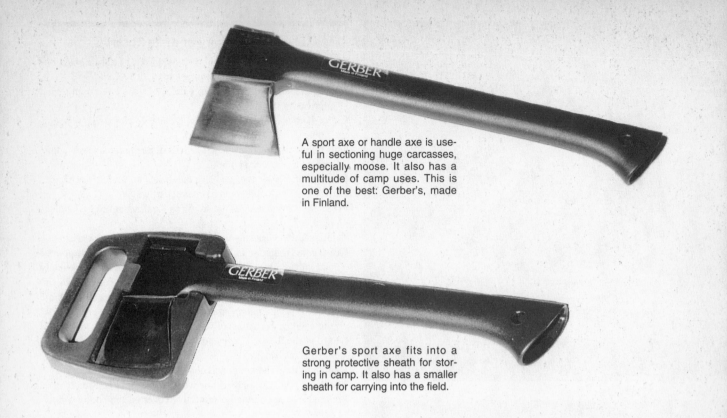

A sport axe or handle axe is useful in sectioning huge carcasses, especially moose. It also has a multitude of camp uses. This is one of the best: Gerber's, made in Finland.

Gerber's sport axe fits into a strong protective sheath for storing in camp. It also has a smaller sheath for carrying into the field.

plus big game in a pinch. Fixed-blade models also run large. I own a Blackjack Brute, a big strong knife just right for building tomahawk shelters (huts made from cut intertwined limbs). The variety of fixed-blade knives is huge. For field work, however, we'll narrow the fixed-blade model down to the sheath knife.

Sheath knife is a generic term for countless fixed-blade knives worn on the belt. Trying to pin down an exact definition is futile. Sheath knives have short, long and medium-length blades. They are light, and they are heavy. Also called "hunting knives," they are just that. The large models are ideal for heavy field work. There are also tiny sheath knives that are superb for field-dressing small game or birds.

Hatchets

Long ago, a hatchet of some sort made up the fighting gear of many soldiers, not only Native Americans with their tomahawks, but also Europeans, as well as Asians. Today, the hatchet, also called hand axe, is more a camp item than a carry-around tool. However, some hunters do pack a hand axe, using it to chop wood for a campfire on the backtrail, as well as sectioning a big game animal, such as a moose. Blackpowder hunters who wish to emulate the tools of the mountain man of the Far West turn to the tomahawk, another breed of hatchet, for their work. A hand axe is a rugged tool, built as the good ones are today, and there is nothing wrong with adding one to a hunting outfit, albeit no knowledgeable hunter requires a hand axe to section any game animal, except maybe an elephant.

Field Saws

Small lightweight saws that take up very little space are popular with today's big game hunters. I have carried a mini-saw for the past couple decades or more, using the saw to part the chest cavity of big game. The saw also sees use on any hunting trail, including backpack trips for scouting and/or small game hunting, because saws are useful

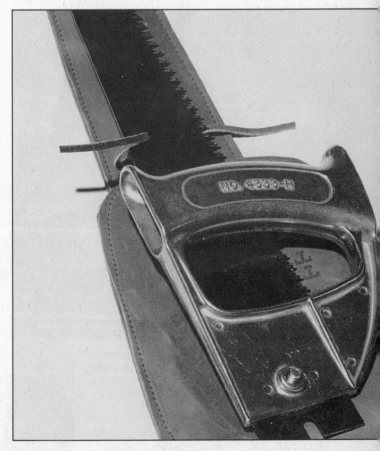

Game saws are extremely helpful in the field. This is one of the best game saws available today. It's called "The Saw" and it's from AFA, Anchorage, AK. Handle folds for fitting into sheath.

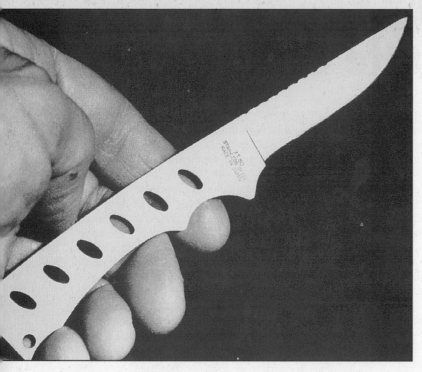

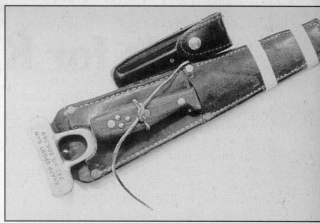

This is a rather compact cutlery kit for all that it does, and it is the outfit preferred by the author for all of his backpack hunts. The knife is a "hardware store" type at first glance, however, it is very easy to sharpen and it remains sharp through the entire work necessary for field care of deer-sized game. The EZE-LAP knife sharpening tool in its convenient pocket-size leather sheath will sharpen a knife, also serve to take the wavy pattern out of a knife blade. The meat saw, by Knapp Company, is very handy, especially for camp chores and for hunters who have not mastered removal of the foreleg by finding and dislocating the proper joints.

The Katz no-handle Caper's Pal knife is designed to cape big game trophies, but it has a multitude of uses, including camp cooking and small game field-dressing.

Field sharpeners are many. This particular model is small and light, and it works.

in building tomahawk shelters, although a strong knife like the Black-jack Brute mentioned earlier is faster-working. There are a number of good game saws on the market today. Buck Knives offers one, for example. It is their Sawbuck & Sheath with 10¼-inch blade and black Kraton handle. Typical of game saws, the two edges differ—a cross-cut design on one side, pruning side on the other.

Field Sharpening Tools

I carry two folding knives on many of my outings because knife blades, no matter what they are made of, get dull through use. I also pack a sharpening device. A good one is the diamond hone in the compact model, such as the Sportsman's Diamond Sharpener from Smoky Mountain Knife Works, which is 8 inches long, but only half that size taken down for carrying. The hone itself fits into the handle of the tool. Another interesting knife sharpener, which I've carried on backpack trips, is the Ultimate Edge Diamond Sharpening Steel. While this is not a compact unit, over 15 inches long, it's extremely lightweight and neatly fits into a backpack compartment out of the way. DMT also makes good knife sharpeners that are compact and easy to carry in the field.

The 4-inch Diafold Diamond Whetstone has a folding handle that doubles as a sheath for the shank of the sharpener. The unit is only 4¼ inches long, folded. It comes in different meshes—1200, 600 and 325. The first is extra fine (green handle) for polishing edges and final blade finish, while 600 mesh (red handle) is fine grade for knife-sharpening, and 325 is coarse. The 600 mesh DMT whetstone is my choice for field work.

Man's earliest tools included cutting edges of stone. Remarkably, ancient obsidian and flint knives, along with arrowheads and spear-points, were capable of extreme sharpness. Furthermore, all of these cutting tools were extremely well-designed. Some of our finest knives and arrowheads are shaped very much like Stone Age counter-parts of the distant past. These knives were used in the field, as we employ knives to this day, to care for harvested game. Of course, technology has brought us a long way down the road to materials and designs that provide us with the best field cutlery ever enjoyed.

Tools for Knife Sharpening

The first rule of knife sharpening is safety. Be extra careful with all cutting implements, just as you are with all shooting instruments. Mostly, this is common sense, but do not forget eye and face protection. Wear a safety shield to protect both face and eyes when sharpening a knife. An excellent source for knife-sharpening techniques is *The Razor Edge Book of Sharpening* by John Juranitch, available from Razor Edge Systems, Inc., PO Box 150, Ely, MN 55731.

For me, failure in knife sharpening centered on two Ps. One P is "Pressure;" the other is "Patience." I have always applied far more pressure than necessary and far too little patience when I experience a knife-sharpening failure. So don't try to ram the knife through the sharpening instrument, or the sharpening instrument through the knife. It's not necessary to create a keen edge. And do have patience. Even with the most modern equipment, sharpening a knife takes a little time.

Razor Edge Systems, Inc., offers a kit that includes the instruction book noted earlier. This is not the forum to summarize that book; however, it is a good time to say that anyone can sharpen a knife—razor sharp—if he follows certain guidelines, so here's how the Razor Edge kit works.

Besides instruction book and instructional pamphlets, the kit, housed in a wooden box, also includes two hones—one coarse, one fine—two guides, one Sportsman's Razor Steel and one Edge Tester. The heart of the system is the guide, which positions the blade of the knife correctly on the surface of the hone. The idea is to use the coarse hone to break in the blade. The fine hone creates the finished edge. There is no need, in this sharpening method, for other hone grits. Coarse and fine do it all. An extra keen edge is gained through the use of the Sportsman's Steel, and the Edge Tester is used for just that—testing to see if the knife is truly sharp. If not, the honing process is continued with guide in place. This is only a reflection of the system, of course, but sufficient for the reader to decide if this is the type of sharpener he wants. Applying the two Ps above, light pressure and patience, I obtained knife edges that were razor-sharp using this kit.

Mentioned earlier as a device useful for backpack hunting trips because of its light weight, the Ultimate Edge steel is not a steel in the sense of straightening a knife edge. It is a sharpener, reducing metal from the surface of the blade to create a new edge. As always, angle is vital to success. The knife blade should be maintained at a specific angle, rather than turned to various angles during the sharpening process.

Yet another system for sharpening a knife, different from either of the two previously mentioned, is the Diamondbuck. The 6-inch model offers a good surface for knife sharpening.

The Lansky Fold-A-Vee Sharpener is highly portable. It folds down for ease carrying. Blade angle is ensured by holding the knife with edge perpendicular to the working surface. Ceramic rods do the sharpening.

The Explorer knife sharpening system from Gutmann Cutlery Company has two main parts, a clamp to ensure ideal blade angle at all times, and sharpening surface, which is a ceramic rod held in a cradle.

The Lensky Sharpening System Kit works on the principle of blade edge alignment with hones. A clamp holds knife in place, while a rod connected to hone presents hone at the correct angle to the knife blade. Slots in the clamp allow for different blade angles.

The Lansky Universal Mount can be permanently fixed to a working surface to hold the Lansky sharpening system in place. Hunters may wish to secure the Universal Mount to their workbench or butchering table.

As always, maintaining the angle of the blade edge is important to successful sharpening of the knife. This type of sharpener is used like a whetstone, the blade of the knife drawn across the surface, where monocrystal industrial diamonds act as an abrasive to reduce metal.

Another method of knife sharpening is the ceramic rod, or in the case of the Katz DCS model, ceramic rods set in a wooden base at specific angles. The angles of the rods determine the sharpened knife edge. To use the ceramic rods, the knife is held so that the blade is vertical, then the blade is drawn back and forth across the rods.

The Lansky Sharpener is one of the most unique knife-sharpening devices of all times. As the illustrations of this device show, the knife blade is secured on the horizontal, while the sharpening stone is guided at a specific angle. Several angles are available, and the guide is simply installed in the slot for the desired angle of the hone. I recommend the use of the Lanksy Super "C" Clamp or other Lansky Mount with this tool. The mount provides full control of both knife blade and hone.

Chef's Choice has three different knife sharpeners sufficiently unique to deserve mention. The first is Chef's Choice Diamond Hone Set 400. It is a sharpening stone with interchangeable abrasive pads. The unit acts as any standard stone—the knife edge is drawn across the surface of the abrasive pad to reduce metal; however, this is not a stone, but rather a surface of 100-percent diamond abrasive.

A second model is the Chef's Choice Manual Diamond Hone 2 Stage 450 Knife Sharpener. The two stages are extremely important to the function of this sharpener. Drawing the knife through the first stage creates a bevel on the blade of the knife, while drawing the knife through the second hones the edge to sharpness. Housed in a plastic body, this sharpener is easy to use on any flat surface.

A third unit from Edgecraft Corporation is the Model 110 Heavy Duty Chef's Choice Diamond Hone Sharpener. This is an electric model with pre-sharpening slots. It is a three-stage sharpener. The first stage is for pre-sharpening the knife, creating a bevel edge with a diamond disk. The stage two and three slots use orbiting diamond wheels to sharpen the knife. Magnets control the blade angle by drawing the knife against the side of the slot. I appreciated Rule 1 of the Model 110 instruction sheet: "Loosen your grip on the knife."

These are a few sharpening devices, all different, yet all entirely workable. Choosing the knife sharpener, and knife sharpening method, for you is a matter of trying different types to see which works best.

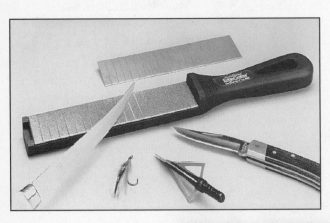

(Left) The Edge-Crafter Set 400 is a unique sharpening tool with two interchangeable sharpening surfaces, both made of 100 percent diamond abrasive pads held flat by special magnets. The Set 400 is useful in sharpening hunting and butchering knives, and also fish hooks and broadheads.

The DiamondBuck knife sharpener comes in two styles, a folding model and a table model. The 4-inch portable model folds into its own handles for carrying. The 6-inch model offers a larger working surface. Both use non-crystal industrial diamonds for abrasive sharpening surfaces.

The Chef's Choice Manual Diamond Hone, Model 450, has a two-stage sharpening feature, along with precise edge alignment through angled slots. The blade is drawn through these slots by hand. Many different types of knives can be sharpened with the Model 450 unit.

FIELD CARE OF big game is a responsibility. As care goes, so goes the succulence of the meat on the table. Field care is also an important part of the hunt. An outdoorsman who does not know how to field-dress his harvest is not complete in his skills. There are many ways to take care of a big game animal after it's down in the field. The methods discussed here are not the last word, nor the only word. They are simply tried and true ways developed over many years. They offer a foundation on which the hunter can build. The goal is always the same: clean meat, free of gastric juices, unspoiled and ready for butchering.

Safety First

Field-dressing a big game animal can be a man-sized job, and a man can get hurt doing it. Chances of injury are about like finding a $100 bill stuck to the bottom of your shoe, but every year, a number of hunters do fall prey to accidents while field-dressing big game. How?

Sometimes a "dead" animal kicks the dickens out of 'em. So, the first rule in field-dressing any big game animal is to make sure that it's truly defunct. Approach with rifle or bow at the ready. If there is any sign of life, stop. Get steady. Take aim and wait for a moment. If the animal continues to move, shoot again. Put a second bullet into the head or upper neck, or an arrow into the chest cavity. Meat waste is minimal with these shots, and dispatch is speedy. If you're not certain of placing the bullet perfectly, go for the "boiler room" behind the shoulder, putting that second bullet into the rib cage.

If you walk up, at the ready, and the animal appears totally finished, approach from the off-side—where the hooves are not. Look

Chapter 6

Field Care for Big Game
Game Care & Cookery

with binoculars first, if you have a pair with you. While a bird's eyes close when it expires, mammals' eyes remain open and unblinking. This can be seen with binos from a distance. If you cannot see eye motion through your binoculars, then move in closer and, with a long stick (such as a downed tree limb), push against the backside of the animal. If the buck or bull is rigid, odds are it still has get up and go, and it might do just that—get right up and go.

Another test: With a long stick, touch the open eye. If the eye blinks or twitches, back off and be ready to shoot again. But wait a minute first. Touch the eye again. If there is any sign of life the second time, then shoot again. More than one hunter has watched his prize rise to its feet and take off on a dead run after initially hitting the ground like a sack of sugar beets. "But I don't want to waste meat," you say. I'm sensitive to meat loss, too, but look at it this way: Better to lose a few more pounds of meat to a second bullet or arrow, rather than watching the entire package of chops, steaks and burgers run over the hill. Besides, the *coup de grace* on any animal showing signs of life is the only right thing to do.

Warning: Suppose you get a bowshot in late afternoon, and you wait awhile before following up. Then you get on the trail, perhaps using a flashlight. By the time you reach the carcass, it's dusk or even dark. Do not bend over to get a look at your game, even though you know it's dead. You may catch an arrow in the eye. It's happened before. The shaft protrudes through the carcass, and the broadhead,

Approach downed game with great care. Even deer-sized game can injure or kill a human. This small bull moose could, with one kick, end a hunter's career.

Get help if you can. Holding a leg up out of the way may ensure you don't get cut trying to do the job of field-dressing big game by yourself.

which may be impossible to see in dim light, is poised in the air. Unfortunately, this is a dangerous and common situation.

Once you know the big game animal is absolutely finished, then it's time to begin the field-dressing operation. Unload your firearm. Set it away from the scene, not only to keep it clean, but so you won't step on it or trip over it. Get your bow out of the way, too. Secure all arrows so that broadheads are safely covered. Don't remove your knife from pack, sheath or pocket, however, until the animal is moved into a working posture. Holding a knife in one hand, while trying to move the animal, is asking to slip and fall, perhaps on your own blade. Now the object is to wield your knife without cutting self or partner. This can be deadly serious. A slip of the knife can deliver severe bodily harm, even death. A deep knife wound can cause bleeding that demands hospitalization, and the hospital, or even a professional first-aid station, may be many miles down the road. Ask yourself, "If the knife slips, which way will the blade go?" Obviously, it will go in the direction of pressure, so cut away from self or partner.

In spite of great care, if you field-dress a number of big game carcasses in a career, you'll eventually get cut. Chances are, it'll only be a scratch. But you must treat it. Compact first-aid kits are the answer for minor cuts. They contain bandages and should have some sort of disinfectant. If you have soap and water along, as I always do, wash the cut well. Apply disinfectant after washing. Liquid soap in tubes is widely available. Then bandage the cut to stop bleeding and keep the wound clean.

Nobody I know, including myself, wears goggles or any other special form of eye protection for dressing out a big game animal. Protective eyewear only weighs a few ounces and easily fits into a pocket or corner of the daypack and perhaps should be worn. Hunters who

41

wear eyeglasses may wish to consider special lenses for extra protection.

Bleeding the Carcass

Old-time hunters apparently bled the carcass as a rule. Perhaps "sticking 'em" got started in blackpowder days when a low-velocity projectile did not disrupt a lot of tissue. Therefore, internal bleeding was minimal, and it was a good idea to vent the jugular to drain body fluids. These days, the high-speed bullet, especially in the chest cavity, promotes a great deal of tissue damage. Simply opening the carcass allows fluids to flow away. Of course, broadheads, by their very nature, open the circulatory system. An animal taken by arrow demands no further "bleeding out." I never bleed a carcass, but some hunters insist on venting as much body fluid as possible, especially on larger-than-deer game, such as caribou, elk or moose. Be aware, however, that if the buck or bull is heading for the taxidermy shop, the cape (head and neck area) should be as cut-free as possible.

Watch Out for Musk Glands

Removal of the metatarsal glands, located on the inside of the back legs between joint and hoof, is wise if the animal is in rut. If the animal is not in rut, slicing the gland away has little value. If the gland is cut out, the knife must be washed free of secretions after the operation. The sometimes rusty-looking liquid from these glands ruins the taste of meat. Test first by sniffing the metatarsal gland. If the gland emits a strong odor, you may wish to cut it away, but do so carefully, making certain that you don't compound the problem by transferring musk from knife to edible meat.

There is one exception to removal of musk glands. Javelina, a small musk hog generally known as a "wild pig," are hunted annually in Arizona, Texas and New Mexico, as well as Mexico and down into South America. These near-sighted creatures are true musk hogs, for they wear a musk sac located on the back toward the hind quarters. Don't touch the gland. Leave it alone. You'll get an argument from 90 percent of the hunters you speak with on this point, because slicing the gland away is a long-time ritual written about for at least a hundred years. In spite of all this history, removing the gland on javleina is a mistake. It promotes the spread of musk, which may find

There are many ways to field dress a big game animal. But in all cases, the carcass should be positioned before any field work is started. Align the animal as straight as possible before beginning.

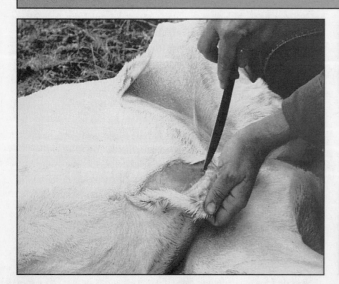

While there is no one way to go about field-dressing a big game carcass, starting with a cut alongside the reproductive organ is preferred. The cut is hide-deep only, and does not penetrate into the body cavity. This cut pertains to the buck or bull carcass only, of course.

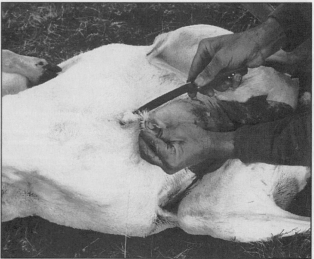

Continue the cut alongside the reproductive organ. With a doe or cow carcass, this step is, of course, eliminated.

On a doe or cow, the pelvic canal can be cored out either before or after making a cut in the abdominal region.

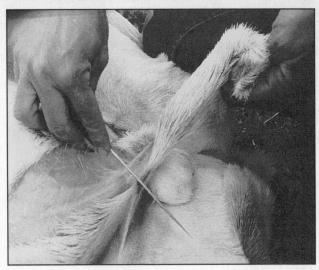

Continue to free the reproductive organ, but do not remove it. Leave it intact, to be drawn through the pelvic cavity later on.

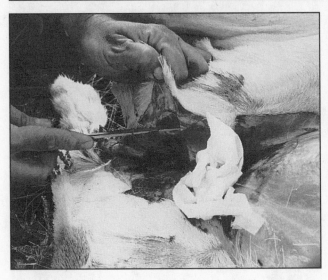

At any point in the operation, a clean rag may be placed in the working region to keep things a little cleaner.

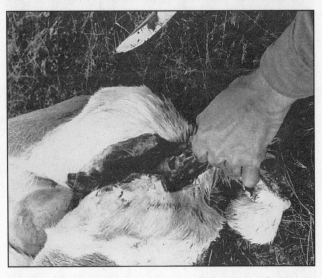

Pulling on the reproductive organ shows where to cut. The idea is to free the organ from its bond with the hide, all the way to the pelvic canal.

its way to the meat. Instead of slicing the gland out, stay away from it. Field-dress the little hog as usual, then strip the hide away. The gland comes away intact with the hide, rather than leaking on the meat.

Field-Dressing Big Game

As noted earlier, this is but one way to field-dress a big game animal. As the hunter gains more experience, he may wish to modify the procedure to suit his own desires.

Step One: Positioning

Position the carcass for ease of operation and safety. Trying to work on a downed animal lying on its side, for example, is awkward.

Prop the animal belly up, back down. On a huge animal, such as a moose, you may need help. Also, a stick or two jammed between the rib cage and the ground supports the animal with its belly upward. Turning the head to one side also helps. If you have a partner, he can help by controlling the front legs.

Step Two: Cutting Along the Reproductive Organ

Now with that sharp knife, slice along one side of the reproductive organ of the male animal. Do not cut deeply. Do not allow the point of the knife to break into the abdominal cavity. The plan is to slice around the reproductive organ to loosen it from its position on the carcass. The entire organ is cut free, (see photos) intact, except for its basal contact point near the rectum. For does and cows, remove the

At this point, the reproductive organ is freed right up to the beginning of the pelvic canal.

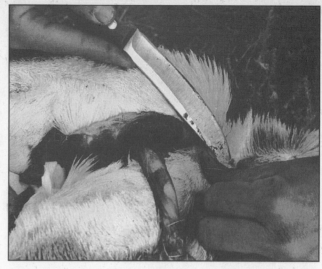

A cut is made virtually behind the reproductive organ to the anal area.

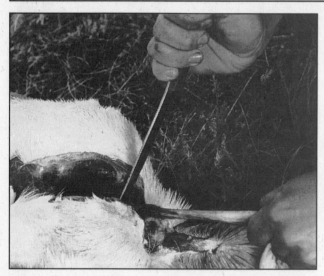

Now the coring process can begin. The knife cuts a circle all around the pelvic canal. Tugging gently on the reproductive organ helps to keep it out of the way during this important coring process.

The coring process is complete at this time. Now a cut is made from the anal region to the sternum, or all the way to the neck. If the animal is to be mounted, stop at the sternum.

udder by slicing it out and discarding it. Do not remove the udder if it is needed for identification purposes.

Step Three: Freeing the Lower Intestine

Now circumvent the bung area of either the male or female carcass with a knife. The object is complete removal of the lower intestine from its position within the inner walls of the bung area in the pelvic region. You can see where we are going with this: The reproductive organ, still attached, will be removed, intact, with the lower intestine *back through the pelvic region.* Imagine this step as a "coring out" process. You are coring the intestine from the walls of the pelvic canal.

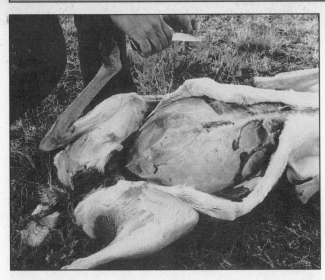 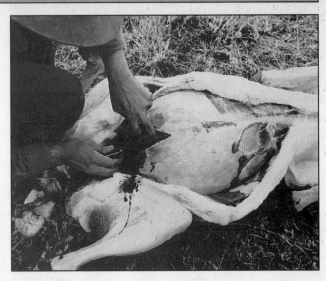

Since this buck is not bound for the taxidermy shop, the cut along the underside was made up to the neck. Now, the skin is carefully worked back off of the carcass to expose the entire belly region. This makes the rest of the job a lot easier because you can see what you are doing without the hide getting in the way. Also, it makes later skinning easier.

Now that all hide is worked back off of the belly of the carcass, the viscera is exposed. This is done with a long cut just under the skin, and not into the body cavity any deeper than necessary.

Step Four: Slicing the Abdomen

Using the sharp point of the knife, make a slit from anal region to sternum (breast bone), being careful not to puncture the peritoneum wall protecting the abdominal cavity. The cut is made as close to the centerline as possible. Cut the hide only, and do not let the knife enter the viscera. At this point, separate the hide from the meat by careful knife work on both sides of the centerline. This is an important part of the operation. By "skinning" the belly hide back out of the way, the entire abdominal cavity is clearly exposed. Plus, cutting the hide back helps to keep hair from getting on the meat. When the hide is not stripped back out of the way, it's very easy to slice the hair, and cut hairs fall on the belly. They also float in the air, landing on the hands and knife.

Step Five: Cutting the Belly Skin

Now, with the very tip of the knife blade only, make a slit from the anal area to just below the sternum to expose the viscera. There are "gut hooks" and other special knives that some hunters prefer for this operation. I find a sharp-pointed knife entirely workable. Only the tip of the knife blade is used, with the blade edge upward, facing the hunter. Fingers lift the abdominal wall tissue, while suppressing the offal (viscera) inside of the body cavity so the knife tip does not cut into the exposed intestines. After this cut is made, the offal are visible within the body cavity.

Now an important choice is made: If the carcass is to be packed out where dust may readily enter the cavity, the heart and lungs can be removed without further slicing of the hide along the sternum. Rather, the hunter works his knife blade along the entire outer area of the diaphragm, slicing through it. The diaphragm is a membrane that separates the viscera of the abdominal cavity from the "boiler room" or chest region. Once the diaphragm is sliced all along its perimeter, the hunter reaches in and cuts the lungs/heart free from their connective tissue. Tugging at these organs helps to release them from their contact points.

The knife does the rest. This is blind cutting, which demands great care because the hunter cannot see very well into the chest region. I reach far up toward the throat from the inside of the chest wall, cutting the windpipe/esophagus free near the throat region. The net result of this operation is the freeing of heart and lungs from the chest cavity, without cutting through the sternum. Air should be allowed to circulate freely into the chest cavity after the organs are removed. The benefit of this operation is two-fold: The carcass is not quite as open to dirt and debris, and the taxidermist has no worries about sewing up a sliced hide along the sternum.

If there is no concern about getting dirt into the carcass, and if the animal is not taxidermist-bound, a second choice can be made at this point—cutting along the sternum to expose the entire chest region. First, slice the hide down the center of the sternum all the way to the throat. Second, use your meat saw to cut through the sternum, separating the rib cage into two parts and opening the chest region so you can look inside where the heart and lungs reside. Obviously, this second choice is not a blind operation. Incidentally, a stout hunting knife can be used to cut through the sternum, instead of a game saw. This can be tough on a knife, but some blades can take it.

Step Six: Removing the Offal

Recall the reproductive organ and scrotum remain attached to the offal, as if by a cord. These are now brought back through the anal canal, but not cut off. Pulling the reproductive organ and scrotum through the walls of the pelvis allows them to remain intact. This is a very clean way of getting rid of these organs. *Important*: Be watchful of the bladder. Do not break the bladder while drawing the reproductive organ and scrotum through the pelvic region. Very often, the bladder will be full. The idea is to pull the bladder free of the body cavity along with the other organs. Keep the reproductive organ pointed away from the carcass at all times. Should urine flow through, it will not get on the meat.

The pelvic bone, also known as cinch or aitch bone, is not split,

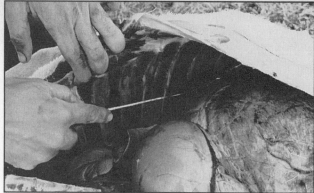

The organs in the chest cavity must be cut free. Work right along the backbone and cut lungs and heart free. These, along with all other viscera, can be tugged free.

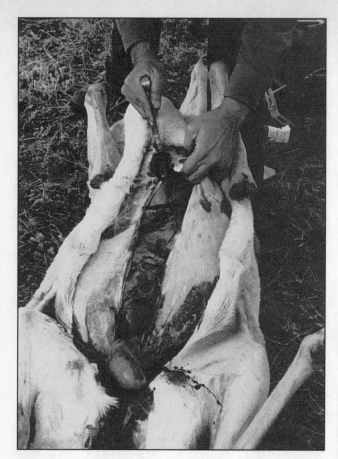

When the cut is made all the way to the sternum, a saw can be used to cut along the sternum, as shown here. However, be certain to skin the hide back first, or the saw will produce a shower of hair that will fall into the body cavity. Since the heart and lungs are lying along the backbone at this time, due to the position of the carcass, the saw will not hit these organs unless it is inserted too far into the chest region.

which keeps the hams intact, rather than flopping open, thus reducing the entry of dust, dirt or debris into the body cavity. Also, leaving the pelvic bone intact protects meat (round steak) that otherwise suffers from exposure to air and elements. On the other hand, splitting the pelvic bone allows for easier removal of offal, plus less chance of breaking the urinary bladder. While I never split the pelvic bone on deer-sized game, neither do I find fault with that method. If the bone is split, a small hand axe is useful, and a game saw is equally good. I've seen good knives ruined as hunters pounded on the back of the blade with a rock while using the blade to part the cinch bone. Heavy hunting knives, however, can handle the strain.

At this point, the reproductive organ and scrotum have been carefully pulled through the pelvic canal. The heart and lungs are loosened from their bonds within the chest cavity. And the abdomen is open with all viscera exposed. Removing the offal is now a simple matter of turning the carcass on its side and pulling all internal matter free and onto the ground. A little knife work directly beneath the backbone may be necessary to free the offal from the body cavity. Lying on the ground at this time, intact, are all of the "innards" of the big game animal. The liver and heart may be retained. If so, the heart is cut free, leaving the sack around it (the pericardium) in place to protect the heart from dirt. The liver is also sliced free from its connective tissue. The gall bladder, looking like a little balloon attached to the liver, should be cut out completely and discarded. "Bitter as

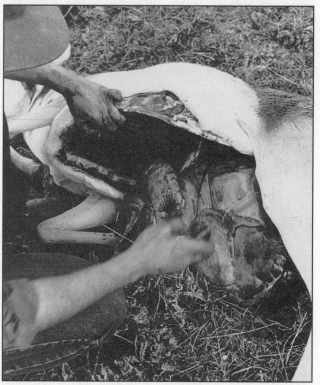

Now the offal can be removed from the body cavity. Gently tug on these to free them, as shown here.

gall" is more than a saying. Prop the heart and liver on a branch or clean rock to allow cooling.

Step Seven: Washing Out the Body Cavity

Deer-sized game can be lifted so that body fluids trapped within the abdominal cavity and chest cavity drain down and out through the pelvic canal. Then the interior of the carcass can be washed with water or snow (which melts from carcass heat into water). This is an important step, because juices from the alimentary canal are washed away. These juices, in the region around the windpipe, can quickly sour meat. A good washout helps prevent this problem. I always carry a clean rag in my daypack. The rag is used to wipe the inner cavity of the big game animal following draining. The rag is used again after a good hand-washing.

Now all of the internal parts are free from the carcass. The cavity can be washed with water at this time.

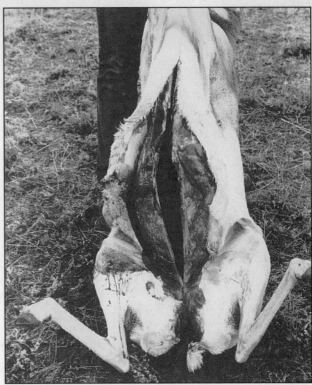

The job is done. The carcass can now be drained, and the cavity washed again with water.

Sometimes help comes in the form of automation. This bison bull could be skinned on the ground, but the job is much easier with the carcass elevated.

Step Eight: Cooling the Carcass

Before attempting to move the carcass, especially if it is to be backpacked, allow it to drain and cool. This makes a cleaner carcass to handle and also slows bacterial growth.

Evidence of Gender

Leaving evidence of the animal's gender intact on a carcass may be the law on some hunts, so check regulations. The most obvious evidence of sex for big game is the head. The antlered or horned head of deer, elk, moose and other game clearly denotes a male of the species, while the non-antlered or non-horned head proves the carcass belonged to a female. However, when boning or disjointing a carcass, it may be necessary to carry the meat from field to camp or vehicle. Then, it's wise to leave a part of the scrotum intact on the hind quarters. With careful cutting, it's possible to leave one testicle with each hind quarter. A reasonable game ranger will certainly see the parts of carcass packed to camp were of male persuasion if the hunter makes a solid attempt to leave parts of the scrotum attached. The udder can be left with the carcass as proof of female gender.

Hunter Cleanup

I carry water, and I don't mind using a little to wash up after field-dressing any game. A surgical sponge, or any small sponge, is useful. Impregnate the sponge with soap at home, then place it in a plastic ziplock sandwich bag.

Keeping the Carcass Safe

Hanging a field-dressed carcass in the sun can spoil the meat. That's as obvious as finding a bullfrog in your tomato soup, but drive by hunting camps and you'll see game hanging in the sun all day long. If you choose to skin the carcass then, wrapping it (skinning is covered

Keeping a carcass cool is important. On a warm day, a field-dressed, unskinned, game animal can be placed in a cool depression like this one, and covered with grass.

Another cooling method is to skin the carcass first, then place it into a cool depression. This one is wrapped in a cheesecloth bag, with a tarp underneath to keep the meat clean.

A small pack saw can be used to cut grass to cover a carcass, as shown here. Covering not only helps with insulation, but also serves as a deterrent to birds, such as magpies, that can cause a lot of damage to a carcass.

more fully in the butchering chapter) in a game bag or other clean porous cloth, like cheesecloth, is a good idea to keep off flies and dirt, but it has nothing to do with preventing the sun from heating the meat up, which promotes bacterial growth. Instead, hang the carcass at night to cool it. Then, lower the carcass during the day, placing it upon a tarp. Cover the top with sleeping bags to insulate the meat. Of course, if it's terribly cold all day long, this step is not necessary. Even then, don't allow the carcass to catch the direct rays of the sun. Sometimes there is no place to hang a carcass. A way to keep it cool is by placing it on the ground, preferably on a tarp, and covering it over with grass or other protection from the sun. Don't leave a carcass lying on the ground for very long, however, and if possible, turn it over so that one side does not remain against the ground all the time.

The Paunch Shot

We all hope it will never happen, but even the finest marksman may someday direct a bullet too far back. The paunch shot makes field-dressing messy and decidedly distasteful, but the job must be done all the same. The steps outlined above are still followed. However, there are some special considerations. First, cut away all hide affected by the bullet, or for that matter, a broadhead. This hide will have intestinal matter permeating it and it must go. Second, remove any abdominal wall tissue where bullet or arrow passed.

Third, after the offal are dumped on the ground, do a meticulous job of cutting away any tissue within the body cavity that shows signs of intestinal matter, or even discoloration from contact with intestinal matter. Fourth, do a special job of washing the body cavity with water, and scrub it thoroughly. Fifth, get the hide off quickly and butcher it as soon as possible. Most importantly, don't be afraid to get rid of tainted meat. Trying to save questionable parts may cause the ruination of good meat. *Hint*: Use your nose. If you suspect tainted meat, put your nose to work. Your sense of smell will tell you when a piece of meat has retained gastric juices.

Boning a Carcass in the Field

Boning a carcass is not that difficult. Do not eviscerate the animal. Prop it on its belly, not on its back. Make a long knife cut under the hide all the way from between the horns or antlers to the tail. Then make cuts across the shoulders and across the hind quarters. Skin the hide free and drape it on the ground on either side of the carcass. Picture this: The skinned carcass appears to be resting on its own blanket (hide). Now remove the backstraps (loins). This is easy, requiring only long straight cuts alongside each loin to remove it from alongside the backbone. Set the two loins aside on a clean surface to cool out.

The simple cut around the lower leg, and then straight up the inside of the leg, provides an excellent start for skinning a carcass, either in the field as part of field care, or in camp or home butcher shop.

Now remove the two front shoulders. This is also simple. Lift and cut. Lift and cut. The shoulder blades are freed from their position against the rib cage and set aside to cool. The hind quarters can be handled in various ways. One is to cut the meat free from the bone by running the blade down along the bone itself and working the blade around it. Or the hams may be cut free by running the knife first along the front of the leg bone and then along the back, removing huge parcels of meat. Further skinning of the neck area reveals neck meat that is simply "boned out" with the knife blade.

Disjointing a Carcass in the Field

This is a slightly different process from boning. First, follow the field-dressing process previously outlined. Then work on the eviscerated carcass. Do not remove the hide in the disjointing operation. Rather, leave the hide on the carcass for protection of the meat. Imagine the field-dressed carcass resting on the ground, hopefully on a grassy spot or a tarp. (I carry a small tarp tucked in between my packframe and my daypack as a matter of course—great for making shade, as well as creating an instant shelter against wind, rain or snow.)

Remove the shoulders as described earlier, leaving the hide on them. The shoulders almost seem pasted on the carcass, rather than firmly attached. They actually slice right off. Set them aside to cool. Then, work the knife down into the joints of the back legs and cut the hams away from the carcass, again leaving the hide intact for protection against dirt. Set the hams aside to cool. Turn the remainder of the carcass belly-down. This time remove hide along the back by making a cut directly down the backbone, exposing the loins. Cut the loins out. They will not be protected by hide. Let them cool, then place them in clean plastic bags, which I always carry.

The white kitchen-type bag is nice for this job. Liver and heart, if you want them, also go into a clean plastic bag for transport. The rib cage and other skeletal parts are normally discarded in the disjointing process; however, I won't leave ribs behind on a whitetail buck deer. They are favorites of mine, so I use my saw to cut down the backbone, separating the rib cage into two parts, and put both into one plastic bag. The ribs go directly against my packframe—flat, followed by the hams, then the shoulders. All are firmly tied on the packframe. Finally, attach the plastic bags containing the other meat parts, plus any meat boned off the carcass. Do this job right, and all you will leave for the coyotes is a skeleton.

The Site of the Harvest

Do not be concerned if the site of the harvest is less than neat and tidy. In moments, many creatures will be at work cleaning it up, while at the same time, getting a free meal. In a matter of a few days, most of the remains will be gone. Bugs as well as rodents and canines will all be at work, not to mention ravens, magpies and, in some areas, vultures and buzzards. Bald eagles also clean up leftovers (golden eagles are more prone to killing their own deer and antelope).

A hunter well practiced in careful field management of big game can take pride in his skill. It's a matter of self-sufficiency and wise use of a valuable resource.

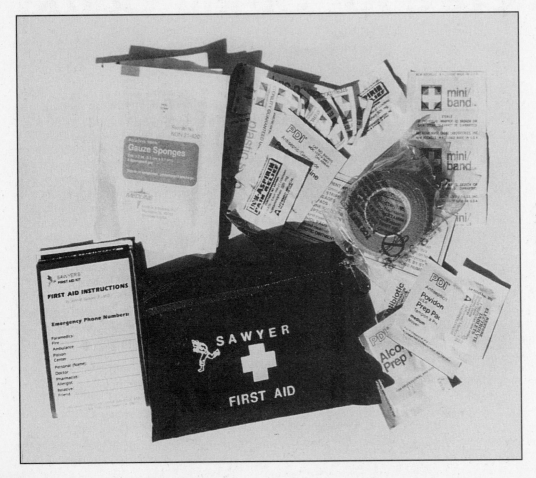

Carrying a pocket-sized first-aid kit like this one into the field provides everything needed to treat cuts.

SMALL GAME MEANS cottontail rabbits, number one in the land, and tree squirrels, second in popularity. However, field care for small game transfers to a number of other edibles, including opossum, raccoon, beaver, muskrat, woodchuck, rockchuck and a multitude of similar animals. Not included are bullfrogs and turtles, which demand special on-the-spot preparation. Small game animals literally provide tons of protein every year. Most hunters can bag some sort of small game near home, at a minimal expenditure of time or dollars. Recreation value is almost limitless as well. But, as with all wild food, field care of small game is the first step to a good meal. What to do with it after you've got it—that's the topic of this chapter.

The cottontail rabbit is the number one small game animal in the land, and probably always will be. Although very short-lived, whether hunted or not, and in spite of natural cycling, cottontails have the ability to build their numbers rapidly. Cottontails live almost everywhere. This one calls the badlands home.

Chapter 7...
Field Care for Small Game
Game Care & Cookery

Before and After The Shot
Choosing Your Weapon

Tender cottontails and none-too-large tree squirrels, as well as a host of similar-size edibles, are easily ruined by overgunning. If hunting with a shotgun, consider #5 shot. No particular shot size is perfect for small game, but I've found #5 a good compromise, providing an adequate number of pellets per load and sufficient to cleanly dropping small game without riddling the meat with hard-to-find tiny globes of lead. I've taken cottontails with #8 shot, even #9s. At close range, these smaller shot sizes are deadly, but there are so many pellets per shotgun charge that there may be a problem finding and ridding the meat of them. So I like #5 shot where and when available, with #6 shot a good second choice.

The 22 rimfire is, in my opinion, ideal for both cottontails and tree squirrels, and I prefer the 22 rifle over the shotgun where it is legal and safe to use. Depending upon the conditions, the 22 Short hollowpoint remains a good choice for small game, sufficiently powerful, but not destructive, quiet and effective. I'm a big fan of target-grade 22 Long Rifle ammo, too. Accurate 22 Long Rifle target ammo makes that all-important head shot easier to accomplish. Some hunters like 22 Long Rifle hollowpoints for small game. While I have no argument with that choice, it just does not happen to be my cup of tea. Head shots only being the rule, I prefer the 22 Long Rifle target round. Costs more, but how many shots do we shoot at small game in a season?

The tree squirrel is the number two small game animal in popularity, but that's more because of a less vast habitat than any other reason. Squirrels are good to eat, and great small game to hunt.

It's easy to recommend the right arrowhead for small game—it's a broadhead. I used to recommend blunts, but I cannot any longer. I've taken enough small game with bow and arrow to know that the broadhead is the better choice. While some bowmen recommend a dull broadhead, I like a sharp one. Which broadhead? It hardly matters because all are good for small game. Some of the tougher one-piece heads are nice because they last longer than modular heads. For example, I have arrows tipped with Abel Grizzly broadheads that have seen field service for several seasons. These tough broadheads are dulled by contact with the ground, but not ruined. There are no replaceable blades to break off, and the simple one-piece Abel Grizzly can be resharpened quickly.

After the Shot

Unload the firearm and safely set it aside, or do the same with bow and arrows. If there's snow on the ground, as often there is when I hunt small game, I place the harvested rabbit or squirrel directly on the snow for a couple moments before attending to the skinning operation. That's because of fleas. Sometimes the small game carcass is home to quite a colony of fleas. That's just a fact of life. It's also a fact that fleas can get on the hunter, and that's not good, so don't let it

Hunting small game in the snow with a Kimber 22 rimfire rifle, the author gets steady for a meat-saving shot.

happen, or you may find yourself breaking out in hives. I set the carcass in the snow for a moment, or if there's no snow on a rock, then I watch. If fleas are abandoning the rabbit or squirrel like sailors on a sinking ship, I let 'em leave for a few moments. Then I start the field-dressing operation.

Field-Dressing Small Game

Cottontail rabbits are simple to field-dress, mainly due to the ease of skinning. There is nothing to it. Watch out for the fine hair, however, as it floats everywhere and sticks to everything. Take your time. Get the hide off without pulling free a lot of hair. Following are steps to field-cleaning the highly edible, high-protein, all but fat-free rabbit.

Squirrels are no real problem, either, but they are not as easy to skin. Usually, limits are held to under a half-dozen squirrels per hunter, so taking time to properly field-dress each squirrel does not harm the hunt.

Step One: Removing the Hide

Roll up your sleeves and use protective gloves if you wish. Watch your hands at all times. If you see a flea, slap it off and let it find a

Bullet placement is highly important to small game field care because only the head shot counts when meat is the object. This shooter has closed the gap on a cottontail. He'll place the 22 bullet from his rifle just right at this range.

(Text continued, page 55)

FIELD-DRESSING SMALL GAME RABBIT

Slit the hide cross-wise on the back, accomplished here with a Puma folding knife.

Pull the hide both ways, fore and aft, to cleanly remove it from the carcass.

Here is the head with half of hide removed from rabbit.

Now pull hide down over hind legs.

Using the tip of the knife only (this is why a sharp point is good for small game work), slice just underneath the belly skin of the rabbit to expose viscera.

Pull viscera out of the body cavity by hand, or swing carcass rapidly in a vertical circle, which uses centrifugal force to remove viscera.

Pull hide over the head, as shown here. Sever head at neck, which accomplishes two things: it removes the head, and one-half of the hide.

Continue to pull hide and fore and aft until the hide is in two parts, one part by the head, the other by the tail of the rabbit.

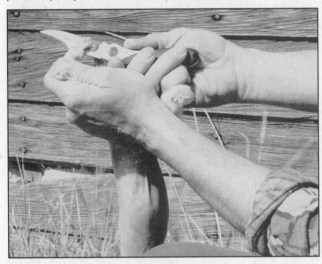

Break the back leg at the joint. This is easily accomplished by hand. Pull downward on the broken joint to expose the leg bone, as shown here. Now cut hind furred paw free. Do this to the other paw and rabbit is entirely skinned.

Cut both front legs off at the joint. This not only removes bony and inedible part of front leg, but also the furred paws.

After viscera are removed from the belly region of the carcass, cut directly through the center of the sternum, as shown here, to expose lung/heart organs. Remove these by hand.

Hold rabbit with belly side facing you. Use knife point to cut through cinch bone (pelvic region). This exposes any remaining viscera in the anal canal. Remove such viscera by hand.

The way a small game animal is harvested is paramount to field care. A modern pellet rifle, like this 17-caliber RWS model, is excellent for small game within range, and very easy on the meat.

Kevin Norcross of Casper, Wyoming displays several meals of cottontail rabbits. The 22 rimfire pistol is good for the artful dodger if the hunter is expert enough to make the head shot.

Step Two: Removing Head and Legs

Let's concentrate on the rabbit first. The hide is resting over the head and hind legs. With a knife, cut off the forepart of the front legs. Then sever the head with the knife. Now half the hide, plus the forepart of front legs and the head, can be discarded. Next, cut off the forepart of rear legs with the hide. *Tip*: The head can be removed with a partial knife cut, then a strong twist. Once again, the squirrel may require more attention, especially more knife work, but the idea is the same—to rid the carcass of the foreparts of legs and head, leaving only the body of the small game animal on which to work.

Step Three: Eviscerating The Game

Getting the offal out of the body cavity is also easy on rabbits. Make a cut with the point of the knife just under the skin to expose the viscera. The cut goes from vent to head, right through the rib cage (sternum). Also, cut through the pelvic bone. Then, loosen the intestine in the pelvic canal so it will fly free when you do the next step. Holding the rabbit by its hind legs, lift the rabbit up and snap it down, as if you were cracking a buggy whip. Centrifugal force evacuates the viscera. The squirrel, once again, may demand more hands-on effort to remove the offal, but make the same incision, from vent to throat/head, and try the buggy-whip method. Free up what viscera remain with your fingers on rabbit or squirrel, including heart, lungs and liver. Clean the body cavity of every internal organ, in other words.

Rabbit fever, or tularemia, is for real. The use of "rubber gloves" made of synthetic materials is highly recommended. These gloves are strong, comfortable, unhampering and reasonably priced. Few of us use them. We should, however, and I'm going to. If a rabbit's liver is highly spotted, I suggest leaving that rabbit behind. This is not unlawful in my region, provided the rabbit truly shows signs of illness.

Step Four: Removing the Tail and Extra Skin

Cut off the tail. This does not mean the furry outer powderpuff of the rabbit, or the bushy squirrel tail, but the bony tail itself. Make a V-cut using the knife blade to cut on one side of the tail toward the hams, then on the other side. This cuts off the tail right at the base so it can be tossed out. Also slice away some of the flap of skin that used to cover the belly of the rabbit or squirrel because it is not good to eat. At this time, do not worry about removing the tough outer skin that

home in the snow. On a rabbit, the easy way to slip the hide is to grab the fur right in the middle of the rabbit on the back or the belly. Make a slit with your small knife. Then pull the skin in two directions—toward the head and toward the tail, simultaneously. This leaves hide over the head and hind feet of the rabbit. In a moment, the hide will split into two parts. Discard both parts right away by tossing them aside. The hair will be found and used by different creatures, including mice which use rabbit fur to line their nests.

Tree squirrels can be skinned in a similar fashion, but not as easily. Squirrels have stronger hides that seem almost glued on at times. I suspect older squirrels are the most difficult to skin. Sometimes it's best to skin a squirrel almost as if it were a tiny big game animal, by cutting from vent to throat, then making cuts from that long incision outward to each of the four legs and peeling off the hide. Don't be surprised if it takes a little tugging. I have resorted to pliers at times.

The 17-caliber pellet is capable of high accuracy and efficiency on small game. Somewhat unique in design is the RWS Superpoint, far left, designed for good penetration on small game.

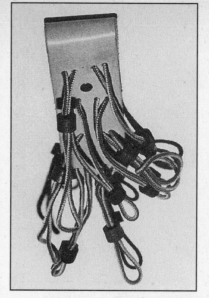

The Lohman small game tote is more than a way to carry small game animals from the field. It's a game care item because it allows the carcass to hang in the open air, rather than "sweating" in a game vest or game coat.

Fadala considers small game hunting with a bow a fine experience. These squirrels were harvested with blunts from a Herb Meland Three-Piece Takedown Pronghorn longbow. Good food. Good sport.

covers the backstraps of the rabbit. This skin will be removed during the butchering process. For now, leave it on to protect this excellent piece of meat.

Step Five: Washing and Cooling

I carry water when small game hunting so I can immediately wash the carcass after evisceration. Then I allow the carcass to cool out for a few moments. On a cold day, a cottontail, weighing about $1^1/_2$ pounds, cools quickly, as does a skinned squirrel.

Step Six: Drying and Bagging

What you have in hand is a rabbit or squirrel carcass, completely free of offal, with no head, tail and lower extremities on front or back legs. Dry the damp carcass with a clean cloth, then place your prize in a clean plastic bag once it has cooled off. This keeps the meat clean. If you don't dry the carcass first, water will collect in the plastic bag and make a mess. Although the cottontail rabbit is the subject of this chapter because of its immense popularity, the squirrel gets the same treatment. It, too, is cleaned and carried in a plastic sack.

Although probably a topic for Chapter 9, "Transporting Game From the Field," it's important to remind hunters that game vests and coats with game-carrying pockets worn on the hunter's back can pick up warmth from the body of the hiking outdoorsman. From time to time, check the contents of your game bag or game pocket to make certain your harvest is staying cool, rather than warming up. You may have to remove your hunting coat or game vest to ensure the coolness of its precious cargo.

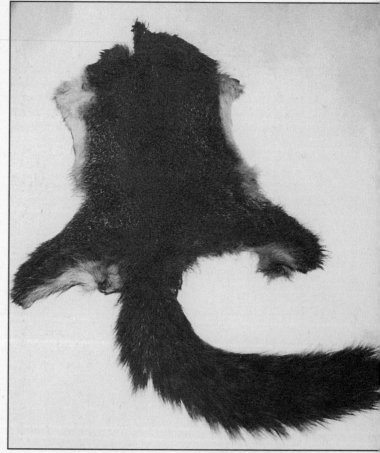

A bonus of doing a nice job of skinning a tree squirrel is the handsome hide, intact, as shown here.

My own small game strategy includes cleaning rabbits and squirrels very soon after the harvest. Even rabbits become more difficult to care for when they "set up." Also, gastric juices can invade the meat, not only from shotgun-taken rabbits and squirrels, but even from head-shot animals. Therefore, it is extremely important to good eating to clean small game as soon as possible after you get it. I'm aware

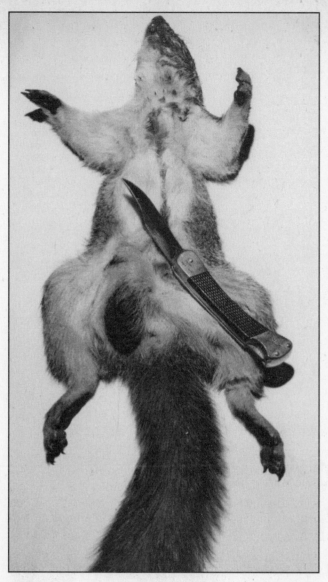

A sharp-pointed knife is right for the skinning operation on tree squirrels, and other small game. The small game animal is first laid out on its back and a cut is made from anal region to neck, which has been executed here.

The squirrel is skinned along the belly (one straight cut from anal area to neck) along with cuts outward along each leg. Then the hide is peeled back by hand, using a sharp knife to slice wherever connective tissue must be cut free.

that sometimes the hunting gets pretty hot, and it's difficult to stop the action for a field job on harvested game, but do it anyway. The result is better meat.

Saving the Pelt

The methods for skinning previously discussed did not take saving the pelt into account. Rabbit pelts can be useful for glove linings, as well as decoration. Squirrel pelts can be extremely handsome, especially the fantastic Abert's squirrel with its tasseled ears and remarkable coloring. The pelt can be saved through careful skinning with a long cut from vent to head, plus cuts going from this main incision out to the pads of all four feet. Then the hide is carefully removed from the carcass by hand, plus careful strokes of a small knife blade.

Squirrel mounts are fairly popular and quite handsome. Rabbits don't get mounted as a rule, although the "lowly" cottontail provides such high-grade food and unending recreation that perhaps we should consider honoring one now and then at the taxidermy shop. Careful skinning is demanded if the small game animal is bound for the taxidermist.

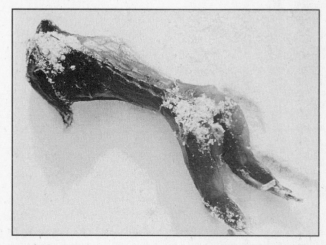

One way to cool a small game carcass is in the snow, as this rabbit is being cooled off before placing in a game bag. Once cooled, the skinned carcass cannot sweat, and will not rapidly or easily spoil.

The enjoyment is two-fold. Taking upland game birds with a Jerry Hill longbow was great; proper field care was also enjoyable because the eating was worth the effort.

Chapter 8

Field Care
For Upland Birds
And Waterfowl
Game Care & Cookery

THESE BIRDS ARE gourmet quality all the way. They'd sell for several dollars a pound on the open market, if you could buy them at the grocery store. Quail, dove, partridge, grouse, wild turkey, pheasants, ducks and geese are included for this chapter on field care. There are hundreds of different types of upland birds the world over, including woodcock, snipe and many other edibles lesser known to the general world of hunters. Field care for birds, in a basic sense, is the same. Butchering is not always identical, but many similarities exist, while cooking can be vastly different species to species. This chapter is concerned only with the first of the trio mentioned above, not butchering, not cooking, but rather the field care of upland birds and waterfowl to ensure that the bird you put on the table is the best tasting bird it can be.

Field-Dressing Upland Birds and Waterfowl

Some simple tools are needed: Water in a container, such as a canteen or bottle, plus cleaning rags, plastic bags, and a sharp knife are the only tools necessary for field-dressing upland birds and waterfowl. You may need a little string, too, if you wish to hang a bird in the field for cooling out.

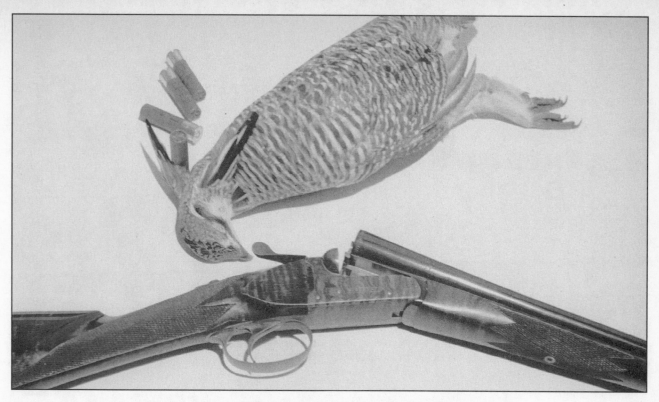

Field care starts the moment the game is in the bag. This fine prairie chicken was harvested with a 28-gauge Hatfield Uplander double barrel shotgun. The light charge of shot was sufficient for a clean harvest, but not damaging to the excellent meat.

Step One: Drawing the Bird

No matter what variety of upland bird or waterfowl, it's imperative to field dress it sooner than later. This is true of ducks and geese, and absolutely essential for the quail/grouse/partridge families, which tend to sour quickly, especially in warmer weather. Twenty-two rimfire rifles and handguns, along with any legal firearm, as well as airguns, are legal for taking mountain grouse and partridge over much of the West. The bow and arrow is entirely legal for game birds where I hunt; check local regulations where you hunt. While it's true that upland birds can be brought to bag with firearms or airguns, and

waterfowl with archery tackle, the fact is, most of these avians are harvested with shotguns.

It's important to understand that shotgun pellets travelling through the abdominal region of any bird cause the flow of fluids, most of them bitter. These fluids wander throughout the cavity of the bird. That's why swift drawing of the bird is so vital. And it's easy to do. Pluck away a few feathers around the anal vent of the bird. I prefer to pull out quite a few feathers, all the way from the vent to just below the breastbone, so that I can see what I'm doing. Then, with the sharp point of a small knife, make an incision from the vent to the base of

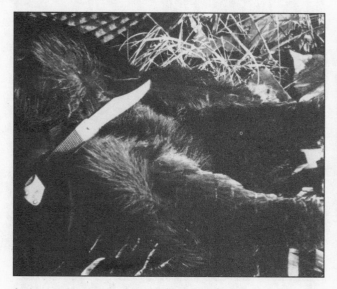

A sharp-pointed knife, like this Puma folder, is used on upland birds. Here, a wild turkey awaits field processing.

Here is the vent area exposed by plucking feathers from the region.

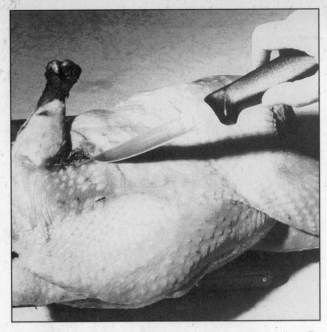

Note where the 36-caliber round ball from a muzzle-loading rifle penetrated. This area needs to be cleared of any bloodshot meat and tissue.

Maneuver the bird so that the vent area can be cut into to remove viscera.

the breast bone. Then, two more cuts are necessary. These cuts begin in between the vent and the breast bone and run outward. The result is a four-way cut exposing the innards of the bird so the hunter's hand can reach in.

The next part of the drawing job is probably where the term originated, because the offal must be drawn out of the body cavity. Human fingers are the best tools in the world for this task. Reach way up into the body cavity and pull all of the innards out, including heart, liver and gizzard. Save these three organs if you wish, but of course discard lungs, and all other inner parts of the bird. The heart, liver, and gizzard can be used for preparing stock, which in turn makes fine gravy.

Step Two: Bleeding Out

It's wise to bleed any upland bird or duck soon after it is dispatched. There are two fast and easy bleeding methods: The neck may be sliced with a sharp knife to cut the jugular vein, or the head may be removed entirely, which is even more certain of evacuating body fluids. Know the law: It may be unlawful to remove the head of an upland bird or a duck, in which case the neck-cutting operation is advised. No matter which method is chosen, body fluids of any type, blood as well as gastric, can be detrimental to the flavor of the meat, so take this step seriously.

Step Three: Removing the Craw

The craw, located in the neck/upper chest region of the wild turkey and similar upland birds, should be removed at this time. The craw is loaded with food, and these foods can sour rapidly, which in turn may harm the quality of the meat. Feel for the craw with your fingers. Find it, then slice all around the craw to pull it free. It's a very simple job. Always study the craw of a bird to determine what it ate. This can be valuable information for future hunting. For example, I noticed that the craw of a wild turkey was loaded with fine grass seeds, which led me to a patch of grass along a creek. Next season, I got another bird there using that knowledge.

Puddle-jumping ducks on the desert rewarded this hunter with a future duck soup treat.

Step Six: Using Baking Soda

Over the past few years, I've added this step to field-dressing all birds. After the cavity of the bird is washed out, I drop about a teaspoon of baking soda into the opening, along with a half cup of water, depending upon the size of the bird (two teaspoons of baking soda and a couple cups of water for wild turkeys). I swish this mixture around. Then I work the baking soda and water with my fingers in a scrubbing process. Although I cannot begin to prove it, I think the baking soda clean-out does a good job of cutting gastric juices. I'm convinced that quail benefit from this step. Quail sour quickly, probably because of the strong gastric juices left in the abdominal cavity of the bird, and baking soda seems to neutralize these fluids. I repeat: proof is lacking, but evidence is not. Evidence suggests the baking soda treatment is worth the slight extra bother of having a little ziplock sandwich bag full of soda in the game vest or coat pocket.

Step Seven: Drying It

Dry the interior of the bird with a clean rag. Leaving the body cavity wet is an invitation to spoilage, even though the baking soda treatment was used.

Step Eight: Cooling It

The vented bird should be cooled. Remember that most of the feathers are intact, and these feathers hold in heat. And sticking the warm bird into the game vest or hunting coat is asking for spoilage. One way to cool any bird, from quail to wild turkey, is to hang it in the shade a while. A piece of string tied to one or both legs does the trick. After fully cooling a bird, you may wish to wrap it with a cloth to insulate the meat from reheating.

Step Nine: Skinning or Plucking

In the field, a bird can be skinned or plucked on the spot. However, do leave evidence of the species intact. For example, where I hunt

Cooling your field-dressed upland game prevents meat spoilage. Hang the bird in the shade by the feet. After cooling, protect the meat by wrapping the carcass in cloth or other insulating material.

Step Four: Cutting Away Loose Skin

The loose skin around the vent and belly of the bird, skin that was exposed by the four-way cut, should be sliced away at this time and discarded. It's of little to no value, and quite often this flap of skin is tainted from contact with bitter visceral juices. Cut the entire tail section off and discard it. Just make a circle with your knife that encompasses the tail and off it comes. Remove the entire vent area. This area can only cause souring and offers nothing edible.

Step Five: Washing the Cavity

The entire cavity of the bird should be washed now with water. I literally scrub the cavity out with my fingers, working down against the interior of the cavity to remove all remaining evidence of offal. Don't try this without water. A water wash is the only way to do this job right. That's why I always have a canteen of water with me when upland bird hunting, or a water container in the duck blind. The value of washing the cavity with water is self-evident—to get rid of fluids.

After a carcass, such as this sage grouse is clean, washed *and dry*, it can be carried in a plastic bag. But it must never be bagged warm or it could spoil. Also, be sure to leave identification (one wing) on the bird until checked by a game warden, as this bird was before removing the wing.

This bird is ready to be plucked. It is free of all viscera, and the gizzard is attended to. Heart and liver are also saved in a plastic bag, along with gizzard, after these parts cool.

Here is the plucked bird. Feathers left on the ground will quickly deteriorate and are not to be considered littering.

sage grouse, the law states that one wing must remain on the carcass for identification purposes. Removing both wings can lead to a fine. I pluck quail. I skin most other birds, including wild turkeys. Using the cooking methods described later, skinned birds turn out fine. They are not dry at all. Quail, however, are worth the extra bother, so I leave their skin intact by plucking out the feathers. The skin on quail helps hold in juices when pan frying is used to cook these delectable birds. Plucking is just that—pulling feathers out, either by hand or machine—it will be by hand in the field, of course. Skinning is rather simple: Just make a slit with a sharp knife right under the keel of the bird. Make the slit as long as you please. Then poke underneath the slit to lift the skin away from the breast meat. Pull the skin free. That's about all there is to skinning a bird in the field.

In camp, other methods can be used to get rid of feathers, but in the field, dry-plucking is the only choice. In camp, a pot of hot water promotes easy feather-plucking. Plunge the bird directly into the boiling water, then pull the wet feathers free by hand. Some hunters use wax. Paraffin is melted, poured over the bird, allowed to harden, then lifted off in slabs. It's best to hand-pull major feathers first. Birds can also be singed, but this method is actually a follow-up after removing feathers. Singeing can be done over a camp stove. Turn the burner to high, then hold the plucked bird over the flames. The flames will burn off any tiny feathers clinging to the carcass. Be sure to wash off the bird after singeing to remove lingering burned feathers.

Breasting a Bird

Another way to handle a game bird in the field is the breasting method. This way of dressing a bird seems wasteful, and on some birds it would be. Quail, for example, should never be breasted. Their plump little legs are worth saving. Dove, on the other hand, are nothing but breast. Dove legs are as meatless as a twig. To breast a dove, hook your thumb directly under the point of the breastbone. Hold the bird firmly with the offhand, and yank upward with the thumb, pulling the breast completely away from the body of the dove. The

entrails of the bird remain within the body cavity. The wings of the dove remain with the breast. Pull only one wing off and leave the other intact on the breast for identification purposes. Now rub the breast with your thumb to remove the feathers and the skin. Rubbing is all it takes. The feathers, along with the skin, come right off intact and are discarded.

I also do the breasting operation on sage hens. The difference is that I may save the legs by simply cutting them off with a knife. Breasting a sage hen, or any larger bird, is not at all like breasting a dove, however. This is a filleting process. The breast is first skinned. Make a cut at the breastbone, through the feathers, and lift all of the skin and feathers away from the breast to fully expose the meat. Then, with a sharp knife, cut straight down the keel to one side, and then again on the other side. Tease the meat away from the keel with your fingers, as well as further knife slices.

The object is to remove the entire breast meat package from the bony keel of the bird. Don't forget, however, that evidence of species must be left intact, so be sure you either leave one wing on, or as I try to do, find the game warden who is working the area and have him check your birds and register them. This is an easy matter where I hunt because there are game stations set up in the field. Once the game warden says it's OK, then breast your birds for camp or home, rather than carrying the feathers and bones out of the field. A good boning or breasting job saves the meat, leaving only the inedible portions of the bird in the field.

The largest bird I ever breasted was a young wild turkey. After checking the young tom through the game warden station, I pulled the feathers and skin away from the breast, boned out the entire breast area, saved the legs as well, and we had fried turkey steaks in camp, rather than the usual roast turkey. Breasting worked fine in this instance, but it is not the usual way to field-dress a wild turkey. On the other hand, many wild birds are best field-handled with the breasting method, whereby the meat is salvaged, while the rest of the carcass is discarded for the use of other wild creatures, from ants to coyotes.

The head is removed now, and discarded.

Hanging Game Birds

Large game birds, from sage hen size to wild turkeys, can be hung in camp after field work. These birds should not be hung without a protective covering, however. I use sections of deer game bags for the job. The long deer bags are cut into shorter lengths. One end is tied shut with string. Then the bag is slipped on the hanging bird, wrapped around its feet tightly, and taped in place. Masking tape, electrician's

The turkey carcass can be completely cooled overnight by hanging it as shown here. However, it must be covered to protect the meat from flies. A double-wrap with a "deer bag" was used to protect this bird.

It's all right to skin the breast of an upland bird like this sage grouse; however, after cooling, the meat must be covered or it will dry out. Leave a wing intact for identification.

Field care of upland game and waterfowl starts with an attitude. Here's a sage grouse. It's a renewable resource and it's "meat on the hoof." Take care of it when you get it.

Field care of the gizzard is easy. The first step is to slice it open *cross-wise*. This exposes the contents of the gizzard as shown here.

Now the contents of the gizzard are completely removed, and the tough skin that lines the gizzard is stripped away by hand. This is very easy to do. The tissue parts readily from the gizzard and is discarded.

The turkey tail can be kept and prepared as a fan.

tape, or any other type of adhesive tape serves to create a seal so flies and other unwanted visitors cannot get to the meat. Hang the bird(s) in the shade, of course, and take them down by day to insulate them with a sleeping bag or blanket to keep them cool.

Doing the Gizzard

Taking care of the gizzard is also simple. First, make a cut about a quarter-inch deep *crosswise* on the gizzard. Now turn the gizzard inside out along the cut. The gizzard will readily do this. Then, dump the contents of the gizzard, after studying to determine what the bird was eating (good reference for hunting information). Now remove the wrinkled skin that forms the inside of the gizzard and throw this tough skin away. Wash the gizzard with a bit of water and dry it. The gizzard is now ready to pack out of the field in a sandwich bag along with the heart and liver, which have also been washed and dried.

Saving Feathers

Leaving the feathers of any bird in the field is not littering. Feathers are biological. They decay and return to the soil. However, you may wish to save feathers of game birds. Primitive-type archery is back in vogue as this is written, and wild turkey feathers are used for fletching. Feathers are also decorative. A small feather on the end of a string, or tied to the upper or lower string of the bow with a piece of thread, is a neat wind gauge. Some feathers are useful for fly-tying as well. By skinning the pheasant, obtaining a "cape" is no problem. These capes are valuable for fly-tying.

The tail feathers of the wild turkey is highly decorative and easily salvaged. Cut off the tail, and this means removing the plump section of meat that holds all of the tail feathers. Slice this off, feathers intact, with a sharp knife. Then salt the meat portion to dry it. Place the tail feather fan on a cardboard backing and pin the feathers in place using straight pins. When the tail dries, you'll have a nice fan to display.

These are just some of the basic field methods for handling wild birds of all species.

The most obvious means of packing smaller edibles from the field is by hand.

Chapter 9

Transporting Game From the Field

Game Care & Cookery

GAME CARE INCLUDES transporting the meat from the field to the camp or the car, then to the home or the butcher shop. This step is just as important as proper field care. Do it wrong, and your meat will reflect the mistake.

Small Game and Birds

After field care, these easy-to-carry edibles require cooling and staying cool. It does no good to properly field-dress and handle a cottontail, squirrel, duck, partridge, quail or any other delicacy, only to ruin the meat through incorrect transportation. Cottontails and squirrels can be carried in the open air. Lohman's Model 884 Small Game Tote is a perfect example of a small game/upland bird/waterfowl carrying strap that attaches to a belt or can be carried by hand. Eight string "nooses" hang from a common leather strap. Small game can be held fast by the head, as can upland birds or waterfowl. I've never had a piece of game slip off my own Model 884 Small Game Tote.

The advantage of open-air carrying is obvious: The game does not warm up in a coat pocket or game vest. But there is nothing wrong with game coats or vests, either. They especially have their place in hunting quail, dove and other birds that have large limits. This is even true of cottontails where limits may run high—ten per day where I hunt bunnies. If a game coat pocket or game vest is used to pack the meat out of the field, great care must be taken to avoid heat-up. Heat from the hunter's own body can invade the coat pocket or vest and spoil game. So stop now and then. Empty the contents of your game vest or coat onto a clean area, such as a carpet of grass, to make certain that your cargo of gourmet food does not spoil. Quail, incidentally, seem especially prone to spoilage through improper transportation.

Another good way to take small game, upland birds and waterfowl from field to home is fully field-dressed, excluding an identification wing where the law demands. All small fare can be treated about the same: skinned or plucked, washed, and placed in clean plastic bags. Cooling and keeping the meat cool is the delicate part of this operation. If the meat is allowed to heat up within the plastic bag, fast spoilage is the rule. On cold winter days, I carry fully dressed cottontails, well-cooled, in a plastic bag or bags. Then, from time to time, when I stop to rest a moment, the bag goes down on the snow. This keeps the meat absolutely perfect.

Ice chests make ideal game meat carriers. A chunk of ice lasts a long time in today's well-insulated ice chests. If the transport is a long one, dry ice may be used. Dry ice cannot be employed to transport game meat by airplane, however. A lot of boned meat can be packed into an ice chest. Styrofoam chests are especially lightweight, too, and ideal for air transport. Freeze your meat first, if you have a chance; then no ice is necessary to transport it a very long distance.

Transport by Vehicle

The day of proudly displaying a buck deer across the fender of a car or truck is long gone and should not have been in the first place. You may be proud as a new father of identical twins, but your harvest is generally of little interest to the rest of the world. Put game inside the vehicle, not on top of it. This goes for any wildlife. A well-cooled

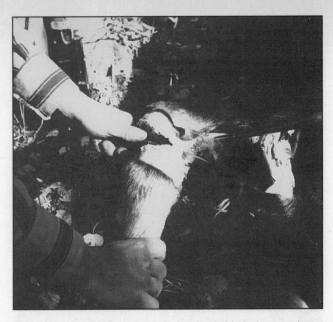

Reduce the weight of a carcass by leaving behind what you do not eat, such as this heavy hock on a moose. The bony lower leg will be left for coyotes to chew on.

game carcass, be it cottontail to moose, can be transported over a fairly long distance by insulating it within the vehicle. Be especially careful to insulate the flooring, such as a pickup truck bed. I carry a batch of old newspapers, plus a couple worn-out sleeping bags, for this work. Cardboard boxes broken down flat also work well for floor insulation.

Place your game in between layers of old newspapers, plus cardboard flats, plus sleeping bags, and it will remain cool for quite a while. I've carried meat across three states in two days without losing one bite by first skinning the carcass, covering it with a game bag, then insulating the meat well, transporting it within the interior of a vehicle. Boned and frozen meat within a cooler is better, but once a large carcass, such as a deer, is well-cooled, it will stay that way for a couple days when properly insulated and carried inside the vehicle. Don't forget to let cool air reach the carcass when possible. For example, if travelling in cool weather, remove insulation at night so that the carcass can receive cold air, if you're staying over a night or two on the way from hunt to home.

Boning/Jointing Big Game

A few notes on getting the carcass from field to camp or vehicle were sounded in Chapter 6, "Field Care for Big Game." Of special importance are the arts of boning the carcass or, at the least, jointing it. It's a simple fact, the edible portion of a carcass, domestic or wild, is only a percentage of the live weight. We do not consume antlers, horns, hides, bones, hooves, body fluids, abdominal content or anything other than specific palatable muscle structure, with the exception of specific internal organs, such as the brain, which is eaten by only a rare few gourmands. Because we use only a percentage of a carcass for food, the load can be lightened amazingly by boning or jointing. Boned or jointed meat can be taken from the field well-cooled in clean plastic bags attached to a packframe. An entire elk can be carried out in only a few trips from the site of harvest to camp by a couple hunters if the meat is boned out.

As always, the letter of the law must be observed. If evidence of sex is the rule, then boning and jointing become less effective than otherwise. Nonetheless, the law does provide for leaving inedible portions of a carcass in the field for other consumers to enjoy, includ-

Game vests come in many styles and sizes. Browning's Turkey Vest was designed for turkey hunters, but enjoys multiple use status and works fine for small game hunting.

Disjointing or boning is the way to carry a big carcass to camp via the packframe.

Sometimes "heavy equipment" comes in handy in transporting a large carcass from the field. This bison was lifted first, skinned, then literally deposited in the bed of a truck to deliver the meat to camp.

ing magpies, crows, weasels and countless other life forms. So bone or joint a carcass when it is appropriate. Don't be afraid to make a couple trips from field to camp, especially if you wish to carry out the hide, horns, antlers, hooves or other useful parts of the carcass. Always disguise your cargo with bright orange before packing out. Never allow your load to look like moving game, for obvious reasons. Although a basic law of hunting is to completely identify a target before shooting at it, as in all walks of life, some people do not follow the rules.

Driving Right Up to a Carcass

In many hunting situations, it's legal, prudent and downright smart to drive right up to a big game animal and lift it directly into a vehicle. It also makes sense to move the vehicle as close to a carcass as possible before backpacking the animal out when you cannot drive up to it. Do not drive across farm fields or, for that matter, any vegetation that can be ruined. And never go off-road when the ground is wet. The ruts you put into the land may last for decades, causing severe run-off problems. In some areas along the Oregon Trail, ruts made by wagons in the last century are still well-established in the earth, some of them eroded by water flow into miniature canyons.

The Pack Animal

Most of my hunting career, I have been my own pack animal, but I'm well acquainted with beasts of burden for the job. Pack animals are not limited to horses, mules and burros, although these animals, especially the horse, are far more popular than others. A large dog can carry a modest load of meat, and a goat can, too. A llama can carry more than a goat. My son, Bill Fadala, uses llamas now and again to hunt backcountry. He finds that a llama can carry a modest load, generally not to exceed a hundred pounds, and usually about half that. Remember that a field-dressed mule deer buck weighs from perhaps 180 to 200+ pounds, but such a carcass can be boned down to a llama load or less when the job is done right.

Of course, we never want to strain and hurt a pack animal. And by the way, don't let a pack animal, especially horse or mule, hurt you, because it happens every year. I know we won't go to crash helmets and neck protectors for backcountry horseback riding (it's simply not

While using horses for packing is an excellent way of getting big game from field to camp, only trained animals are right for the job. This horse knows the ropes, including hitching a ride back to the ranch.

Horses do a great job of getting to downed game, but they have to be trailered to the vicinity first.

Well-trained horses, like these Mexican steeds, do a great job of getting game from field to camp. The cowboy in this picture carried whitetail bucks out (Coues deer) strapped behind his saddle.

the cowboy thing to do), but I know people who wish they had been wearing a crash helmet and neck protector when a horse has balked and sent them flying to the ground with lifelong injuries. So consider such protection, even though you won't look like Roy Rogers when you're riding.

The Game Cart

Also known as elk carts in the West, these wheeled vehicles work quite well, depending upon the terrain. A custom-made elk cart built by Bud Sprenger of Casper, Wyoming, is an especially effective model. This particular cart can be operated by human leg power, or pulled by winch and cable, or cable attached to a vehicle. Sprenger and friends have used the special cart to pull bull elk from canyon to roadside many times. So the game cart is another option in getting meat from field to vehicle for transportation home.

Backpacking the Carcass

Because my family and I tend to hunt away from major roads for a lot of our big game, the backpack method has served to transport most of our big game from field to vehicle. My latest packframe is a

Before attempting to backpack this mule deer buck to camp, it is literally cut in half, sectioned at the ribs to divide the load into two parts. The front half will weigh a little more than the back.

modified Camp Trails Freighter model. Starting with the standard unit, I added brace work for additional strength, plus side padding to safeguard the riflestock, plus a padded hook to accommodate a sling for carrying the rifle in the field. There are many ways to attach carcass to frame. The following is but one method.

Step One: Minimizing Weight

Reduce the weight of the carcass as much as possible. Make two trips instead of one. If you do carry an entire unboned carcass from the field, be certain that you can handle the weight without injury to your back, knees or any other part of your body. Never jump down with a loaded packframe, not even from the height of a log. Step down carefully instead, allowing your body to slowly absorb the weight of the pack. Jumping causes extra strain and can cause serious injury, including a hernia.

Step Two: Sectioning the Carcass

If an entire carcass is carried out of the field, do it in two steps, unless it's on the lighter side. The weight a person can safely manage without injury is entirely personal, and a hunter must know his own limits. I feel that antelope weighing about 100 to perhaps 120 pounds are within my limits, and I still carry out deer whole up to 170 pounds, but will not attempt heavier loads. How do I know when my own limit is reached? First, I look at the carcass. Experience tells me roughly what the animal weighs. Then I strap the field-dressed carcass to my packframe and rise with it loaded on my back, getting to my feet very slowly. I can tell in an instant if the load is beyond my ability. My knees speak first. If I feel pain in my knees, I immediately sit down with the load, slip out of the frame, and go to work cutting the carcass into two pieces, or boning it out, or disjointing it.

In most cases, halving the carcass makes more sense than carrying it whole. I find myself going to this system more and more as I grow older. It's safer in terms of injury, much easier as far as strain is concerned, and can even be faster. Two quick trips from field to camp may take less time than one extremely slow one. A half deer, for example, is not an overload for a seasoned outdoorsman, provided the buck's not a monster. Of course, a dressed weight of over 200 pounds still results in a hefty load. So after halving the carcass, load one of the halves on the frame, rise slowly, and if there is any indication of strain, go to work with your cutlery kit to reduce the carcass. Get rid of hide, at least some bone, and so forth, until the halves are entirely manageable.

Halving a big game carcass is easy. After field-dressing, cut through the ribs where the backstraps (loins) of the animal leave off. If you have your saw, use it to sever the spine at this juncture. The result is a deer in two parts, the front half weighing a bit more than the back. For example, a deer that weighed 170 pounds field-dressed went 90 and 80 pounds in halves, the upper section going 90. I've weighed the halves of other carcasses as well, finding the same situation. Halving a deer or other similar-sized carcass is not only sensible for a lone hunter, but ideal for partners. Each sportsman carries a half, and this way the whole deer makes it in one trip.

Step Three: Picking a Route

Although I like old-timey things, such as longbows and muzzleloaders, I also have a great respect for modern technology and high-tech helpers in the field. My own global positioning unit from Eagle is a perfect example of a high-tech tool I greatly admire. I've used it to help map the safest route from field to vehicle by pinpointing my destination. I'm less a woodsman than many others, so the global positioning instrument is a great tool for me and the rest of us who do not have a Daniel Boone sense of direction. If you know the terrain

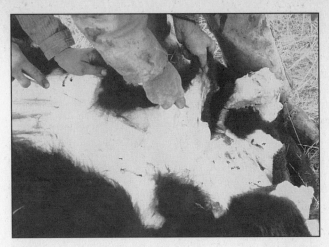

Be prepared to skin large animals on the spot, reducing the weight of the carcass. Also be ready to section a carcass. There is no rule that says a big game animal must be taken to camp in one piece.

One way to rise with a load is to kneel first, as shown here.

Using the walking stick for support, the hunter begins to rise slowly to the standing position. There is no need to hurry. Waist belt is not cinched at this time.

Now waist belt is cinched in place and the hunter is ready to hike to camp. Cabela daypack is slung over the top struts of the frame, where it rests on the meat. Even in steep country like this, a hunter can get a large big game carcass from the field to camp if he reduces the size of the carcass to cut the weight, and if he doesn't try to get the whole thing back in one trip.

well, then you can all the better choose a safe way to your vehicle. But do take a moment to consider the best route from the site of the harvest to the camp or car. It's very important. One time I decided on a shortcut to camp, my back loaded with about 150 pounds of carcass. I ran into a canyon, made the huge mistake of trying to negotiate it instead of walking around the long way, and ended up taking a ride to the bottom the fast way, on my backside. No bones were broken, but my pride was severely damaged.

Step Four: Tying Up the Load

In a moment, we'll talk briefly about tying the carcass onto the frame. But first, another safety point demands attention. That is rising to your feet after the carcass is tied onto the frame. My way of doing this is sitting down with the packframe behind me. Then I slip arms through the straps and buckle the frame belt. At this point, the frame is secured to my body. Then I lean forward, rolling my body and placing both hands flat on the ground. I end up on my hands and knees at this point. Getting off my knees and onto my feet is accomplished one foot at a time. In order to rise, I either have a partner help me up, or I use a walking stick to pull on.

But before rising, the load must be securely tied to the frame. I rest the packframe flat on the ground first, pulling the carcass onto the

frame with head up, legs down. My pack has a shelf on it. The bottom-most part of the carcass is lodged against this shelf. It's not a bad idea to remove the lower limbs of all four legs entirely by cutting them off at the joint, but they can also be left on and tucked in. I used to use $1/8$-inch nylon cord for the tie-on, but not any more. I've moved up to $1/4$-inch. The larger diameter cord requires fewer wrap-arounds and does not tangle as easily as the smaller cord. At this point, about 20 feet of the nylon cord is slipped under one longitudinal strut of the backframe, then under the body of the game animal, and out under the opposite longitudinal strut. About half the cord sticks out on either side of the carcass.

The rest of the procedure is more common sense than rules. It's a matter of tying the carcass onto the frame so the legs are tucked in and the head strapped down. That's the entire goal of the operation: head strapped down, legs tucked in, so nothing protrudes out to the side, or as little as possible. If you are packing a buck deer, the antlers can be used as tie-on points. A buck antelope offers the same with its horns. The nylon cord goes around the upper body, lower body, middle, horns or antlers, and legs, until the carcass is securely tied on board. It's not a bad idea, if a section of rope remains after tying the carcass, to run a line longitudinally, from the top of the frame to the bottom of the frame. If the frame has no shelf to help support the butt-end of the carcass, the longitudinal tie is even more important. Sometimes, I take several longitudinal runs with the cord. This provides good support, plus a location to make a final tie-off point right in the middle of the carcass.

Carrying Quarters

If you can pack out a moose or elk whole, you were born on the planet Krypton and can leap tall buildings in a single bound. The only way the rest of us can backpack out an elk or moose is by reducing the size of the beast. Quartering is one way to do that. The disjointing process described in Chapter 6, "Field Care for Big Game," is employed to reduce the carcass into sections: head with antlers, if you wish to keep the antlers; two front quarters consisting of shoulders,

upper legs, and half of the rib cage; and two rear quarters; along with the hide, if you want. Also separate are the heart and liver, cooled and placed in plastic bags. The hide can be left on, and this is not a bad way to go because the hide keeps the meat clean during transport. Describing how to tie quarters on is unnecessary. It's quite a simple matter. I tuck the big end firmly down against the shelf of my packframe and use ordinary wrap-arounds with $1/4$-inch nylon cord to retain the quarter on the frame.

Walking Out

I use a Moses Stick, which is no more than a walking staff. Mine are made from agave stalks. The agave plant is a cactus with a long center stalk. It looks very much like the familiar Century Plant of the Southwest. I take only dead stalks. It's wrong, and unlawful as well in some regions, to cut a living agave stalk, so never do it. Further-

Here, the front half of the buck is tied onto the packframe. Now the hunter has to gain his feet and start packing. A Moses Stick helps maintain balance and is good for support while walking and when stopping for a rest.

Even half a deer is a load, so the hunter has to take his time. The walking stick is used effectively here.

Smaller deer can be packed out whole, but a hunter should never take a chance of hurting himself, either with a strain, or by falling down. Don't pack more than you can comfortably carry.

more, the dead stalk is aged to perfection. If worked on by carpenter bees, it's especially ideal. Carpenter bees burrow into the stalk to make a home. This hollows the stalk out to a degree, making an already light stalk even lighter. Agave stalks are strong. I scrape the stalk clean with an ordinary butcher knife, followed by coarse sanding.

Then a crutch bumper is fixed to the lower tip, and a tanned leather handle is glued and nailed to the upper end of the stick. Under the top of the handle, I place a rubber or foam pad as a binocular rest. The Moses Stick is useful for hiking, binocular searching for game, shooting rest, and other tricks, including signalling, and it's also ideal to lean on when carrying out game via the packframe. My walking staff has saved me from would-be fast rides down canyon sides, as well as simple stumbles that can result in not-so-simple bone fractures. I strongly recommend some type of walking stick when getting game out via the packframe method.

In my daypack, I carry a number of essentials, including marking ribbon to mark my harvest site. I also have an extra fluorescent orange game vest with me. I tie this onto the antlers or horns of the carcass after it is loaded on the frame. A bit of marker ribbon on the frame never hurts, either. Be safe. Make sure your game animal does not look like one as you pack it from the field to your camp or car.

Mark Your Harvest Site

Never leave the site of the harvest without marking it well, even if you are related to Dan'l Boone. I carry rolls of fluorescent ribbon for the purpose in my daypack. Pick the ribbon up on the return trip so you don't litter. I learned this marking trick the hard way. I'd cut a buck mule deer in half, intending to return for the second part that same day. It was early afternoon when I set out for camp with the first half of the carcass. Once there, I unloaded and then started back. Unfortunately, I missed the path and found myself off by one hill. I spent the rest of daylight looking for the second half of my buck. When I finally loaded the carcass on my frame, it was dark, so I had to make the trek to my vehicle by flashlight beam. Had the site been marked, I would have immediately seen the second half of the deer carcass, for it was actually in plain sight, just one hill over.

The Packframe and Its Value

More good packframes are around today than ever before. My first packframe was a homemade job built of heavy-duty marine-grade plywood and rope. It worked, but comfort was only a word compared with today's great models. There are numerous tube-type frames, as well as flexible plastic types. Use what you like. But do get the right size. The hunter who goes for moose and elk should buy a large frame. I like the large frame all around, as it accommodates deer-

sized animals intact. I would recommend large for every hunter, but the individual outdoorsman must choose his own frame size in accord with what fits him.

Backpacking stores are commonplace these days, and packframes are also sold in sporting goods shops and department stores. Try several frames for size before buying yours. Buy a daypack, too. The daypack is loaded with good gear and simply slips over the struts of the packframe, or otherwise attaches to it. If hunting true outback country, consider taking lifesaving gear with you. I carry a small tent into this setting. Mine is the Camel SST Sixty Second model, and it truly takes but a minute to set up. It weighs 7 pounds, and well worth the carrying, especially in territory known for snowstorms. This particular tent is available in three sub-models: Genesis, Exodus and Explorer.

The first two are dome-shaped; the last one an A-frame style. Mine is the Exodus with a center height of 57 inches and overall dimensions of 7 by 11 feet, enough size for two to three hunters caught in a storm. A nylon tarp, good for instant shelter, can also be carried via a packframe without knowing it's there by tucking it between the frame and daypack. Consider a lightweight sleeping bag, too, for far-away hunting hikes. I have a Peak 1 that serves me well. A sleeping bag plus tent provide shelter against everything from gentle rain to blizzard snows. The packframe is a fantastic unit for the meathunter who wants to get off the beaten path, or follow a trail into far-off places. Mine goes where I go, and it sees use on almost every big game hunt.

Getting meat from the field to a vehicle and to the home is just as important as any other aspect of game care. It requires a clear understanding of purpose—to care for the meat in all phases—and execution of a plan, plus good gear, not the least of which is a packframe. While packing big game from the field is often hard work, it's also a part of the hunt's challenge. Knowing the art is vital to anyone who considers himself a meathunter.

An orange vest is tied to the carcass before packing. This is a safety precaution that should be followed.

Meathunters and cooks need a large variety of knives to do many different tasks, but author's son Bill Fadala used his Buck folding knife one hunting season for everything from small game to large, including field-dressing, skinning, and full butchering of big game.

THROUGHOUT THE HUNTING season of 1993, my son, Bill Fadala, ran a little experiment. He used one knife, a Buck XLTi folder, for everything from field work on small to big game, plus boning out every carcass from deer to elk. It worked. The meat he packaged for the winter was superbly prepared for the freezer. However, in spite of this successful experiment, we won't use one knife for everything, because there are too many excellent options that make the work go smoother and faster. At the same time, it's wise to remember

Chapter 10

Tools for
Butchering and Cooking
Game Care & Cookery

that a hunter does not need every butchering tool in existence to do a professional job of meat preparation. The same is true of cooking gear. It's impossible to list all cooking tools from garlic crusher to stove. This chapter deals with many butchering and cooking tools, but, of course, not all of them. There are so many options that a 500-page catalog would not be large enough to list every one.

Butchering Tools

Skinning Knife

Assuming the hunter does his own butchering, as we do, a skinning knife is in order. The hide of a big game animal can be removed in the field or in camp, or in the home butcher shop. It all depends upon the nature of the hunt. No matter where the job is done, however, a skinning knife is ideal for the work because of its unique blade shape. The skinning knife blade is rigid, rather than flexible. The back of the blade is comparatively thick, and the edge is rounded so only part of the blade makes contact at any given time. The blade is heavy rather than light, and overall weight of a skinner is not a concern, since the knife is not generally carried in the field by the hunter. The work of the skinner is to part the hide away from the meat without slashing either one, using the wedging effect of its blade style. A skinning knife does not require a sharp point.

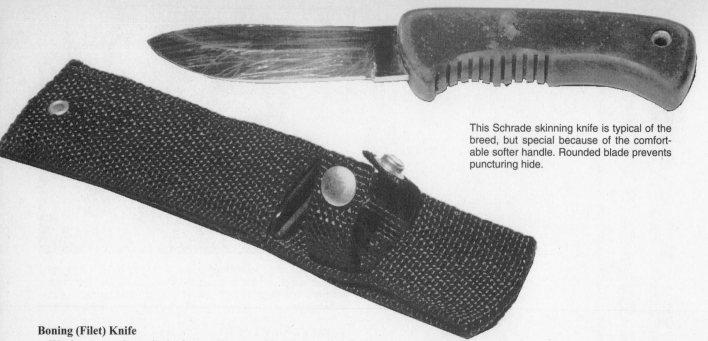

This Schrade skinning knife is typical of the breed, but special because of the comfortable softer handle. Rounded blade prevents puncturing hide.

Boning (Filet) Knife

We do not store bones in the freezer. However, this does not mean that bones are worthless. They can be used to boil for stock, and while we won't do it (let's be honest), the marrow within the bone itself is good food, so we could boil the bones and crack them open as the Mongolians (Tartars) did, and still do. The boning knife is vastly different from the skinner because its work is entirely different, removing meat from the bone. The blade is flexible, rather than rigid, and shaped much straighter than the skinner's blade. By nature, the flexible blade is thin instead of thick. Boning knives are usually lighter in weight than skinners, with much narrower blades. The blade's flexibility allows a wrap-around effect, curling around a bone to some degree so that meat is sliced free. The point of the skinner should be on the sharp side, so the blade deeply works its way into the carcass.

Anza's boning knife has a long blade with great flexibility. The blade is easy to sharpen, and it stays sharp through a great deal of work. The boning knife blade must be strong and capable of holding an edge, because much of its tenure is spent working against bone.

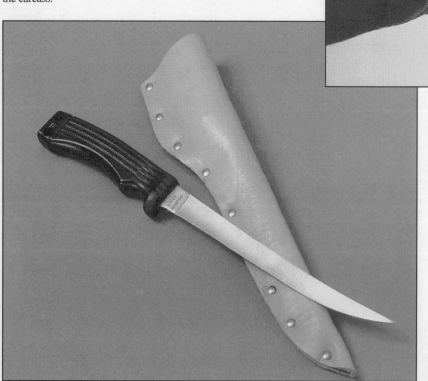

Buck's fish filet knife also works as a boning knife. Care must always be taken with thin-bladed knives, of course, because the blade sometimes bends and it's easy to lose control of the knife.

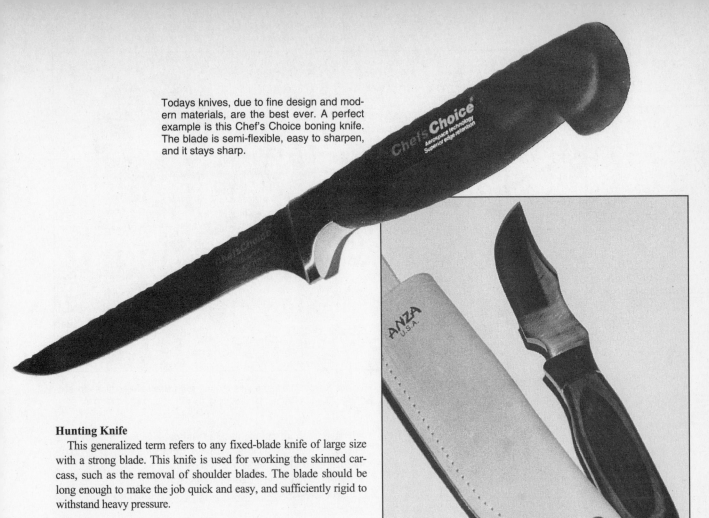

Todays knives, due to fine design and modern materials, are the best ever. A perfect example is this Chef's Choice boning knife. The blade is semi-flexible, easy to sharpen, and it stays sharp.

Hunting Knife

This generalized term refers to any fixed-blade knife of large size with a strong blade. This knife is used for working the skinned carcass, such as the removal of shoulder blades. The blade should be long enough to make the job quick and easy, and sufficiently rigid to withstand heavy pressure.

Meat Saw

The meat saw goes into play soon after the carcass is skinned. It can be used to reduce ribs to packaging size, for example, or to cut through the aitch bone (hip or pelvic bone) of the carcass. The saw is also useful in removing hocks quickly and neatly, as well as sectioning any part of the carcass. The meat saw goes to work again even when a carcass is home, for it creates working-size pieces. For example, a ham can be cut into two or three pieces for easier handling by cutting with a meat saw. This is especially important on elk-sized carcasses.

The Meat Cleaver

The butchering methods shown in this book do not include cutting through the backbone to create chops, but for those who wish to do so, it's easy with a meat cleaver. First, the spine is cut down the center with a meat saw, and then a cleaver is used to cut out each chop. We also use the meat clever to prepare ribs for packaging. After the rib cage is cut with a meat saw, each rib is further separated with a meat cleaver. A small meat cleaver is also ideal for working with small game, such as cottontails and squirrels. A large cleaver can be used for small game, but a tiny cleaver is not that handy on a large carcass. If only one cleaver is purchased, it should be a large one. *Be especially careful with a cleaver. It will remove a finger just as readily as it removes the lower legs of a rabbit.*

Caping Knife

Gaining popularity is the caping knife, which is a small model used to remove the cape for taxidermy work. Some hunters are finding application for these small knives in butchering little carcasses, such as rabbits, squirrels and even birds (boning out breast meat).

There are so many fine cutlery tools offered today that it's impossible for a gamehunter to keep up with them all. Anza, for example, offers a special heavy-duty hunting/skinning knife made from file blades that are specially tempered.

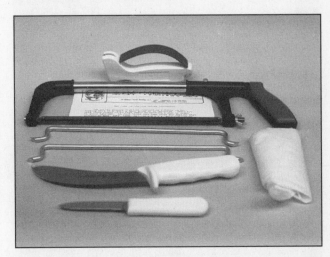

The Sausagemaker company of Buffalo, New York, has a special Deer Field Processing Kit that contains full instructions for use, along with how not to handle a harvested deer in the field. Included: special "anal removing knife," skinning knife, two stainless steel spreaders, gloves, sharp meat saw, and accu-sharp sharpener.

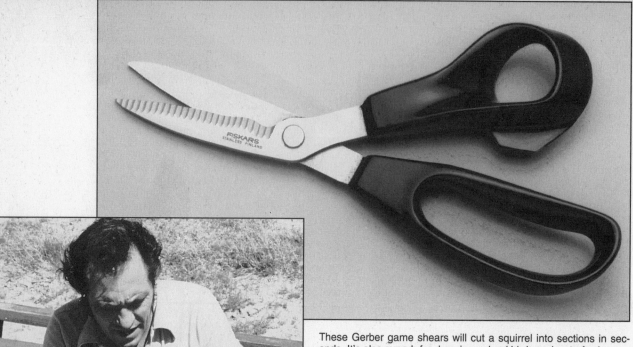

These Gerber game shears will cut a squirrel into sections in seconds. It's also superb for dressing upland birds and waterfowl.

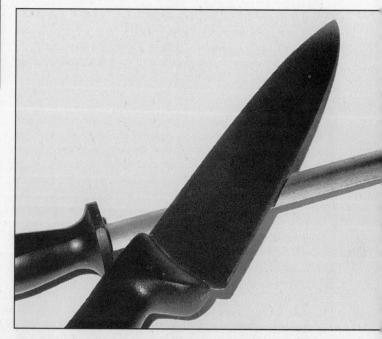

Game shears are made to for relatively heavy-duty work. Here, game shears are used to snip the wings from a duck.

Game Shears

Sometimes called kitchen scissors, because they are basically large, strong scissors, game shears are extremely useful in butchering small game and birds. Game shears have a notched blade, which is perfect for severing the lower legs of birds to remove inedible parts.

Knife Sharpening

A steel is handy to have during the butchering process. A steel is not truly a knife sharpener. It's used to maintain edge straightness. As a finale in sharpening a knife, the smoother the steel, the better. However, for butchering work, I still like a steel with some serration. If only one steel is purchased, it should be the smooth style, for it will serve not only in the butchering process, but also in the final stages of knife sharpening.

All butchering operations demand sharp knives. Sharp knives are not only easier to work with, but also safer. Knives that require con-

siderable force for cutting can slip and cut a person. Several knife sharpening tools and their functions are included in Chapter 5, "Tools for Field Care." Please refer to that section.

Here are a few simple rules of knife care:

1. Put the knife away dry, not wet, even if it has a stainless steel blade.

2. Oil all wooden handles from time to time using a drop of linseed oil or a furniture oil. Finish with a clean cloth so that only a trace of oil remains on the handle, and do not get oil on the blade of the knife for the obvious reason of tainting meat with the oil.

The steel, shown here with a chef's knife, is useful in keeping a knife edge straight. The chef's knife is ideal for chopping parsley, onions, and other vegetables for cooking.

Also better than ever, the modern frying pan. With non-stick surfaces that truly don't stick, it's hard to beat a state of the art frying pan. Heavier models, like this one, have thicker bottoms that hold heat well.

The use of special cooking tools is essential with modern coated frying pans like this one. The plastic spatula resting in the pan will not scratch the surface like a metal one will.

Here is an excellent frying utensil, an old-fashioned cast-iron skillet coupled with a close-fitting cover. With cover in place, food can actually be steamed tender by slow-cooking.

3. Finish the wood handles. Some wood-handled knives come from the factory with very little finish. Do not create a deep, hard finish on these handles. Merely touch them up with a little Birchwood-Casey Tru-Oil to make the handle less susceptible to moisture.

4. Do not cut paper, wood or any other object with a butcher knife. Cut only meat with it.

5. Do not use a knife for prying or as a screwdriver.

Follow these simple rules and your knives will last.

Choosing Butchering Knives

The previous information concerning knife types, such as boning knives vs. skinning knives, should serve to direct a home shop butcher to the right models. However, don't forget that there are many models within the genre. Consider knife size when choosing your own models. Try a knife in your hand for comfort before buying it if

you can. Also, consider the handle structure. If your hands get tired using wood handles, look into the many new knives with softer synthetic handles.

Hardware stores usually have a reasonable supply of knives for butchering. Restaurant supply houses normally carry an even greater number, as do specialty knife shops, which are a part of many malls and shopping centers. Finally, don't forget your local library: There are a number of good books on cooking and butchering tools. These are worthwhile catalogs for browsing.

Cooking Tools

Frying Pan

Part of the great modern world of super cook gear, today's fry pan is better than ever. I still love the old-time cast-iron skillet, and I own four that see use. However, it's difficult to bring out the old-timers when I can grab my new non-stick, heavy-bottom pan. The two keys are non-stick cooking surface and heavy bottom. The latest models are truly non-stick. I do own a couple thin-bottom non-stick fry pans for the trail, but these do not see service in the kitchen. Another tip: Check the handle of the fry pan. It should be designed to remain rigid. Handles that rotate when loose with age are troublesome.

Knives for Cooking

The butcher knife is useful in taking a boned hunk of meat and turning it into steaks or cubes. A paring knife is valuable for peeling potatoes, carrots and other vegetables. A Chinese cook knife is great, I know, but I have not yet familiarized myself with its use. But it deserves mention, for it works very well, as we all know from watching cooking shows on TV. A chef's knife is valuable for many tasks, including chopping and dicing (chopping parsley, dicing onion). And a thin-bladed boning-type knife is useful for cutting thin steaks for various dishes.

Standard or Glass Roaster

A standard roasting pot, with lid, is valuable. It serves well for wild turkeys and any game roast. The glass roaster is excellent for preparing boned meat like a pot roast dinner. This is due to the excellent seal created by the tight fit between the lid of the glass roaster and the body. Roasts prepared in these are always moist.

Modern glass cookware is better than ever. This fine cooking utensil is large enough to prepare a roast for several people, and it cleans up quickly and easily with hot soapy water and a cloth.

The crock pot is a highly useful cooking tool. As this illustration shows, the crock pot is a four-piece device. It consists of the heat source (base), far left, plus electric cord, container and lid.

The heart of the crock pot is the control switch, shown here. This crock pot has 5 settings. The lower settings are used for very long cooking times. On the higher settings, the cook will have to check the food more frequently to ensure that is does not burn.

Crock Pot

The crock pot is used for several recipes in this book that require slow cooking. After a few hours, the result is delicious.

Wok

My wok is really a standard frying pan, but the wok deserves mention because many cooks use these excellent utensils to great advantage, especially for stir-fry dinners. Also, electric woks are available, but you must be near an outlet to use it.

Dutch Oven

Useful indoors as well as outdoors, the Dutch oven is good for everything from a tasty roast to baking a cake. There are numerous books on Dutch oven cooking. I often use a Dutch oven, without lid, on the cookstove for making stews.

Pressure Cooker

The pressure cooker is so valuable that it has its own well-deserved chapter. See Chapter 23, "Pressure Cooker Cookery," for the uses possessed by this amazing cooking utensil.

Microwave

The microwave has earned a special place in the American kitchen. It has also earned a special place in this book, see Chapter 24, "Microwave Cooking."

This Presto pressure cooker will finish carrots in a minute or so, and it will "parboil" a rabbit dinner to tenderness in 10 to 20 minutes. A pressure cooker is one of the best cooking utensils on the market—fast, efficient, easy to use.

Stock Pot and Others

The stock pot is my spaghetti sauce maker. I seldom use the stock pot to make stock, not when my pressure cooker is available for that task. Other pots are also useful in game cookery, in assorted sizes.

Meat Grinder

We've gone to a commercial-type meat grinder because gameburger is so important to our overall meat supply. While this type and size grinder is right for our particular operation, it is not correct for most hunters. Commercial meat grinders are very expensive. There are many good kitchen-type grinders, however, that work fine for modest quantities of meat. These are available in electric or hand models. A good hand-grinder is still one of the best investments a hunter cook can make. We still have ours for small jobs.

Cutting Board

My own cutting boards are two, both wood: One is thin and hard for slicing, such as bread; the other is thick, softer and much heavier, for cutting steaks and cubing meat. A note on wooden cutting boards: Unless they are maintained with thorough cleaning after every use, they can cause trouble because wood may harbor harmful bacteria. When my wooden cutting boards wear out, I'm going to a hard-sur-

This commercial grade meatgrinder is ideal for preparing gameburger and high cost of unit demands considerable use. This is extremely lean gameburger that will be packaged and frozen without fat. Gameburger meat without fat is ideal for making chile and a multitude of other dishes.

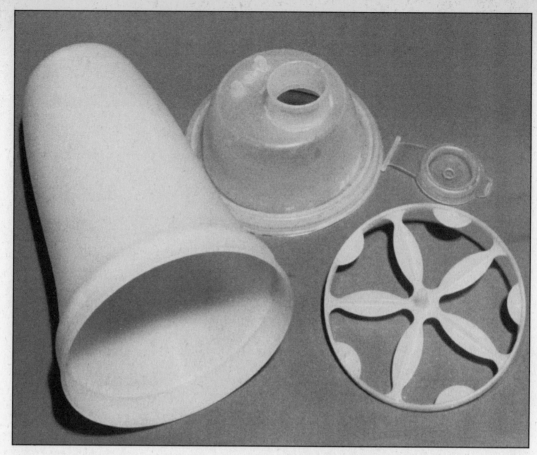

This particular type of shaker is among the best. Corn starch or flour is placed in the shaker with water, stock, broth, or other juice, and after shaking, the result is a milk-like fluid that is used as a thickener for stews, chile con carne, gravy, or any other dish that requires thickening.

face synthetic for new ones, and I have to suggest the same for others. Consider the polyethylene cutting board for its hard, non-absorbent, odorless surface. These come in various sizes. We also use several large cutting boards for butchering. These are sections of formica countertops. They are used to cover our regular countertops for indoor butchering, after the meat is sectioned from the carcass, which hangs on gambrels attached to rafters in an outbuilding.

Butcher Block

Our own butcher block is a heavy, movable (on wheels) block that serves for butchering in an outbuilding. There are also smaller butcher blocks that are even more portable.

Spatula

This is an important item in cooking breaded game meats. Use a good stainless steel spatula for standard-surface pans and a special plastic, such as exo-glass, spatula for non-stick fry pans.

Spoons

Wooden spoons are useful for stirring sauces. A tip: wet the wooden spoon before using it. This will help seal the surface so the spoon will not stain so readily, nor take on food aromas so quickly. The wooden spoon must be washed with soap and water after use, then dried before storing.

Skim Ladle

Although game meat is non-fatty for the most part, the skim ladle is another good tool to have around anyway, especially when work-ing with domestic meats for our wild-and-tame recipes where the two kinds of meats are combined for certain dishes. The skim ladle is lowered into the sauce or broth to collect the fat off the surface of the food. The skim ladle I am familiar with is made in Denmark and offered through the Williams-Sonoma company of San Francisco.

Corn Starch Mixer

I bought mine at a hardware store. This simple container mixes corn starch with stock to make gravy. It also helps to prevent lumps in the gravy, which is important.

Many Little Things

A multitude of cooking tools remains unmentioned, and most of it will continue to go unheralded in this work. Anyone who cooks knows what he needs for the job, and if he's in doubt, a walk through a restaurant supply house will offer two dozen ideas in a half-hour. Peelers, strainers, collandars, garlic press, larding needles, aprons, gambrels for hanging game, brining buckets, latex gloves to keep hands clean, pepper grinders, oil cans, cheese graters, pasta forks, stir-fry pans, rice cookers (rice is great with venison steaks), potato mash-ers, whips, hand held mixers, large standing mixers, wrap dispensers, ladles, measuring spoons, canisters, spice containers and dispensers, measuring cups, mixing bowls, rolling mincers, meatloaf pans, roast-ing racks (for ducks and geese) and much more.

These are some of the tools the game butcher and cook need to make his work light and easy, as well as fast. As promised, the list is incomplete. But anyone who owns all of the tools mentioned is certainly off to a great start as a game care and cookery expert.

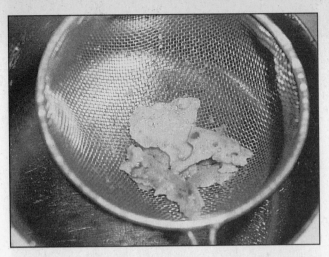

A simple strainer is an important cooking utensil used here to separate fat from broth. The broth is placed in the freezer until the fat hardens on the surface. Then the broth is poured through a strainer like this to catch the solidified fat, which is discarded.

This flat separator is made of dark, transparent, plastic. Note strainer top. Juice or stock is poured first through the strainer lid, then the juice is poured out through the spout of the separator. Since juice is heavier than fat, the good juice pours out of the spout first. The cook watches through the transparent plastic container until fat begins to enter the spout, -then stops pouring, leaving the fat behind in the separator.

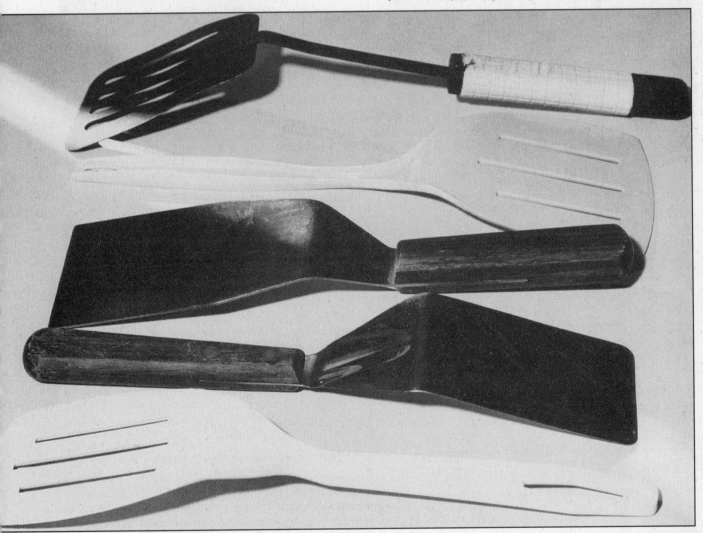

Spatulas are important cooking tools, but they can differ widely in design. The top-most spatula shown here is coated to reduce scratching non-stick surfaces. However, it is made of metal, not plastic. The next in line is also protective of non-stick surfaces; it is made entirely of plastic. Below that is a metal, and very heavy thick spatula with a sharp edge. It is useful in grilling meat. Next is a thin-bladed metal spatula. The blade is flexible, allowing it to work especially well in the skillet. Finally, there is a second all-plastic spatula, however this one is not nearly as wide as the other in this photo, and works well in smaller frying pans.

While some hunters hang a carcass by the head, the author prefers hanging it head-down, as shown here. Notice that this hunter has begun the skinning operation with circular cuts around the hind legs near the joint, as well as cutting back the hide from the front legs. Deer is hanging from a gambrel.

Chapter 11...
Butchering Big Game
Game Care & Cookery

THE GOAL IN butchering big game is to reduce the carcass to manageable storage size, resulting in cuts of meat easy to use in the kitchen. Boning wild game does this. Bones have value, but we modern consumers do not take advantage of the bone marrow. At least, we don't most of the time. I have made stock by cracking bones and boiling them, but more often than not, bones are not used, so why store them? I don't. My freezer packages contain boned meat, period. Therefore, the butchering process described here is not what you'd find in a professional butcher shop, where most cuts contain bone. I don't make chops or T-bone steaks because my family and friends do not eat the bone integral to these cuts. The boning procedure is not the only way to butcher, of course. Many books show the standard butchering procedure, with bone-in cuts, and if the reader likes taking up freezer space with bones, he's free to do so.

Hanging the Carcass

I wouldn't know how to skin a carcass hung by the neck or antlers, but obviously others do know how, as I often see big game hung in this manner. My way is to hang a carcass head-down. Gambrels (iron rods that support the carcass at the hocks) are suspended on the beams of my work area. A carpenter built my system, with five large metal hanging eyes, plus a movable pulley, which allows me to lift a large carcass into working position by myself. A big game carcass must be well-supported before butchering, or the job can be time-consuming and difficult.

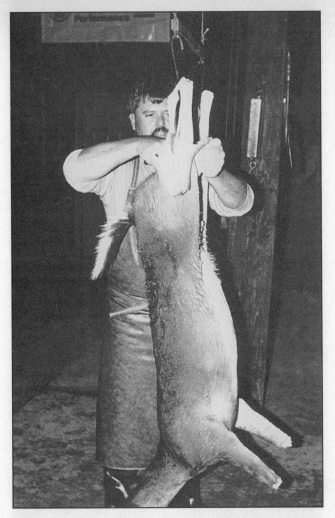

In many instances, big game taken far from a road is boned out in the field. In this case, hanging the meat is difficult if not impossible. Field-boned game goes directly from the vehicle to the butcher block. In some cases, when the meat cannot be attended to quickly, chunks are placed on a cold cement floor covered with newspapers and clean nylon tarps. Then, the chunks of meat are, in turn, covered with the tarps. When it's quite cold, with temperatures hovering near the freezing mark, chunks of boned meat will hold a day or so. Naturally, if temperatures are below freezing, boned meat will hold even longer. But I much prefer taking care of field-boned meat as soon as possible, taking no chances on spoilage that way.

Disjointing the Carcass

Disjointed carcasses, whereby the hind and fore quarters are cut at the joint and removed in the field intact, can be hung. I hang two hind quarters on one gambrel, one quarter on each side. Front quarters may require tying, and if ribs were salvaged, they can be hung by piercing the rib cage with the sharp ends of the gambrel. Normally, jointed carcasses are not fully skinned in the field, especially the hind quarters, so the parts should be hung to make skinning cleaner and faster.

Skinning the Carcass

Chapter 10, "Tools for Butchering and Cooking," mentioned the importance of a skinning knife to remove the hide from a carcass. It's wise to skin the rear hocks back to expose the entire area. Do this while the carcass is still on the ground, then slip the gambrel through the hocks and hoist the animal aloft for work. If the situation allows, the carcass can be lifted only part-way up, allowing the butcher to work at eye-level. Then, when the rear portion of the carcass is skinned, it can be hoisted higher. Skinning a carcass requires making the proper first cuts, called ripping, such as on the inside of the hocks inside of the front legs. Then the hide is worked off by pushing your fist between it and the carcass, as well as using the skinning knife to part the hide from the meat.

A little judicious tugging is also in order. Once the hide is freed up around the hocks and tail, oftentimes it can be pulled downward for

(Text continued, page 86)

This deer, hanging on an adjustable gambrel (goes up or down), is ready for hide removal. Circular cuts above the ham start the operation, and the hide is removed downward from that location.

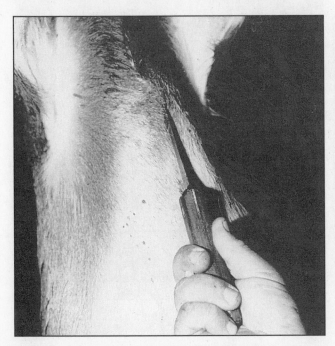

A single cut up the inside of the ham divides the hide at this point for further skinning downward.

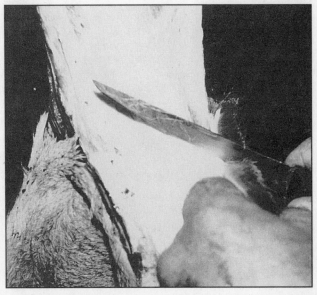

Although the hide can be removed, in part, with careful pulling and handiwork, much of the effort is accomplished with the blade of a knife. An expert can use almost any knife style for the job, while most of us should use a skinning knife with a blade designed for removing hide.

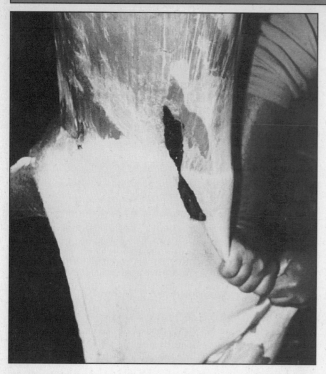

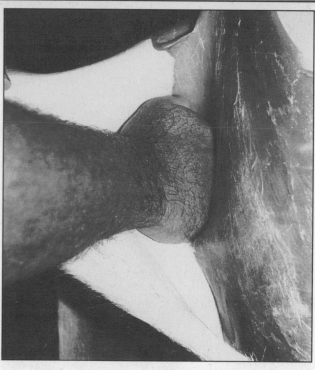

In part, the hide is removed by pushing downward, as shown here. In places, the hide will strip away cleanly from this action, but in other spots only a knife will part hide from tissue.

Using a fist to force the hide off is useful. The object is to push the fist between hide and carcass, as shown here. Notice, too, that the hide is being tugged gently outward at the same time.

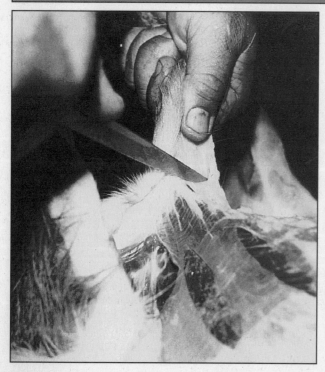

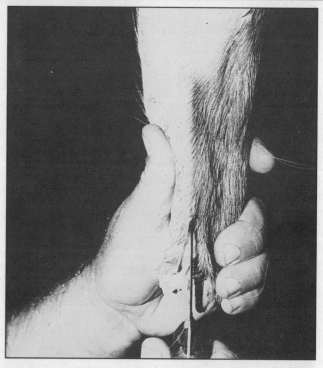

Here is removal of hide along the brisket area. The brisket is pulled outward with one hand, as shown here, and the hide is cut away by knife with the other hand. The hide can be fairly tight to the carcass in this location. The method shown here, however, will work, no matter how tight the hide is.

At this point, the skinning operation is all the way down to the foreleg. A cut is made on the inside of the foreleg upward, as shown here.

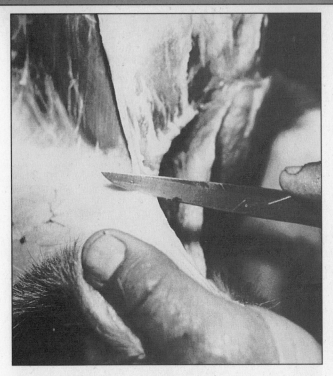

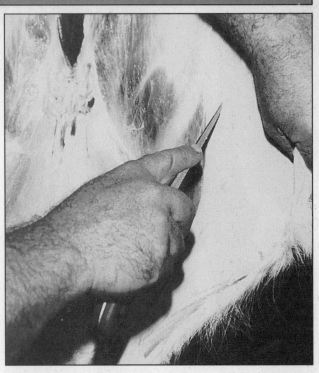

This is a good close-up example of using the knife to remove hide. The knife cuts more into the hide than the carcass, which parts the hide away from the carcass without meat loss. This is important. Cutting in toward the carcass can slash the meat.

Careful knife control is essential in removing the hide of a big game carcass. See how the blade is controlled with the tip of a finger in this illustration. As the knife cuts *against the hide*, at the same time, the hide is pulled outward and away from the carcass with the other hand.

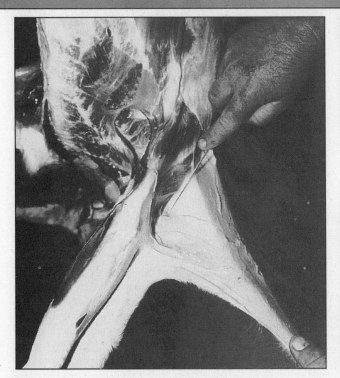

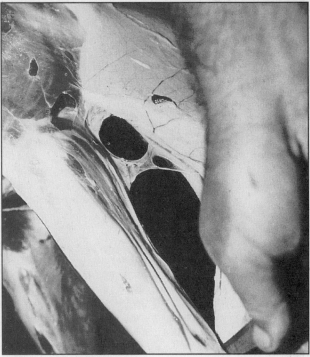

After making the long cut on the inside of the leg, the knife is used to separate hide from foreleg.

At this point, the hide is completely stripped away from the foreleg.

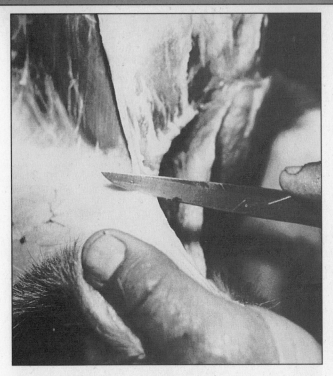

85

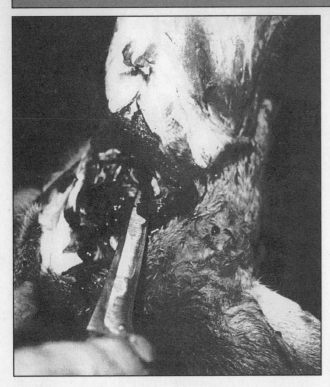

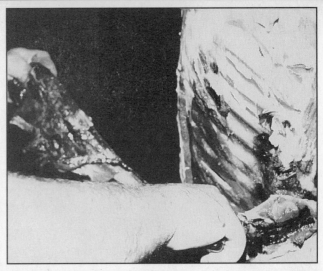

The hide is entirely stripped off of the carcass at this time. The first step now is removal of damaged tissue, as shown here on this deer struck in the rib cage with a broadhead.

The entire hide is removed down to the head. Now the head, along with attached hide, is removed intact. The head is removed by cutting through a vertebra.

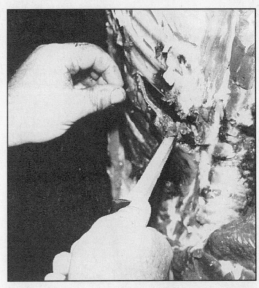

All damaged meat in the region of the broadhead strike is removed by knife. Failure to remove this meat is a mistake. Bad meat mixed with good ruins the good.

quite some distance. Some hunters prefer to carefully skin with the knife to ensure a fat-free hide because they intend to have the hide tanned for use. Others do not care how much fat is left on the hide, so they'll tug as much as cut to remove it. A local hide-selling agency in my area buys big game hides, or trades finished gloves for them. They do not care how much fat remains on the hide, as they take care of that problem themselves.

The front legs can be ripped as well before the carcass is hung. This makes later work much easier. Also, front shanks and hind shanks can be disjointed and removed before hanging, which also makes skinning easier later on. The hide on the underside is already ripped because this was accomplished in field-dressing when the initial belly cut was made from the anal region forward to at least the brisket or all the way to the head. Now that the carcass is hung, preferably with fore hocks and rear hocks ripped, the tail can be ripped, which is done with a simple cut down the length of the tail and then a tug to remove the hide from the tail itself. Next, the tail can be removed by cutting it through the final vertebra, or sawing it off close to the carcass.

The next skinning operation is called siding. It's the removal of hide from the flank area of the carcass, which has been mostly completed during field-dressing. Then comes backing, which means stripping the hide off of the entire back region of the carcass. The skinning operation is actually easier to do than to explain, because the goal is always clearly in front of the butcher: to cleanly remove the hide without getting hair on the meat. There is no other goal in hide removal, other than salvaging the hide itself, which means avoiding puncturing the hide and getting it free in one full piece. Removal of the hide in sections is poor workmanship, plus it means cutting through the fur, which causes hair to fly everywhere. Remove the hide in one intact piece.

The hide is worked all the way down around the head. If the harvest is bound for the taxidermist, then it was already caped in the field. However, our concern is not a trophy, but rather a meat animal. Therefore, the hide can be cut right to the head or jawbone. Then, the head can be sawed off, with hide attached, or disjointed and broken free, also with hide attached. If the hide is to be kept, it can be cut in a circular fashion all around the head/neck area to remove it. The head is then discarded. If the hunter wishes to keep the antlers or horns, these can be sawed off beforehand. Brains are edible, but as a rule we do not use them in our recipe list, so I'll not include saving them. The hide can also be cut entirely free while the head is still on the carcass. This is a matter of personal choice, as either way works fine.

Washing the Carcass

Water does not ruin meat, but leaving a carcass soaking wet may promote bacterial growth. I prefer to wash the skinned carcass with a mixture of one quart of water and one cup of white vinegar. Using a clean cloth, the carcass is scrubbed with vinegar-water starting at the topmost section and working downward. Use plenty of water. I place an old tarp underneath the carcass to capture everything, including wash water. Now, let the carcass dry on its own, or if you plan to age the meat, dry the carcass thoroughly with a new clean rag like a discarded bath towel, which works exceptionally well in sopping up moisture.

Aging the Carcass

I have experimented with aging everything from ducks and rabbits to moose, and while the conclusions stated here may not agree with those found by others, I'll stand by them all the same. I never age antelope, not so much as a day. Antelope is already tender and requires no further aging, plus it spoils easily. Supposing you bring an antelope home from the field on a Sunday night; then it better be packaged before Monday ends. Deer can stand a day or two of aging, but I see no great value in aging venison longer than that. Under ideal conditions, venison can hang quite a while, of course. At 35 to 40 degrees Fahrenheit a carcass may be hung in a dry area and literally eaten as it is butchered. But freezing breaks the meat down anyway, so my deer meat generally goes into the freezer within 24 hours. Elk and moose can stand a little aging, however. At 35 to 40 degrees, a week of hanging can improve the tenderness of these coarser-grained meats. Buffalo—the same holds true. The old idea of letting meat hang until it has a green cast should not be called aging. A better word for that is "rotting." Aging is an important part of game cookery, however, and that is why a special short chapter, Chapter 17, is devoted to the process.

(Text continued, page 90)

Butchering Non-Field-Dressed Game

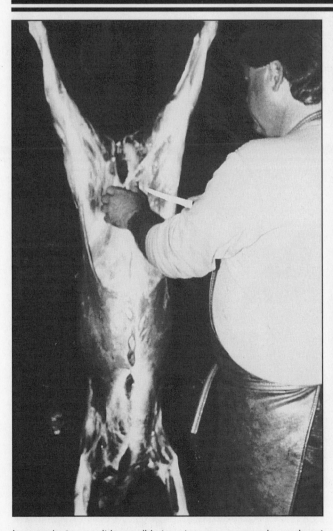

In some instances, it is possible to get a game carcass hung almost immediately after harvesting so that the hide can be stripped off the carcass before removal of viscera. That is the case here. The deer carcass is now ready for dressing. The first step is detachment of reproductive organs, as covered in the chapter on field-dressing a carcass.

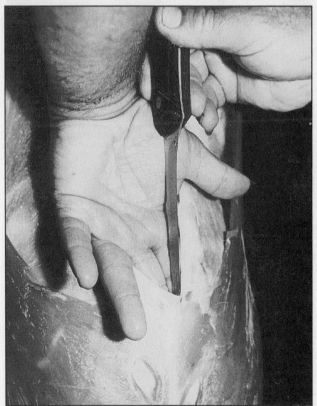

A longitudinal cut is made into the abdominal cavity. Fingers underneath the non-cutting edge of the knife help guide the cut, keeping the point of the knife just under the skin to prevent slicing into the viscera.

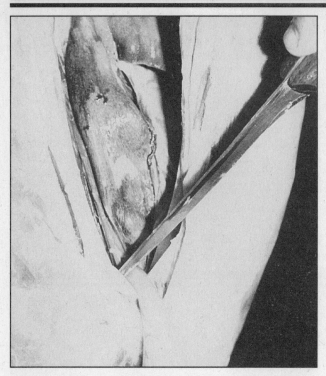

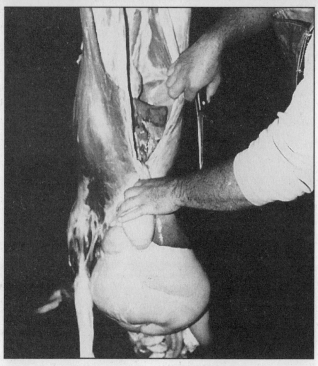

Showing continuance of the longitudinal cut. The viscera are now exposed.

The abdominal cavity is entirely opened now, and the viscera are spilled outward down to the sternum.

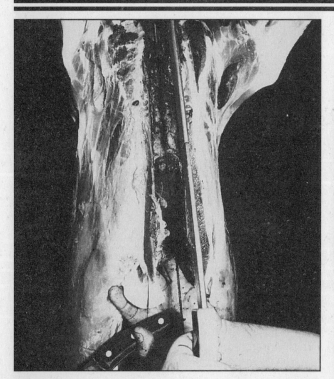

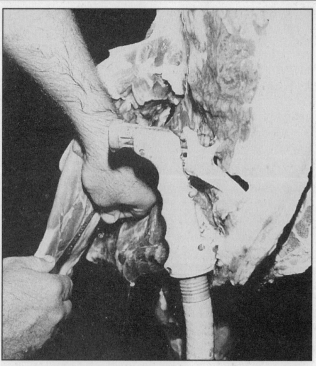

The saw cut can be continued all the way through the sternum now, severing the rib cage in half. At this time, removal of rib cage contents, including heart and lungs, can be accomplished very easily.

The front legs with shoulders attached can be cut loose by pulling outward on them and cutting in between shoulder area and rib cage. Hose is handy for washing meat clean.

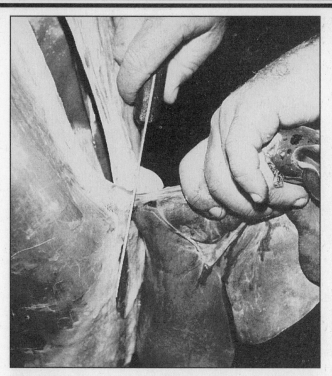

The entire contents of the abdominal cavity are now dropped out with one knife cut to sever the connective tissues.

The aitch bone (pelvic bone) is cut with a saw to separate the hams of the carcass. Remember that the pelvic canal has been cleaned out and its contents removed with the viscera.

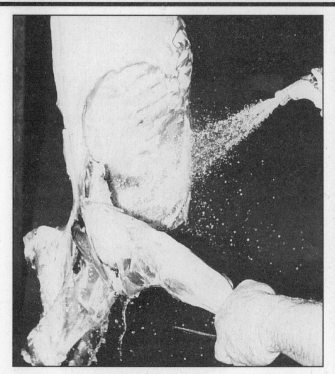

The front legs and shoulders are mostly freed from the rib cage now. Only a little tissue holds the front legs and shoulder blades to the carcass. At this time, the butcher is hosing the carcass off to remove any foreign matter entirely.

The carcass is now free of hide and head, and entirely cleared of viscera. It is now completely washed out, including the inside of the rib cage, as shown here. Now it's time to butcher the meat. Note that two front legs plus shoulder blades are attached only by a little connective tissue. Legs and shoulder blades can be removed with one small slice of the knife.

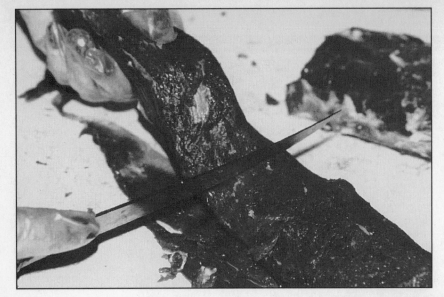

After shoulder blades are removed for boning or turning into roasts, the ribs can be cut away, leaving the backbone. The loins are easily removed from the backbone by cutting them out. After they are cut out, they should be cleaned up as shown here. This is one long loin that has been removed from the spinal area.

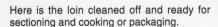

Here is the loin cleaned off and ready for sectioning and cooking or packaging.

Conventional Piecing or Sectioning

While my way is never the conventional method of piecing the carcass, others may wish to have traditional cuts. The following description pertains to head-down hanging only. These cuts include hind shank soup bones; heel of round for pot roasts; an intact rump piece for rump roasts; round steaks taken in between the heel of the round and the rump roast; plus a small flank steak section on either side of the carcass; the sirloin steaks that lie beneath the rump roast; porterhouse, T-bones, and club steaks; and then rib roasts follow down the backside of the carcass; ending with pot roasts; plus neck meat for grinding or boning. On the belly side of the carcass, below the flank steaks, are boiling pieces made from the larger flank; then short ribs and boiling pieces; down to soup bones in the fore shank.

The standard cut is alright for elk and moose, as well as bison, but I find it difficult and impractical to consider porterhouse steaks and rib roasts on a deer-sized carcass, much preferring my own boning-out method of butchering. In order to provide standard cuts, a lot of sawing is necessary, too, including a longitudinal cut straight down the backbone of the carcass. My boning method does not require the longitudinal cut down the backbone. Plus, the boning process provides the cook with ready-to-use cuts for a multitude of dishes, not to mention the compactness of the final product. Note: Boning seems wasteful at first because you're left with so little of a carcass, but this is normal.

You can throw the bones away before dinner or after—that's the only difference. I prefer getting rid of the bones before the meat is packaged, rather than from the dinner plate. Having kept close records, I can attest to the fact that an antelope doe yields about 20 to 25 pounds of boned meat, or about 25 percent of the weight of the carcass. A buck deer may provide up to 50 pounds of boned meat, but once again, that represents not much more than 25 percent of the carcass. It's simply a fact of nature that hide, viscera, head, body fluids, bones and hooves constitute the greater part an animal's weight. However, getting rid of inedibles before packaging, rather than off of the dinner plate after the meal, is not wasteful.

How to Bone a Carcass

The following is but one way to bone a hanging carcass. Some butchers may wish to take steps out of sequence, going with their own tried and true methods. That's fine. *Important: Refer to photographic illustrations for a better understanding of the butchering process described below.*

Remove Shoulder Blades

As previously noted in field-handling a carcass, the shoulders of a big game animal are quickly and easily removed. It's a simple matter of cutting them free by pulling outward on the shoulder and cutting

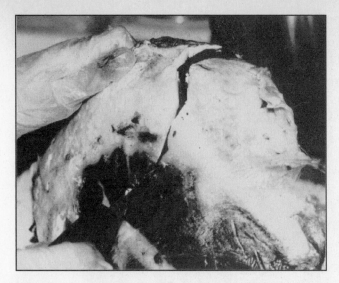

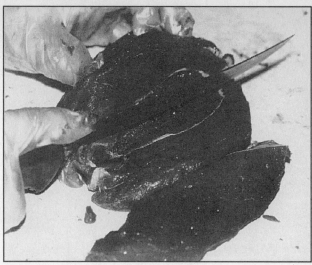

The large ham can be cut in half for easy boning. Different butchers will differ on where the cut is made, but removal where pelvis and thigh meet is good.

A big hunk of boned meat is cut into steaks. Of course the steaks also have no bone in them.

the inside between the shoulder and the rib cage. The shoulder will part company from the carcass with only a few sweeping cuts of a standard-type knife with a longish blade (6 inches or so). You can immediately work on the shoulders if you wish. Cut off the lower shank section. Discard the truly tough pieces, but remove the better chunks for grinding into burger. The rest of the shoulder blade can be boned out, a rather simple matter. Or, the ends can be cut off and boned, while the centermost section is retained for a shoulder roast.

Cut Off the Neck

I use a saw. It's easy to see where it ends and no explanation is necessary. The neck can be retained and cooked intact as a roast, especially slow-cooked at low oven temperatures for several hours with a good complement of condiments. Or it can be boned out for

burger meat. If the neck is from a rutting buck deer, get rid of it—that's my best advice. I have, in the past, saved neck meat from rutting bucks, but must admit that it's second-rate to downright poor eating. Do not under any circumstances bone the neck meat from a rutting buck and add it to the rest of your burger meat. You may ruin the entire batch of boned meat. If the neck is good, you can bone it by cutting from the top straight down to the vertebra, then on both sides of the vertebra to remove the meat from the neck bones. Obviously, a boning knife is used for this operation.

Cut Forepart of Vertebral Column

Behind the neck, a section from where the neck was sawed off to the beginning of the backstrap (loins) should be cut out for stew meat or burger meat. Cut on either side of the backbone and remove the

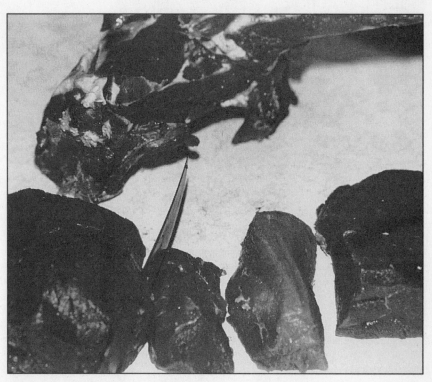

Cutting with a boning knife right along the thigh bone and into the pelvic region removes meat from bone. The large chunks of boned meat can be frozen intact, or sliced into steaks.

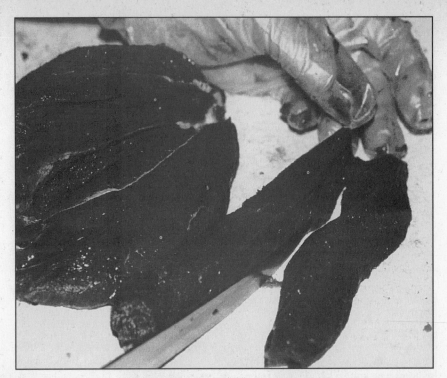

Here is a nice piece of boned meat that can be cut into stew pieces, used for burger, or in some instances, shaped with a meat hammer for steaks.

Bone meat can be cubed, as shown here, for excellent stews.

Removal of tougher tissues is easy. Separate tissue from meat with boning knife. If good meat is left intact on tissue, scrape meat away and use for gameburger.

hunks of meat. The flexible blade of a boning knife is perfect for this work, bending just enough around the backbone.

Remove the Loins

Now cut off the remainder of the backbone just beneath the two hanging hind quarters. This gives a long section of spine that contains the loins. These are carefully boned away from the carcass by running a sharp boning knife alongside the full length of the vertebral column. Keep the boning knife blade up against the bone at all times so that your knife removes all of the loin. It takes several careful cuts to get the job done, but it's really quite easy to do. After the long strips of loin are free, carefully tug off the tough outer tissue that covers the top of each loin. This can be stripped off by hand, but a knife may be required to get it started.

Important: Do not cut the loins into serving pieces. Cut them only once in the center for deer, or two to three times for larger animals. Then, package and freeze these larger sections. The meat will last much longer in the freezer in these bigger uncut hunks, rather than as medallions. Cut the loin into medallions after thawing the package and just before cooking. The loin meat will then be fresh and juicy.

Remove the Tenderloins

After the loins are removed from the spinal column, turn the spine over. You will see two pieces of meat that look like mini-loins, which is what they are. These tenderloins are aptly named because they are very tender. They are terrific sometimes, and less than terrific other times. Paunch-struck carcasses may provide tenderloins of low quality, because they've been attacked by gastric juices. I've had both excellent and poor tenderloins, however, from well-harvested game. The last tenderloins I ate were superb, butterflied, marinated and quick-fried in butter and wine.

Cut and Bone the Hams

I prefer to cut the hams apart with a saw, going straight down through the aitch bone (if still intact) and what is left of the backbone of the carcass. This yields two separate hams, ready for boning. There are various ways to bone the hams. I prefer sawing off the uppermost and lowermost part. These are boned out by simply following the muscle division lines. That leaves a large center ham section, which can be further boned or left intact. If left intact, do not remove the bone. In this instance, the single thigh bone is left in the meat and the entire ham is used as a roast. This is an especially excellent cut for antelope. Alternatively, the hams can be boned without making the two cuts mentioned above. Just follow the muscle division lines, which look as if they were drawn on the carcass just for that purpose. A boning knife plunged deeply along these lines divides the ham of the carcass into natural sections. The bone within the ham is easily removed and discarded.

The hams are now reduced to boned-out chunks of clean, superb meat that can be cut into steaks. As always, I recommend leaving the meat in large hunks for packaging and freezing. However, the meat should be trimmed of excess fat so that, after thawing, every cut will turn into a steak. The excess trim can be used for burger meat or stew.

Burger and Stew Meat

The boning process reduces the carcass into meat-only chunks, but it also leaves scraps, pieces with amorphous shape that don't fit into any specific category—not stew, not steak, not roast. These scraps are used for gameburger and stew meat. For burger, the scraps are ground up, then carefully packaged and frozen for later use. For stew, the small pieces can be cubed ahead of time, then stored. If the scraps are larger chunks, then do not cube the meat. Remember, the freezer is kinder to bigger parcels of meat, especially with regard to what we

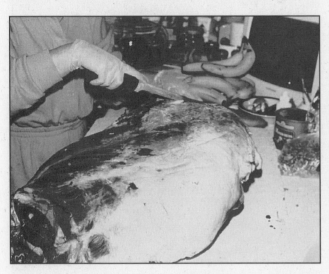

Here is a beautiful deer ham waiting to be boned. The key to success in boning is to follow natural muscle divisions. These are readily visible.

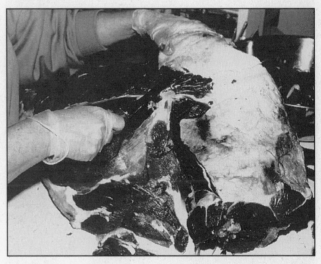

In boning the haunch, natural muscle division lines are followed, as shown here. Here, the haunch is divided along the bone, making two distinct parts.

The dividing of the haunch is continued here. Now the haunch is severed into two "logical" portions, the word logical applying to the natural division line that is clearly visible, almost as a white line of tissue separating muscle groups.

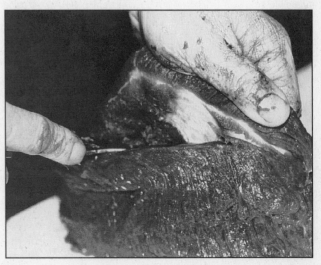

Here is a good clear view of a dividing line that separates two parts of meat in the boning process.

call "freezer burn." Freezer-burned meat is meat which has been attacked by gases within the refrigeration unit. Careful wrapping prevents much of this problem, but freezing meat in larger pieces leaves fewer surface areas for the gases to attack.

Very Large Carcasses

Common sense dictates that large carcasses demand slightly different treatment. However, the basic boning plan still works great with bison, moose, elk, caribou and other larger animals. The difference lies in the number of cuts made. For example, the neck of a big animal may require two cuts instead of one. The same applies to the fore-part of the spinal column in front of the loins. Loins are handled in the same manner, but cut in several pieces because of their large size.

In cutting the hams, they are still separated by sawing through the aitch bone, then sawing down both ends of the spinal column. Then, the two huge hams are further reduced in size, as they hang from the gambrel, with a cut to remove the sirloin steak region and a cut straight across in the area of the round steaks. This leaves the heel of the round, plus what we'll call the pot roast section, which is boned into beautiful hunks that can be turned into steaks or roasts, with the scrap going to stew meat or burger.

The individual can modify this home butchering system to fit his own needs. Conventional cuts can be made, instead of boning. Or a combination of the two may be used. Perhaps loin chops are especially appealing to a cook. If so, leave the spine intact rather than boning it out. Then cut the spine longitudinally, and again cross-wise, to remove each loin chop one at a time. Meanwhile, bone everything else. It's your big game carcass, butcher it the way you want. But handle all cutting tools carefully; and remember that proper handling of meat during butchering means a more enjoyable meal later.

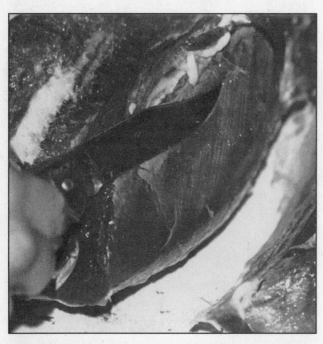

On beef this round steak would be considered a somewhat less desirable cut (than a T-bone steak, for example). But on this nice venison haunch, the round steak shown here will slice into perfectly fine steaks.

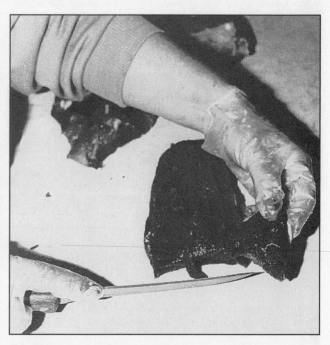

The boned chunk of round steak venison shown here will be cut into excellent steaks.

Here is a close look at a piece of bone meat from the haunch of a deer. It's easy to see that this meat will cut into steaks across the grain, not with the grain of the meat.

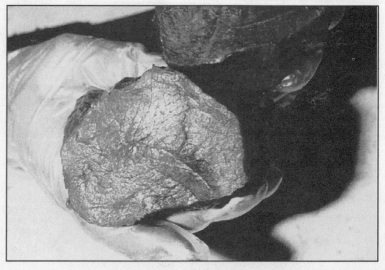

THE SMALL GAME carcass should arrive in the home butcher shop skinned, washed, cooled and ready to go, as explained in Chapter 7, "Field Care for Small Game." Now, it can be cut up and prepared either for cooking or packaging. Ideally, cottontail rabbit and squirrel are prepared fresh; however, both will remain in good condition in the freezer, when properly wrapped, for about six months. After that, cottontails, in particular, lose their tasty "edge" with the meat possibly taking on a somewhat oily sheen. But whether served promptly or stored for later use, certain butchering methods apply for all small game, not only the ubiquitous rabbit, and squirrel, but also the less popular species such as armadillo, porcupine, woodchuck, beaver, muskrat and others. Chapter 15, "Preparing the Exotics" deals with some of these edibles, but that chapter is more concerned with preparation and handling for palatability, while this chapter tends to proper butchering techniques.

Age Determines Use

The first thing to consider before butchering small game is the age of the animal. Why? Because of cooking style. Older small game animals can be cooked with terrific success if the chef knows he is dealing with a mature animal. For example, an older rabbit can be tenderized through par-boiling or, better yet, pressure-cooking for 20 or 30 minutes. Also, small game animals can be segregated by age for packaging and freezing. Then the cook can treat a package accordingly—young small game for a quick-fry supper, older ones par-boiled or pressure-cooked as noted above.

Age determination begins in the field before the head is discarded. First, look at the teeth. Old teeth are more stained and yellowish than

Chapter 12...
Butchering Small Game
Game Care & Cookery

young teeth, showing a bit more wear. In most cases, you probably won't remember which carcasses had old-looking teeth and which did not. However, it's worth a quick glance. And if you see signs of maturity, you can mark the animal. I arrived home with ten bunnies from a bowhunt a couple seasons ago, and one of them was marked with a bit of string on one leg, because in glancing at the teeth it was obvious that this rabbit was a senior.

A number of other ways may be used to estimate an animal's age, all with varying levels of reliability. Older small game may have tighter and even tougher hides. Again, this determination is made in the field. Another field-test is by ear: Young animals have pliable ears, while older ears are stiffer, as a rule. At home, the cook can try a pliability test on his small game: younger animals are more flexible, even after rigor mortis sets in. They tend to bend more readily than older ones. Also, a pressure test can be done. Using an index finger, put pressure on the center of the hind leg of the animal. Older animals may show more toughness than younger ones. Unfortunately, there is no foolproof age test, but this is a starting point. These same methods also apply to upland birds, the subject of the next chapter.

Butchering Small Game

After separating by age, it's time to section/soak/trim. The cottontail rabbit is used as a model for this chapter, because anyone who can properly butcher a rabbit can do any small game quadrupeds.

Safety First—You'll probably use a meat cleaver for small game

Proper care of small game begins the moment after the game is harvested. These beautiful tree squirrels, shown with Fadala's Herb Meland Three-Piece Pronghorn longbow, are destined for the table and good eating.

Cottontail rabbit is cut with a cleaver. Here are the back legs. Note that lower portion of leg is removed. This prevents jagged bone, which can cut through the finished freezer package.

butchery operations. Be careful because a meat cleaver has no conscience. It can break a finger, or worse, so keep digits away from the impact of the blade.

Obviously, the hunter can reverse some of the procedure; however, I've listed each sequence in an order that works in my kitchen. Also, some hunters will find game shears worthwhile for small game butchery. The notch on game shears is useful for cutting off the ends of legs, or other butchering duties.

Sectioning

Place the carcass on a butcher block or stout cutting board, with backside down. A large knife with heavy blade can be used for sectioning, but I prefer a meat cleaver, the smaller the better. Two initial cuts are made. First, remove the back legs right where they join the loin region of the back of the rabbit. With what remains of the car-

cass, make another cut separating the front legs/ribs from the loin. You now have three pieces on the cutting board: two front legs with rib cage attached; one mid-section consisting of the back of the rabbit; two hind legs intact as one piece.

Take the hind legs and hold them vertically with the butt end down against the cutting board. Keeping your fingers out of the way, slip the cleaver between and alongside one of the hind legs and press down hard, cutting into one leg. The pelvic region and the other leg remain together. Next, slice the remaining leg so the tail (if it remains on the carcass) and the pelvic canal can be removed and discarded. Now the back legs are separated.

Now turn to the section of front legs/ribs. Make one cut with the cleaver between the two front legs and right down the spine, leaving an end result of two front legs, each with one-half a rib cage attached. Leave each piece this way; they cook perfectly together. There is a nice little piece of meat along the topmost of the front leg/rib cage that is actually an extension of the loins or backstraps.

Now turn to the remaining third of the rabbit, which is the animal's midsection. Turn it spine-up on the cutting board and make a slice, either with the meat cleaver or the point of a sharp knife, right down the center of the spine. This cut leaves two flaps of thick skin, one on either side of the back.

One at a time, grab each flap of skin and pull it from the back. Usually, the skin can be literally ripped off, but if it does not come

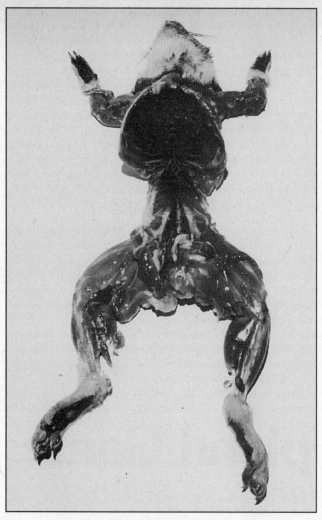

Here is a squirrel carcass completely skinned. It's clean and ready for butchering. Head and feet will be cut off and discarded.

away clean, cut it off with a sharp knife. The back is now free of the tough over-tissue. At this time, use the cleaver to clip off the lower extremities of all four legs. These bony extensions are no good for anything. Make the cuts clean and square, avoiding jagged edges that will cut through your package when you wrap the carcass for the freezer. After spending all that time hunting, dressing and butchering, you don't want it to end in freezer-burned meat.

This little butchering sequence results in five beautiful pieces of small game edibles: one piece of fine meat tenderloin from the back; two tasty front legs with half a rib cage attached, and two meaty back legs.

Soaking

After all of your small game is sectioned, it's time to soak 'em out. Plain cold water will do, but I find that cold water with a little white vinegar is helpful in removing over-tissue from all the parts. The amount of water needed depends upon the amount of game to be treated. The limit where I live is ten cottontails per hunter, and it takes a pretty good-sized container and a gallon or so of water to properly cover that many. As a rule, add about a cup of white vinegar to a gallon of cold water. Let the game meat soak for some time, at least a few hours. I've left the pieces as long as overnight, when it's cold enough to leave them in the garage. But don't put them on the back porch as a friend of mine did. His neighborhood cats had a feast. Incidentally, the vinegar/water treatment turns rabbit meat fairly white.

Trimming

After a good soak, remove the pieces from the solution. I pour the entire contents into a colander. This allows the vinegar/water to run off, so the pieces can dry off a bit. Then I toss the still-damp pieces onto a clean towel or paper towels. After drying, it's time to trim each piece. This is best done with fingers and a small knife. Pull away and trim all loose tissue from the parts. This tissue is worthless. You now have rabbit, or other small game pieces, fit for a king's dish—clean, free of unwanted extraneous tissue and ready to cook or package.

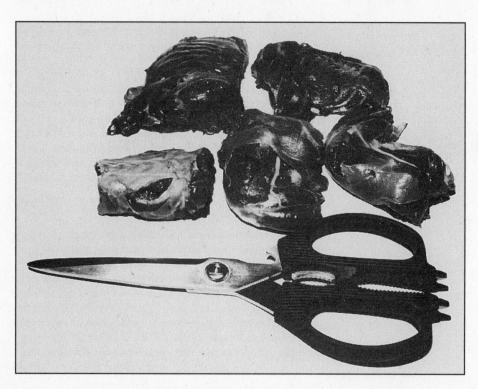

These Gerber's scissors were used to cut a squirrel carcass into proper sections. No knife or cleaver was used.

AS WITH ALL game, the flavor of upland birds depends greatly upon field care, followed by careful treatment in the home butcher shop. For several reasons, flavor can be ruined rapidly on all upland birds from dove to turkey. First, birds have a high body temperature. They must be completely cooled in the field before home butchering. Second, because shot often penetrates the body cavity, gastric juices are a problem. Third, birds must be well-bled, because blood can spoil the flavor of the meat. Fourth, birds must be transported under cool conditions from field to butchering site. While this factor is true of all game meat, birds seem even more susceptible to heat spoilage than small or big game. Feathers are great insulation, and they hold in body heat. But birds can be cooled by opening the body cavity, especially with a cool water wash to further remove natural heat.

Initial Handling

Once home, the bird, especially larger tablefare such as the wild turkey or grouse, should be checked for tissue remaining in the chest cavity. Sometimes it's difficult to remove all of this tissue in the field. At home, reach inside and literally scratch out (with fingers) or scrape out (with spoon) all matter along the backside of the chest area up along the spine. Then, flush with cool water. Materials left here are non-edible and spoil rapidly.

Also, while the crop was removed in the field, the windpipe may remain intact within the neck. It's a good idea to remove it because it spoils quickly and has no food value. The neck itself may be retained for making stock, which is a base for gravy.

The liver, heart and gizzard, used to make stock for gravy, should be soaked overnight in the refrigerator in a container of salt water,

Chapter 13...

Butchering Upland Game
Game Care & Cookery

then allowed to drain. Dry these parts before packaging. Be absolutely certain that the gall bladder, a small green appendage, is not attached to the liver.

The wild turkey can be hung overnight in a cool place if it is impossible for the hunter to begin butchering right away; however, aging is not necessary, nor recommended. For more notes on general aging, see Chapter 17: Aging Game Meat. If the head is removed, hang the bird by its legs, but if the head is intact, hang a wild turkey by the head/neck to allow body juices to drain away. Place a small tarp or newspapers underneath the hanging bird to catch drippings. If the bird is to be mounted, it must be hung by feet only. Taxidermy tips are listed at the end of this chapter.

Age Determines Use

It's good to know how old your birds are for reasons of cooking style. The younger the game, the more tender the meat tends to be. So older game shouldn't be prepared in a way that can further dry out the meat, such as the uncovered oven method. This is especially important for wild turkeys, which can grow a little tough with age. While experts can look at feather patterns to distinguish between juvenile and mature birds, most of us are better off relying on size and other factors for age information. It's quite easy to tell a young tom turkey from a mature tom, and no problem distinguishing a young grouse from an old one, by size alone. Birds smaller than

Boned breast meat, upland bird steaks, fully breaded, and frying in canola oil.

As part of the butchering process for this chapter, cooking boned and steaked upland game bird is shown. This is step one. The universal marinade is used to make the boned breast meat steaks delicious. Discard marinade after use. It will be contain unwanted juices.

turkey and grouse are a little more difficult to assess. Dove, for example, have a mature look quite early in life. One trick seems to work across the board, however, and that's the hardness of the keel (breastbone). A young bird has a rather pliable keel, while a more mature bird has a rigid keel. Also, poking the breast meat is somewhat revealing of a bird's age. Mature birds seem more firm than younger birds. I've had good luck on dove and quail with this simple method.

Another excellent way to determine the age is to pick the bird up by its lower beak. If the lower bill almost breaks in two, or at least bends considerably, the bird is young. If the beak is well-set and rigid, bending little, and in no way offering to break, the bird is mature. Also, cock pheasants have spurs. On mature birds, the spurs are long, sharp and rigid; a young male has shorter, blunt and pliable spurs.

Feather Removal

There are a number of ways to remove the feathers from upland birds. Here are a few of the more popular methods:

Skinning

I prefer skinning upland birds whenever possible. The theory holds that leaving the skin on makes for a more moist cooked product; however, the recipes provided for upland birds in this book take dryness into consideration—so skin away.

Breasting

Dove are normally breasted in the field. Just about any other upland bird, including pheasants, may be also breasted, either in the field or home butcher shop. Breasting is listed here as a defeathering procedure because the first step in the process is to slice with a knife along the keel (breast bone), just underneath the skin, producing a slit. Part the slit with your fingers, then tug the skin, along with the feath-

Using a rolling pin, as shown here, work crackers into a flour-like consistency. Then mix with flour, 50 percent saltine cracker, 50 percent white flour. This is for basting marinated upland bird breast steaks.

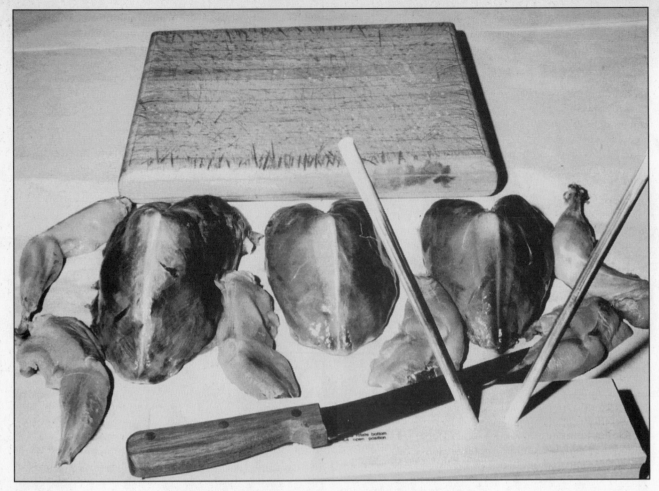

Butchering upland birds is easy. First, divide the carcass into breast meat and legs/thighs, as shown here, using a sharp knife.

ers, free from the bird. Then remove the breast meat from either side of the keel, preferably with a filet knife, its flexible blade working to part meat from bone.

Dry Plucking

This basic method is clean and easily accomplished on most birds, but not so readily undertaken on them all. Dry plucking a quail, for example, is not impossible, but the delicate skin of this bird may peel back unless the plucker is very careful. Dry plucking an old tom turkey runs from difficult to "I'm going to skin this thing." Dry plucking, as the name implies, is simply pulling the feathers out by hand without water.

Scalding or Wet-Plucking

Hard-to-pluck birds get the hot water treatment. Perhaps there is a magic temperature for this process, I don't know. I boil a big pot of water underneath a camp stove outdoors for the job. As soon as the water rolls, I cut the heat and let the pot sit for a couple minutes. Then I dunk the birds into the drink. There's no trick here. A single dunking usually does the job. Pull the bird back out of the water, let it cool off for a few seconds so you don't burn your fingers, then pluck the feathers by hand. The hot water loosens the feathers, making removal an easier job. I don't use paraffin in the water very often for upland birds; however, ducks do get the paraffin treatment (see Chapter 14, "Butchering Waterfowl").

After dry or wet plucking, tweezers work well for pulling out small remaining feathers. It's not quite as tedious as it sounds, however, because there are seldom many feathers left after a conscientious job of plucking.

Another way to get rid of remaining small feathers is to singe with a flame. I use a camp stove outdoors for this job. Touch the remaining feathers to fire and watch them retreat. Be sure to wash the bird off after singeing, and don't burn the meat.

Sectioning

Most birds do not require sectioning of any kind; however, there are reasons to section some upland avians. A young wild turkey or pheasant can be fried, for example. It sounds almost ridiculous, but it works, if the bird is tender. And these large birds demand sectioning before they can be fried up.

This is one way to do the job: First, lop off the neck, close to the body. Now run the blade of a knife inside each leg and cut close to the body and down to the hip joint, removing the legs. Separate the leg into thigh and drumstick by slicing through the joint that separates these two parts. That takes care of the two legs. Now cut the wings off close to the body, also directly through the joint. Lop off the tips of the wings with a knife, if you wish, or cut them off with game shears. There's not much meat on them, even the wild turkey.

Next, cut off the lower back of the bird by running the knife blade from vent region to mid-back. Game shears work well on this task, too, but only for smaller birds. Use a large knife on larger birds and only one cut will get the job done, the long blade spanning the breadth of the bird. Cut across and free this bony piece. With two cuts, one running down each side, remove the rest of the back. This leaves the breast standing alone. It can be cut once, length-wise right along the keel, for two parts; or it can be cut twice, once length-wise and again cross-wise, to produce four breast parts.

Practice on a whole chicken in the off-season, and when hunting time arrives, you'll be an expert at sectioning any upland bird. Also remember that when you get to the point where only the breast stands, it can be boned out very easily. Just throw the bony keel away, or plop it into the stock pot or pressure cooker along with gizzard, heart, liver and neck for making stock. Partridge, grouse, quail, and other birds can be cut in half with a large butcher knife. This simple sectioning leaves a bird that can be slow-fried or smoked to perfection. Small birds can also be sectioned into the same parts as described for larger ones. It all depends upon the dish being made.

Removing Leg Tendons

This step is a dandy when it works, but it takes a little practice and personal experimentation. The object is to remove as many tendons from the turkey leg as possible before storage or cooking. Start by making a slit in a circle around the lower end of the drumstick. Then insert a metal skewer into the slit and lift a tendon. Grab the tendon end with pliers and pull straight outward. Sorry to say, this worthy plan does not work as well as I wish it did; others may have better luck than I with it, so I had to put it in.

I have had better success removing tendons in the field, however. The entire lower leg is intact at this time, and a knife is inserted about 2 inches above the ankle of the bird. The knife is thrust all the way through the leg, then withdrawn, leaving a hole. Don't cut the tendons with the knife. If you feel tendons with the blade, back off and go for another entry, but leave the tendons intact. The idea is to pull the tendons free one at a time by teasing them out of the hole with a metal skewer or the point of a jackknife, then tugging them free with needle-nose pliers.

Washing

Whether an upland bird is sectioned or not, consider a final washing of the meat. This is a worthwhile step. Prepare a bath of water and baking soda—about two quarts of water and four tablespoons of baking soda mixed thoroughly. Drop the bird parts into the wash for an hour, then rinse, drain and dry each part. Now you can cook or package the washed meat. On large birds, such as a wild turkey that is not sectioned, use a sponge. Soak the sponge in the water/baking soda mixture and wash the inside and outside of the bird. This will reduce any leftover acetic juice.

Taxidermy Considerations

Hunters have learned that quail, grouse and many other wonderful upland birds make beautiful mounts. On the smaller birds, the wisest maneuver is to leave them either entirely intact, or remove viscera very carefully through the tiniest possible slit in the vent region. Then, the birds are placed head-first into a "newspaper cone." Leave the newspaper several sheets thick and simply roll it so that it forms a cone. Then, the tip of the cone is folded back where the beak rests. The back of the cone is also folded, and the bird is tucked in with feathers running the right way. Now either freeze the bird or get it to the taxidermy shop as soon as possible.

The wild turkey is quite another proposition. Although it, too, can be tucked into a large paper cone, there are certain special considerations for this king of the upland avians. Here are a few steps to consider in bagging a wild turkey for a super mount for your den wall:

Hunt wild turkeys when the birds are fully feathered, meaning in the spring or late fall. Avoid early fall hunting because turkeys do not have fully mature feathers.

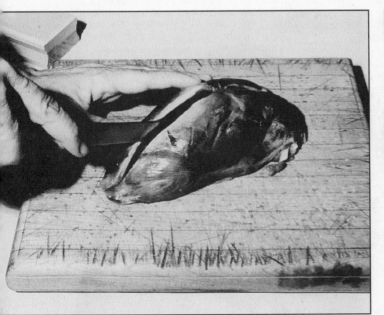

An excellent way to process larger game birds is boning of the breast meat. This works especially well on pheasants and grouse, as well as other larger upland birds, such as partridges. The first cut is made right along the keel (breast bone), as shown here, using a thin-bladed knife.

This photograph shows the breast meat being boned from the keel.

Carry your bird by the legs, not the neck. Carrying the bird by the neck can permanently mat down the feathers, possibly jamming some in such a way that they can never be re-straightened.

Never wring the neck of the bird. This also jams feather butts into the skin, and those feathers may never be the same.

Plug large shot holes, as well as the mouth and the nostrils of the bird, with cotton or tissue immediately after it is down. This helps block leakage that may stain and mat feathers. With a stick, just stuff cotton or tissue directly into these openings.

Keep your wild turkey clean. Do not place your prize on the bed of pickup truck or other flat surface without an absorbent cloth or other material under it. Try to cushion the bird's ride; it's more delicate than you think. Hang the bird by the feet as soon as possible. Obviously, it must never be hung by the head or neck because of possible deformation and permanent matting of feathers.

This point goes against our love of hunting for food, but in good conscience I have to advise getting your wild turkey to the taxidermist immediately and without evisceration for the best possible job. The bird can be put on ice and taken right in. Then the taxidermist can retrieve the cape, and the meat will be salvaged. I realize this goes against our cardinal rule of getting a bird eviscerated and cooled rapidly for best eating, but a big turkey mount is once in a lifetime. If you get the bird to the taxidermist quickly, the meat will still be edible.

If you cannot reach the taxidermist immediately, then carefully wrap the bird in newspaper. Use the cone method as much as you can. After the turkey is well-wrapped with newspaper, place it inside of a large plastic garbage bag and freeze the packaged bird solid. Even though the bird is frozen, get it to the taxidermy shop as soon as possible. The quality of the mount depends on it.

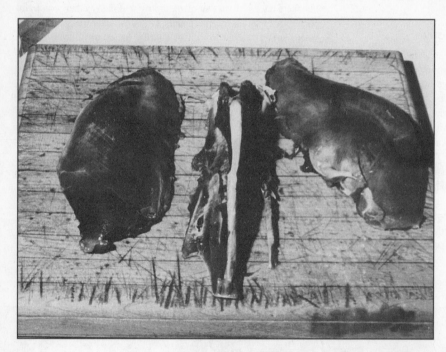

Here is the breast meat boned away from the keel, showing the two pieces of meat, plus the keel itself (center), which will be discarded.

On large upland birds, such as sage grouse and pheasants, breast meat can be sliced into steaks, as shown here. The steaks are cut thin so they can be fully marinated.

AS ALWAYS, AS game care quality goes, so goes tablefare quality. Butchering waterfowl is not so different from butchering upland game birds, but there are a few special points worth considering.

Initial Handling

Geese and ducks should be well-bled in the field, their heads removed when and where legal to do so, or a neck incision made to sever the jugular vein. Naturally, birds destined for the taxidermist do not receive either treatment. Usually, ducks and geese are hunted in cold weather, but that does not mean they cool out quickly without proper attention. Their feather/down covering is super insulation, designed to retain body heat. So drawing is accomplished as soon as possible in the field, and hopefully the birds are cooled in the open air, and kept cold on their journey to the home butcher shop.

Once home, ensure that lungs and all internal organs are removed from the chest cavity, as these spoil rapidly. Reach inside and scrape against the chest cavity, backbone side, with fingers or a spoon to remove leftover tissues from field cleaning. Flush with cool water afterwards.

The long windpipe in the neck of waterfowl also tends to sour rapidly. Remove it after the duck is devoid of feathers. This requires one long slice into the exposed neck with a sharp-pointed knife. It's easy to distinguish the windpipe, as no other organ in the region looks like it or feels like it—a long rubbery tube.

There's controversy over aging waterfowl. Some of the best old-time books on the subject go into explanations of how to improve the meat of ducks and geese through hanging. I cannot go along with prescriptions that call for several days, but I have hung geese and ducks

Chapter 14...
Butchering Waterfowl
Game Care & Cookery

under cover, not in the open, well-protected from dust or dirt, and at temperatures just above freezing, for three days. Did it help? Hard to say. The birds were delectable, and probably would have been so with or without aging. As for tenderizing through aging, preparation of waterfowl includes slow-cooking methods that soften even old ducks and geese. However, aging may be worthwhile for those birds that will be cooked in the open oven style.

Age Determines Use

As with most game, the animal's age gives clues as to the best way to prepare the meat. Older game tends to be tougher, requiring parboiling or pressure cooking to restore tenderness. One age determiner is the lower bill (jaw) test. Hold the bird up in the air suspended by the lower bill only. If the bill is rigid, the bird is most likely mature. If the bill bends, or tends to break, the bird is young. The keel area of ducks and geese also hardens with age, so press against the keel to see how much give it has.

Feather Removal

Skinning

Both ducks and geese can be skinned. For ducks, use a sharp-pointed knife and run the blade underneath the skin from vent straight up the front of the bird, following the edge of the keel as a guide and stopping just below the head of the duck. Then the skin is tugged

SKINNING

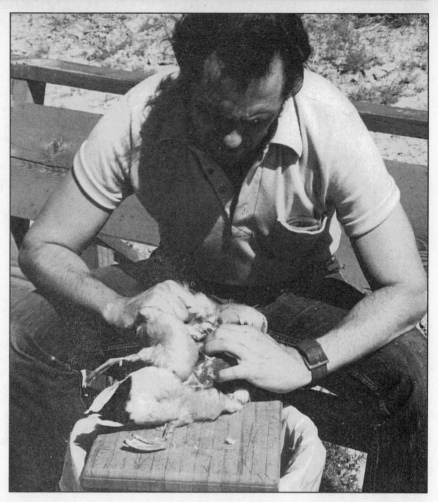

For the skinning operation the ring-around-the-neck step is left out. Instead, the feathers of the breast region are parted *with the skin*. Note how fingers pull in opposite directions to part the skin.

from the centerline cut toward both sides of the bird. On older birds, the sharp knife may be necessary for further skinning, just as a knife is used to remove the hide from a big game animal. The difference, of course, lies in the type of knife and in the smaller cuts. Instead of a skinning knife, a narrow-bladed, sharp-pointed jackknife or other smaller knife is used, and the cuts are short and delicate, more like teasing away the feathered skin.

Geese are skinned somewhat differently. Here is one method that comes out of an old tradition called "shinding," which means skinning, but with the purpose of rendering goose fat for cooking and other uses. Goose fat is highly prized for its unique flavor and low melting point. The skinning process on a goose begins down the backbone, just the opposite of the duck. But the same type of knife is used, small and sharp-pointed. The cut runs from the tail straight up the backbone, then around the bottom-most part of the neck where neck and body join. Then a butterknife is used to pry underneath the goose skin, lifting it off. In some places, the butterknife will not suffice, and the sharp knife must be used to cut connective tissue. But all in all, the prying method suffices for separating the feathered skin from the meat. This is not the only way to skin a goose, but it is one way. Some hunters may find the duck skinning method more to their liking, where the skin is virtually pulled away from the carcass by hand after a major cut is made up the breastbone of the bird.

Dry Plucking

Dry plucking a goose or duck is not quite as grim a task as may seem. One way to dry pluck waterfowl is to lay the bird on a flat sur-

face with the head facing toward you. Then tug about an inch of feathers out by hand, forming a bare ring around the neck of the bird where it joins the body. This bare ring of flesh is the key to the rest of the job. Bend the neck back against the body, pulling tight the skin on the upper body. Use steady pressure to hold the skin firmly, then starting at the bare ring around the neck, pluck feathers out of their hold using your other hand, working toward the bottom of the bird. Try not to tear the skin in the process. Little by little, feathers will disappear, except for some down and a few stubborn pin feathers that can be removed with a propane torch. The key to success is keeping the skin taught and intact with one hand, while plucking and pressing feathers out with the other hand. The inch circle is the starter point every time, the bird rotated around and around as you work to remove feathers with finger pressure.

Wet Plucking

Boil a big pot of water outdoors on the camp stove as you would for upland birds, only this time add paraffin to the hot water. One source notes three twelve-ounce cakes of paraffin to six quarts of water. I've never had a recipe, always boiling a big kettle of water and dumping in four or five cakes of wax. Don't try to do the ducks in super-hot paraffin/water because it won't work. The water and paraffin must be hot, but not at the boiling point. If the water is too hot, the paraffin tends to run off the feathers. Don't depend upon the paraffin to do all the work. Do a little preliminary dry plucking before dipping the duck or goose, especially the tail feathers. Cut the wings off, too—they only get in the way. Ideally, the birds are cold when

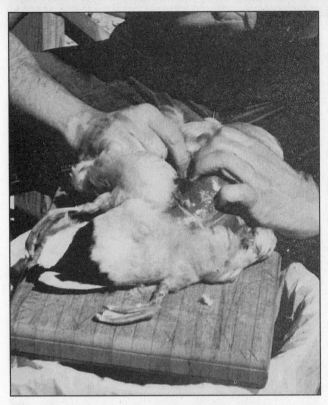

At this time, most of breast skin is either loose, or entirely free. Now the skin can be tugged free from the carcass, bringing the feathers with it.

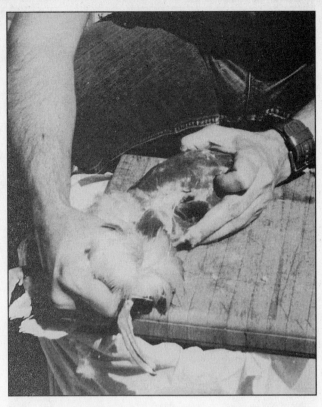

The skin, along with feathers, is tugged downward in this illustration. It's easy to see that the meat is left intact here, and not torn.

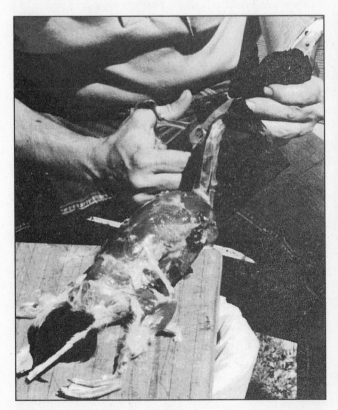

After the duck is skinned, the head is removed using game shears. This makes a neat job of it.

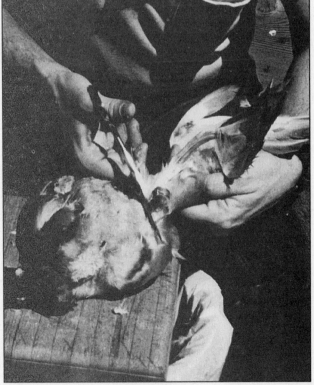

The tail may be removed before the skinning process begins, using game shears. However, this is an optional maneuver. The tail may also be removed at the end of the skinning process. It really does not matter.

PLUCKING

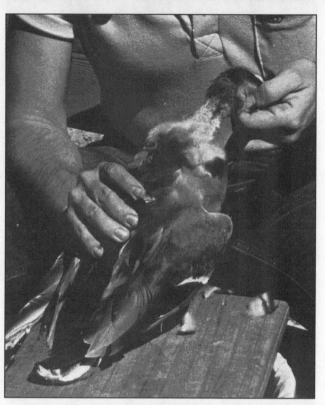

The duck is firmly positioned on a cutting board for plucking. A tiny ring of feathers is removed around the neck in a circle, plucking with fingers.

As the initial step goes, so goes the rest of the job when defeathering a duck or a goose. The ring of feathers removed from around the neck, as illustrated here, allow a good starting point for the rest of the job.

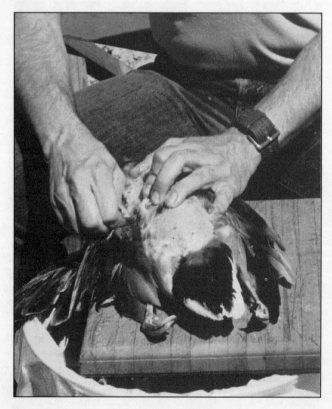

Feathers plucked by hand along entire breast, starting at neck region, then working down, then back up, then down, back up, and so forth.

In this illustration, the feathers around the legs are tugged free. The entire breast area of the duck is done before the back is plucked.

dunked. That's what makes the paraffin stick to the feathers, coating them with the warm wax. Dip the birds two to four times, in order to build up a coating. *Tip:* If you dip the birds in very cold water after the final paraffin application, it helps the wax harden on the feathers, so when the wax is pulled free, it takes the feathers with it. They should come free in large bunches. This is not a perfect method, but then no defeathering job is perfect. Sometimes, ducks can be defeathered without the paraffin, too, with the same kind of hot water soak noted for upland birds, but I like the paraffin way better. It's more certain.

After a dry or wet plucking, remaining down and small feathers can be removed by singeing. A propane torch is handy, or the flame of a camp stove can be used. Some hunters ignite a tight paper roll and singe with that. Any controllable flame will do, but don't burn the meat.

Tweezers can be used to withdraw some stubborn feathers; however, they don't work well on down. Singeing is the more reliable way to finish defeathering.

Boning or Sectioning

Depending on the preparation methods that will be used, the meat can be butchered either way. Any waterfowl can be boned, and this method comes highly recommended for open (uncovered) oven cooking, where the duck or goose is prepared in hunks, not whole. Start by

BONING OR SECTIONING

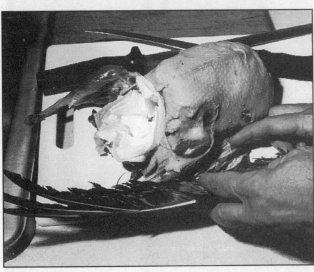

The first step in butchering waterfowl is laying the bird out on a clean surface, such as the synthetic cutting board used here. Note that one wing remains attached to this snow goose (one of the smaller species of geese). The wing remains attached to comply with the law. It is used for game department identification.

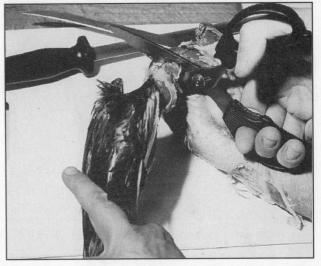

Game shears are extremely useful in waterfowl butchering. Here, game shears are used to remove wing that was left on for identification purposes. The cutting notch on game shears is used to sever the joint.

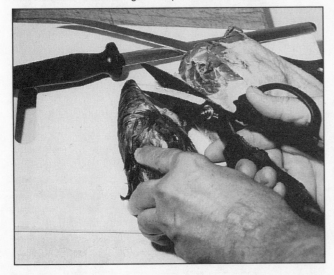

The cutting notch on the game shear is also useful for stripping meat from bone.

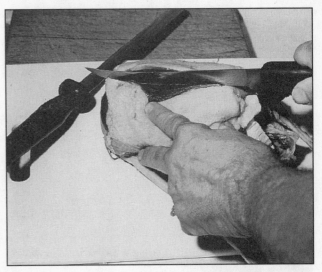

The next step in butchering waterfowl is removal of breast meat, since this particular carcass is destined for duck soup, which can be made with snow geese as well as ducks. A thin-bladed knife is used to part meat from the keel or breastbone area of the waterfowl. The first slice is being made here.

skinning. Then, cut off both legs close to the body. Use game shears to remove the bony back of the bird, but don't toss this part out, even though it carries very little meat. It cooks up crisp in the open oven and is enjoyable to chew on. The breast area is left. Using a thin-bladed boning knife, cut along the breast to one side, holding the blade in against the keel at all times, separating as much of the breast meat on one side as possible. Then, do the same with the other side.

Sectioning is very similar to boning, with the exception of the breast area. First, skin the bird. Follow by cutting off both legs close to the body. Also, use game shears to remove the backbone. Then, begin work on the breast. Leave the bone in the breast when cooking ducks, especially with the uncovered oven method. Instead of working breast meat away from the keel, cut the breast of a duck into four equal parts and the breast of a goose into six or eight equal parts. Incidentally, the open or uncovered baking method for geese pertains to younger birds, because this preparation method tends to dry out the bird, and the younger the game, the more tender the meat.

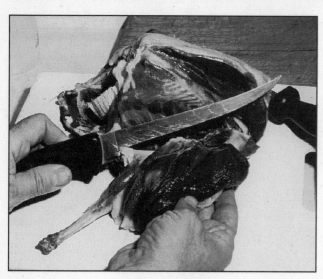

Here is one-half of the breast completely removed from the carcass.

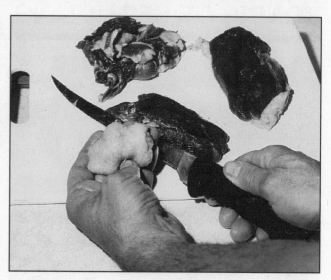

Fat is easily removed from waterfowl carcass using a combination of filet knife, plus pulling with fingers while cutting fat free. Removal of fat leaves a completely boneless chunk of breast meat to be cubed for duck soup.

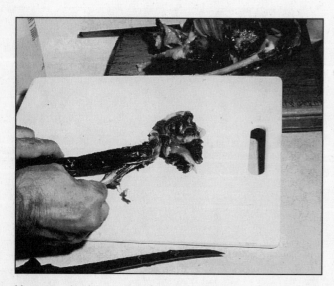

Meat can also be removed from leg using game shears. In this operation, the points of the game shears are put to work, snipping small cuts to remove meat from bone.

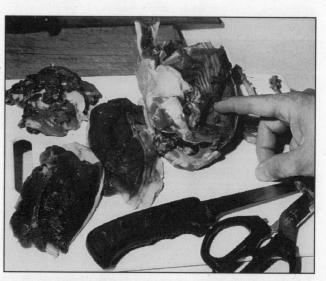

At this point, the carcass is examined. Note that breast meat is removed in two large chunks and has not yet been rid of fatty skin. The carcass can be boiled for stock now. Meat has been, for all practical purposes, removed.

Washing

Ducks and geese can be washed in light salt water. Pour a gallon of cold water into a container, more water if you need it to cover all parts, and add about a half-cup of salt. For sectioned duck or goose, soak the parts in this solution for an hour, then rinse off and dry each part. For whole birds, make up a quart or so of water with a couple tablespoons of salt and give the duck or goose a bath with this solution, inside and out, using a sponge. Then rinse with cold water and dry the bird well with a clean rag or paper towels.

Taxidermy Considerations

The taxidermy-bound duck or goose requires the same care given other birds. Stuff cotton or tissue down into the throat and shot holes to prevent leakage of body fluids, then tuck the bird into a newspaper cone, as described in Chapter 13: Butchering Upland Game. Take care to prevent feather matting and keep the bird cold, frozen if possible. Ideally, the bird should not be eviscerated. Once again, I realize this goes against the tenets of good game care, but we mount very few waterfowl specimens, and you want the job to be done right.

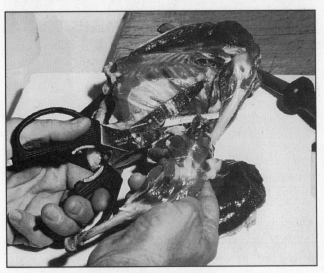

Game shears are used to remove leg at joint. Once again, the cutting notch is employed.

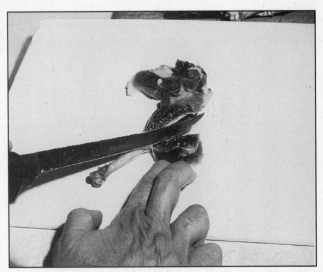

Filet knife is put to work removing meat from leg bone, as shown here.

After fat is removed from breast, boned breast meat is cubed for soup. Note stripped meat above the breast half being cubed; this is meat from the legs that has been cut free using filet knife and game shears. Upper right is intact boned breast meat, not yet defatted.

This illustration shows the finished job. All of the boned meat is placed together; this is meat from the legs as well as from the breast. To the right are the legs, stripped of meat, and above is the carcass. Carcass and leg bones can be boiled or pressure-cooked to make stock.

109

The mountain lion is a delicious exotic, but most hunters will never eat one. That's a matter of food prejudice and failure to give the meat a chance.

Chapter 15...
Preparing the Exotics
Game Care & Cookery

EXOTICS PROBABLY AREN'T. After all, what we call exotic edible species live right here in North America, but the name holds because these edibles are not on anyone's list of daily fare. Our lineup of edible "different things" is far from complete, either, and it also leans to the personal. No one can guess what another dinner guest might enjoy for food, so the comments rendered here come from individual information, based on individual taste buds.

Mountain Lion

I'll vouch for this one, having partaken of three. The meat is extremely light in color, with fine grain. Cuts look like the best loin pork, but taste nothing like pork. Describing the flavor of mountain lion meat is difficult. It is mild, rather than strong, and while I'm sure some cats provide tough meat, the ones I've tried, including one older specimen, were extremely tender. Mountain lion has a tendency to go dry on the gas grill unless marinated and treated exactly like grilled antelope steaks. The best-eating mountain lion treat (again based on personal taste only) is breaded steaks cooked in half margarine/half canola oil on medium heat. Simply delicious.

Field care of the mountain lion is typical of other four-legged animals, with the exception of hide care. The hide on any mountain lion is valuable, and care should always be taken to preserve it. Therefore, clean neat cuts are necessary. The cut from vent to chest should be as straight as possible, with four cuts going out from this longitudinal slice to all four legs. The paws should be left intact on the hide, and

Mountain lion cooks up into tasty boneless morsels when handled properly, and especially when treated to Universal Marinade. Use paper towel, as shown here, to blot excess oils.

Handling a porcupine requires gloves.

John Fadala poses with a large porcupine (in hand) and a smaller one (on the ground). The porcupine is an exotic that is edible, but does require careful cooking.

the entire package—hide, head and paws—rapidly taken to the taxidermist, since it is on the thin side and can spoil easily. If this is not convenient, the hide can be frozen for short-range storage. But it must be wrapped first, not in newspaper, but in a clean discarded white sheet, and then into a large plastic garbage bag. Expel the air from the bag, then tape it shut before freezing the cat hide.

Raccoon

Raccoon has long been admired as good food in our Southern states, and that's where the recipes listed in this book came from. Field care for coons includes careful skinning because the pelt can be, in season, valuable. Even when not salable, the pelt is decorative. Some old-timers insist the jugular should be cut to bleed the carcass thoroughly for the best-eating meat. This must be done with care, if at all, to avoid damaging the pelt. Ideally, the hunter quickly skins the raccoon, and by dressing it out, also bleeds the carcass without making a neck incision.

If the hunter goes to work on a coon right away, he's wise to dehide it before evisceration. We'll assume that to be the case here. The best way to skin a coon: First, ring the hind legs with a sharp knife; then make incisions from the inside of both hind legs to the vent. Do the same with the front legs, going from the inside to the mid-chest of the coon. Next, a cut is made from vent to mid-chest, which joins the leg incisions. This cut runs all the way to the jawbone. The tail is then longitudinally cut on the underside only with a straight incision that meets the first leg incision. The hide is slowly and carefully stripped from the tail, pulling gently and using a sharp-pointed jackknife wherever the hide refuses to slip free under modest pressure. Next, skin the hind legs downward. This is rather self-explanatory because the previous cuts outline exactly where to go. Now that the hind legs are skinned back, a gambrel can be used to hang the coon for the rest of the operation.

The skinning operation continues downward to the front legs until there is nothing left to do except work the hide off of the head or cut the head off at the neck, which is the normal procedure. If the raccoon is going to the taxidermy shop, bring the hide in with feet and

Rattlesnake is good food, although there isn't a lot of meat on this delicacy unless the snake is very large.

head attached. The taxidermist can finish the job of working the hide free from the head and feet. What you have left is a skinned coon carcass hanging on a little gambrel or suspended by each hind leg with cord. Remove the skinned tail and feet with a sharp knife; they are of no value.

Once the pelt has been saved, it's time to butcher the raccoon. The carcass still contains offal, which must be removed. This maneuver is little different than doing a squirrel. The usual cut is made from vent to breastbone, then through the breastbone, and all innards are removed. The aitch bone is cut and the canal is freed of all matter. A toothbrush is handy for working through the canal, with water, to clean this area completely. Now the inside of the carcass is flushed with water. A water hose is ideal, using good pressure. At this point, look for two small pear-shaped musk glands. You will find them under the forearms. Cut them out carefully and get rid of them. Then, close the carcass and wash your hands. A heavy salt water soak is the next step, using two gallons of very cold water with two full cups of salt. Soak the carcass for several hours, followed by draining and drying. You're ready for parboiling or pressuring, then cooking.

Porcupine

One day not long ago, I grabbed my little Herb Meland Pronghorn longbow and struck out on a mountain trail. Before long, I came upon a weathered old porcupine ambling along the same trail. No reason to take him, I figured, because the "spined pig" has never been a favorite of mine on the table. But I'd told the rancher down below that if I saw a porcupine, I'd shoot. They were destroying trees at quite a clip, and the area had many porcupines roaming in it. One Grizzly broadhead later, it was mine, quills and all. "I'll bring the hide to Charlie," I said out loud, "so he can do his quill work with it." The quills make fabulous decoration.

Porcupines are easier to skin than they look. Turn the animal over on its back, work from the belly, and in moments the hide is free. There is nothing tricky about it, so I'll skip the details. The usual vent to neck and inside leg cuts do the trick. The hide peels off rather handily. Now, I had one hide, but didn't want to toss the carcass away, even though it would have been legal to do so. "OK," I said. "Let's try one more time." And try I did. The meat was sectioned into several large chunks and soaked overnight in a bucket of ice water

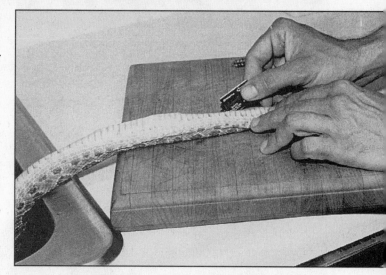

A single-edge razor blade is safer to use for evisceration of rattlesnake; however, author prefers sharper, and thinner, double-edge blade. Great care must be exercised when using a razor. A slit is made from vent to neck, in as straight a line as possible.

and heavy salt. Then I pressure-cooked the hunks with condiments, and the meat was roasted. Best meat I ever ate? No, but "tolerable good," as they say. Lamb-like, if a comparison can be made.

Opossum

Or just plain possum, these odd little animals provide food for man. The following comes secondhand from a back-East friend who says he likes to eat these little critters. The possum is well-bled immediately after taking and can be skinned or not, as the consumer sees fit. If not, it's scalded in boiling water before preparation. The water contains lime or ashes about a half-cup to a gallon of water. After scalding, the possum is scraped until hairless and then eviscerated, like other four-legged small game, if the job has not been done already. Musk glands beneath the forearms, as on a coon, are removed, and the carcass is soaked in heavy salt water for several hours. Then, the little beast is cooked, as our single recipe describes later in the book.

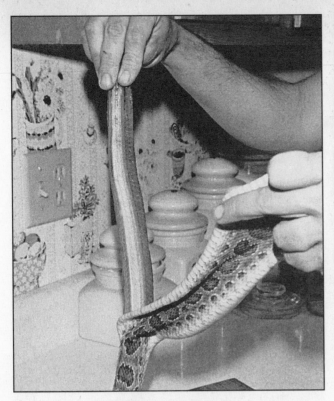

Skin is stripped carefully from the carcass of the rattlesnake by simply pulling gently from head downward toward vent. The skin will not tear if reasonable pressure is used in removing it from the carcass. Viscera are easily removed with the fingers, simply stripping the contents out and discarding.

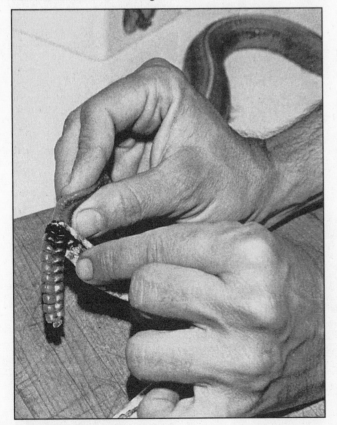

After all skin is freed from tail area using razor blade, it is pulled downward gently all the way to the rattles of the snake, as shown here. Use gentle pressure only.

Do not try to strip skin away from lower tail region of snake. It will probably tear in the process. Instead, cut all around with razor blade to free skin from tail region.

Rattlesnake

My last rattler, a large one from the prairie, was taken by arrow using a Black Widow recurve bow on an extended hike through Wyoming badlands. One problem with rattlesnake: there isn't enough of it. The meat is white, delicate and tasty, not unlike frog's legs. Also, field care is easy.

Remove the head and bury it or place a heavy rock on it. Dead rattlers are still dangerous. Their poison sac remains loaded with venom, and this can get squeezed out. Also, rattlers retain reflex action long after dead. Sever the head and put it where no one can come into contact with it.

Next, slit the snake the full length of the belly from anal opening to neck, using a sharp single-edge razor.

Peel off the skin by hand, slowly and carefully, right back to the anal opening. Make certain the cut is centered down the plates, so there is equal plate showing on either side. The hide is a prize well worth saving. It can be enjoyed as a keepsake, studied or used to make hatbands and other decorations.

Cut off the rattle intact with the skin. Just make one sharp cut with the razor, right through the backbone of the snake just in front of the rattle.

Later on, after taking care of the meat, stretch and tack the skin full-length on a board. Salt the skin heavily and then when dry, rub off as much salt as possible by hand. Apply glycerin or hand lotion containing glycerin, and rub well into the skin to soften it.

Back to the carcass—deepen the long cut made on the belly, if it did not penetrate fully into the cavity of the snake. Then, strip out the innards, followed by a cavity flush with cold running water, using your fingers to clean at the same time.

Cut the snake into serving pieces. The number of pieces depends upon the length of the snake, but they should be short, about two to

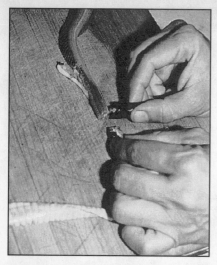

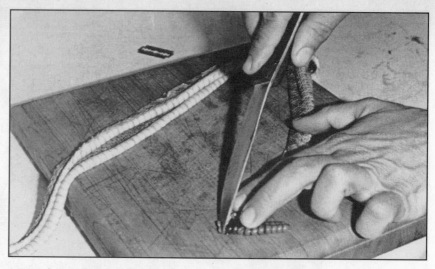

After skin is pulled all the way down to the rattles, the carcass is separated from the skin and the rattles with one clean razor cut.

A little meat will be left in the tail section of the skin. This meat can be carefully teased away using the point of a knife as a scraper only. Scrape major meat away, but do not work the blade of the knife too hard, or the skin will tear.

Here is the skin of the rattlesnake, completely removed from the carcass, with rattles intact on the skin.

To cure the skin, tack it on a board for drying purposes. The underside of the skin has been salted. Later, the underside of the skin will be treated with glycerin to soften the entire skin, making it supple.

The rattlesnake divides into two useful sections. Here is the carcass of the snake, which will be cut into sections and cooked.

four inches. This is important, because if left in long strips, the meat looks like snake, which may turn off prospective diners. When cut into shorter pieces, the sections of meat look more like filets.

Now dunk the cut pieces of meat into cold water plus salt and vinegar. A quart of water, two tablespoons of salt and a half-cup of white vinegar will do it. Let the meat soak for two or three hours, then remove, drain and dry. The meat is ready to cook. See the recipe on fried rattler in the recipe section of the book.

Turtle

These highly edible creatures can be great fare, especially as turtle soup. As always, pre-care is the key to success. The head is first removed with a small hatchet. Then—it all depends. If camp or home are nearby, the turtle goes directly into a pot of boiling water. The water should be well-salted, about a half-cup of salt per gallon of water. This seems to relax the muscles, making the rest of the job easier. Also, turtles, like snakes, tend to have considerable reflex action long after dispatched, and the salt water boil calms this reaction. Let the turtle roll in the boiling water for fifteen minutes, then pull it out for deshelling. If no hot water is handy, allow the dispatched turtle to sit an hour or so before continuing the field care process.

Cut along the two shell haves to slice the muscles. Remove the lower half with careful cutting and work the meat out of the upper half of the shell. Make certain that only nice edible meat portions are retained. Lop off the claws and lower part of the tail, then skin the rest of the legs with a sharp knife in the usual fashion. You do not have to remove the offal. It will remain intact with the upper half of the shell.

Next, chunk the turtle meat into about 1-inch cubes. Place these pieces in salt water with vinegar—about a quart of water, two tablespoons of salt and a half-cup of white vinegar—for a couple hours, then drain and dry the pieces. The turtle meat is ready for cooking. See the recipe section for further instruction.

A couple more turtle tips: You won't end up with cuts of meat from the usual land turtle, although this is not the case with sea turtles. Instead, the meat ends up in chunks, their shape unimportant. Also, be sure to remove entirely the anal opening by slicing it away and getting rid of it, but don't forget to salvage the hunk of good meat at the base of the tail. Also, bone out the neck meat, which is good. Turtles have good meat, but not an awful lot of it, so don't be disappointed when you discard so much of the animal. What is left is well worth the trouble.

Bullfrog

Quiet walks along the drainage ditch that follows the main canal near my hometown remain an important part of my growing-up memory book. It was legal to hunt bullfrogs with a 22 rimfire rifle, and that's how we got ours, head shots only. Bang! And the frog sank. Then you leapt in and retrieved it from the muddy bottom of the ditch. The field care of bullfrogs is simple and easy because you want only the back legs. These are disjointed neatly and carried home in your game bag. Our frog leg recipe is simple and delicious.

Woodchuck and Prairie Dog

These along with rockchucks, are edible, although older specimens can be tough and strong-flavored. Game care includes immediate small game field-dressing and cooling, followed by washing, draining and drying of the carcass. Skinning right away makes the job much easier. Later, the animal is sectioned much the same as a cottontail rabbit, with all parts soaked for about four hours in salt-water with vinegar—about a half-cup of vinegar per gallon of water, plus a quar-

Prairie dogs were food for Native American tribes, and they remain food fit for humans to this day. Of course, proper care and cooking is essential to success.

The rockchuck is closely related to the woodchuck. Both are edible.

ter-cup of salt. After soaking, remove the parts, dump the water and replace with plain cold water plus a quarter-cup of baking soda per gallon. Leave for thirty minutes. Then lift out the meat and wash each piece under cold water, drain and dry. The meat is ready to cook.

Muskrats

Known at times as the water rat or musquash, muskrats have provided meat for many north country trappers when other edibles were impossible to come by. "The skin is taken, but the flesh is cast away," said Martin Hunter in his 1935 Harding book, *Canadian Wilds*. Martin added that "This is for no other reason but the name." Of course, muskrats aren't rats. "They live on the same food, roots, grasses and twigs as the beaver," Martin reminded. The muskrat is field dressed like any other small mammal. Refer to Chapter 7: Field Care for Small Game.

There are, as promised, many more exotics than listed here, as game cookbooks prove, especially older books that treated what we call exotics as common tablefare. Truth is, most wildlife is edible, right down to the common house sparrow, and certainly beaver, many different snakes, crayfish, alligator, feral pigeon, coati-mundi, crows, blackbirds and others. Once food prejudice is conquered, these and a multitude of other wild things taste just fine, as proved by fancy restaurant names for dishes many of us wouldn't touch if we knew what they really were! So enjoy your escargot, while I eat my snails.

A VITAL STEP in properly caring for game from field to table is the middle sequence in between the harvest and cooking—wrapping and storing the product of the hunt. Ill-packaged game meat suffers reduced storage life and a decline in table quality. But "freezer taste" or "freezer burn" is avoidable for a longer period of time through proper packaging and storage. Here are a few tips for increasing the longevity of freezer-stored game meat.

Double-Wrapping

I began double-wrapping game meat at least twenty years ago. At the time, commercial game packaging plants did not double-wrap as a rule. I know, because I asked at least ten different establishments about the process and none contacted at the time did it or felt it necessary. Today, that's changed. Our last informal survey in Idaho and Wyoming turned up eight of ten shops double-wrapping meat.

The system is simple: Lay out a piece of plastic wrap on a flat working surface. This can be any brand of plastic wrap normally used in the kitchen to package anything from sandwiches to leftovers. In the past, we had ready access to a special heavy-duty plastic freezer wrap, but our local source dried up. We then located a new supply of this special plastic freezer wrap in Idaho; however, in the meanwhile, we discovered that ordinary plastic food wrap works as well, costs a little less, and is easier to find.

Place the piece of meat in the center of the plastic wrap and neatly fold the wrap over the meat. Do not trap air inside. Doing a package free of air pockets is easy with a nice chunk of boned meat, as well as

Chapter 16...
Wrapping and Freezing Game Meat
Game Care & Cookery

burger, but not so easily accomplished with odd-shaped pieces, such as rabbit or upland bird/waterfowl parts. So work at it until your skill improves. Try various arrangements with odd-shaped pieces, fitting them together like a puzzle to form a neat package as free of air as possible.

Place the wrapped meat in the center of a piece of freezer wrap with the shiny side up, lying against the plastic wrapped package. Neatly fold the wrap to form a tight package.

Use masking tape to hold the package together. Freezer tape is generally more expensive, and does no better, if as well, in securing a package of frozen meat. Half-inch-wide masking tape is excellent, but narrower tape also works. If there is any doubt that the package is intact, use more tape. On rabbits, upland birds and waterfowl, an extra wrap of tape may serve to create a better unit, because odd-shaped parts cause an irregular-shaped package. Use enough to create a solid package. The content of the package is worth a lot more than an extra piece of masking tape, a bit of plastic wrap, or a little freezer wrap.

Vacuum Packaging

Worth mentioning is the vacuum food sealer, which promotes storage life by excluding air from the package, while thwarting freezer burn. Cabela's Professional Food Saver is one such unit, selling, as this is written, for roughly $200. Vacuum food sealers can be used for

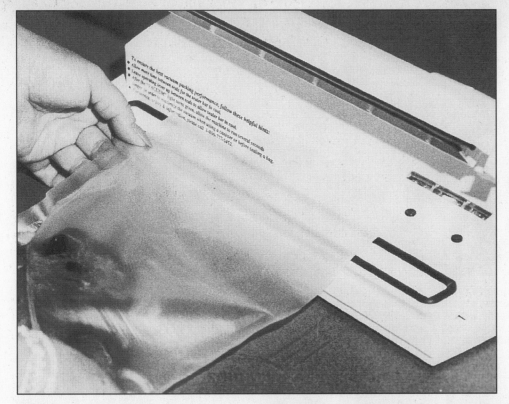

A modern approach to wrapping game meat for the freezer is vacuum packing. Here, a section of plastic bag has been cut off and is now being sealed on one end in the vacuum packing machine.

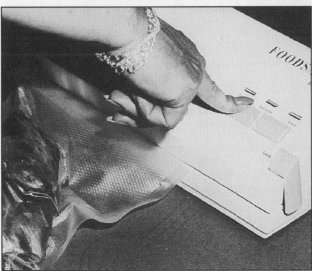

The meat is placed in the freezer bag. In this step, air is withdrawn from the package.

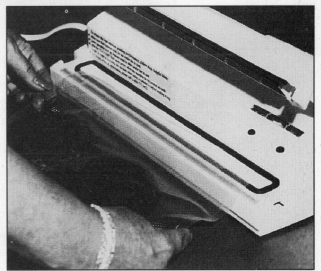

The vacuum unit seals the end of the package after air is withdrawn. This gives the vacuum pack effect.

a multitude of products, even non-food items that you wish to keep dry. These sealers are fully adjustable to accommodate different foods—fish, fowl, game meats—and feature a non-corrosive pump. Although I am now experimenting with vacuum sealing food, I have no data on storage longevity. The literature, however, indicates that freezer burn is eliminated or at least greatly delayed, which suggests that vacuum packaging may be an answer for long-range freezing of game meats.

Marking a Package

With a marking pen, jot down sufficient data about the packaged product. Obviously, the species is vital information—deer, boar, bear, elk. What's in the package? It's also important to note the date of packaging for several reasons. Is a deer taken in September tastier

than a similar deer tagged in November? Was the animal bagged during rut, before, after? How long has this package been frozen? Dates are absolutely critical. The cut—roast, steak, burger—is also vital. Other data are not as important, but may prove valuable. We've learned much about game meat by including site of harvest. Is game from one region better-tasting than game from another? How about the size and condition of the animal per region? You'd be surprised at some of the geographic differences we've noted in the same species.

It's useful to write down the name of the hunter, especially for youngsters, who gain a special appreciation for the wise use of game meat when they see the fruits of their own labor served on the table. Sometimes, specific instructions are useful. If a game animal was particularly young, mark it so; you may wish to use that meat for cutlets or other dishes that benefit from tender meat. The reverse is equally

117

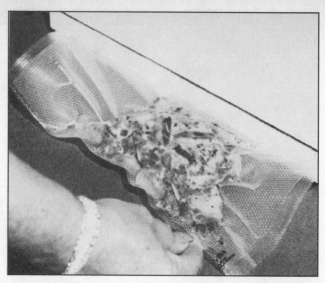

The vacuum packing method is useful for just about any game meat and shape, including waterfowl. *Important:* The package can be frozen as shown here, or it can be wrapped with standard freezer paper for extra duration. The vacuum bag takes the place of the initial plastic wrap, as well as excluding air.

After preparing a game dinner, such as this casserole, part of it may be vacuum packed and frozen for later use.

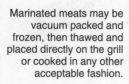

Marinated meats may be vacuum packed and frozen, then thawed and placed directly on the grill or cooked in any other acceptable fashion.

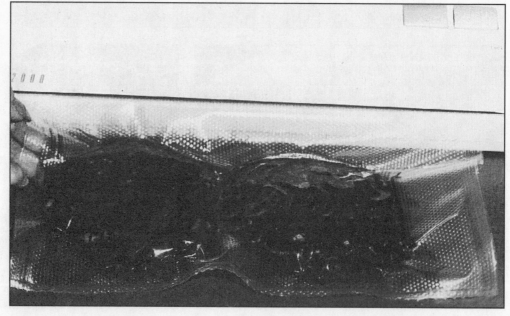

true: If you bag an older goose, make note of it. Then cook it accordingly. Of lesser importance is the manner of harvest: shotgun, 22 rimfire, bow and so forth, but it can be interesting.

What to Package

Don't package bones unless you particularly enjoy cooking standard cuts. It makes no sense to store what will inevitably be tossed out. Don't package fat, either, because it deteriorates faster in the freezer than meat. I found this out by testing. Chapter 18, "Processing Gameburger," mentions the no-fat system I use today for grinding and packaging ground meat. So don't add fat to your burger meat before packaging. And be sure to trim fat from meat before wrapping the cut. As a rule: trim now, not later. If the piece of meat requires trimming before cooking, trim it before packaging. A little "rind" is all right, but leaving large amounts is wasteful of freezer space.

Dealing with Bloodshot Meat

Generally, packaging bloodshot meat is unworthy of time and effort. Some hunters, however, insist that bloodshot meat is good if cooked properly. Even Nessmuk, the great old dean of camping, offered a recipe for cooking with meat cut from the bullet's channel. However, Nessmuk hunted with a muzzleloader, and I suspect his bloodshot meat was quite unlike what we see today from high-velocity bullets. If a hunter insists on saving such meat, here is one way to improve upon its quality: Soak it out. If it is a large piece, put cold water plus a couple cups of salt well-stirred into the bathtub and drop the hunk of meat into it. Let the meat stand in the water for a couple hours, turning it now and then. This will whiten the darkened meat quite nicely. But I still recommend cutting away the most severe bloodshot meat before trying to salvage the rest of the hunk for packaging and freezing.

Derek Rochat of Mkashi Ranch, Zimbabwe, Africa, is put to the important task of marking packages for the freezer. When marking packages for the freezer, ask yourself what you will want to know about that package a few months later: species? where taken? by whom? weight of package? approximate age of game animal?

Gameburger is labeled as to species, in this case, deer, as well as date of harvest. Also, weight will be printed on the package, which is important when a specific amount of gameburger is needed for a recipe. A baby scale is ideal for the job.

Storing Frozen Meat

Packages should be placed in the freezer according to cuts instead of species. At least this is one way to do it. I like all of my steaks in one area, roasts in another, chili/stew meat in yet another section, and so forth. Of course, rabbits go with rabbits, squirrels with squirrels, and ducks with ducks. Put the packages close together in the freezer with as little space between each package as possible. Free-standing packages seem to take on freezer burn faster than packages stacked closely together.

Defrosting

There are several ways to safely defrost frozen game meat, but first how not to do it. Do not allow a hunk of meat to stand open on the counter for hours in a warm environment. This happens all too often when a cook takes a package of meat from the freezer, leaving it to thaw all night long. By the time he gets back to the meat, it may be warm. That's bad. Ideally, the meat should go from frozen to cold, but not to warm until the meat is cooking. Here are some better ways to thaw frozen meat: Place the package, still frozen solid, into the microwave oven on the defrost setting. This knocks the edge off of the package. Then, the package can be left out in the open for a while until it is *partially thawed*.

There is nothing wrong with cooking partially thawed meat. Roasts do especially well when cooked from a partial thaw to done. Steaks can be cut from a large hunk of steak meat while that meat is only partially thawed. Steaks may even cut easier when very cold, as opposed to cutting them when fully thawed out. If time is not critical, another way to thaw a frozen package of meat is in the refrigerator overnight. The package will still be hard by morning, but it won't be quite as solid as it was twelve or so hours ago. In the morning, remove the meat from its package, and then return it, well-covered with plastic wrap, to the refrigerator for further thawing. Cook later in the day either partially thawed or remove an hour or so before cooking time to allow further thawing.

Another good way to thaw meat is in water. First, remove the meat from the package, then plop it directly into cold water, no salt added. When the meat is partially thawed, remove and place covered in refrigerator until cooking time. Also, combinations of the various methods are worthwhile. Meat-thawing can be started in the microwave, for example, just long enough for the frozen meat to break its bond with the wrapping paper around it. Then the meat can be removed from its packaging and placed covered in the refrigerator or into cold water for further thawing. Ultimately, the important thing is to keep the meat good and cold from freezer to cooking.

How Long Will it Last?

Meats vary in their freezer longevity. My data are unscientific and based solely on personal experience. Furthermore, the experiences of others could differ with mine. However, the following offers the reader at least a few guidelines for the expected freezer life of different game meats.

Burger Meat with 10 to 20 Percent Fat

I've found that burger meat ground with 10 to 20 percent fat lasts about six to eight months with full color and flavor. After that, the quality drops. The meat is still edible, and apparently safe for several months more, but top quality is compromised.

Burger Meat Without Fat

Burger meat ground with no fat, which is how we do all of our hamburger meat these days, lasts a full year or a bit longer in excel-

Robert Rosenfels of Zimbabwe takes part in a game wrapping operation. Note that the package is tightly wrapped, with air expelled, and the corners are well-taped.

In preparing any meat for wrapping and freezing, trimming is vital. Here, the bony backplate of the waterfowl is cut away with game shears and discarded.

lent condition. As previously mentioned, fat breaks down quicker in the freezer. So the less fat in your burger, the longer it will last.

Red Meat with Fat

Red meat, such as deer, with fat left attached to the pieces, is good for about eight months, and after that it begins to lose flavor. More accurately, the fat seems to deteriorate within this time frame and flavor falls off.

Red Meat Without Fat

Red meat without fat (well-trimmed) lasts a year with full flavor intact. A full eighteen months later, the meat is still palatable. After eighteen months, this meat loses some of its character, not only in color, but in flavor.

Cottontail Rabbits

In spite of extremely careful wrapping, even with two layers of plastic and one of freezer paper, top quality disappears after six months with cottontail rabbit meat. At that period, the meat seems to exude a bit of oil and the flavor falls off. Perhaps part of the problem is in the wrapping process itself. A future experiment with vacuum-sealed rabbit meat is in order. In the meantime, the reader is invited to try vacuum sealing rabbit meat as his own experiment in freezer longevity.

Squirrel

My tests suggest that squirrel meat outlasts rabbit by a month or two in full flavor, color, texture and overall quality, but after about eight months squirrel meat is less than perfect. As noted above, the problem could be with the wrapping as much as the meat itself, and vacuum sealing may be the answer.

Upland Birds

The freezer is no kinder to upland birds than to cottontails. I find that after six months the highest quality of the meat diminishes. This goes double for wild turkey. In one test, wild turkey cooked after eight months of freezer storage was decidedly reduced in quality.

Waterfowl

A friend gave us a goose that was frozen one full year. It was good, but probably not as good as it would have been six months earlier. Ducks, the same applies. I place waterfowl life at six to eight months for full flavor and texture, with declining quality after eight months.

Other Meats

I do not have a record of freezer life for all wild meat from rattlesnake to moose, but as a general rule, red meat without fat is good for a year in the freezer when wrapped correctly, while cottontail pieces, frog's legs, turtle chunks, and upland birds are better cooked within a half-year, with waterfowl lasting six to eight months at top quality.

Testing Two-Year-Old Meat

Knowing the meat would still be safe to eat, I set aside a few packages of boned venison steak meat and burger meat with and without fat. These were purposely left in the freezer for two years. Then I ran my informal taste tests, with several of us doing the judging. Steak meat, boned and without fat, was edible after two years, but decidedly reduced in quality. Served alongside a piece of the same kind of meat frozen for only six months, everyone picked the older meat as less tasty, even though cooked the same way in the same pan at the same time. Two-year-old burger meat with fat was even easier to detect, while the two-year old burger meat without fat tasted much better, but was not as good as burger meat frozen for only six months.

The importance of this chapter is multifold: Wrap game meat carefully; store it well-compacted in the freezer; thaw the meat carefully, never allowing the meat to get very warm before cooking; use red meat within a year, and most other meats within about six months.

Aging game meat depends on the game. Antelope do not require aging since the primary goal of aging is tenderizing, and antelope meat is tender on the spot.

Chapter 17

Aging Game Meat

Game Care & Cookery

THE CONCEPT OF aging is steeped in myth. A cook might brag, "I like to hang a pheasant by the neck, feathers on, until it drops to the ground. Then the bird is aged just right." It's a matter of taste and culture, and there are probably cooks and consumers who would like a pheasant so ripe that the body pulls away from the neck by virtue of its weight alone. Not me. And probably not you. Aging is dangerous for two reasons: It's often ill-understood, and it can be done all wrong. Some aging methods are better called rotting, for that's just what it is. It is better not to age meat at all than to spoil it.

Aging is the process of allowing meat to mature, which is generally accomplished by letting it hang in open air for a specific period of time at a specific range of temperatures. Aging can bring out flavor, albeit not always a flavor we like. Aging can also promote tenderness, for as meat gets ripe, it softens. If you don't think so, check a carcass shortly after it's harvested and again after a few days of hanging. The meat will be a bit more tender with time. To carry the point further, consider a piece of meat that has gone too far. It is totally spoiled. Yet, it's also tender.

Hanging Game Meat for Aging

A dressed and skinned carcass can be hung in a dry place for a specific period of time to age the meat. A *dry* place, mind you, not damp, because moisture promotes spoilage. The meat must be protected from flies, dirt or any other negative element—a game bag may be useful.

121

The most important part of the aging process is maintaining the correct temperature. Even if meat gets dust on it, it may be salvageable, but once rotten, it stays that way. Hot meat rots; it does not age. Ideally, the temperature should remain hovering around 40 degrees Fahrenheit at all times. I've aged meat successfully at barely above freezing—around 34 to 35 degrees, and up to about 45 degrees for a short period of time. But 40 degrees seems to be a fine compromise. *Important:* If you do not have a clean, dry place to age your meat at the proper constant temperature, do not age your meat at all. To do so risks spoilage.

Washing a carcass after skinning is wise, prudent and will never hurt the meat. But if that carcass is going to be aged, I suggest drying it with clean towels. Damp meat left to hang is inviting trouble, probably because the water on the meat is a possible home to unwanted

Never forget that aging begins in camp. These javelina, hanging after a light snowfall in Arizona, are already in the aging process. Hunters should remember that aging does not always begin after returning home.

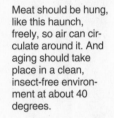

Meat should be hung, like this haunch, freely, so air can circulate around it. And aging should take place in a clean, insect-free environment at about 40 degrees.

Aging meat begins in the field, but the hunter must find the right location to age meat. This abandoned building offers shade to hang a carcass. Look for such places, rather than allowing a carcass to hang where it will be sunstruck.

guests from the microbe world. So the meat should be clean before aging, free of hair, and wiped down if not washed down, but it should also be dry. Be certain all gastric juices are washed away from the carcass. Imagine the effect gastric juices would have if allowed to work on meat over a period of time.

During the aging process, a dark rind called casing builds up on the meat. It's outer tissue that has air-dried and is no good to eat, and is cut off before preparation. On a ranch during my youth, we hung our deer in the tack room or other out-building not so much to age it, but to secure it for daily eating. A deer was gone in less than a week anyway with all of us working on it. Meat was cut from the hanging carcass, most of it boned and fried, eaten with batches of fresh flour tortillas and refried beans made by the Mexican cowhands who worked on the ranch. In time, the casing became thicker and thicker, and toward the end of the week, it grew to as thick as 1/4-inch, sometimes thicker. That meat, hanging in a cool, clean place that probably hovered between 35 and 45 degrees (never did check it for sure, but winter weather in that region ran that way) was good to the last bite, but definitely a little stronger flavored toward the end.

Case-Aged Meat

Meat can also be aged within a case or other enclosure, and butchers lovingly call this dark meat case-aged. It usually sells for less per pound than fresher meat, because of its dark color, but some people prefer case-aged meat over fresher meat. It's a matter of personal taste. A hunter can case-age meat, too, by placing the meat in a refrigerator and leaving it for a while, always checking for progress. Refrigerator-aged (same as case-aged) meat is fine if not allowed to go too long.

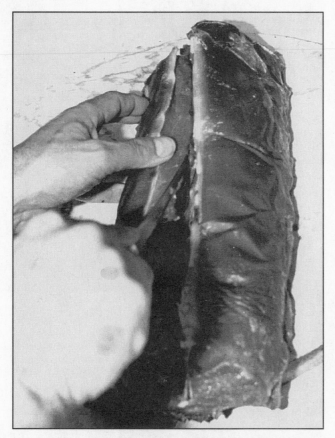

Casing is a dried covering of tissue over a piece of aged meat. This deer loin shows casing very clearly, with a dried slightly crinkled effect. This meat was aged only three days in a dry area at about 40 degrees. Cutting into the chunk reveals moist meat just behind the casing.

Walk-In Cooler Aging

A walk-in cooler, as found in meat processing plants, can be an ideal aging compartment. It's clean, insect-free (or easy to make that way) and temperature controlled. A hunter bent on aging meat may inquire about leaving the carcass at the local locker plant for a specific period of time, well-covered with cheesecloth or in a game bag. There is a fee for this, and it varies with processing plants.

Freezing to Age Meat

While freezing is not an aging process, and in fact is designed to cease all aging of the meat, the freezing process can tenderize meat. Supposedly, this is due to cell breakdown, whereby the liquid of the cell expands (as liquids do when frozen), thereby breaking down the cell wall. Maybe so. I can't prove this theory, but I believe it works. This fact is highly important to game care, because there are some meats which are best treated to a quick trip from the field to the freezer. If a major reason for aging meat is tenderizing it, then freezing may be an ideal replacement for aging with some species. Antelope is one such meat, as explained later.

What Meats Need Aging?

If a rule of thumb is necessary, let's agree that coarser-grained meats enjoy aging more than finer-grained meats. As with any generalization, it's not entirely accurate, but it has merit.

Antelope

At one time, I had an opinion that went, "Maybe you should forget aging antelope meat." Now, I feel more strongly than ever about aging this type of meat, and I'm willing to make a flat statement and stand by it: "Do not age antelope meat at all." Field-dress your antelope as soon as possible. Get the hide off and let the carcass cool overnight. The next day or the day after if it's cool in the hanging spot, butcher the carcass, package the meat and freeze the packages. Antelope meat does not require aging. It's already tender, and freezing makes it more tender than necessary. One complaint I often hear about antelope meat concerns its texture—too soft, people say, almost mushy. This can be true and aging would render antelope meat even softer, ruining its texture. This fine-grain meat does not, therefore, demand aging.

Black Bear

Black bear meat is on the coarse-grained side, yet may be the exception to the rule. At this juncture, we've had bear meat from several different carcasses, and most of the meat was butchered and frozen. The one carcass that was aged did not seem, to us, more tender or tasty than the previous non-aged meat. So, this one hangs in limbo. On the basis of personal experience, I'd say age the meat for two or three days at 40 degrees, then butcher, package and freeze, but if aging conditions are not available, don't worry about it.

Buffalo/Bison

Two bison of my acquaintance were treated to aging at 40 degrees constant temperature for a period of seven and ten days, respectively. Both bulls were similar in maturity and size. The week-long period of time seemed sufficient to me, but the ten-day aging period did not damage the meat either, although I did not see any further value in the additional three days. Two carcasses does not a study make, but this coarser-grained meat does do well with judicious aging. My family ate bison meat as it aged, and the flavor did not seem to change as aging proceeded. However, we all agreed that the meat was more tender after four or five days of hanging.

Aging depends on the species. Should bear meat be aged? For a day or two, but not a week. It's not necessary. Remember that aging does not mean hanging a carcass in a warm place. Forty degrees is about right.

To age or not to age? That is the question. This buck, in spite of its two-point rack (six-point Eastern count), was judged several years old by a study of its teeth, yet the meat was not aged, and it turned out to be delicious and tender.

Caribou

I lived on caribou almost exclusively for two weeks off the Denali Highway in Alaska, about thirty miles away from the road, living in a tent. While there, I ate plenty of caribou meat—some the day a bull was harvested, and some ten days later. It was all good, but after a couple days, the meat gained no improvement I could detect. I think two or three days of aging caribou meat is sufficient. The grain is about medium, more coarse than antelope, but finer than moose or bison.

Deer

Deer aged for two weeks may be prime to someone else, but it's strong to me. Deer meat aged for five days (as a test) was tender and tasty, but few of our deer receive so much as five minutes of aging. It's generally too warm during our deer season to properly age the meat, plus we've found little benefit in aging venison. As a rule, if temperatures permit, a three- to five-day aging period is fine. If conditions do not permit, don't worry about it. Butcher and package the meat, then freeze it. Freezing will take care of what little tenderizing most venison requires. As another test, whitetail deer ribs taken from a November buck were eaten at intervals of two, four and six days of aging, with temperatures ranging from 35 to just under 40 degrees. The ribs were equally good at all three aging periods. No one noticed a marked difference in taste or quality.

Elk

Elk meat is more coarse-grained than antelope or caribou, but not as coarse-grained as bison or moose. In testing aged and non-aged elk, however, the aged meat won. The fourteen-day aging period recommended by some cooks is probably too much of a good thing, however. A week is long enough.

Javelina

This little "wild pig" of the Southwest and Mexico is actually a musk hog, and he earns every bit of the reputation with his musk sac located on his backside near the rump. As noted elsewhere, the musk sac should be avoided entirely during the field-dressing process, then removed intact with the hide. As for aging this fine-grained meat, forget it. The meat does not need aging, and may be the worse for it.

Moose

Moose meat greatly benefits from aging. It's coarse-grained and rich-flavored. The excellent taste of the meat is enhanced by a week of hanging at 40 degrees, as is the tenderness. As a test, we aged

Be certain to clean a carcass thoroughly before aging the meat. This deer, struck in the chest region with an arrow, required removal of bloodshot meat before aging. Also, shoulder blades have been freed and are hanging.

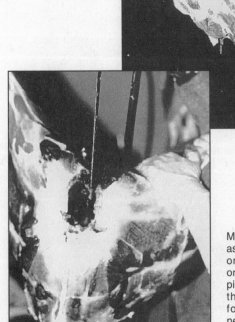

Meat can be aged as a whole carcass, or in large pieces, or in quarters. This piece was aged for three days in the form of two connected hams.

124

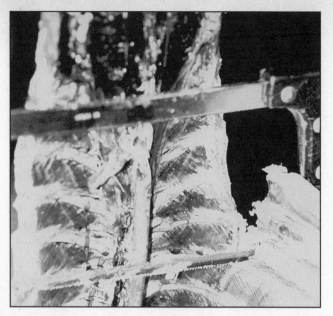

Ribs are cut free of this carcass for immediate cooking before aging the rest of the carcass. Pieces of meat can be consumed from a carcass as it ages. This is no problem.

moose meat from seven to fourteen days. After a week, it was impossible for any of us to note further changes in either flavor or texture.

Sheep

Wild sheep meat is great. I've eaten Rocky Mountain and desert varieties, and found both to be superb. Recently, a friend provided several pounds of prime sheep meat, aged in the locker at 40 degrees for four days. The meat was prime. But was it better for being aged? Can't prove it by me. I contacted the same person who helped me previously with the question of aging sheep meat, and this Alaskan guide and hunter gave me the same answer he provided several years earlier: "Can't see much difference in the taste of the meat."

Upland Birds

Some upland gunners believe in aging pheasants and other birds, so I decided to give it a try. I hung two pheasants—field-dressed, body cavities washed thoroughly with water and vinegar—for four days at temperatures that ranged from 35 to 45 degrees. If the birds improved with aging, I could not tell it. In fact, I feared for the meat after the second day, but it did not spoil. The next experiment was with quail. Two birds were hung for two days. Improvement in flavor or meat texture, if there was any, escaped me. I see no reason to age upland birds: grouse, partridges, quail, doves or any other. On the other hand, neither can I say that pheasants or quail, the only two birds I aged for testing, lost any quality from aging. I suppose this one has to remain at the personal level. Hunters who believe in aging certain upland birds should do so—carefully. The rest of us probably won't bother.

Waterfowl

"Hang 'em by the neck until the body weight of the duck or goose causes separation." The same advice given by some pheasant hunters applies to ducks and geese, and I don't buy it. In recent times, I did have a chance to age a goose, and my findings were inconclusive at best. I still don't know if it was a good idea or not, because it was only one bird—hardly a test. But after three days of hanging in ideal

conditions, the goose was cooked (not frozen), and it was great. It probably would have been great anyway, however. If a hunter has a clean, dry place to hang waterfowl for a couple days at 40 degrees, and he likes the idea, I cannot veto it, as I have no experience to suggest a problem with aging waterfowl. On the other hand, I don't think I'll age mine. If I change my mind, the aging period will be three days.

Exotics and All the Rest

Rattlesnake, turtle, muskrat, beaver, raccoon, possum, prairie dog, bullfrog and all the rest labeled exotic for our purposes are not aged. Could these treats be aged? I suppose so, but having no data on the results, I'm going to make the call that they need not be aged.

The game species included here do not constitute a complete list of wild edibles by any means. If in doubt about aging, err on the side of caution. Age only part of an animal or only one game bird out of the bag to find out if the process is worthwhile on that specific animal or bird.

Aging Meat and Individual Taste

Hunters must experiment individually with the aging process because aging meat is personal, a matter of taste. The "almost gone" tenderness and strong flavor of certain well-aged meats is a treat in various cultures and among specific cooks and consumers. Properly aged meat makes a dish fit for kings, but not all kings agree on taste, so dictating how long a specific species should be aged is, in the final analysis, impossible. It is possible, however, to offer starting points for hunters, and that's what we have here.

The next deer you get, hang the carefully dressed carcass, well-skinned and clean, in a dirt-free, fly-free environment at a controlled temperature hovering right around 40 degrees. Cut off a few round steaks after a couple days and give them the taste test. Let the meat age another day. Is the venison getting better, or do you detect that it's only getting stronger? If the latter, butcher right away and package the meat for the freezer. One deer may not make a valid test, but I think even that one experience is enough to bank on. You may find that aged meat is a treat to your taste buds, or that aged meat is not for you. If in doubt, use the general aging information provided here to help you understand the process and what it can, or cannot, do for meat in terms of flavor, texture and tenderness.

You must keep an eye on aging meat. Or maybe a nose would be smarter. Check out the meat at least twice a day. If it seems to be drying out rapidly, with casing getting fairly heavy, perhaps it would be best to stop the aging process, processing the meat immediately.

To cook burger meat on the gas grill or over coals, add a little fresh beef fat after thawing the meat. This gameburger was frozen fat-free. A little fresh beef fat was added just before cooking and *voila!* a juicy burger.

GAMEBURGER IS GROUND red meat, any kind of meat actually, but for our purposes it is meat from larger quadrupeds such as deer and elk. Ground meat is highly versatile—the main ingredient of chili dishes to meatloaves, not to mention the good old American hamburger with special sauce, lettuce, cheese, pickles, onion on a sesame-seed bun. Gameburger is also the heart of a special turkey stuffing recipe noted later in the book—gourmet all the way without much

Chapter 18...
Processing Gameburger
Game Care & Cookery

fuss. Special spaghetti sauce made with gameburger is rich without being greasy. Meatballs are good in soup, too, and the list goes on and on. In the two previous editions of this book, the chapter on gameburger dealt with various fat content at different levels. This edition notes a big difference—no fat at all, but don't panic. The new gameburger cooks up great in the fry pan, over coals, on the gas grill, and is better in all dishes than ever before, especially spaghetti sauce.

Choosing the Meat

Meat scraps of all kinds turn into good gameburger, but don't fool yourself. If you put questionable scraps into the pan for grinding, you may spoil the entire batch, so don't do it. Choose only sweet meat for your gameburger. Bloodshot meat should be discarded. So should lower shank pieces that wouldn't grind up correctly in the largest commercial meatgrinder in the country. Forget such scraps. Use only clean, sinew-free meat for gameburger. You are not making also-ran, half-fat ground meat here. You're creating top-grade food, just as good as, if not better than, the most lean ground sirloin steak you can buy at the supermarket meat counter. The only difference between prime stew pieces and chunks of meat destined for the grinder is shape. Irregular bits go into gameburger; pieces that can be cubed nicely become stew meat.

Preparing the Meat

There's not much to getting gameburger meat ready for the grinder. Bone the meat and set it aside. Do make certain that it's clean and entirely free of hair. Much of our gameburger meat comes from

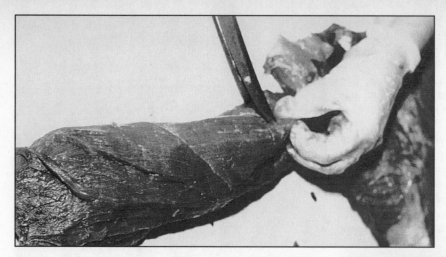

This fine chunk of boned venison is an obvious candidate for steaks. But the tip, being cut off here, will turn into gameburger.

These chunks of boned meat are ideal for steaks, but they cannot be turned into perfectly uniform cuts due to their shape. That's fine, because all irregular pieces, especially the tips, will make great gameburger.

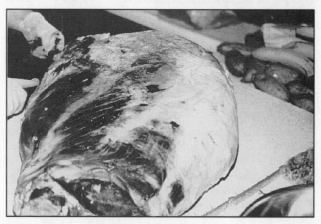

the hams, where large chunks destined for steaks are whittled, leaving smaller chunks for stew or gameburger. Neck meat also makes good burger, but a word to the wise: Don't mix neck meat with meat from the quarters. Sometimes neck meat, especially during rut, is stronger-flavored than meat taken from other parts of the carcass. If you mix the two types, your entire batch of burger may be stronger flavored than you may like. Sometimes this slightly stronger meat is ideal for chili and similar dishes, but not best for burgers or meatloaf. Keep the neck meat gameburger separated and mark your packages carefully so you'll know which is which when it's time to cook.

Blade meat also makes good gameburger. However, they're good as roasts, too and I suggest keeping a blade or two intact just for that purpose. But for those who find more use for burger meat than roasts, the entire front shoulder region can be boned out easily and quickly, then turned into chunks of meat for stew and/or burger meat.

Trimming

A boning knife is ideal for trimming gameburger meat because the thin blade easily separates unwanted tissue from solid meat. One way to do this is by firmly holding the chunk of meat against the cutting board and sliding the boning knife away from your hand while trimming meat away from tissue, or tissue from meat. Home-type meat grinders have a terrible time with tough tissue. Larger commercial grinders will handle such tissue, but I suggest trimming down to lean meat anyway.

Get rid of all natural fat in making gameburger. Fat goes rancid far easier than solid meat, and it seems to freezer burn quicker, too. Also, while game fat is a feast for some of us, it is bad-tasting for most others. Whitetail deer ribs, which are well-laced with fat, are a delicacy when properly spiced and cooked over hot coals. However, I doubt this particular dish will find favor with the majority of eaters. And even though I find whitetail deer rib fat delicious, I trim all fat from meat destined for gameburger.

No-Fat Burger Meat

Cooking with no-fat burger meat requires special care for some dishes. In spaghetti sauce, chili, casseroles, meatloaf, meatballs and any other similar dish, the no-fat burger meat is actually easier with which to work. I've spent plenty of time and effort degreasing fatty burger (and sausage) by cooking the meat in a frying pan, draining off the fat, then placing the meat on a dish loaded with paper towels, the dish going into the microwave for a couple minutes on high pow-

This nice venison haunch will turn into many good-eating steaks; however, many irregular pieces will also make great stews and gameburger.

er. This cuts fat in a hurry, the melted fat running into the paper towels. But with no-fat gameburger, degreasing the meat is not necessary. Just use it in your dish without a thought.

About the only place a lack of fat poses a problem is in making the American hamburger. But here's how to work with no-fat burger in the fry pan, over coals or on the gas grill. Rub both sides of the burger with canola oil before dropping the burger into the frying pan. Do not pre-heat the pan above medium. If you want to brown the burger toward the end of its cooking time, turn the heat up for the last minute or two, but not before. Since there is no fat in the burger meat, it can burn more quickly than fatty burger meat. The same oiling method can be used for burgers on the grill. Rub canola oil on both sides of the burger and place the meat on the grate over coals or gas flame (lava rock), but don't go away. While oiled burger meat cooks up fine on the grill, it can burn more easily than burger with fat. Lower heat does a better job than higher heat with no-fat burger meat, cooking but not burning it.

Also, fresh beef fat can be added to the burger meat just before cooking. This works with patties in the frying pan, as well as over coals or gas grill with lava rock base. The freshly ground beef fat prevents the burger from drying out or burning, while at the same time adding that nice familiar flavor of beef to the patty. I especially like a little fat in a burger cooked over coals. The fat drips down on the hot surface below, smoke rises, and it all adds to the aromas and flavors of the backyard cookout.

What Fat and How Much?

Fresh fat is the key, rather than what kind. However, beef fat is the choice for the standard hamburger. Pork fat is an excellent addition to gameburger, but definitely provides a different flavor. The reader may wish to try half-beef/half-pork fat for something different. The amount of fat depends upon personal taste. If you wish to be precise, first weigh your no-fat burger meat on a scale, then weigh the fat you wish to add. If you have 2 pounds of no-fat ground meat, you can easily compute how much fat to add. A very lean burger has about 10 percent fat content. Over hot coals, 20 percent fat won't harm anything either. Much of the fat melts, running down on the coals or hot lava rock.

Fat vs. Suet

Suet is generally located around the kidney region and loin area. If you ask the butcher for suet, you may or may not get it. Most of the time, he'll just grab fat that was trimmed from beef steaks. For example, the standard rib steak is trimmed of some fat (and some is left on). This type of fat is often for sale, and sometimes free if you're a special customer, at the local meat counter of your supermarket. I prefer beef trim over suet for my own gameburger. It's tastier, I think, than suet, and suet can sometimes have a waxy texture that I don't like. So I recommend ordinary trim fat for your gameburger.

How to Grind Fat

Fat for gameburger should be ground fresh and added on the spot. The reason for excluding fat from burger in the first place was explained in Chapter 16: "Wrapping and Storing Game Meat." Fat deteriorates faster than meat, and therefore no-fat burger lasts longer in the freezer. Moreover, those wishing to cut fat from their diets have a perfect gameburger in the no-fat version. There is no reason to add fat, then try to get rid of it later. Don't add it in the first place, until ready for cooking hamburger patties. Then grind the fat fine and mix it in completely. It's that simple. You now have prime gameburger, devoid of fat until you want the fat, and then you're in full control of how much fat, not to mention what kind, goes into your ground meat. You also have the pork fat option as a different twist.

Pre-Spicing

I add spices *before the meat is ground*, not after. Do not overdo spicing because the burger, even in its frozen state, may become overwhelmed. This is especially true of garlic salt or garlic powder. In a large bowl holding 10 pounds (roughly) of meat chunked for grinding, lightly sprinkle garlic salt or powder, with a similar treat-

Gameburger meat without fat is ideal for making chili and a multitude of other dishes.

ment of black pepper, freshly ground from your pepper mill if you like, plus a tablespoon of Worcestershire sauce. This makes a good initial spicing. If you find later that your taste buds call for more or less spicing, alter the amount to suit yourself or try different spices. A prime candidate is paprika, which works very well in pre-spicing gameburger. Onion salt judiciously applied is also good. Some people like a little oregano.

Grinders and Grinding Meat

For our purposes, there are three kinds of grinders: electric home units, hand-powered home grinders and commercial models. Small electric home grinders, normally with plastic housing and low-power motors, are fine for doing modest quantities of meat. These grinders are much slower than commercial types, but also far less costly. A full-scale commercial-type meat grinder can cost ten times more than a small electric kitchen model. Of course, it also works far harder than the little grinder. We graduated to a commercial grinder several years ago, giving our small electric grinder to friends. Our hand-powered tool remains with us and always will. A good hand-powered grinder can do a lifetime of work, especially if it's one of the bigger models. And it can be set up anywhere, unlike the electric types. Used hand-powered meat grinders are not too difficult to locate, and I've seen many in second-hand shops. They're a good buy and a lifetime investment.

The high-powered commercial meat grinder works well the first time through, especially if the cook has taken time to develop nice chunks of meat free of connective tissues. The heavy-duty commercial model will grind these tough tissues, provided the blade and plate are sharp, but it's worth a little extra time in preparation to end up with a pure, high-quality product. Small electric grinders may require two passes for finer-cut burger meat. The first pass is through a plate designed for sausage (large hole). Then a small-hole plate is installed in the grinder for the second and final pass. The same can be true for hand models, depending upon the "cranking power" of the individual.

Keep a grinder clean and it will last a long time. Heavy-duty commercial models never wear out. If an electric motor goes, it can be replaced, and the unit will go on grinding meat for another long period of time. Hand-powered grinders don't wear out either, not inside of a single human lifetime, at least. Small electric meat grinders may not provide lifelong service, but they do work for a very long time with proper maintenance. No matter which type you choose, all grinders require a little upkeep. As noted, keeping them clean is vital. Along with that, grinders demand a little bit of lubrication. The little electric grinder has instructions for upkeep, so read and follow them. The hand-powered grinder uses a touch of vegetable oil on working parts for continued good service. The commercial unit has an oil reservoir that must be kept at the proper level, plus, it's wise to dry the grinder's parts in the oven, applying a little vegetable oil afterwards.

Packaging Ground Meat

Chapter 16: "Wrapping and Storing Game Meat" covered the basics on this subject, but a special word about ground meat is in order. By all means, double-wrap, as described in Chapter 16, but also

ensure that all air is forced from the initial plastic wrapping. This is important because pockets in the meat trap air, which is not good for top-quality longevity. I'm also not so sure that these pockets aren't good places for freezer burn to get started, although I cannot prove the point. So wrap tightly and neatly for long-lasting top-quality gameburger.

The many recipes that call for ground meat, including chopped sirloin steak, do well with gameburger because of its exceedingly low fat content, as prepared here, and its great flavor. Smoked on the grill, fried in the pan, used in casseroles and spaghetti sauce, gameburger is one of the more important meats a hunter gains from his deer and other larger quadrupeds. It deserves all the care and attention suggested in this special chapter.

Dale's Seasoning is used here to pre-season chunks of boned game meat to be ground into gameburger. Pre-seasoning enhances flavor. Many liquids can be used, including soy sauce and teriyaki marinade. Worcestershire also works in very small quantities.

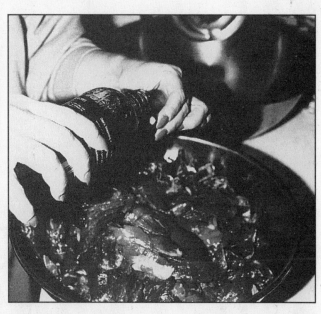

Go easy with any liquid used for pre-seasoning gameburger. Even though the burger is frozen, it seems that seasonings grow stronger in character over time.

Garlic in powder or salt (granulated) form works extremely well for pre-seasoning gameburger, but must be used with special care. A few sprinkles will handle this entire pan of boned meat. Garlic flavor grows more robust with time.

A little black pepper, prior to grinding gameburger, adds flavor. Here, freshly ground pepper is added to meat chunks.

WONDERFUL BOOKS HAVE been written on camp cookery in all its glory— some in great detail, others distilling the subject to its most basic components.

> *The Slow Smoke rises, and in it are hidden mysterious pictures that none but the children of the woods can see...Food, warmth, protection—life itself—depend on precious fire. Cold, dismal, wet, the gloomy woods in one brief moment turn to coziness. Enough to hail a priceless gift, but more than creature comforts—mere animal needs—is found in this flickering magic! There is spirit power.*
> Bernard S. Mason, Woodcraft and Camping

The spirit of the campfire captured in Bernard Mason's words is doubled as the fire also provides tasty, nutritious food for campers. This chapter leans to the simplistic in cooking good food in camp or on the trail.

Open Campfire Cooking

Starting a fire is so simple that often it's accomplished by accident with catastrophic results, yet building the right fire for camp cookery is not always the simplest chore. Probably, that's because there are so many different ways it can be done. My own open cooking fire is ultra-basic: a mere circle of rocks for safety, a compact fire within the rock wall, simple utensils, and age-blackened pots and pans, worthless to everyone except me. A long-handled frying pan can be held directly over the flame to cook bacon and eggs in the morning, if the flame is low and the cook watchful. If the pan gets too hot, move it

Chapter 19...
Camp Cookery
Game Care & Cookery

aside for a moment. That's all there is to the open campfire thermostat. Move the pan here and there to locate more or less flame, or back out altogether for a moment. Residual heat in the pan will continue the cooking process, and when that heat diminishes too much, hold the pan back over the open flame.

This kind of cooking sounds simple because it is. A covered Dutch oven can be set down in an open fire, too, provided the cook can retrieve it at will. For example, Dutch oven soup can be made on an open fire in one of two ways. Rest the covered Dutch oven in the center of the flaming fire and go away for a while. The soup will boil and then simmer down as the flames dwindle. You may have to stoke the fire again to finish your soup, unless you live in hardwood country. I've cooked Dutch oven soup over a mesquite fire, a big one, that was never refreshed once from start to finish. Wood fires using softer woods demand rekindling. But at all times, the cook must be ever watchful. That's the secret. Things can happen fast with open flame, and the chef has to be ready to move a pan in or out of the heat. But with proper attention, food is cooked, not burned, on the open fire.

Cooking on Coals

A favorite of mine, this simple method relies on hot coals to form a cooking surface. Ideally, coals are born of a hardwood fire. Softer woods provide sufficient coals to cook a meal, but the coals will have

A well-supplied hunter can do a great deal of camp cooking. The Mountain Chef stove, shown in the foreground still folded in its case, will provide a cooking surface in this modest camp, which is about to be set up.

and allow the retained heat to continue the cooking process. When necessary, return the utensil to the bed of coals for further heat.

Cooking Over Coals

This is an entirely different process. Coals are again raked from the hot bed of the fire, or the fire is allowed to diminish into a pile of glowing coals. Then a grate is placed over the hot coals and food is cooked on the grate. Extremely hot coals from hardwood fires can provide sufficient heat for cooking food in a pot or pan sitting on the grate, but mostly, cooking *over* coals means direct broiling of food. A favorite outdoor dish of mine is strips of game meat, well-marinated and larded, placed on the grate over hot coals, then eaten hot, with refried beans and flour tortillas, but that's a recipe for later.

In soft-wood country, such as the pine tree forests of North America, as well as woodless regions like some badlands and high plains deserts, a hiker may have to bring along his own coals for cooking. I do it all the time. Use aluminum foil, or a plastic shopping bag plus aluminum foil, or a Tupperware container with a well-fitting lid, to house some self-lighting hardwood charcoal briquettes and to prevent soiling your clothing or daypack. Superlight grates are also available for backpackers, perfect for trail cooking with coals.

Place the charcoal on a hard base, if possible, such as a rock. Ignite, wait for full glow, then rest the grate over the coalbed using small rocks for support. *Warning:* Choose only a hard, smooth rock for your coalbed. Otherwise, the rock may heat and crack violently, possibly hurling a piece at high speed and injuring someone. You can cook many fine meals over a backpacker's grate with a bed of coals beneath. One of my favorites is trail-cooking small game and birds with a method described later in this chapter.

Flame from a campfire offers sufficient heat for all kinds of cooking. Meat can be cooked on such a flame; however, the piece of meat should be held "upwind" from the fire. Otherwise, unwanted smoke flavor may permeate the meat. This is especially true for soft wood fires, such as pine.

to be replenished when they cool. This is not a problem with a hardwood fire, such as oak. Coals are simply raked from the fireside to a clear, safe spot, where they form a solid bed of heat for cooking. Frying pans, pots, and even pressure cookers function on a bed of coals, as long as there is sufficient heat. Should the bed be too hot, that's easy to handle. Move your coffee pot or frying pan, or other utensil, off the bed for a moment, or to one side away from the hottest coals,

The "mountain rock stove" is an excellent camp-out cooking option. Note warming rock and rock beneath frying pan handle to keep handle cooler. Use a glove when working around hot coals like these.

Here is another useful stove made of rock. Be sure to select rocks that won't crack under heat. Only the back portion of this rock stove is covered. A grate can be placed over the forward part, and the rock to the back can be used as a surface for spoons and other cooking utensils.

Cooking over coals is much easier than cooking on an open fire, especially where broiling meat is concerned. The idea is to let the fire burn down to coals, as this outdoorsman is patiently doing.

Living Off the Land

My friend, the late Ted Walter, and I made an annual or semi-annual outing we called "survival hunts." Truly, there was little survival to it. The closest we came to going hungry was traversing a vast section of high country in Arizona, beautified by blue spruce forests, but offering little in the way of small game or birds. Finally, we found some grouse, and our bows provided a feast for kings. We carried hardwood coals, quite a supply, plus a grate. The birds would have been dry as unbuttered popcorn without oil, but we had that, too, and condiments. The recipe can be found elsewhere in this book, but for now the important point to consider is the cooking oil. These days, I have a Cabela's daypack with two elongated compartments, one on either side of the pack. One side is for a container of denatured alcohol for my alcohol stove; the other is for a bottle of cooking oil. (Canola oil works extremely well because of its neutral flavor.) The oil, plus spices, is the secret to great small game and birds roasted over coals, slowly, without drying out.

Living off the land means cooking wherever you happen to be, and using minimal utensils for the task. My camp-cooking tools have long been the previously mentioned old pots and pans, but slowly these are giving way to the new no-stick surface utensils, both for frying and boiling. They make life on the trail a lot easier, so forget the romance of the old-time cooking pot or pan and latch onto the latest non-stick offerings. You may also wish to carry a small stove. There are dozens of good ones available now. Peak 1, for example, has several from which to choose. Coleman offers a couple, too. I also like the simple alcohol stove such as the Safesport Alcohol Stove.

Foil Cooking

On the survival outings, my partner and I did a lot of foil cooking. Although we relied on small game and birds for meat, we carried some food with us, especially a couple potatoes, and now and then a few ears of corn. These were wrapped in foil, then thrust into live coals on the fire, where they cooked to perfection. In camp, many foods can be prepared in foil, including complete meals, especially with gameburger. An entire meal in one foil package is quick and convenient. Also, the foil cooking container doubles as your dish. After the meal, the foil is disposed of properly—no dishes to wash. Incidentally, a piece of heavy-gauge foil extended between the forks of a stick makes a miniature frying pan, good for thin strips of meat and other smaller fare. *Tip:* Buy heavy-duty aluminum foil for cooking; light-gauge foil tears too easily.

Camp Stove Cooking

The camp stove is an obvious choice for outdoor cooking. Currently, camp stoves fuels include "white gas," which is unleaded gasoline; Coleman fuel, another liquid; or propane. Other possibilities exist, such as kerosene and butane, but they are not popular. Camp stoves come in different styles from different companies. The final choice should be based on individual application. While the larger stove is ideal at base camp, compact units are better for the trail.

A rock stove can also be turned into an oven by covering it. Cooking foil dinners in a covered rock stove is especially simple. Place the foil dinner on a coal bed. Rake a few coals on top of foil package. Then place rocks on top of stove to further hold heat in. Remove rocks with gloved hands when dinner is ready.

Cooking on a Stick

The recipe listed in this book, called "Marinated Venison Kabobs on a Stick" says it all. Marinated chunks of any red meat—deer, elk, antelope or moose—are impaled on the point of a whittled stick and held near hot coals until cooked to taste. An open fire can also be used, provided the chef cooks his meat on a stick upwind from the flame. If not, the meat can take on the unwanted taste of smoke from pine and other soft woods.

Grate and Griddle Mobile Kitchen

A grate is a framework of parallel metal bars used to hold food that is cooked over coals or any other heat source, while a griddle is a flat pan or plate used for frying. Both of these tools can be used "on the go." The grate I carry in my chuck box is from an old oven. The met-

al bars are close enough to retain burger meat as well as steak. The griddle I have came from a junk shop. It's a foot across, and no more than a frying pan without handles. The grate is obviously ideal for all types of broiling, as well as for holding boiling pots over an open fire or bed of coals. The griddle is ideal for making bannock and other breads, plus bacon and eggs and any other food normally cooked in a fry pan. The sources of heat beneath grate or griddle include open fire, coals, camp stove, gas stove—just about anything that creates heat.

Portable Gas Stove

This particular type of stove is super in camp, but it's not really the typical camp stove. The unit I have is Cabela's Camp & Blind Stove. Imagine two burners removed from a home gas range with a drip plate underneath. This particular propane stove cooks just like the top of a kitchen gas range. I carry it in the back of my hunting vehicle, attached to a 20-pound propane bottle. Along with my chuck box, the stove cooks up meals on the go, as well as in base camp.

The Sheepherder Stove

The concept is old—a metal box that burns wood and/or coal, as well as just about any other combustible. This stove has a chimney and works well inside a tent that can accommodate it. My particular stove is from the Mountain Chef Stove Company of Colorado. It collapses into a totally manageable package and, when fitted together, offers excellent heating as well as a cooking surface. The chimney rises up tall enough to clear the roof of any standard tent. Usually, this type of stove is used by guides and outfitters, and today is often called an "outfitter stove." Cabela's offers several styles, including the Outback Stove, a takeoff on the sheepherder, which is a large, semi-permanent half-barrel unit capable of burning large logs. Also available is Cabela's Alaknak Stove, which is a collapsible model in two sizes, regular and extra large. The former measures 18x18x8 inches when set up; the latter is 16x16x21 inches. The regular size closes to only 2½ inches thick; the other collapses to 2 inches. Both have dampers for regulating air flow.

The sheepherder-type stove has grown from the little outfit popular

Camp cooking convenience depends upon utensils, plus how a camp is set up. This Badlands camp offers no hardwood coals, so a bag of coals has been brought along, plus most of the cooking will be accomplished on a propane stove.

Here is a camp well set up for cooking. The major source of heat here is a Coleman camp stove (center) resting on a table for easy reaching. Other containers keep utensils out of the weather.

A grate is ideal for camp cooking with coals. The simple grate here is being used as a "stove top." Coals in the pit provide heat, while the grate allows the heat to strike the bottom of the pot.

with sheepherders in their small wagons to a multitude of models that offer great versatility and utility. As camp cook units, they are heavy-duty in nature.

Standing Gas Stove

There are two differences between the standing gas grill and the aforementioned Cabela's Camp & Blind Stove: set-up and durability. Instead of the unit resting on the ground, tabletop or other flat surface, this outfit has its own built-in stand. Also, the standing grill is much more heavy-duty in nature. The propane burners are large and sturdy, and come in single- and double-burner models. Cabela's calls its offering the Outdoor Cooker.

Dutch Oven

The Dutch oven is a world unto itself. Many books cover the subject, and this is not the forum to relate every detail. In its most basic form, the heavy-gauge cast-iron Dutch oven, with a lid, can be used on open fire or with a bed of coals. An expert can mix up some stew or soup, place the oven in a pit of coals, put more coals on top of the lid, go away, and come back to a meal cooked unbelievably well. Little to no steam escapes from a good Dutch oven, and that's part of the secret to its success. Food is "deep" cooked, but not dried out. Naturally, insufficient moisture can cause trouble, because despite the

Here, a Cabela's two-burner propane stove is this camp's sole cooking utensil. The larger propane bottle will last quite a while.

sealed system, enough steam will eventually escape. If heat continues under these circumstances, food will burn.

Cookie Tin Cookery

The cookie tin is simply a container of coals that turns into a stove. The beauty of this simple device is its portability, coal-saving nature (put the lid back on to smother coals after cooking), ease of use—(just stick a grate over the glowing coals), cleanliness (coal dust does not get on your camp gear), and its effectiveness. A full-scale meal can be cooked over a large cookie tin with coals.

Jackknife Cookery

The philosophy of jackknife cookery is simple: "With a jackknife as an only tool—or almost—I can make a tasty meal outdoors." In 1929, James Austin Wilder wrote the book on this subject: *Jack-Knife Cookery*, published by E.P. Dutton & Co., Inc., of New York. Long out of print, copies are still available for campfire cooks who want them badly enough to go through an interlibrary loan or a used-book store. Condensing a book in a paragraph or two is unfair. Instead, here is but one method from Wilder's text on the topic of cooking in a hole, called an "eemoo." Wilder says just about any fuel will work in his eemoo, but believes that you can't beat hickory charcoal.

First, dig a hole. Austin calls it a "Plug Hat" hole, because you can plug it up with a tophat, the kind worn by high society in the middle to late 1800s. Then, line the bottom of the hole with small hard stones to hold in the heat. Wilder's outdoor savvy shows when he says, "Choose 'non-pop' stones the size of an egg. Certain kinds explode." Small dry twigs are placed on the rocks, graduating to larger fuel that turns into a heap of hot coals. Leave air space around the wood to encourage a draft for the fire. As the wood is reduced to coals, start your kabob. Wilder isn't fussy about the meat, anything from beef to duck, quail, grouse or, if you like, lizard meat.

Cut a green stick of wood and peel away the bark. After sharpening both ends, cut your meat into chunks of about half-inch size. Then, string the pieces on the stick, pushing them to the middle. For well-cooked meat, leave a trace of sunlight between each meat chunk on the kabob; the meat hunks should touch if you want them a little more rare. Before cooking, lightly roll the kabob in flour. Now that the coals are ready and the meat is impaled, it's time to cook. A mound of dirt should be near the hole from digging. Pack it down a little with your boot heel and stick one end of your green wand of

meat into the dirt, leaving the meat above the coals in the hole. Jab it well into the ground so it'll hold.

This cooking tip from *Jack-Knife Cookery* is indicative of the book's spirit. I like to modify things, so I set my meat into a container, laced in a little soy sauce, a spray of garlic powder and ground black pepper, before flouring the chunks. Then I impale the meat on the kabob. My first attempt was just about perfect. I learned that Wilder was right about well-done/less-done meat. Stick the chunks right up against one another, and they cannot cook nearly so fast. A good compromise: Leave air space, but don't let the meat overcook.

Of course, the idea of jackknife cookery is utter simplicity—even the hole can be dug with an old jackknife. But I prefer a little Army shovel for the job. Another way to cook meat over the hole is with a longer green stick, sharpened on one or both ends. The long stick is placed over the hole, either end leaning on the edge of the hole for support, the meat right over the hot coals. Cooking both sides is easy—just turn the stick over.

The Grub Box

Since the grub box was mentioned as a camp cookery item, it's only fair to say a word or two about it. My grub box is a hinged-lid wooden box that fits across the back end of my venerable Jeep hunting vehicle. Inside there is, as one might expect, grub, or food—cans of soup, vegetables, fruit, even canned bacon as well as a couple MRE packages (Meal Ready to Eat—Army fare). But that's not all. A Peak 1 sleeping bag and a Russian army coat (should I get stuck someplace and have to walk out), a coffee pot, an alcohol stove, denatured alcohol (well-sealed so it won't leak out or evaporate), a big cookie tin filled with coals, and a few odds and ends, including minor cooking gear and eating utensils, can all be found inside. The grub box is a potential lifesaver—for real—if broken down in the outback, but it's also a convenience box. I wouldn't be without mine.

The Nested Cooking Kit

A multitude of utensils work on the trail and at home camp for outdoor cooking. The nested cook set, however, is classic. These are available at Army surplus stores, with kits not only from our own military, but from other countries as well. There are also many commercial nested cook sets, such as Peak 1 cookware in stainless steel. Even the lids do double duty—you can fry foods in them. The Trekker model can be used as a double boiler. Peak 1 also offers

A proper camp setup allows the preparation of just about any food. This is an especially well-run camp in Africa, with a large working surface. These large pieces of boned meat were turned into biltong (jerky) and sausages.

Here is the superb Mountain Chef stove set up. Note that legs elevate stove bottom off of the ground to prevent a fire. A great deal of camp cooking can be accomplished on the top of a stove like this one.

This U.S. Army-issue cooking kit, turned out at the end of World War II, is capable of doing a great deal of cooking, mainly frying. Author carries bottle of cooking oil and kit like this one on the backtrail.

The cookie tin makes a neat stove for cooking outdoors. It's easy to use.

A lot of on-the-trail cooking can be accomplished if a hunter uses a packframe and pack. Fadala prefers a daypack slipped over the struts of the packframe in a modular fashion.

stoves that fit inside these cooking sets. The Outfitter Cook Kit has six pots and pans with a Peak 1 Multi-Fuel stove fitted inside.

Backpack Cooking

Today's packframes and packs are superb: well-designed, superbly built, lightweight, comfortable and made to last. My own modified Camp Trails Freighter frame has served me well for years. I added aluminum cross members for extra strength. I like a modular system for backpacking, with frame, daypack instead of full-size pack, sleeping bag attached on the shelf of the frame, tent (sometimes), nylon tarp between daypack and packframe, and certain other gear attached, such as my Gerber Sport Axe, a tool I've come to favor on the trail for many chores. Cooking from a backpack includes many of the aforementioned methods: open campfire, on coals, over coals, foil, cooking on a stick, small cookie tin with coals (easily carried), jackknife cookery methods and others. Living off the land leans toward the lifestyle enjoyed by hikers who backpack. Nested cooking kits, along with compact stoves, add to cooking ease and pleasure.

There are literally hundreds of different ways to cook in camp or on the trail, and no one chapter in one book can cover them all, nor does any single author know all of the means and methods of cooking outdoors. This chapter, therefore, is offered as a starting place for the outdoorsman who aspires to become an excellent camp and trail cook.

COOKING UNDERGROUND IS an ancient practice, centuries old, yet a viable and exciting way to make special meals today. Pit cooking is admittedly time-consuming, and not in keeping with the majority of methods in this book, which hinge on fast and easy fare with gourmet quality. With pit cooking, the gourmet quality is there, but at the price of a little digging and a bit of waiting. Cooking in the ground is a social affair with delicious results, great for a family gathering or having friends over to watch your culinary talents at work. Just about any red game meat cooks fine underground, so do upland birds, especially pheasants. The wild turkey makes an especially excellent pit-cooked meal. But first, a little history, because your dinner guests and family will want to know about this interesting cooking style and you'll have the time to tell them.

Polynesians still do it, burying large parcels of wild boar or goat meat underground, wrapped in large green leaves along with herbs and spices, plus plenty of moisture to prevent drying. The process is ages old on the Islands. Native North Americans also prepared food underground. Chief Plenty Coups, famous leader of the Sioux nation, spoke with writer/historian Frank Linderman about pit cooking. In Linderman's book, *Plenty-Coups*, the great Chief's own words describe the "meat-holes" of his people.

My mouth waters when I remember the meat holes. We used to dig a hole in the ground about as deep as my waist. You have seen many of them along the creeks and rivers. We would heat little boulders until they were nearly white hot and cover the bottoms of the hole with these stones. Then we would cut many green boughs of the chokecherry trees and cover the hot stones a foot deep with them. Upon these we would place thick chunks of buffalo meat, fat and fresh from the plains, sprinkling them with water.

Chapter 20...

Pit Cooking

Game Care & Cookery

The pit is made deep enough and wide enough to hold plenty of coals, plus the wrapped turkey.

The first wraps of aluminum foil around the turkey are as much to hold liquids as to protect the bird. So use plenty of foil up top so it can be secured.

Wrapping properly is vital in cooking a wild turkey underground. Long sheets of aluminum foil provide a buffer zone between bird and hot coals.

This is one of the most important steps: the ends of the foil are folded together to form as much of a seal as possible. A good seal holds steam in, which is necessary for proper cooking, tenderness and moisture.

The Chief's words clearly explain the basic concept of cooking underground: Dig a pit to hold hot rocks or coals as a heat source, then bury the meat in the pit, protected in some way to keep it clean, and be certain to include moisture so the meat does not dry out or burn. Of course, there are many ways to accomplish the task. The Crow Indians covered their meat with green boughs first, and then the fresh hide of the animal to prevent burning or drying out, and to help hold in moisture. To further generate heat, I understand they built a fire on top of the pit, after covering the animal hide with earth. Our modern method trades aluminum foil for animal hide and green boughs, but retains the same concept. There is no fire built over the pit, because we use plenty of glowing coals underneath to generate heat for cooking.

There are two steps to pit cooking: pit prep and meat prep. Digging the hole is done the old-fashioned way—you work at it with a shovel. The environment is not scarred by the process, because afterward the pit is covered, the earth tamped back in place and, in no time, traces of the pit are gone. As for meat prep, the entire plan hinges on retaining moisture underground to prevent drying, with the spices penetrating into the meat, resulting in incredible tenderness, but more of that in a moment.

Let's get back to the hole in the ground. For our example, the wild turkey is the guest of honor, so the pit should be about 2 feet deep and about 2x3 feet wide. After digging the hole, fill it with hardwood like oak or mesquite. If hardwood is not available, softer woods will suffice, but that's risky. If the wood does not generate large, glowing coals of long duration, the meal may surface undercooked. Hardwood is hard to come by where I live. Pine is poor, while aspen and poplar are better. But a bag of hardwood coals is better yet. For our purposes, let's assume you have hardwood. Start the wood ablaze and keep adding more wood until the pit is about half full of coals. A large bag of hardwood charcoal briquettes will do the same job. Burning wood in the hole not only provides the necessary coals for cooking, but also heats the pit and the surrounding ground.

Now that the fire is raging and you are waiting for hot coals to appear, it's time to finish preparing the meat. The wild turkey is washed for a last time. By the way, although this is a book about game care and cookery, if you wish to use a domestic bird, I won't tell. Then, completely dry the bird with a towel, clean cloth or paper towels. Follow by massaging the turkey inside and out with pure lard. So little lard is used for the process that any concern about cholesterol should be forgotten. Now sprinkle the cavity of the bird with black pepper, onion salt and garlic salt. The amounts are difficult to establish; I generously powder the inside of the carcass. Then, apply the same three spices to the outside of the bird, along with a fourth—paprika. Don't overdo the paprika, but sprinkle enough to color the breast area.

Continuing with the bird's pre-pit prep, stuffing can be used. Consider the prime rice/meat stuffing with giblets recipe provided elsewhere in the text. Standard bread stuffing is also excellent, and there are some good ready-to-go stuffings in a box that save time. But don't stuff the turkey just yet. *Caution:* Whatever stuffing is used, it must be moist. Add a little canned chicken broth to your stuffing if it seems a bit dry.

Now it's time to wrap the bird. Place several sheets of heavy-gauge aluminum foil on a flat surface, such as a camp table, and rest the bird in the center of the foil. At this time, smash a cube of butter or margarine directly upon the breast of the bird. Also, if the bird will not be stuffed, put a can of chicken broth inside the cavity of the bird, along with two cups of water and four chicken bouillon cubes. As an option, a cup of sherry wine can also be added to the body cavity. If the bird will be stuffed, add one-third of a can of chicken broth as

Even though it seems that the bird is well-secured within an aluminum foil chamber, yet another sheet of foil is used. Note how the well-wrapped bird is set down in the center of this foil sheet for yet another layer.

Inspect the foil wrapping as you go. If there is any tear at all, place a piece of new foil on top of the tear and cover with two or three additional sheets of foil.

The full-wrapped bird is laid into the pit. Notice the use of gloves to protect the hands from getting burned.

well. A little butter or margarine in the neck cavity is next. After moisturizing and/or treating to butter/margarine, the body cavity and neck cavity are stuffed.

Now it's time to pull up the sides of the aluminum foil around the bird so it rests in a "boat." Now place one cup of water and one cup of canned chicken broth (approximate amounts) alongside the bird. The aluminum boat will hold the liquid. Follow by wrapping the bird like an Egyptian mummy, using at least six sheets of aluminum foil. When the turkey is totally wrapped, it's time to place it in the pit.

It's important to place the meat package in the hole before the coals lose their intensity. Burying the meat will not extinguish the coals, although eventually the air will diminish and the coal or briquette will die out, hopefully after its work is finished and not before.

Shovel out one-half of the hot coals and set them aside, next to the hole, because they're going right back into the pit. Place a flat rock upon the coals remaining in the pit; this will be a base for the wrapped bird. After resting the package on the rock, shovel the waiting coals back into the pit, all around and on top of the bird. Then, place one final sheet of aluminum foil directly on the coals that cover the bird. This single piece of foil is an insurance barrier to prevent dirt from getting on the wrapped bird. At this point, the dirt by the side of the hole is carefully returned to the pit, directly upon the piece of foil. Since the turkey and coals take up a lot of space in the pit, the dirt shoveled on top makes a mound of earth, which is excellent for insulation. That's the whole point of the pit method—holding in heat for cooking.

Be sure to start pit cooking early enough in the day to give about six to eight hours of cooking time. I've never burned any food cooked underground with the method described here. When the bird emerges from subterranean seclusion, it should be cooked through and tender, but the smart cook tests the product before serving it. If done correct-ly, the legs of the bird easily pull away from the carcass. Also, run a fork into the breast meat. It should be juicy, but well-cooked. Any red color means back to the pit. Cooking underground is not for those in a hurry, and if more time is needed, then another smaller fire is necessary, or more hardwood briquettes must be added to the pit.

Birds must be cooked completely. Red meat can be served less than well-done, although the nature of the pit is thorough cooking. Ideally, the meat falls away from the bone of the bird, or with red meat, the product is juicy and so tender that only a fork is needed for cutting.

The possibilities are endless with underground cookery. As noted earlier, just about any meat can be used. One wrinkle is making the underground cookout a barbecue. A big hunk of red meat is browned in the largest fry pan you can find. Heat the fry pan on high and add canola oil. If it smokes when it hits the pan, all the better. Now sprinkle garlic salt or powder, either one, all over the hunk of meat and drop it directly into the hot oil. Completely brown the meat on all sides. Be watchful of spattering oil because you're working with a hot skillet here. After browning, place the meat upon several layers of heavy-gauge aluminum foil and pour on plenty of your favorite barbecue sauce. Then thoroughly wrap the meat, just like the turkey, and put it in the hole. Cover with coals, a sheet of foil, and dirt. Hours later, the barbecue sauce will have penetrated the meat for a real taste treat.

A miniature version of the pit is also an option. Foil dinners, mentioned in Chapter 19: "Camp Cookery," are perfect candidates for the mini-pit. The dinner is prepared—especially with ground meat patties, carrots, onions and potatoes—and wrapped not as usual with a couple layers, but with several layers. Then it's dropped in the mini-pit, covered with coals and earth, and allowed to cook for about two to three hours. The usual six- to eight-hour pit cooking times for large

Now the wrapped bird is completely covered with hot coals, but carefully. Do not shovel the coals recklessly, and be especially careful not to shovel a rock onto the wrapped bird, which can break the foil seal.

parcels of meat are not necessary and, in fact, may overcook, burn or dry the foil meal.

A note on unearthing the meal: This part of the process is handled with great care. The top layers of earth are gingerly shoveled off and set aside. Then the upper coals, which are on top of the meat package, are slowly removed. I've used a well-gloved hand along with a garden trowel for this job, ensuring the foil wrap is not penetrated. The last thing you want is dirt or coal dust inside the package. After the package is unearthed, it's set aside on a clean, flat surface and the outer foil is removed. Discard this right away—it's covered with coal dust and dirt. Gently peel away layer by layer until the meat is exposed.

As alluded to earlier in this chapter, pit cooking is more than a good way to prepare a tender morsel. It's historical and interesting. It also provides the chef with a little bit of show-off time. I've yet to see the dinner guest who wasn't excited to see the package of meat unearthed from the pit. Of course, pit cooking is possible just about anywhere a hole can be dug. The method is excellent for camp, but works just as well in the backyard, and pit cooking on the trail is also a treat. I often carry a folding Army shovel, which is entirely sufficient to dig a cooking pit, and there's not much to toting a roll of heavy aluminum foil. Carrying spices is no problem on the trail as well. Two cans of chicken broth aren't that heavy, either. And we'll assume some sort of water source for further moisture.

I've pit cooked mountain grouse whole with excellent results, and these culinary adventures took place at high altitude on a mountain. I've also prepared javelina in camp, half a hog at a time, albeit modified slightly with the addition of a disposable wet cloth around the foil-wrapped carcass to further slow the cooking process. Such a large parcel of meat requires quite a bed of coals and a good-sized pit, about 2½ feet deep, and about 3½x3½ feet wide. Mesquite wood provided very hot and very long-lasting coals.

Given the patience and time to pit cook properly, this style of preparation is one of the best and, as promised several times in this chapter, certainly one of the more interesting methods of preparing game meat in an outdoor setting.

The last step is to carefully shovel a dirt mount over the top of the buried bird. The dirt serves as insulation to hold heat in around the bird, instead of allowing heat to escape through the top of the hole.

There's nothing like hardwood coals "on the spot," like these mesquite coals born of a hot fire. The coal bed in the background is an all-night supply. In fact, there'll be hot coals in the morning from a bed as deep as this one.

Chapter 21...
Cooking with Coals
Game Care & Cookery

COOKING WITH COALS is explained in one way or another in many parts of this book. This little chapter is a brief roundup of a few coal-cooking ideas. Cooking with coals is efficient, resulting in good-tasting food, especially broiled game meats. Here, methods for preventing meat dry-out are included, because game is so lean it can turn into shoe leather over coals. Marination can prevent that problem, and so can larding the meat before cooking. Basting is another way to prevent drying, as well as pumping juices into the meat using a meat pump.

How to Cook With Coals

Ideally, coals come from hardwoods burned right on the spot. I was raised in the Southwest, where hardwoods abound, especially my two favorites, mesquite and oak. Many other parts of the country enjoy a bounty of hardwoods, too. The best feature of hardwood coals is their long-lasting heat. For example, many times I've camped in the desert, open style—nothing but stars for a roof, with heat rising from a bed of buried coals beneath my sleeping bag and a roaring oak or mesquite fire corralled in rocks off to the side, preferably against a rock wall for heat reflection or with a built-up reflector of wood or tin sheeting. In the morning, the fire is out, but rake through the "dead" white ash and smoke curls up. Pop a few fresh pieces of wood on the ash and soon flames leap out from a fire newborn.

141

No hardwood here for a coalbed, so pack your own. Carrying a modest supply of hardwood briquettes is no problem on a pack-in trip.

The other means of obtaining coals is to buy them packaged. These are charcoal briquettes, and they work perfectly well. You can buy them in most grocery stores by the bag. Self-igniting briquettes require only a match to get them started, and these are handy for cookie tin cookery.

Cooking with coals is simple. Rake 'em out of the fire glowing hot and neatly arrange them on barren ground where they won't start a brush fire or forest fire. Have a rock corral ready for the hot coals and put them inside the circle to prevent the wind from blowing an ember into dry grass or brush. Then rest a frying pan or cooking pot directly on the coals and you have a natural range top with super heat. You'll have boiling water, or a pot of hot coffee, in no time. To cool the coals down, layer a little dirt over them. This insulates the hot coals, while allowing a transfer of heat that will slow-cook an egg or medium-cook breaded meat without burning the breading. You can also sprinkle a little water on hot coals to cool them down. Soon enough, the water will evaporate and the coals will burn hot again. Of course, don't completely douse the coals. Use a spray bottle for best results.

Another way to manage a hot coalbed is by moving the cooking utensils. If a pan is getting too hot, pull it off and set it aside for a moment. Still another method is to pick out the hot spots in a coalbed.

Coals are perfect as a hot cooking surface. A frying pan full of elk steaks and potatoes is treated to an even supply of heat. If the pan gets too hot, it's simple matter of removing it from the coals for a moment. Coffee pot, upper right, has special handles at side, plus top-mounted wire for cooking outdoors.

If you want to boil a pot of coffee, find the hottest, freshest embers; for slow frying, select a cooler spot. The uneven heat a coalbed provides is like having a cooking range with choices. Another fine way to cook over coals is with an ordinary clean metal sheet. Cowboys in Sonora cook almost-transparent flour tortillas on the tin, and it is also useful as a flat surface for heating pots and pans. Ultimately, cooking over coals is a management process. The cook manages the coalbed to suit his specific needs.

Coal-Cooking Utensils

It all depends upon your goal. Obviously, the best utensil for making a fresh pot of coffee is a coffee pot, although any pot will brew up a cup of java. The Dutch oven is especially useful with coals because its heavy walls hold heat for a long time. A few coals beneath, on the sides and on the lid go a long way. Also, the lip around the lid of the Dutch oven is ideal for retaining coals, so take advantage of it if yours is so designed. Using coals, you can cook up many different dishes in a Dutch oven, including stews, which come out unbelievably tasty. All other pots and pans work on coals, too, including double-boilers.

The grate is ideal for coal-cooking, and these come in many different forms. One of the best grates I own is a rack from an abandoned oven. The bars aren't too far apart for anything I've cooked, including hamburger meat. Another utensil, the cookie tin, has already been mentioned elsewhere. I now have several covered cookie tins filled with hardwood charcoal briquettes in my hunting vehicle, ready for use. At home, the hibachi, as well as any other grill-type cooking unit, is perfect for coal-cooking. These units retain the coals for specific heat direction and, even more importantly, control the coals for safety.

And don't forget aluminum foil. A hiker with only aluminum foil and hardwood for coals, or a supply of charcoal briquettes, can cook

The cast iron skillet is ideal for cooking over coals. Only part of the frying pan is on the coals. In this way, food can be moved from hotter to cooler areas of the pan.

There are dozens of different grate designs. The one on the fire is rigid and simple. The grate in hand has hinged legs that fold to various heights, so that the grate can be positioned over coals high, medium or low.

On a short day-hike, carrying canned goods is no problem. Here, the cookie tin cooker is stoked up for a meal. When the fire dies down, the tin will be ready to serve as a stove.

an amazing variety of foods. Simple sticks can make good coal cooking tools, too. Sharpen a green stick, impale a spiced piece of meat on the end, hold the meat over the coalbed, and cook the morsel.

This brief list of utensils for coal-cooking is light years from complete. Only the cook's imagination limits the possibilities of coal-cooking. I've made bannock and other breads over coals, fired up a homemade oven built of scrap found near an ancient mining site with coals, and one time tried a mud oven that worked perfectly when coupled with hot coals from a hardwood fire.

Coal-Cooking with Smoke

Smoking is a specific means of using wood to provide smoke, which in turn either cooks and/or dries food. But there is also much to be said for the smoke that rises from a hardwood coalbed in the outback. I guarantee that marinated quail over mesquite coals tastes far different from the same gourmet meat cooked over other types of coals.

Preventing Meat Dry-Out

Marbled meat cooked over coals poses no problem. The fat within the meat literally melts, flowing downward upon the coalbed. There it fires up, smokes and is eventually burned off. But game meat is different because it's not marbled, and cooking such lean meat over coals can be a disaster, unless you know how. There are many ways to prevent dry-out of game meat over coals, and here are four to consider: marination, larding, basting and pumping juice into the meat before cooking.

There are dozens of different marinades, if not hundreds, but not all work over coals. For example, our Universal Marinade with milk base is superb, turning antelope and other meats into tender feasts;

Any boneless meat, such as these loin pieces, cooks up perfectly over coals, provided some source of liquid or juice is supplied to prevent drying. Here, each piece is wrapped in bacon fat. Note potatoes wrapped in foil located within the little grill.

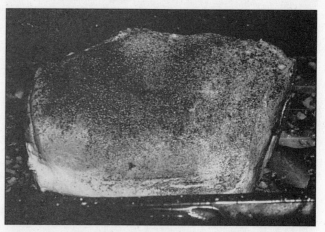

A large piece of meat can be marinated and cooked over coals. Place in a roasting pan first, with plenty of stock and spices. Allow the meat to rest for a few hours, then turn it. Turning the meat is the same as basting it. When cooking over coals, baste meat with juices from pan. Also excellent: slicing off individual pieces (small steaks) to eat. Slice, then turn chunk of meat and cook other side until another piece is ready for eating, then slice it off, and turn the meat again.

however, it's all wrong for coal cookery. On the other hand, teriyaki marinade is excellent on game meat cooked over coals, as is soy sauce, or soy plus Worcestershire sauce, and similar combinations.

Larding meat is another simple, yet effective means of preventing dry-out. Our recipe called Leg O' Lope is a perfect example of larding to keep an extremely lean meat moist and tender when cooked over coals. Larding for our recipes includes lard, beef suet, beef fat, pork fat, salt pork and bacon, but other fatty elements will also work. Larding is a simple process requiring only a knife. Rather than wide cuts, deep incisions are made into the chunk of meat before cooking, and into these niches, fat is literally poked or stuffed. Lard works fine, and so does suet, but I like ordinary beef fat better because it holds up, rather than breaking down.

Larding has two advantages: It keeps the meat from drying out, but

The first step in larding meat is cutting a deep recess or pocket with a thin-bladed knife, such as this filet knife. Larded meat cooks beautifully over coals.

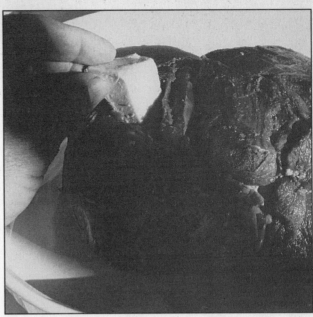

After a hole is cut in the meat, a chunk of butter, margarine, pork fat, beef fat, salt pork or bacon, as well as many other enhancers, can be inserted into the crevice. As the meat heats on the grill over coals, the fat produces moisture to prevent drying of the meat.

at the same time, when the cooking is done, the fat can be discarded because it does not entirely melt into the meat. Pork fat works similarly and can be used for a flavorful change of pace. Salt pork and bacon are *interesting*, because they can almost take over the flavor of game meat. That's either good or bad, depending upon taste.

If larding is simple, basting is simpler, although it demands a little more watchfulness because liquid can cook off and dry out. At that point, basting ceases to work and the meat dries out. Basting is accomplished by brushing or by dripping liquid onto meat. A basting brush can be used to apply oil or other liquid directly on the meat, just like applying barbecue sauce. On the other hand, basting can mean dripping a liquid right on the meat a few drops at a time. Then, a fork is used to rub the liquid all over the meat.

Canola oil makes a good basting liquid because it does not leave a distinctive taste. Some prefer olive oil, but it can leave a flavor of its own on the meat. Butter is useful when the coals are kept on the low side. Super-hot coals may cause butter to run right off the meat and flame up. Margarine holds better than butter as far as flaring up is concerned, but here again we have personal preference. In the end, it does not matter what is used for basting as long as the meat is kept moist and the flavor of the finished product suits the diners.

A meat pump can be used to literally force fluids into lean meats, which prevents drying out on the grill. It's like giving the hunk of lean meat a great big vaccination. Ordinary beef or chicken broth is perfectly useful for injecting, but any stock works as well. One of my favorites is stock (juice) left over from a lamb roast, although not everyone enjoys the flavor of lamb. Antelope meat, which is very lean, takes on a super taste when cooked over coals after pumping in lamb juice. Any overflow burns off on the coals, so you can't really over-inject. Of course, stock is not the only choice; barbecue sauce works well, too.

These are a few ideas for cooking with coals—a simple and effective process. The heat from coals, plus smoke, do a great job of cooking. Coals make a fast and handy cooking surface, and their use is limited only by our imaginations. After all, any old bucket, even with holes in it, turns into a cooking utensil of merit when it's filled with coals.

Meat cooked on the grill over coals can be moist and tender. It can also be dry and tough. The difference is primarily in the cooking style. Marinated meat, basted often, turns out fine over coals.

Coleman fuel is ideal for gasoline cooking, not only because of the excellence of the product itself, but also due to the safety and convenience of the can. A special pouring spout is offered by Coleman for this can.

Chapter 22...
Cooking with Gas
Game Care & Cookery

THIS CHAPTER DEALS with an extremely popular means of cooking food, just about any food from game meat, domestic meat, vegetables, pies, cakes, pancakes to breads. It's cooking with gas or gasoline stoves. Campfires are more romantic, and hardwood coals broil meat better, but gas and gasoline stoves do a great deal of cooking for millions of people in the field or at home. The home gas range is hard to beat, although some people have switched to electric ranges because they are supposed to be cleaner. The single greatest advantage of cooking with gas is control of the flame. There is no question about how much fire is beneath the cooking utensil because you can see it. Gas allows a tremendous range of heat, from a flicker to near blowtorch power from certain liquid fuel stoves.

But our goal here is not a discussion of the home gas range, but a look at cooking with gas in camp or in the field. Gas and gasoline cooking units are especially welcome when the sky clouds up and raindrops are on the menu, because these stoves function under cover a lot better than smoky fires or coals. Gas camp stoves generally use propane fuel, while gasoline stoves ordinarily burn unleaded gas or specifically prepared combustibles, such as Coleman fuel, which burns cleanly and efficiently. Other fuels are entirely possible. Denatured alcohol and Sterno, a "jellied" gasoline, also work wonders in cook stoves designed to burn them. Obviously, each specific unit requires specific fuel(s) and must be operated only with manufacturer-suggested products, for efficiency as well as safety.

Full meals can be cooked on this excellent Peak 1 Multi-Fuel stove. This model has a level ring so that stove can be used on somewhat irregular surfaces.

The Coleman Ultralight Stove is a dual-fuel model. It produces ample heat to cook full meals, yet it is packable at the same time.

(Right) The fine Peak 1 Apex One-Burner Stove is attached to a fuel bottle that has a regulator. This is a stable and efficient gasoline-fired cooking unit.

(Below) The Peak 1 Apex II Stove is lightweight and easy to pack, yet it will cook a complete meal on its high-efficiency burner. Note the fuel bottle with attached regulator.

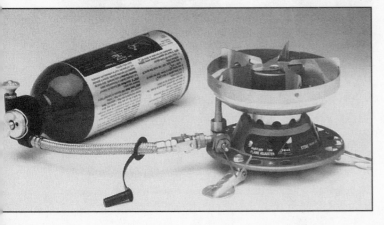

Compact cook stoves have been around for many decades. Outdoorsmen are familiar with the famous Primus stove, which functions at high altitude as well as sea level, providing a blowtorch effect that delivers heat far greater than the tiny stove seems capable. The Primus, and models like it, are self-generated; there is no pump. There are also pump-up compact stoves, such as the Peak 1 Multi-Fuel model, which burns unleaded gasoline, Coleman Fuel or kerosene. This stove weighs under 21 ounces, holds over 10 ounces of fuel, and provides about 7,500 BTU. It burns for an hour and a half with Coleman fuel on full power, and almost two hours with kerosene on full power.

One of the neatest compact units to come along in a while is the Safesport Alcohol Stove. It weighs less than 9 ounces, runs only 2.75x3.5 inches in dimension, comes in its own leather zippered case,

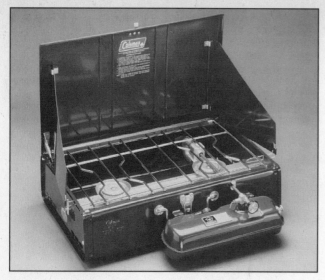

The famous Coleman Two-Burner gasoline stove has been around for years. The current model is the best ever, with greater efficiency and ease of operation. It will cook a full meal on fully regulated burners that can simmer, boil or fry anything.

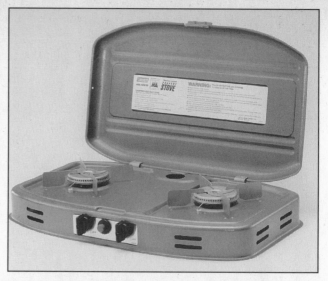

State of the art is the only way to describe the Coleman Propane Stove with two burners. Propane is clean and easy to use. It cannot spill. Of course, the original Coleman gasoline stove still has a place in the outdoor kitchen because it is very economical to operate, and it does the job, as this fine stove does for all camp stove cooking.

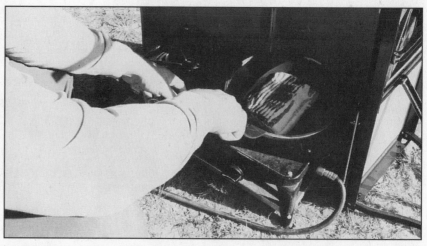

Propane fuel, as packed by Coleman here in disposable bottles, is clean and efficient. The net weight of these bottles is 16.4 ounces each.

The Cabela two-burner stove cooks for days from a large propane bottle. Here, the stove is sheltered from the wind with a picnic table turned on end.

and burns denatured alcohol. It'll also fire on rubbing alcohol, but not nearly as well. The compact Safesport easily cooks up a full meal, one entree at a time, including a pot of coffee after the main courses are ready. A pint of water boils in much less than five minutes at sea level, and 4 ounces of fuel will boil 2.5 quarts of water. A full tank of fuel will burn for about twenty-two minutes. The double-wall design is ingenious and simple: As the stove warms up, it produces hot multiple flames that resemble the burner on a kitchen gas range.

Competition has driven manufacturers to produce compact gasoline stoves that are better than ever in all their diversity. The new Peak 1 Apex is the perfect example of a high-quality compact unit. It has a fuel line running from a metal bottle with a regulator. It does not require a spirit or priming cup for pre-heating the generator. This modern fuel bottle has a sealer cap that really works. I have yet to experience a seep-out with one, and I carry a full fuel bottle in my Cabela daypack all season long. One of the best features of the Apex is a wind-guard system, comprised of built-in fins and a circular metal fence around the burner. The entire Apex system weighs less than 19 ounces, and the fuel bottle weighs 4.7 ounces.

Elk burgers are treated to a little margarine during cooking on a gas grill. Lava rock over gas flame lies below the cooking meat.

Bobbi Wade cooks for a number of hunters in her outfitting camp in Wyoming. Bobbi has a full-fledged gas range to do the work. It uses propane.

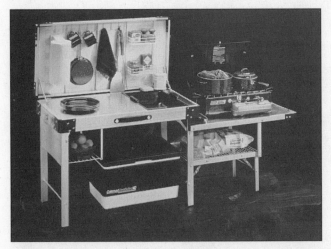

The heart of the handy Coleman Kitchen is the gasoline-operated cooking stove on the right. The Coleman Kitchen is ideal for long stays. It operates easily and keeps everything neat and tidy, plus easy to find.

Compact propane stoves are not only still with us, but their designs have improved in recent years. There are many models available, but I'm most familiar with the Peak 1. It weighs more than the Apex, mainly due to the disposable propane fuel cylinder which runs 16.4 ounces. The beauty of propane is no spillage (there is no liquid fuel to spill), plus convenience and ease of operation. Turn it on, light it up, and that's it. Quite a number of outdoorsmen turn to propane for this reason, in spite of additional fuel cost and added weight in the backpack. The Peak 1 weighs a bit less than 50 ounces with fuel cylinder. It brings a quart of water to a boil in four minutes at sea level, and the flame is adjustable over a wide range, including a simmering level. This unit has a rating of 8,000 BTU.

Compact cooking stoves are superb for backpacking or incidental camp cooking; I use my own alcohol stove to boil a pot of coffee, tea water, or heat a can of soup. But there's also a time and place for the full-scale gas or gasoline camp cook stove. You can only expect the smaller models to do so much cooking in so much time, and that's why the famous full-size Coleman stove remains popular today. Of course, these larger units, too, have escalated in excellence of design. For example, Coleman's Dual-Force Gas Stove burns liquid fuel at a

Professional master camp chef, Clifford White, hires his services to hunting camps all over North America and Canada. He prefers a gas range like this one for full control of heat. Here, he prepares another great meal in an Alabama hunting camp.

fraction of propane's cost. The two-burner Model 414-700 provides up to 17,000 BTU. The familiar pump-up reservoir rests in the front section of these new Coleman stoves and remains detachable for compact transportation.

Larger gasoline-operated camp stoves are ideal for long-stay camps and are by far more economical than propane stoves. Estimated fuel costs for fifty hours of running time at current USA prices are $12.50 for unleaded gasoline, $45 for prepared camping fuel, and $172 for propane when using $3.29 disposable propane cylinders.

That latter figure can be reduced by using large refillable bottles instead of the small disposable ones. While propane costs more than gasoline, it is tremendously popular because of convenience. Large propane bottles take up more space than disposable cylinders, but last a long time. If size is a consideration, a smaller 11-pound bottle may be an option.

A standby cook stove in my camp is a two-burner Cabela gas model that burns propane. I connect this stove to a 20-pound refillable propane bottle and look forward to many outings before running out of fuel. The Cabela stove goes just about everywhere I do during hunting season. It's sufficiently rugged to withstand a fairly hard ride in the back of my Jeep station wagon, and it works hard everyday, many times a day. This particular stove resembles the top of a standard kitchen gas range without the oven, and works like one. One match and I'm ready to cook just about anything from fried rabbit to pressure cooker game stew.

Finally, the gas grill has come a million miles since its inception. My grandfather had his gas grill custom-built in his backyard in Arizona, where on any sunny day he might be found cooking up a great meal of wild or domestic meats. Today's gas grill offers tremendous temperature control, including electronic ignition. Generally, the gas grill relies on a bed of lava rock positioned above the gas jets to evenly distribute heat and to prevent flame from direct contacting with the meat. It's a super arrangement. When the lava rock finally breaks down, a replacement bag is purchased and put in place.

For a number of reasons, there is no point going over the details of gas grill cooking: First, the methods of cooking over heated lava rock do not differ much from cooking over coals; second, there are so many different gas grills available it would take several pages to cover only some of them; and third, every new gas grill comes with full instructions for use which are very helpful and informative. Although my grandfather's custom-made grill used natural gas, today's gas grills get their fire from propane bottles, which are readily refillable. Have an extra bottle on hand, however, because Murphy's Law says you'll run out of propane when your meal is half-done.

These days, there are literally dozens of different cook stove models that burn all sorts of different fuels. The outdoor chef's job is to choose the right ones to match his needs. He'll need more than one stove, requiring at the very least a compact model, not only for backpacking, but also for that midday hot lunch or quick pot of coffee, plus a larger unit to accomplish the bulk of his camp cooking. Preparing edibles and hot drinks on gas/gasoline stoves makes camping and back road travel that much more enjoyable.

The Coleman Propane Stove can be carried in the back of a hunting vehicle for on-the-spot cooking, with no chance of fuel spillage. The neat disposable propane fuel bottle, at the right, is the reason.

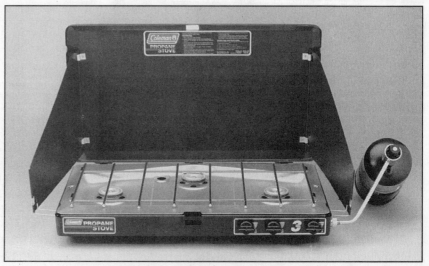

THE PRESSURE COOKER is an often-used item in my kitchen. I wouldn't be without one because a pressure cooker satisfies a basic cooking need: Good-tasting food that seems to have taken all day to cook, but didn't. Not enough people use this type of cookery and I don't understand why. Cottontail rabbit and squirrel do especially well in the pressure cooker. The venerable "par-boiling" technique that used to take a lot of time is greatly cut down with a pressure cooker. In fifteen to twenty minutes, rabbit and squirrel pieces are tender. Then, it only takes a few moments of pan frying to turn out nicely browned, fried meat that melts in your mouth.

The pressure cooker also works well for side dishes, like refried beans, a delight from the wonderful world of Mexican food. Tossing canned refried beans in a frying pan to prepare them is fine, but making them from scratch is less expensive. Usually, boiling beans until tender for mashing takes a long time. But the pressure cooker cuts down that time, plus most of the remaining liquid is incorporated into the mashed beans. Then the beans are treated to the full refried bean recipe. These are just two examples of the advantages of the pressure cooker.

The pressure cooker functions with super heat and pressure in a sealed container. Steam does the work, and very little of it escapes because beneath the lid of the pressure cooker is a rubber ring, which serves as a gasket. The food is cooked with temperatures higher than that of boiling water.

Although there are exceptions, the usual sizes of pressure cooker run 4-, 6-, 8-, and 10-quart capacity. The 6-quart model is most popular because it's just about right for the so-called average family.

It really is a unique tool because there is nothing else exactly like

Chapter 23...
Pressure Cooker Cooking
Game Care & Cookery

it. And it's right for the times, because our society is in such a hurry. I can think of at least seven good reasons to use a pressure cooker, not only for game meals, but for any food: speed, nutrition, taste, tenderness, no fat, stock-making (broth), and simplicity.

- The pressure cooker makes food fast. Depending upon the model, a few pounds of potatoes are soft enough for mashing in about ten minutes; a batch of carrots cook in three minutes; rabbit and squirrel tenderize in about twenty minutes; a hunk of boned meat is edible within an hour or so; beans cook soft in less than an hour; and soup is a snap, too. The pressure cooker is a real time-saver.

- Nutrients do not escape from the sealed pressure cooker, so the resulting broth is rich with the good stuff. Very little water, comparatively, is used, so only a very little nutrient-laden water is poured off of the finished product.

- And the taste of the broth is rich as it comes from a pressure cooker. But anything cooked this way tastes good. Of course, tasty food has to go in before tasty food can come out of the pot, but that's understood.

- The pressure cooker is ideal for tenderizing "hard food" that needs softening. This is obvious with a potato or a carrot, but tenderness is also assured with meat, and the cut of meat doesn't matter much. Tough cuts of meat, domestic or wild, are brought to tenderness in

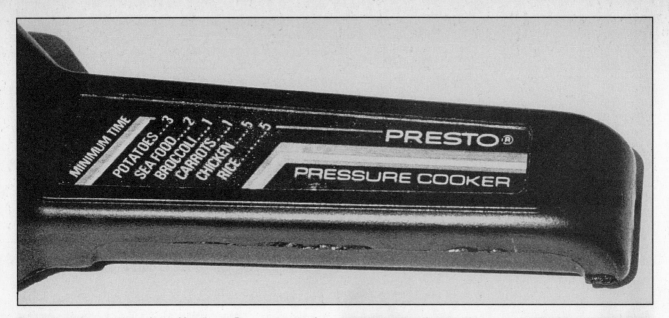

Pressure cookers can vary in cooking times. Be sure to note the correct times for your specific model. This Presto pressure cooker has a few popular foods noted right on the handle. Of course, you must adjust times to suit yourself. You may like carrots a bit more on the done side, so you may wish to add one minute to the time noted on this cooker.

the pressure cooker. Most game meat is tender to begin with, and if tough, it is often made that way through improper field handling or cooking. But some old-timers are tough. A ten-year-old bull moose can be made as tender as veal in the pressure cooker. The key is time. The longer the meat is cooked, the more it tenderizes. Naturally, cooking may have to be done in stages: Let the pressure cooker work for twenty minutes, then cool it down, check water content, add more water or broth if necessary, and let the heat and steam build up again. Cook for another twenty minutes and check again. Remove the meat from the pressure cooker when it's tender.

- No fat is needed for cooking in a pressure cooker. The unit works on the principle of heat and steam, and does not require oils or fats, although in some instances a bit of oil may be used in pressure-cooking.
- Meat scraps can be pressure-cooked into broth, and the same is true for giblets. Wild turkey giblets, along with scrap parts as neck and wing tips, turn plain water into gravy-making stock in about a half-hour.
- Simple is the byword with pressure cooker cookery because the work is done by steam. Condiments can be added, and in many instances, full meals emerge with little effort.

Safety

Anything that gets very hot can cause a problem, and this includes the cooker. Here are a few points for proper handling:

- Be sure to install the pressure regulator before allowing the cooker to heat up. Do this immediately after putting on the lid. Today's new models are easier to use than ever, but may work differently from older models. *You must read and follow the instructions with your pressure cooker. Never rely on general information only.* My new Presto pressure cooker is much more advanced than my old one, for example, and they do not function exactly the same.
- Use the correct pressure regulator at all times, because they are not necessarily interchangeable. If you lose the one for your unit, be

Be sure to learn each part of your pressure cooker and use each part correctly. The unit with the holes in it goes on the bottom of the pressure cooker. It prevents food from sticking to the bottom.

certain to obtain the correct replacement. Once again, be certain to understand how your model functions; there are countless older pressure cookers around—they just don't wear out—and the pressure control on the latest models can be different from older models. The photos and captions in this chapter reveal information concerning a late model Presto pressure cooker.

- Do not bump the pressure cooker when it's working. This could jar the pressure regulator, causing it to loosen or fall off. After all, you wouldn't bump any utensil on a hot stove, so the rule applies across the board for all cooking tools.

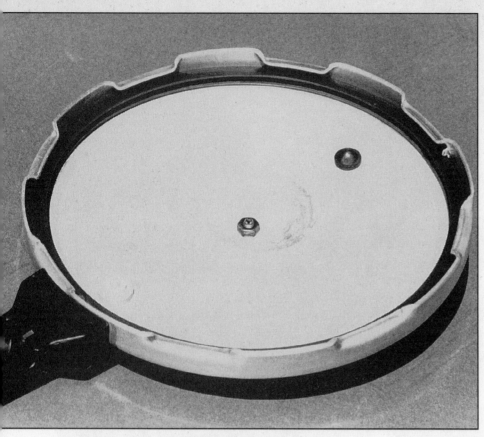

Pressure regulators are not necessarily interchangeable on pressure cookers. If the pressure regulator for your cooker is lost, be certain to replace it with the correct one.

The rubber sealing ring is vital to the proper function of the pressure cooker. Learn proper maintenance of the rubber sealing ring; some do not need to be oiled.

A modern Presto pressure cooker exhibits a special built-in release valve. Do not attempt to open this cooker unit until the valve is fully depressed as shown.

- Properly cool the pressure cooker. While you should always follow the directions with your unit, there are three general ways to cool the cooker: Run tap water along the top of the cooker until all steam is bled off; tilt the regulator slightly to allow the slow escape of steam, *but never open the cooker until all the steam is entirely gone*; or leave the unit on the stove and let the steam dissipate over time. This latter method is perhaps the best way to reduce pressure—the natural way. However, it does not work with foods that must be carefully timed, and cooking times vary for each specific model. For example, if your carrots need one to three minutes, you must get the steam out of the unit in one to three minutes. If you let the unit cool naturally, your carrots will be mush. Letting the cooker cool on its own, however, is good with meat and other products, such as beans, that do not readily overcook in a pressure cooker. In fact, the extra time is usually beneficial in the further cooking of such foods. *Note:* Specific pressure cookers may offer additional means of bleeding off steam. Read instructions for your unit.

- Never force the lid open on a pressure cooker. If, after ensuring that all pressure is relieved, the unit will not open, let it rest longer. Cool it again with tap water. The older method of returning to the stove, and reheating the unit to break a vapor lock, is no longer recommended.

- Follow the guidelines in the instructions and do not overfill the pressure cooker with water. Actually, very little water is needed. The pressure cooker is not a boiling pot; it's a steam machine.

- Make sure the handle is tightly fitted to the pressure cooker. If you notice the handle getting loose, fix it or have it fixed. A loose handle may cause the pressure cooker to rotate when you remove it from the stove, possibly knocking off the pressure regulator. Newer models are designed better than older ones because the handles do not readily loosen. But do check the handle on your model to ensure it is tight at all times.

- Be sure all parts of your cooker are functional. For example, you should be able to see light through the steam vent pipe. The pressure regulator rests upon this pipe, and in order for the regulator to function correctly, the orifice must be clear at all times. Also, make sure the cover fits correctly and has not been damaged. In short, check all parts to make certain each is in perfect working order.

- Be certain the sealing ring is intact. If not, it may leak steam. Also, check the overpressure plug to see that it's in place.

153

Beans can take a very long time to cook, especially at higher elevations. The pressure cooker produces juicy cooked beans in a much shorter period of time. Do be careful about burning the beans, however, which will happen if the water level gets too low. Cook in intervals, adding moisture to the pressure cooker. These delicious pinto beans are ready for a ranch bean dish, or refried beans, or...you name it.

- At start-up, bring the pressure cooker to high heat, but do not leave it on high heat for the duration of cooking because it is not necessary. Once steam is established, the unit does the job without a lot of heat beneath the cooker. Even though modern pressure cookers incorporate new safety features, it's smart to avoid any possible problem by using medium to lower heat levels once high heat has brought the unit to a functional level.

- Buy a new model if you have a very old one. No one is more sentimental about old-time cooking gear than I am, but the modern pressure cooker is much better than the older type. I purchased a new Presto to replace my old Presto, and as good as my old one was, the new one is better. It's a modern cooking device in every sense, with old-fashioned high standards of manufacture.

Special Safety Notice: Everything is very hot in pressure cooker cookery—the steam, the unit, the food—so don't get burned. Use a pot holder to transport the unit from stove to sink for cooling (letting off steam). And be sure the food has cooled down sufficiently before diving in. Also, if cooking a large hunk of meat, do not thrust a fork into the center of the meat when it's done. Always let dense foods, such as a large piece of meat, cool for a while before poking. The center of the food can be so hot that you get a mini-explosion when you poke into it.

Some of the previously mentioned notes also pertain to maintenance, such as keeping the steam vent pipe clean and clear. Also, using a little vegetable oil on the rubber gasket was once advised, to help prevent drying out of the rubber, but the more modern units don't require it. Oil does not help preserve the new material and, in fact, causes more rapid deterioration. So wash the gasket and dry it. Also, wash the unit as you would any other good pot. I use mild steel wool pads with soap.

Don't forget marinades when using the pressure cooker. Marinades, such as these extremely good commercial products, can be poured directly into the pressure cooker at various time intervals to enhance foods.

Recipes

The recipe section of the book contains many interesting dishes prepared in the pressure cooker, either entirely or in part. These are meat dishes of many kinds, stews, soups, vegetables, broth (stock), and more. Use your imagination. If a food is normally boiled, it can probably go into the pressure cooker. And don't forget to use your pressure cooker for tenderizing meats that you would otherwise parboil. The pressure cooker is faster, and often does a better job, than parboiling. I think you'll find the pressure cooker a modern utensil worthy of a place in every kitchen. I even use mine in camp and in my travel trailer.

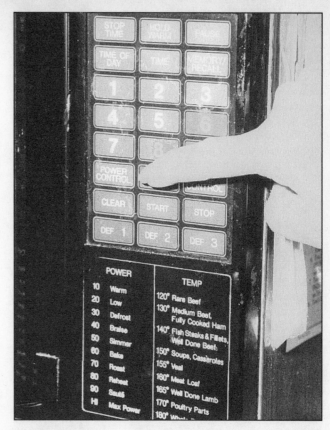

Microwaves vary in many ways. The cook must know how to make his unit function properly and over a wide range of applications. The control panel on this microwave clearly shows a power option, as well as three levels of defrosting capability.

Chapter 24...
Microwave Cookery
Game Care & Cookery

MICROWAVES DATE BACK to the 1940s. Original models were expensive, and very few were sold until the last few decades, but today the microwave has come of age. And current microwaves are the best ever. Just about everyone has one. Even our travel trailer has a built-in microwave. No day goes by without using it many times. There are a multitude of reasons for meat hunters to own and use a microwave:

- Today's microwave is versatile. It can be used to cook up a full meal, heat leftovers and drinks, get side dishes ready, and more.
- The microwave is very fast, which is a big plus for today's busy cook who needs to save time.
- Nowadays, microwaves go just about everywhere. I already mentioned the one in our travel trailer. A friend has one in his hunting cabin in western Wyoming. "I got electricity to the place in mid-June, and by the first of July, my lights were on, inside and outside," he said, also adding, "On the same day, my microwave went in."
- Microwaves are programmable, which is just right for our high-tech society. The microwave is an obedient servant that can be told what to do, when to do it, for how long, and at what power.
- Microwaves are superb for thawing meat. Most units have thawing modes that are put into operation with a simple push-button technique.
- The microwave not only heats leftovers, but it can freshen bread and pastries which have dried out.

- Finishing foods has become, perhaps, the most important use of the microwave in my kitchen. I make several dishes that are cooked on the stove part-way, then finished in the microwave oven. Two of these are Antilocapra Italiano and Easy Rellenos. Without the microwave, both of these recipes must be changed dramatically. With the microwave, the former is a gourmet dish without the investment of the usual gourmet cooking time, and the latter is a taste treat made in minutes.

- The microwave oven is ideal for reducing fat from certain meats, as well as extracting water content. This is supremely important in our red spaghetti sauce recipe, where store-bought Italian sausage is first pan-fried, and then treated to a couple minutes on paper towels in the microwave. This reduces fat from the sausage, making the final sauce a much better product. Gameburger is also pre-fried and given a minute or two in the microwave, not for fat reduction, but to remove moisture.

- Not terribly important, but useful nonetheless, the microwave can be used as a timer when cooking food in a stove or oven, or over an open fire. Some units have a separate timing element, but for those that do not, the oven's timer may be used if some food or liquid is inside the microwave. Never operate an empty microwave. Often, I place a glass of water inside the unit at 20 percent power and set the timer for a specific time, such as three minutes. At the appropriate time, touch the button on the microwave, and in three minutes the bell goes off.

Many side dishes can be prepared entirely in the microwave. One of the best is rice; however, the cooking dish must be covered. This is step one in properly covering the dish with plastic wrap. Note that the wrap is taut over the top of the dish, but not stretched to the breaking point.

Getting to Know the Microwave

All cooking utensils, right down to the common frying pan, require a little practice. Imagine a cook who had never used a frying pan. Would he know that on high heat he can quickly brown food, but a hamburger would be burned on the outside and raw in the middle if the heat were not adjusted? The same is true for the microwave oven. Read the manual that comes with your model, and follow it. Being a high-tech machine, the microwave functions in a precise manner. Correctly programmed, it will do its work very well. Community colleges and many other institutions often have special cooking courses for microwave beginners, as well as veterans. Check in your area for these courses if you're interested in becoming a real pro with your microwave. Of course, you can experiment, but learn the basics of your particular microwave oven first.

Use the Cook and Look Method. Go with absolute minimum cooking times, even less, and continually check the progress of a dish. This does not detract from the finished product. For example, if a dish calls for ten minutes on full power, set for eight minutes; check progress; set for one more minute; check progress; set for another minute; check progress, and so forth. Cook and then look.

Stir and mix. Many dishes come out better when stirred or mixed in between cooking times. Soup is a prime example. Mixing and stirring seem to make microwave cooking more uniform. Microwave ovens do not cook the center of the food first, as popularly believed. Heat starts on the perimeter and works inside. So mixing more evenly distributes heat to the cooking food.

Move the food around. Suppose cooking time is ten minutes. After four minutes of cooking, turn the dish or rearrange the food in its cooking vessel. Then cook for three more minutes and move the food again. Then go for the final three minutes. Microwaves with turning tables require less food shifting, but I still recommend moving foods during the cooking cycle.

Don't forget resting periods. Some recipes call for a specific running time, then a resting time, when the food continues to cook from its residual heat.

Carefully arrange food. Inside the microwave, place larger parts toward the outer edge, with thinner or smaller parts in the center. Remember, heating takes place from the outside.

Cover food. Depending upon the dish, covering can speed up cooking time. I also use a single thickness of wax paper over food to keep the interior of the microwave oven a little cleaner.

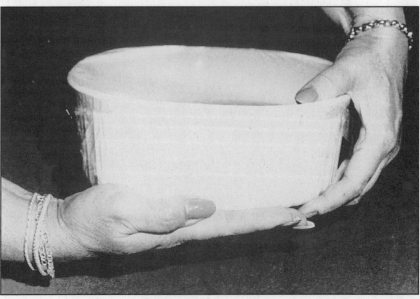

Shown here is a very important step in microwave cooking of rice. The plastic wrap is brought *under* the cooking dish for a seal.

The microwave is all anybody needs to turn a simple can of green beans like this one into a tasty side dish. Note that about one-half of the water is removed from the can first, and then a microwave-safe dish sized properly for a single can of green beans is used, not just any dish.

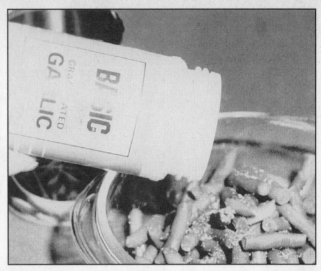

The secret to making side dishes in the microwave is often in the pre-seasoning process. Season before microwaving. Here, a little garlic salt is added to the green beans. Sweet basil was already applied, and a pat of margarine will go on top before microwaving. This side dish will be ready in two minutes.

Microwaves come in different powers. Think of higher wattage as more power. All microwave recipes are prepared at a specific wattage, and your unit may be more or less powerful than the one used by the recipe-writer, so don't be surprised if you must adjust cooking power and/or time. Start by exactly following the recipe. Then you can experiment from that starting point. Here is a simple test for determining a microwave's power: Place a container of room-temperature water in your microwave, two cups even, then cook on high power for three minutes. Afterward, if the water is boiling, your unit is 600+ watts of power. If it takes longer than three minutes, your unit is less than 600 watts.

Thawing Meat and Other Food

Be careful to use the proper defrost setting on your microwave for meats. If you heat for too long on too high a temperature, you'll cook parts of the meat, which is not what you want at this time. As for thawing other foods, again make certain your settings are correct. For example, I thaw frozen juices in my microwave, as follows: Remove the lid and place the frozen can of juice in the microwave on a folded paper towel to catch any spillover; run on high for thirty seconds to a minute and the juice will be thawed enough for mixing. (The tiny rim of metal on the base of the frozen juice container does not cause a problem in my microwave.)

Safety

As noted many times in this book, safety is absolutely essential to all game-handling and cooking. The microwave is a cooking machine; therefore it gets hot, and so does the food it makes. Common sense shouts, "Don't get burned!" However, there's a bit more to microwave safety than getting burned. The first rule is to make sure the door closes properly. If anything causes the door to warp, have the unit checked by a professional. Microwaves have a built-in safety feature: They will not operate with the door open. If your unit turns on with the door open, it's broken and must be repaired before further use.

Also, use the correct microwave-safe cookery and utensils in your microwave oven. Many glass utensils will work fine, but check your instruction manual for the final word. Never under any circumstances use metal pans or utensils, or aluminum foil, in the microwave. You could ruin the oven or, worse, start a fire.

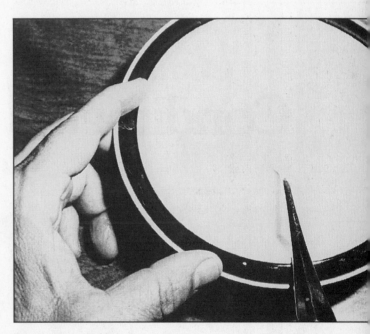

Sauces can be made in the microwave from scratch. They turn out smooth and complete, provided directions are followed carefully.

Forget cooking large stuffed birds of any kind in the microwave. Microwave ovens are like any other tool—ideal for certain applications and not necessarily perfect for others. Large stuffed birds require sufficient temperature throughout the carcass to ensure complete cooking. Incomplete cooking (cool spots) can be troublesome. Also, when cooking your game sausage or Italian sausage for our special spaghetti sauce, pierce the skin before microwaving, otherwise the sausage may explode, which won't hurt anyone, but will leave an unwanted cleanup job in the oven. This last piece of advice goes for all food with skin, such as potatoes.

This chapter only scratches the surface of microwave cookery, because its versatility is almost endless. The microwave is another good way to prepare food, including game dinners, and it is unique in application, just like any other cooking tool. So use it where it shines, and choose other cooking utensils for other applications.

Chapter 25...
Condiments for Cooking
Game Care & Cookery

CONDIMENTS—SPICES, HERBS and liquid enhancements—are so important to cooking that trade routes were opened just to secure them. I have a list of liquid condiments I use over and over again.

There are numerous spices and herbs I use for cooking wild game. I'm not interested in distinguishing spices from herbs, or going into the histories of each specific plant, although there are interesting stories to tell about most of them. For example, rosemary was transferred by a bride from her father's to her husband's home to bring along the memories of where she was raised; chives were used as a remedy for bleeding in ancient Europe; and eating basil made you a happier person. Our interest in the following spices is purely kitchen-oriented.

The World of Herbs and Spices

Spices are classified as aromatic or pungent vegetable products, like cinnamon, cloves and others used to flavor foods and beverages. Herbs are known as plants with woody tissue that withers and dies away after flowering, this tissue is then used as medicine or in cooking. For our purposes, herbs and spices are condiments, along with a host of vegetables and liquids. Cooking without them is like a bow without arrows, a rifle without cartridges, a camp without a campfire. Although a plain chunk of meat roasted over coals can be good, even that simple fare is best enhanced with condiments.

Soy sauce, bay leaves, boullion, garlic powder, lemon and pepper seasoning are all excellent spices for game cooking.

Garlic

Garlic is essential to the fine preparation of game meat. That's only my opinion, but I'll stick by it. Garlic is normally used in one of four forms: garlic clove, garlic salt, garlic powder and the newer minced garlic in a refrigerated glass jar. Any recipe that calls for garlic can use any of the four forms, but they are different and should be treated so.

Garlic cloves and minced garlic can be overwhelming if mishandled because fresh garlic is powerful stuff. The clove can be used in various ways. One way is to break off a section, trim the ends, peel it, and then cut it in half. Do not use a garlic press or dice the piece any further. A split garlic section is ideal for lacing the top of a roast in the following manner: Make a small slit in the roast, insert the chunk of fresh garlic, and leave it there until the roast is done cooking. Baste the roast in its own juices as it cooks, pouring the hot liquid over the top of the meat. When the roast is finished, pick out the garlic chunks and throw them away. Their work is done.

A fresh piece of garlic can also be squashed in a press, forcing out its juices. This reduces the strength of the clove, so it won't take over the flavor of the recipe. But don't overuse garlic. A little crushed garlic in spaghetti sauce, for example, is ideal, while too much overwhelms the sauce. Furthermore, garlic cloves can also be diced after peeling. Diced garlic can be cooked in oil, then the oil, now well-flavored with garlic, is used to fry game meats.

Garlic salt and powder are used more than cloves these days by most cooks. They save time and are easily applied to foods while imparting excellent flavor. Garlic salt and powder also store well, so they're easy to use at home, as well as on the trail or in camp.

Garlic salt and garlic powder can be used for the same meats, but the two styles do differ and aren't interchangeable. Garlic powder is stronger than garlic salt, so it is used more sparingly. On the other hand, use garlic powder, not garlic salt, if there is any question about

the dish taking on an overly salty flavor. For example, a wild/domestic mix of antelope meat and lamb make a super roast that is best treated to garlic powder, not garlic salt, because a considerable amount of bouillon is used to form a tasty brown juice (not a gravy), which results in a salty taste. Garlic salt carries this salty flavor too far. When the roast is done, the juice is ladled over slices of meat at the dinner table.

Pepper

Ordinary black pepper is the best all-around choice, but white or red pepper is excellent in some dishes. I make the choice depending upon how spicy I want the meat. White pepper, I think, imparts the stronger flavor when both are used in the same quantity, and both have a slightly different taste as well, but the difference is subtle. Red pepper adds zest and flavor, but not everyone likes the taste, so don't overdo it. Ideally, ground peppercorns are the best option. It takes only seconds, and the result is definitely a fresher-tasting pepper. Pepper is used in the majority of game meat recipes because it imparts a familiar flavor and enhances the meat. It can be overdone, but that goes for every condiment.

Salt

I very seldom cook with salt, or not at all. This is not a medical choice, but a cooking choice. The latest study I read on salt and the hardening of arteries revealed that salt does no such thing. On the other hand, there are reasons to avoid salt, such as water retention in body tissues or high blood pressure. I don't add extra salt to my recipes because many of the spices mentioned here render a salty flavor as is, and further salting may ruin the dish entirely. Garlic salt—or garlic powder, for that matter—imparts sufficient flavor for cooking, and since I use garlic in many recipes, salt is not added. Furthermore, it seems to me that cooking with salt does not add as much flavor, or "extract" as much flavor from game meats, as sprinkling a little salt on the meat after it's cooked. Let the individual diner salt his food to taste, in other words. For these reasons, salt is not a major additive in the majority of recipes presented in this book.

Paprika

Paprika is great for coloring the top of game roast and wild turkey breast because it cooks up brown and handsome. Use enough paprika, and it adds more than color. Too much paprika results in a flavor I do not particularly like, but as always, we're dealing with personal preference in all matters of taste. Paprika is excellent on gameburgers cooked over coals or on the gas grill. While not on the main list of must-have condiments, paprika is deserving of inclusion on every spice shelf.

Onion

In some kitchens, this is more important than salt and pepper. I do not employ onion as heavily as other cooks, but I love this pungent plant and use it often. Onion can be treated in many ways: whole, sliced, diced, dried, and as onion salt or onion powder. A whole onion is great in a roast, and it can be left in the dish after cooking, just for looks, or discarded, its purpose served. Or the whole cooked onion can be sliced and served with potatoes and carrots (which I prefer). A raw onion also can be sliced or diced and fried, not only for meat dishes, but also as a compliment to mushrooms. Moreover, dried onion works extremely well in numerous recipes and is excellent for camp or trail cooking. I wouldn't make a game soup without onion, and dried onion works about as well as fresh for soup. Onion salt and onion powder are used in much the same manner as garlic salt and garlic powder. The powdered version seems a little stronger to me, and less apt to make a salty dish even saltier.

These Virginia Olson spices are multi-varied. The Poultry Blend worked well on upland game birds.

Garlic powder and onion powder make a roast like this one what it is. Without spices, an otherwise palatable meal can be mundane at best.

Juices from a roast are tasty because of spices. The roast cooks with stock and spices for a few hours, and the resulting juice is delicious. Soy and teriyaki marinade are a base for this tasty juice, but boullion, garlic powder, onion powder, and other spices make the juice special.

Green Onions and Chives

True gourmet chefs, which I do not profess to be, say that chives and green onions are quite different, but I use the two identically in cooking. Many soups are lacking without these condiments to top them off. I think of chives and green onions as a mild way to impart onion flavor and also as a way to add color to a dish.

Marjoram

Also known as sweet marjoram, this herb works well with some game meats. I do not use it in quantity, preferring only a hint of its flavor. Marjoram is a possibility in meatloaf, but not an essential ingredient.

Parsley

I find this essential for spaghetti sauce, and welcome in soup or as a garnish. Parsley is often treated as decoration, but it is not; parsley has real flavor. Although dry parsley is useful, I prefer fresh stuff. Here's how to pop out the flavor of parsley: Cut off the lower stalks and leave only the leafy part (some stalk is all right). Now hold the fresh bunch of parsley under warm tap water. Then, squeeze the parsley by hand, forcing the water out, and take a whiff of that green bunch. It will taste as good as it smells. See side dishes in the recipe section for a special rice dressing used in wild turkey and gamebirds.

Green Chiles and Jalepenos

Although not a condiment, I'm inserting green chiles here because they can be used to flavor a dish like no other vegetable. Green chiles are terrific for Mexican cooking and superb in many other dishes. To roast a green chile, use your outdoor camp stove. Place the green chile directly upon the flame of the stove until the waxy skin turns dark brown, or even black. Then let it cool off a little and peel it by hand. Running water helps to remove the outer skin of the chile. Of course, green chiles are also sold in the can, roasted and peeled, or diced.

Not a spice or herb, jalepenos can be used in Mexican cooking, especially with a chile con carne. Not everyone goes for this sometimes powerful chile, however, so be careful.

Chile Powder

Red chile powder is the heart of chili con carne, but it can be used as a condiment in various ways. For those who truly love this flavor, a little can be added to a game roast, red meat or wild bird. As a powder, red chile is easy to use, but watch the label. It will say "mild," "medium" or "hot" and believe what it says.

Bell Peppers

This also is not a spice or an herb, but I have added bell peppers here because they can be used as a condiment to flavor food. I like dried bell pepper because it is easy to use, although I use it sparingly.

Celery Salt

Celery is not a condiment either, but when it's dried into celery salt, it becomes a flavor enhancer. Celery salt can be added to soup when fresh celery is not available. And in camp, celery salt is ideal because it lasts for a very long time and is easy to use.

Lemon Pepper

This prepared condiment can be sprinkled on frying meat and roasts, or used in soup. The lemon and pepper mix is also ideal for certain jerky recipes.

Sage

I use sage with respect. Over-applied, sage can overwhelm a dish. A little sage goes well in many different dressings, but I don't use this strong herb very much. Sage can also be applied on a lamb/antelope roast recipe, but that's optional. A little sage in our rice dressing for wild turkey is also acceptable.

Basil

Also called sweet basil, it is fabulous when fresh, but speaking in practical terms, dried basil is the way we use this herb. It comes that way from the grocer and applies easily with a pinch or two. It's worthwhile on game meats and in marinades, and also for preparing side dishes such as green beans and red kidney beans. It works well in Mexican dishes, and for a host of other applications, but is absolutely essential in spaghetti sauce.

Oregano

I think of oregano as stronger basil. Actually, the two are absolutely unique, but I use them in the same types of dishes. Every spaghetti sauce I make has oregano in it, and the herb can also be used to dress up fried game meat. If too much is applied to the meat, however, the effect can be negative.

Mint

Some cooks like a little mint sprinkled on their venison roast. I don't use it in this fashion, but the herb deserves inclusion for those who do.

Useful Spices Seldom Used

Here are a few spices that are worth mentioning, but used little in this particular game care cook book. That's because they are a bit "special" in the kitchen, and our goal is superb "down-home cooking" more than anything else.

Rosemary can be used with venison roasts, but it's a matter of personal taste, as always. Trust your nose. Crush a little rosemary with your fingers and give it a whiff. Do you like what you smell? This is a good test for many condiments.

Not found in my recipes, savory is well liked by some cooks. It can be added to meatloaf.

Tarragon can rule or ruin a dish. Be careful. However, this is one herb I use to advantage in a few recipes. Just remember to apply it sparingly because it has a very sharp flavor.

Thyme is another fine herb, but it is not widely used in this book. Thyme fits with a bean/meat dish. See the recipe section for other dishes that use a touch of thyme.

Bay leaf is useful in roasts and spaghetti sauce. If used intact, the entire leaf is dropped into the juices resting in the roasting pot or into the red sauce. Then the leaf is removed and discarded after cooking.

Liquid Enhancements

Now, a few liquids that deserve high praise: soy sauce, teriyaki marinade, teriyaki glaze, Worcestershire sauce and, possibly, sesame oil in small quantities. They dress and top meat, making it taste better and more interesting. These sauces are essential to stir-frying certain game meats, but are also excellent for basic pan-frying, which doesn't use the high heat and swift stirring action of the stir-fry. They double as marinades, too. I use soy sauce, teriyaki marinade and Worcestershire a great deal, especially in stews and on roasts, where the resulting juices are important for making gravy or stock to ladle over the slices of cooked meat. If I had to live without one of the three, it would be Worcestershire. And if I had to get by with only one, I'd have a hard time choosing, but probably soy sauce would win.

Along with these excellent cooking liquids comes a tiny, but solid, brick of tastiness called the bouillon cube. Bouillon comes in two popular flavors: beef and chicken. It also comes in powdered form, as well as cubes. Give me soy and beef bouillon, and I'll strain juice from a roast for a brown gravy a chef would be proud of. For roasting game birds, chicken flavor is the obvious choice.

Condiments on the Trail

One of my favorite outdoor adventures includes backpacking into an area where small game and bird seasons are open. I'm especially fond of bagging these edibles with bow and arrow, or blackpowder smallbore rifle. Inside my daypack is a frying pan, cooking oil and a few condiments. Along with a heat source, I can cook a delicious meal of fresh cottontail rabbit, or grouse, or partridge, on the spot, oftentimes only an hour or two after the harvest. I can't take the whole spice shelf with me from home, so I've condensed condiments. Salt and pepper? Sure, but also garlic powder and a little bottle of teriyaki marinade go along. The difference between rabbit cooked "as is" or with a little garlic powder and teriyaki marinade is amazing.

In closing, it's only proper to admit that this chapter is but a leaf on a tree. There are hundreds of different herbs and spices that apply to cooking of all types. Here are only a few that you may wish to look up, test in your own cooking, and add to your spice shelf: Angelica is more for fish than meat, but can be used sparingly with game roasts; balm or lemon balm is good in a sauce applied to antelope or venison steaks; chervil can be used as a major herb in soups; coriander is another interesting, but little-used herb in this book, although our "Rabbit Nepal" dish does call for it. Cumin is from the parsley family, and it's used in a number of dishes, including Mexican recipes; dill can be used on some meats; fennel is used in some soups; juniper berries are unique and interesting to cook with, but not widely used; lovage is another little-used and often hard-to-find herb that can be used with meat, especially ground meat; saffron is also used in some meat dishes, especially venison loin chops.

This excellent meal includes antelope shoulder roast plus chunks of lamb. The lamb cooks on top of the antelope, juices running down into the meat below. Garlic powder makes this roast taste great.

COOKING WITH WINE or other spirits may be European-born, but wine cookery is worldwide today, and probably has been for some time. The whole idea behind cooking with wine is to add flavor. Of course, flaming desserts are for pageant as well as taste appeal, but the recipes for cooking with spirits in this book are aimed at flavor, not show. The alcoholic content is primarily cooked off in most wine-flavored main course dishes, so it is taste and taste alone that supports cooking with wine. It works well with many different domestic meats and is especially ideal with game, both red meat and bird. Furthermore, most people like the flavor imparted by wine, especially those who "don't like game meat."

In all wine recipes, timing is vital. Never add wine to a recipe at will. Add only when appropriate. While I favor wine cooked into the meal, this is not necessarily the only way to use wine. Others may prefer a much stronger wine flavor. When added late to a dish, wine imparts a much stronger taste. The wine is not cooked in the food; therefore, it tastes like wine. Wine added at the beginning of the cooking cycle and blended in loses its original wine flavor. It is altered by cooking to a different taste.

Wine Choices

Personal preference plays a huge role in choosing wines for cooking. I prefer drinking-type wines over "cooking wine," which often has salt and other additives. I do not care for truly sweet wine in most cooking, while dry wine is not always ideal, either. A medium wine is often the best choice. Remember that table wine (roughly 13 percent alcohol) spoils after it is left open for a week or so. They come in red, white and pink, and can be used for cooking, but I prefer and recom-

Chapter 26...

Spirits for Cooking

Game Care & Cookery

mend standard "beverage" wines. Here are a few wines worth having in the kitchen: burgundy, ruby port, medium sherry.

Marinating

Wine is a part of many different marinades. It serves as a tenderizer because its acid content aids in breaking down meat fiber. But once again, flavor is the major objective here. Marination opens the door to experimentation, and other spirits can be used as well. Chapter 27 also offers a few ideas on marinating with wine.

Basting

Wine makes an interesting, useful and worthwhile baste, but is also dangerous because it can be overdone. Basting requires ladling wine directly over the cooking food or pouring wine into the cooking vessel, then ladling the contents over the cooking food. The first method can result in a strong wine flavor; the second method is safer.

Deglazing

This process is done to the pan that cooked the food, such as the roasting pan that recently contained that big chunk of boned game meat. Port wine works well, and so does sherry, medium to dry, but some like white wine. First, remove the cooking juices from the roasting utensil and strain them. Return the strained juices to the same cooking vessel and heat on the stovetop, adding wine. It's difficult to say how much without knowing the amount of meat that

Wine is stirred into the broth of the stew very deliberately, to mix the wine well, and allow it to cook into the dish. Note cornbread on the side with this stew.

Wine added to bits of boned fried meat add terrific flavor. The state-of-the-art Silverstone frying pan makes adding wine to the dish, or deglazing the pan, very easy.

was cooked, but a cup of wine is normally enough to deglaze the average-size roasting pan. Add the wine slowly, cooking it right into the broth. I especially like deglazing the frying pan, and it's easy because there is no need to strain. Just heat the pan and add wine, slowly, stirring all the while. A pat of butter never hurts the flavor, but this does represent added fat. A $1/2$-cup of wine will usually serve a 10- to 12-inch frying pan. When the wine and juices are combined well, remove the pan from heat and let it rest a moment. Then serve the wine/juice with dinner. Be sure to strain the finished product.

Stir-Frying

For our purposes, stir-fry differs from ordinary frying because the pan is very hot and the food is moved in it very quickly. Stir-fry works with bits of boned meat from just about any wild fare, and adding wine spikes the flavor. You don't need much wine, and I prefer medium sherry most of the time, but port wine is also workable. When the food is almost ready to emerge from the frying pan, splash in $1/4$- to $1/2$-cup of wine, according to personal preference, and continue stirring until the wine blends well into the juices in the pan. Do not leave the wine uncooked.

Frying

Here the meat is fried in a normal fashion, at the usual medium heat levels, rather than rapidly at high temperatures. Wine is added toward the end of the frying process. The meat can be removed from the pan first, rather than leaving it in to cook with the wine—just like deglazing the pan. Or the meat can be left in the pan. Sherry is my favorite choice for pan-frying meat, as usual, but port wine works well, too.

Roasting

This is not deglazing. This is cooking meat with wine directly in the roasting pan. It is added toward the last twenty or thirty minutes of cooking time and is allowed to cook right into the meat, leaving a terrific flavor. Basting the juice/wine mixture is recommended only after the wine has cooked and blended for ten minutes. Don't over-

do it, however. A $1/2$-cup of wine is generally plenty for a normal-sized roast.

Stewing

Wine added toward the end of the cooking process lifts stew from the ranks of stick-to-your-ribs ordinary food to gourmet dining. Port is often the better wine here. And once again, it is cooked into the stew, not added at the last moment and left uncooked. When the stew is ten to twenty minutes away from completion, pour $1/2$-cup of wine into the pan (considering at least 2 quarts of stew). Finish cooking while stirring to blend properly. Then the stew can be thickened, after the wine has cooked into the broth.

Making Soups, Gravies and Sauces

Add wine toward the end of the cooking cycle, and while the soup has been returned to a rolling boil. Sherry and port, as usual, are my favorites.

Gravies can be made from the stock left after roasting with wine, or wine can be added directly to stock that is destined for the gravy

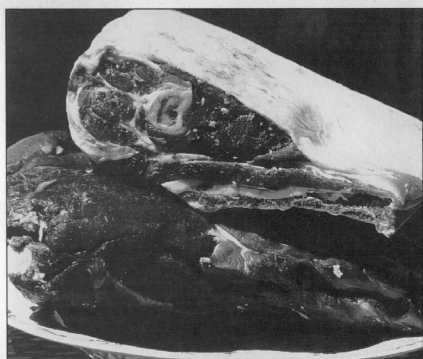

One of the more interesting game recipes is the mixing of domestic and wild meats. Pork or lamb atop venison, antelope, or other game meat allows juices to mingle. Wine fits into this recipe perfectly, coming in at the end of the cooking cycle, but with enough time to cook well into the juices, resulting in a fantastic sauce to pour over the meat.

One of the author's favorite wines is Madeira. It cooks nicely *into* recipes and delivers an excellent flavor.

boat. I don't care for the raw flavor of wine in gravy. I prefer cooking the stock/wine mixture first, then making gravy with it.

There are numerous wine sauces, far too many to include as part of this chapter. Any meals listed in this book using a wine sauce have the sauce included as part of the recipe. For example, orange sauce with wine: Heat and mix a cup of orange juice, a $1/4$-cup of orange marmalade, a $1/2$-cup of port wine, a $1/2$-teaspoon ground ginger and a sprinkle of powdered cinnamon. Bring to a boil. Then lower heat and thicken the stock with corn starch. This can be doubled. This recipe will generally handle about 2 pounds of meat, but can be doubled for larger portions. It is especially good with venison chops or medallions.

Sauteeing

Wine works well with sauteed meats if you add a pat of butter in the process. Raise heat level, add the wine, and enjoy the burst of aroma that is released. Then remove meat and pour the sauce over it.

Other Liquors

This chapter has dealt with wine as a condiment. But remember, many other spirits are useful in cooking, including brandy. Each one has its own merits and demerits, and the wise cook will experiment carefully before adding any spirit.

Bourbon

Any red meat can be enhanced by bourbon. The stir-fry technique with wine can be substituted with bourbon, in fact. The amount used, however, is considerably less than that of wine. Colorful cooking means experimentation. Try bourbon in a small way first, and then add or delete the spirit from your recipe file as you prefer.

Beer

Beer has long been used as a condiment in cooking and, as mentioned in this book, an agent for the beer marinade. Beer can be added

Sometimes a fine roast can be cooked with wine, but it is also possible to make a wine sauce to grace such a roast.

when sauteeing any red meat. Amounts again vary with taste. I have found that less is better than more, for my family's preferences, and suggest only 1 cup of beer with 4 pounds of meat. Remember to "cook out the beer" in your recipe. Unlike many wines, which require only seconds in a hot fry pan to turn into a "gravy," beer may take a few minutes before it blends with the rest of the ingredients. A recent fried rabbit dinner was complimented with the addition of beer at the end of the cooking cycle, the beer "cooked out" during the last several minutes of frying.

Brandy

Many brandies have been used quite successfully in artful cooking for a very long time. Amounts are again less than that suggested for most wines. One of our recent elk roasts, which weighed 6 pounds going into the pan, was treated with $1/4$-cup of brandy during the last one-third of its cooking time. Once again, experiment to discover what works best for you, your dinner guests and your family.

Gin

Gin is at home in the cooking of rabbits and upland game birds. Again, it's a matter of personal taste, and the amount of gin added should be, at least in the beginning, much smaller than wine. Gin can be added toward the end of a gamebird stir-fry in which the birds—grouse, quail, partridge, and upland flier, including pheasant—have been pressure-cooked ahead of time and completely deboned.

Rum

Rum is often considered by the baker (rum cake, for example), but it can be used in the cooking of red meats. It is employed exactly as wine; however, the previously mentioned warning about amounts is sounded again. Experiment with care. Use less rum than you figure you'll need to enhance the dish. Next time you can add more.

Cognac

Cognac may be used in many different ways to enhance game cookery. One good use for this spirit is as a marinade when frying game meat. After browning the meat, remove it from heat and place it in a cold cognac marinade for thirty minutes. Then resume frying. This is only one of many options.

Marinades are many. This one uses beer, along with onion, garlic, dry mustard, oil and black pepper. Inventing marinades is also entirely possible. Think up one for yourself. It may be a winner.

THIS CHAPTER LOOKS at four important cooking areas that enhance game meat meals: marinades, game sauces, barbecue sauces, and gravies. The proficient preparation of these enhancers can make all the difference between a bland meal and a gourmet dish, and none take a great deal of time or effort to mix.

Chapter 27...
Marinades, Sauces, Barbecues and Gravies
Game Care & Cookery

Marinades

The marination of game meat serves three major purposes: tenderizing, "soaking out" and adding flavor. A marinade can be a wise mixture of spices in a liquid medium, such as our "universal marinade." This recipe can be found elsewhere in the recipe section of this book and satisfies all three of the above requirements. A marinade may also be nothing more than wine with no added spices, or soy sauce, or prepared commercial teriyaki marinade used all by itself. Or a marinade may be as simple as saltwater, which is brine. This type of marinade is useful because it does a good job of soaking out unwanted juices. Brine also helps loosen outer tissue, another important aspect of marination.

Tenderizing

Meat is tenderized in marinade, and it need not be made of wine, although wine marinade is known for its tenderizing qualities. However, this is a rather small consideration, because it takes quite a long time for meat to tenderize in a marinade. The exact time is impossible to quote, but a couple of days or longer is the rule. Nevertheless, game meat can be tenderized through marination, as long as there is

Marinating does not always mean soaking meat in a solution. Sometimes marination can be rubbed in. In this case, a light touch of sesame oil, plus black pepper, are rubbed well into these shaped boneless venison steaks. A couple hours later, the meat can be fried normally.

Shaping boneless meat with a meat hammer thins the pieces, offers a tenderizing effect, and prepares the meat for marination. These boneless steaks are "pounded" and ready for marinating.

some acid content, as from wine, lemon juice or some other acetic element.

Soaking Out

This means drawing from the meat unwanted fluids and flavors. This is an extremely important aspect of marination, because most people do not eat game meat every day, so the flavor of certain game is not fully appreciated. But, if the meat is marinated, that unfamiliar taste is reduced or eliminated. In a way, soaking out is a flavor enhancer, but game meat is not soaked to *add* flavor in this case. It is soaked to remove a flavor already there. Soaking out also cleans the meat extremely well and loosens unwanted tissues that can be removed later with no trouble at all. This factor is especially important for small game, such as rabbits, but also is useful on upland game and waterfowl, which may have unwanted tissue covering good meat.

Adding Flavor

Most marinades add flavor to game meat, but this does not mean all game meat should be marinated. The flavor of the meat "as is" may be exactly what the cook and his guests want. However, marinade flavors can be enhancers that improve upon the taste of the game meat.

After Marination

Some marinades continue to have value after marination, while most do not. For example, some marinades may be used as part of a dinner juice to spoon over meat, mashed potatoes or other foods. Marinades may also serve as a base for preparing gravy, although I find this use limited. While certain wine marinades do work for deglazing a pan, many are worthless after they do their work, like universal marinade. It should be discarded, not cooked, after its use. Remember, one reason to use marinade is to extract flavors that some, if not all of us, do not appreciate. After absorbing these flavors, marinades should not be used for making gravies or ladling over meat and other foods.

Marinade goes a long way when placed in a plastic food bag with the meat. The bag is then placed in the refrigerator and turned over from time to time to distribute marinade.

Along those same lines, the vacuum foodsaver can be a great mari-

Here, marinated meat is cooked on the gas grill over lava rock.

nation device. The meat is placed in the vacuum jar, along with marinade, and air is forced out using the foodsaver. Marination takes only minutes instead of hours. Check the instruction sheet with the foodsaver for more details.

Numerous marinades can be found in the recipe section of this book. You'll want to try some or all of them, because there are many different kinds of marinades that work well with various game meats. In fact, why not invent a few marinades of your own? Or study cookbooks for different marinade recipes? Some cooks may believe that marinating game meat to alter its flavor is cheating. I disagree. The object of game cookery is turning wild meat into delicious gourmet dishes, and if marinades promote that end, then why not use them?

Game Sauces

Sauces can turn an ordinary meal into an adventure. Happily, there are more sauces than pebbles on a beach, and many of them work beautifully with game meals. The reader is invited to invent some of his own sauces, too, just as he might think up a few of his own marinades. Many sauces are presented in the recipe section for approval.

If the roux is uncooperative, a simple spoon like this one can come to the rescue, blending flour and oil perfectly.

The brown sauce is ideal for many game meats.

But do remember that most sauces are easy to prepare. Don't let a fancy-sounding sauce throw you. Some begin with a simple roux, for example. Note, however, that a roux is not a sauce, but rather a base for a sauce made of a 50/50 mixture of oil and flour. From a roux, a fine white sauce can be made using a 50/50 mixture of butter and flour, or margarine and flour, plus cream, as shown in the recipe section of this book.

Sauces often fail, not because the cook hadn't blended the correct elements of the recipe, but because of *how* the ingredients were blended. It's vital to prepare a sauce exactly, and not haphazardly. A sauce may be ruined just because an improper utensil was used, for example. Sometimes wooden spoons are needed, whereas metal spoons may affect proper blending. So follow the directions when preparing your sauces. As always, experimentation is encouraged, but when it comes to sauces, experiment on the side of caution. Most sauce-making suggestions are there for a reason.

Barbecue

Cooking over coals is often called a barbecue, but in fact it is a broiling method, as is cooking on the gas grill. Broiling along with a special sauce to enhance the meat is barbecuing. Nobody knows how long the practice of coating meat with sauces for broiling has been around. Igor the Caveman may well have ladled some form of barbecue sauce over his mastodon steaks. I suppose we will never know, nor does the history matter. What does matter is that we are blessed with dozens of different sauces straight from the store shelf, as well as recipes to make our own. The recipe section of the book offers a number of barbecues. Also, the special KO Barbecue dish is presented, a recipe that produces a tender, tasty meal with a high-spice flavor.

Pre-Treatment

Any wild meat is a candidate for barbecue sauce. Red meat is usually first on the list, but anything from quail to moose, along with ducks and geese in between, can be enhanced by barbecue sauce and broiling. So most game meat is great for barbecue, but not all types. Treating cottontail rabbit and squirrels to most barbecue sauces, then broiling these small game treats, is not my idea of enhancement. But that's personal. Even when pre-marinated before barbecuing, these meats tend to dry out on the grill, and if repeatedly laced with barbecue sauce to prevent dryness, the sauce can overtake the meat altogether.

The major problem with barbecuing meats is dryness. That may seem strange, since the meat is treated with a moist sauce as it cooks; however, as suggested above, in order to keep low-fat (unmarbled) meats from drying out, heaps of sauce may be required, and this may not be desirable. This is why the pre-marination of barbecue-bound meat is suggested.

Dozens of fluids do the trick. Three good ones are soy/Worcestershire mix, 5:1, five parts soy, one part Worcestershire; commercially prepared teriyaki marinades used straight out of the bottle; and wine-based marinades.

Do not use the soy/Worcestershire mix as a long-soak marinade because it can entirely overtake the meat's flavor. Simply rub the 5:1 mixture on the meat with your fingers, working it in, but nothing more.

Prepared teriyaki marinade (not teriyaki glaze) can be used like any marinade, soaking the meat for a while. However, this does not mean you should pour a bottle of teriyaki marinade into a container and drown the meat in it. Rather, put the meat in a plastic food bag, pour a little over the meat, and let it go at that. This method saves on marinade and prevents over-doing it. Remember, timing is important. Leave the meat in the teriyaki marinade for only ten minutes before barbecuing. That is long enough.

Just about any wine-type marinade works fine as a pre-barbecue treatment, but remember that wine marinades affect flavor. The barbecue grill will not remove all wine flavor from the meat. Under no circumstances should you soak barbecue-bound meat in wine for more than a few moments.

Do not use universal marinade for the pre-marination of meat for barbecuing. Universal marinade is milk-based, and milk cooked into the meat on the grill can spoil the flavor. Also, milk may cook up on the outside of the meat in a less than satisfactory manner. Universal marinade is ideal for flour-coating meat for frying, however.

Game Gravies

How many times have you had a guest applaud your gravy over and above every other food item on the dinner table? If it hasn't happened yet, perhaps you should think about making either a pan gravy or standard brown game gravy on top of the mashed potatoes and meat. Many different gravies grace our recipe section, so here are a few hints concerning gravy making.

Commercial marinades and barbecue sauces are extremely popular today and better than ever. This exciting marinade is from Lawry's. It works wonders on game meat cooked over coals or on the gas grill.

Gravy Sauces

Domestic turkey provides a lot of juice, and some of this juice will no doubt go toward making gravy for dinner. However, not all of it is needed, because stock or juices from cooked giblets, as well as potato water, are also used in making standard domestic turkey gravy. So save what juice is not used, strain it and store it frozen in a well-sealed food jar. When ready to use, discard the solidified fat from the top of the jar and strain the juice once more. This is a good base starter for gravy served with upland birds and waterfowl.

Roasting a wild turkey will not produce the amount of juices generated from cooking a domestic bird. However, a fine juice base is prepared by adding chicken broth or stock to the roaster during the cooking process. Additional bouillon also helps to produce good wild turkey gravy juices, as does a little soy and/or teriyaki marinade added to the roasting pan.

Roasts not only produce some of their own juices, but many liquids, as well as bouillon, can be added to a cooking roast to make a super base for game gravy. The usual soy sauce, teriyaki marinade, stock, canned broth and other juices, along with some water, produce plenty of juice out of the roasting pan.

Gravy can be made from stock, and a recipe is given elsewhere in this book. Prepared stock is a good starting point for making gravy, and it can be enhanced in various ways, as with additional bouillon, soy sauce or teriyaki marinade.

The pressure cooker is ideal for extracting all of the good from upland bird, wild turkey and waterfowl giblets. However, domestic turkey and chicken giblets also produce an excellent juice for gravy making.

Pan drippings are truly the remains of meat bits and flour coating left in the frying pan after frying. These leftovers can be used to make a taste treat that uplifts the flavor of mashed potatoes, meats and other foods.

Whether you cook potatoes by pot-boiling or in the pressure cooker, the result is water with starch. This water is useful in small quantities to help thicken a fine game gravy, so don't toss all of your potato water down the drain.

Preparing Gravies

Use your hand-operated egg beater or hand-held electric mixer to promote a smooth gravy. They can be employed either after the game gravy is completed, to blend in any lumps, or during the addition of flour/water or corn starch/water for thickening of the gravy.

Straining standard gravy helps find any small bone pieces that may have worked their way into the juices used to make the gravy. Also, straining catches any lumps of flour or corn starch that may not have blended properly. Either way, it never hurts to strain a standard gravy. Of course, this is not done with pan gravy because it is born of the little leftovers in the frying pan.

Getting Rid of the Fat

Greasy gravy is unnecessary. It doesn't have to happen. Game meat is so lean in the first place that gravy made of pan drippings or juices seldom contain a great deal of fat. However, when preparing any juices for game gravy, get rid of fat first. One way is by freezing. Actually, the juice need not be frozen hard for this trick to work. Cooling the juice in the refrigerator or freezer for a while will cause fat to solidify atop the juice. This cluster of solidified fat is then removed and discarded. Also, there are fat separators available on the market. If your local department store does not have one for sale, check restaurant supply houses. These are usually plastic containers designed to pour the fat off the top of the juice. Finally, if the juice is not loaded with fat, it may be skimmed off the top with a spoon. Place juice in a glass container and look at it from the side. You should be able to see exactly how much fat comes to the surface.

Gravy Additives

Milk does at least two things for gravy: it gives a handsome color and offers a little more body. Milk also extends the amount of gravy by a little bit and helps promote smoothness. Don't overdo it, however, as milk can also reduce the flavor from "meaty" to bland.

Butter or margarine also helps to flavor a gravy. Again, don't overdo either of these, as you may end up with what you worked hard in the first place to avoid—a greasy gravy. But a little butter or margarine really gives a brown or white gravy an extra touch of class.

Thickening Gravy

Gravy is just flavored juice if you don't thicken it. There is nothing wrong with meat juice as is, of course, but in order to have a real gravy, it must be thickened. Two readily available and ideal thickeners are white flour and corn starch. About 4 tablespoons per pint of liquid generally makes a good thickener.

If you plan to use white flour to thicken gravy, be aware that the flour must be *cooked* into the gravy. Corn starch demands cooking into the gravy, too, but not nearly as much as white flour. If uncooked, white flour gives the gravy a raw texture and a downgraded flavor. It is entirely possible to thicken gravy base liquid by simply adding a little bit of flour at a time, mixing and cooking into the liquid until the mixture is just thick enough. However, a safer way to add flour, and avoid lumps, is by pre-mixing with water, juice, canned broth, stock or milk. If the gravy base liquid is very rich, water will do. However, if you don't want to reduce the richness of your gravy by adding water, use the same juice with which you plan to make the gravy. *Tip*: Make sure the juice is cold before mixing with flour. If the juice is hot, it will cause a lumpy glob that is almost impossible to blend into gravy.

Canned broth, cool, works just as well to mix with white flour for gravy. Likewise, cold stock mixes perfectly with white flour to act as a thickener. Finally, milk works well, too. But juice, canned broth or stock seem to do the job nicely and are all considered first choices in preparing a thickener for game gravy.

Corn starch is used exactly like white flour and can also be carefully added directly to the gravy base liquid. But as with white flour, mixing corn starch with a liquid beforehand makes for a certain lump-free gravy. Corn starch must also be cooked into the liquid to make gravy, but this can be done in only a few minutes.

While an ordinary spoon works well for mixing liquids into white flour or corn starch, a mixer works better. Or try a very simple plastic container with a lid. After mixing the ingredients, place the lid on the container and shake vigorously. Whether made with flour or corn starch, the thickener should look very much like whole milk, perhaps a bit heavier, but should not pour like heavy cream, or you'll want to add more liquid.

Ruben Sandwich á La Venison

Serve with potato salad and garlic pickles.

1-2 lb. leftover venison roast, sliced	2 eggs, beaten
12 slices rye bread	1/2 cup milk
6 slices Swiss cheese	Salt and pepper
1 jar sauerkraut, drained	Olive oil, margarine or butter

On one slice of rye bread, layer roast, cheese and sauerkraut. Top with another slice of bread. In small bowl, mix egg and milk. Dip each side of sandwich into mixture. In skillet with small amount of olive oil or margarine, brown each side of sandwich until golden brown. **Servings: 6**

Alternate Meats: Elk, moose, antelope, caribou, deer

Texas-Style Hoagies

Good for lunch or dinner. Serve with baked applesauce and sweet corn.

2 lb. ground venison
1 onion, minced
1 can Mexican-style stewed tomatoes
1 4-oz. can green chiles, diced
4 Tbsp. brown sugar
Salt and pepper
1/2 cup catsup
6 fresh onion buns or 6 long hoagie buns

In skillet, brown meat and onions. Drain on paper towel. Add remaining ingredients except buns and simmer for 30 minutes until all flavors are blended. Spoon mixture onto toasted buns.

Servings: 6

Alternate Meats: Elk, moose, antelope, caribou, deer

Chopped Vension Sandwich

Serve this dish with pride and in-season fruit.

3 cups leftover venison roast, cubed	1 cup mayonnaise
1 1/2 cups celery, minced	Fresh onion buns
1/2 cup pickle, minced (sweet or dill)	1 cup sharp cheddar cheese, grated
Salt and pepper	

Preheat oven to broil. Combine venison celery, pickles, salt, pepper and mayonnaise in bowl. Mix well. Toast each bun half. Spread with meat mixture and sprinkle with cheese. Place under broiler until cheese is bubbly. Top with remaining bun half. **Servings: 6**

Alternate Meats: Elk, moose, antelope, caribou, deer

Big Game Recipes...

Your Very Own Venison Sandwich

This is a very simple recipe that serves in making delicious cold cuts.

2-4 lb. gamemeat, boneless	1/8 tsp. onion salt
1 can beef broth	2 dashes Worcestershire sauce
1 can water	1/8 cup teriyaki marinade
1/4 tsp. garlic powder	

Preheat oven to 300°. Place all ingredients in roasting pot. Cover and cook for 30 minutes. Turn meat and cook for another 30 minutes. Check for doneness. If meat is still red in center, cook at 250° until meat is done. Remove and slice for sandwiches. **Servings: 12**

Alternate Meats: Elk, moose, antelope, caribou, deer

Cooking Tips: Save juice for stock. Freeze in proper jar.

Earl of Venison Sandwich

Serve by itself or with a tossed salad.

2 lb. leftover venison roast, sliced	6 Tbsp. Thousand Island dressing
6 English muffins	1/4 cup olives, sliced
2 tomatoes, chopped	1 onion, thinly sliced
1 cucumber, minced	Salt and pepper
1 cup fresh sprouts	6 slices sharp cheddar cheese

Preheat oven to broil. Slice each muffin in half. Layer with meat, tomatoes, cucumbers, sprouts, salad dressing, olives, onions, salt and pepper. Top with cheese. Broil until cheese is bubbly. Top with other half of muffin. **Servings: 6**

Alternate Meats: Elk, moose, antelope, caribou, deer

Draining fried meat on a paper towel removes most overt cooking oil. This is important in a low-fat diet.

"...This can be prepared in a flash should unexpected guests arrive..."

Venison Tenderloin Kiev

Serve with rice or boiled potatoes, an in-season vegetable and mixed green salad.

6 venison tenderloins
Salt and pepper
1 tsp. garlic powder
1 tsp. olive oil
1 can chicken with rice soup

Preheat oven to 325°. Soak venison in cold water for 30 minutes. Drain on paper towel. Season meat with salt, pepper and garlic powder. In skillet, brown meat in olive oil. Place meat in baking dish and top with soup. Cover tightly and bake 1 hour. Remove meat and save juices for gravy.   **Servings: 6**

Alternate Meats: Elk, mooose, antelope, caribou, deer, buffalo

Stuffed Venison Steak

A fresh fruit medley and in-season vegetables complement this dish.

6 venison steaks
Salt and pepper
1 tsp. garlic powder
1 pkg. commercial stuffing

1 12-oz. can tomato juice
1 Tbsp. lemon juice
1/4 cup brown sugar

Preheat oven to 350°. Cut venison steaks to about 2-inch thickness. Slice each piece through middle to allow space for stuffing. Season with salt, pepper and garlic powder. Prepare stuffing mix according to package directions. Stuff each steak and tie with string. Place in shallow baking dish. In small bowl, mix tomato and lemon juices and brown sugar. Pour over steaks. Cover and bake 30 minutes or until done. Baste occasionally.   **Servings: 6**

Alternate Meats: Elk, moose, antelope, caribou, deer

Almond Javelina

This dish works nicely with steamed rice and stir-fried vegetables.

3 lb. javelina meat, boned
1 cup port wine
2 cloves garlic, minced
1/2-1 cup olive oil
3 bunches green onions, diced
1 cup almonds, sliced
See *Almond Javelina Sauce*

Cut meat into thin slices. In bowl, blend wine and garlic. Marinate meat in liquid for 4 hours. Heat skillet with olive oil. Stir-fry meat and onions for 3-4 minutes. Add *Almond Javelina Sauce* and cook for 3 more minutes. Stir in almonds.   **Servings: 6**

Almond Javelina Sauce

2 Tbsp. soy sauce
2 Tbsp. sherry
1 Tbsp. teriyaki glaze
1/8 tsp. white pepper

Mix all ingredients in small bowl.

Smoked Antelope Steaks

A good old-fashioned barbecue couldn't be better.
Serve with baked beans, sweet corn and biscuits.

2 lb. antelope steaks	Fresh ground pepper, sprinkle
Garlic powder, sprinkle	1/4 cup soy sauce
Onion powder, sprinkle	3/4 cup sherry

Slice steaks to about 1/2-inch thickness and pound with meat hammer. Sprinkle lightly with garlic powder, onion powder and pepper. In bowl, combine soy sauce and sherry. Marinate steaks for 6-8 hours, turning once or twice. Barbecue over coals or gas grill. Baste lightly with marinade.   **Servings: 4**

Alternate Meats: Elk, moose, caribou, deer

Cooking Tips: Because lean game meat can dry out on the grill, remember not to overcook. Adding damp hickory chips to volcanic rock of gas grill or on top of coals adds flavor. Set grill on high; meat will have a golden brown finish when done.

Venison Tenderloin with Honey and Ginger

Baked applesauce enhances this flavorful meal.

1 cup Lawry's Lemon Pepper Marinade
2-4 lb. venison tenderloin
1/2 cup honey
1 tsp. ginger

Preheat oven to 350°. Pour marinade over tenderloin in baking dish. Cover and refrigerate 4-6 hours or overnight, turning occasionally. Discard marinade. Mix honey and ginger and baste meat. Bake 25-35 minutes, basting often.

Servings: 6

Alternate Meats: Elk, moose, antelope, caribou, deer

Cinnamon Venison Steak

For those who want something different, this is it.
Serve with rice and baked squash.

2 lb. venison steaks	1/4 tsp. cinnamon, ground
1 cup port wine	Canola oil
1/2 onion, sliced	Margarine
1/8 tsp. white pepper	1/2 can beef broth
1/8 cup soy sauce	

Slice venison into serving pieces, shape with meat hammer and rinse in cold salt water (1 qt. water with 1/8 cup salt). Rinse meat in clear water and dry. In separate dish, mix port wine, onion, pepper, soy sauce and cinnamon. Add meat and marinate overnight. In skillet, fry meat in canola oil and margarine until desired doneness. Drain meat, saving drippings. Add beef broth to juices and boil briskly for 5 minutes, stirring. Use as sauce for meat.   **Servings: 4**

Alternate Meats: Elk, moose, antelope, caribou, deer

Fried steaks, especially venison and antelope, are tasty and simple to make. This meat has been shaped with a meat hammer and treated with condiments.

"...This recipe rates high in the flavor department..."

Spicy Javelina

Serve with sauce over white rice and garnish with steamed asparagus spears.

2 lb. javelina meat, boned
1/2 cup lemon or lime juice
4 cloves garlic, crushed
Olive oil
1/2 cup chicken broth

Thinly slice meat. In small bowl, mix lemon or lime juice with garlic. Add meat and let stand 6-10 hours. Remove meat from marinade and allow to drain; do not blot dry. Fry meat in skillet over medium heat using enough olive oil to prevent sticking. When meat is cooked through, add broth and cook 3 more minutes on high.

Servings: 4

Pan-Fried Caribou Steaks

This great outdoors dish is best served with baked potatoes or pasta laced with Parmesan cheese and glazed carrots.

2 lb. caribou steaks	**Pepper, sprinkle**
Garlic powder, sprinkle	**Flour**
Paprika, sprinkle	**Olive oil**

Cut meat across the grain to about $1/2$-inch thickness. Pound with meat hammer to shape into even thickness. Sprinkle with garlic powder, paprika and pepper. Work flour into meat by hand. In skillet, heat olive oil (enough oil to cover bottom of pan). Fry steaks to medium doneness. **Servings: 4**

Alternate Meats: Elk, moose, antelope, deer

Cooking Tips: Do not overcook the caribou. An alternate method of preparing the steaks is to flour and spice the meat first, and then use a meat hammer for shaping. Flour and spice again; pound again. Other cooking oil options include canola oil, lard, 50/50 lard and margarine or 25/75 bacon fat and canola oil.

Antelope Teriyaki Steaks

Stomachs will be growling when the smell of this dish permeates the room. Serve with baked squash and an orange mandarin salad.

2 lb. antelope steaks	**Onion salt, sprinkle**
Garlic powder, sprinkle	**$1/4$ cup soy sauce**
Pepper, sprinkle	**$1/4$ cup sherry**
Tarragon, sprinkle	**Teriyaki sauce**
2-3 Tbsp. olive oil	**Teriyaki glaze**

Cut antelope steaks to about $1/2$-inch thickness. Pound with meat hammer to shape. Lightly sprinkle each steak with garlic powder, pepper and tarragon. In skillet, heat olive oil, add steaks and sprinkle one side lightly with onion salt. When steaks are almost cooked through, splash on soy sauce and sherry and turn. When soy and sherry mixture turns brown, like light gravy, add teriyaki sauce and glaze. Stir well to blend and cook for only 2-3 minutes. **Servings: 4**

Alternate Meats: Elk, moose, caribou, deer

This is how flour and spices are "pounded" into meat. The steaks are cut and placed on a board, spiced and then floured. The meat cuts are then shaped with the hammer, driving the spices and flour into the meat.

Elk Nuggets

This highly prized elk meat is tasty with steamed carrots and mashed potatoes, which can be prepared quickly in a pressure cooker.

2 lb. elk meat, cubed	**$1/4$ tsp. paprika**
$1/4$ cup soy sauce	**$1/4$ black pepper, coarse-ground**
Garlic powder, sprinkle	**Sweet basil leaf, hand-rubbed**
$1/4$ cup teriyaki marinade	**Canola oil**
2 cups flour	**Margarine**
Onion powder, sprinkle	

"...Excellent camp food as well as home tablefare..."

Pressure cook nuggets covered with cold water for 20 minutes with soy sauce, garlic powder and teriyaki marinade. In paper bag, combine flour, onion powder, paprika, black pepper and sweet basil leaf and shake to mix. Add nuggets and shake to coat meat evenly. Over medium heat, fry floured nuggets in skillet with canola oil. Add margarine to brown nuggets thoroughly. To determine if meat is done, a light pink color in center is fine; running juice means more cooking time.

Servings: 6

Alternate Meats: Any red game meat.

Cooking Tips: Elk nuggets are normally taken from steak cuts rather than roast cuts. However, any cut can be used provided meat is tenderized in a pressure cooker before frying.

Hand-rubbing basil leaves releases fragrance and reduces the size of each bit, which is preferable to large hunks of leaf.

Grilled Antelope Steaks—The Easy Way

Serve with in-season vegetables such as sweet corn or squash and add a mixed green salad.

2 lb. antelope steaks	Teriyaki marinade (or)
Pepper, sprinkle	Sherry
Paprika, sprinkle	Margarine, squeeze-bottle type
Garlic powder, sprinkle	

Cut steaks into strips. If using loin, cut with the grain; if using round, cut against the grain. Lightly sprinkle each piece with pepper, paprika and garlic powder. Put steaks in plastic bag and pour in teriyaki marinade or sherry. Close bag and refrigerate 2-4 or more hours. To ensure meat absorbs sauce, turn bag over several times. Remove steaks and grill. When one side has browned, turn and dot with margarine. Turn and apply margarine again. This keeps meat moist. Cover grill to finish cooking. **Servings: 4**

Alternate Meats: Elk, moose, caribou, deer

Cooking Tips: Do not overuse pepper, paprika or garlic with antelope.

It is always a good idea to clean the grill with wire brush and paper towels before barbecuing. It keeps steaks looking nice, as well as tasting better.

"...The marinade makes this dish fit for a king..."

Garlic Javelina

This spicy garlic dish needs steaming rice and a fresh tomato and onion salad to make it complete.

2-3 lb. javelina, boned
4 Tbsp. olive oil
6-8 cloves garlic, chopped
Thyme, pinch
Tarragon, pinch
2 cans chicken broth

Cut javelina meat into strips. Cross-cut those strips into small pieces and then chop fine. Heat Dutch oven or heavy cooking pot with olive oil. Add chopped meat and garlic, stirring rapidly with wooden spoon. Keep meat and garlic moving. Do not allow garlic to burn because it will change the flavor dramatically. Stir in thyme and tarragon. Add chicken broth and stir to mix. Heat through. **Servings: 6**

Cooking Tips: To liven up this dish, add 1 lb. chorizo, a Mexican sausage. Buy prepared chorizo and cook well. Microwave on paper towel for 1-2 minutes on high before adding to pot. In addition, 1 lb. of cooked macaroni can be added with the chicken broth.

Garlic is currently seen as a healthy food. The garlic used here cooks into the meat fairly well and is not as overwhelming as it may seem.

Venison Steak Parmesan

Serve with your favorite pasta, a fresh salad and hot garlic bread.

2 lb. venison loin	1/2 lb. mozzarella cheese, sliced
Salt and pepper	1 onion, sliced
1/4 cup dry Italian bread crumbs	1 clove garlic, minced
1/4 cup Parmesan cheese	1 16-oz. can tomato sauce
1 egg, beaten	1 tsp. sweet basil, rubbed
2 Tbsp. milk	1 tsp. oregano, rubbed
2 Tbsp. olive oil	

Preheat oven to 350°. Pound venison thin and season with salt and pepper. Combine bread crumbs and Parmesan cheese in bowl. In another bowl, mix egg and milk. Dip venison in egg/milk mixture and then into bread crumb mixture. In skillet, brown steaks in hot oil and drain on paper towel. Place meat in baking dish and top with mozzarella. Bake 10-15 minutes, depending on desired doneness. In skillet where meat was browned, sauté onion and garlic. Stir in tomato sauce, basil and oregano. Bring to boil and then simmer until thick. Pour sauce over steaks and sprinkle with additional Parmesan cheese. **Servings: 6**

Alternate Meats: Elk, moose, antelope, caribou, deer

"...There's nothing like smothered steak on a cold winter night..."

Smothered Venison Steak

This is a tasty treat when served with rice, steamed broccoli and a green salad.

2 lb. venison steak	2 Tbsp. Worcestershire sauce
Salt and pepper	1 can beef broth
Flour	1 cup low-fat yogurt, plain
2 onions, sliced	1 lb. fresh mushrooms, sliced
1 tsp. garlic powder	

Preheat oven to 325°. Salt and pepper steak and dredge in flour. Place meat in roasting pan and top with onions. Sprinkle with garlic powder and Worcestershire sauce. Pour in beef broth. Cover and bake 1 hour or until meat is tender. Remove meat to platter and keep warm in oven. Add yogurt to drippings in pan and blend. Add mushrooms and simmer 10 minutes. Pour over meat. **Servings: 6**

Alternate Meats: Elk, moose, antelope, caribou, deer

Bouillon-Fried Antelope Steaks

*A steaming baked potato and fresh green beans
are filling side dishes to this saucy steak.*

2 lb. antelope steaks	2 tsp. beef bouillon crystals (or 3 cubes)
Paprika, dash	1/8 cup stock or beef broth
Garlic salt, dash	1/8 cup soy sauce
Onion powder, dash	1/8 cup sherry
Olive oil	

Shape meat with meat hammer and dust with paprika, garlic salt and onion powder. Fry in skillet with olive oil over medium heat. When browned on both sides, lay beef bouillon crystals over each piece and pour in stock. Heat 1 minute, add soy sauce and turn. Cook through. Add sherry and cook wine down.   **Servings: 4-5**

Alternate Meats: Elk, moose, caribou, deer

Cooking Tips: The frying pan can be deglazed with port wine for a nice juice to ladle on meat.

Breaded Vension Steak

*This steak is best served with a green salad, baked potato,
fresh green beans and rolls.*

2 lb. venison steaks	2 Tbsp. olive oil
Salt and pepper	1 tsp. Worcestershire sauce
1 egg, beaten	1 cup water
1 Tbsp. milk	1 can cream of celery soup
1 cup cornflake crumbs	1 tsp. fresh parsley

Cut steak into serving pieces and season with salt and pepper. Mix egg and milk in separate bowl. Roll pieces first in cornflake crumbs, then in egg and milk mixture and again in cornflakes. Heat pressure cooker and add oil. Brown steaks; drain on paper towel. Pour Worcestershire sauce, water and soup in pressure cooker. Add steaks and sprinkle with parsley. Close lid securely and set pressure regulator. Cook 10 minutes with regulator rocking gently. Let pressure drop.

Servings: 4-6

Alternate Meats: Elk, moose, antelope, caribou, deer

> **"...There is nothing quite like the imagination of a good cook..."**

Marinated Venison Kabobs

*This dish is great for summer barbecues.
Serve with rice, tossed salad or coleslaw and fresh bread.*

1-2 lb. venison steaks, cubed	1 lb. cherry tomatoes, washed
12-oz. Lawry's Teriyaki Marinade	1 green pepper, cubed or wedged
1 sweet red pepper, cubed or wedged	1 lb. small mushrooms, washed
1 can pineapple cubes, drained	

Place cubed venison in large container and blend with teriyaki marinade. Cover and refrigerate for a few hours or overnight. Drain meat, saving marinade. On skewers, alternate meat with red peppers, pineapple, tomatoes, green peppers and mushrooms. Broil 6 inches from heat or grill, turning occasionally and brushing with marinade. Remove when meat is cooked as desired.   **Servings: 4**

Alternate Meats: Elk, moose, antelope, caribou, deer

> **"...This quick dish is a taste treat that takes very little time to make..."**

Roma Venison Loin

Serve with noodles or rice, Italian salad and cheese bread.

2 lb. venison loin	2 eggs, beaten
Salt and pepper	1 cup Parmesan cheese, grated
1 tsp. paprika	4 Tbsp. olive oil
1 tsp. oregano, rubbed	

Cut loin into serving pieces and pound thin. Season with salt, pepper, paprika and oregano. Dip in beaten eggs. Press Parmesan in meat with hands. Brown loin in heated skillet with olive oil. Drain on paper towel.   **Servings: 6**

Alternate Meats: Elk, moose, antelope, caribou, deer

Big Game Recipes...Steaks & Roasts

Wild Boar Loin Teriyaki

*A delicious main course when accompanied by a green vegetable,
boiled potatoes and the juice from the meat as gravy.*

2 lb. boar loin	1/2 cup teriyaki marinade
1/8 tsp. white pepper	1/8 cup teriyaki glaze
Canola oil	1/8 cube margarine
2 cloves garlic, crushed	1/8 cup Madeira wine

Cut loin into medallions, cross-grain, and shape with meat hammer. Sprinkle with white pepper. Brown both sides of meat in skillet with canola oil over medium heat and remove. Add garlic cloves to pan and stir. Return meat to pan and heat for 2 minutes, turning several times. Lower heat and cook for 2 more minutes. Add teriyaki marinade and let cook into meat. Remove meat and place in serving dish. Add teriyaki glaze, margarine and wine to pan, stirring constantly. When heated through, pour over meat. **Servings: 4-5**

Cooking Tips: The teriyaki marinade adds a sufficient amount of salt to this dish; an additional amount is not needed.

Wild boar are "pork-like" in taste. This recipe is ideal for young specimens because it relies on meat tenderness.

Oriental Tenderloin

*Delicious with spinach salad with sliced
almonds and sesame seed dressing.*

1/2 cup sesame oil
1 Tbsp. sherry
3 cloves garlic, minced
2 lb. venison tenderloin
12 large mushrooms, sliced

Set oven to broil. Mix sesame oil, sherry and garlic in large bowl; add tenderloin. Marinate in refrigerator 2-4 hours, turning occasionally. Broil meat on both sides until desired doneness. Before removing meat, add mushrooms and broil 1-2 minutes. **Servings: 4**

Alternate Meats: Elk, moose, antelope, caribou, deer

Swiss Steak á la Pasta

*This simple recipe is just right with pasta. Save the juices to pour over noodles and
serve with a mixed green salad and Italian bread sticks.*

2-3 lb. venison steak	Flour
2 Tbsp. olive oil	1 large can tomato juice
Salt and pepper	1 can tomato soup
1 Tbsp. garlic powder	2 cans stewed tomatoes

Heat pressure cooker and add olive oil. Cut steak into serving pieces. Sprinkle with salt, pepper and garlic powder. Dredge in flour and brown in oil; drain on paper towel. Return meat to pressure cooker and add tomato juice, soup and stewed tomatoes. Close lid securely and set pressure regulator. Cook 30 minutes with regulator rocking gently. Let pressure drop. Remove meat and save juices for serving. **Servings: 4-6**

Alternate Meats: Elk, moose, antelope, caribou, deer

This finished *Swiss Steak* dinner is handsome and delicious. All big game meats can be used in this dish, especially when the meat is pressure-cooked until tender.

Parmesan Venison Loin

*This zesty dish can be accompanied by sautéd
zucchini and warm bread.*

2 lb. vension loin
Salt and pepper
1 tsp. garlic powder
1 1/2 cups Parmesan cheese, grated
2 cups dry Italian bread crumbs
1/2-1 cup Dijon mustard

Preheat oven to 400°. Slice meat into serving pieces and pound thin. Season with salt, pepper and garlic powder. In small mixing bowl, combine cheese and bread crumbs. Coat meat with mustard and dip in crumb mixture. Bake 15-20 minutes or to desired doneness. **Servings: 6**

Alternate Meats: Elk, moose, antelope, caribou, deer

Elk Medallions Carbonari

Serve with rice pilaf, spinach salad and fresh-baked bread.

2 lb. elk tenderloin	1 cup celery, julienned
Salt and pepper	1/2 cup green pepper, julienned
3 Tbsp. unsalted butter	1/2 cup red pepper, julienned
4 Tbsp. green onions	1/2 cup brandy
2 cloves garlic, minced	1 cup demi-glace
2 cups fresh mushrooms, sliced	4 Tbsp. heavy whipping cream

Season elk with salt and pepper. In skillet, melt butter and sauté onions and garlic for 1 minute. Add elk and brown on both sides. Remove meat to baking dish and keep warm in oven. In same skillet, add mushrooms, celery, green and red peppers. Sauté 3 minutes. Deglaze skillet with brandy. Reduce liquid by 1/2 and add demi-glace. Reduce liquid by 1/3 and add whipping cream. Stir until smooth. Spoon over meat. **Servings: 6**

Alternate Meats: Moose, antelope, caribou, deer

"...This medley of medallions is mouth watering..."

Roasting boned meat with spices and finishing with wine makes an otherwise ordinary game meat a very special treat.

Madeira Venison Steaks

Top this dish off with your favorite pasta, green salad and Italian bread.

2 lb. venison steaks	2-3 bunches green onions, chopped
Olive oil	2 pats butter or margarine
Parmesan cheese, grated (or)	Lawry's Seasoned Salt, sprinkle
Romano cheese, grated	1/4 cup Madeira wine
1 clove garlic, pressed	1/2 cup whipping cream

Cut venison steaks to no more than 1/8-inch thickness. In skillet, heat enough olive oil to cover bottom of pan. Fry steaks over high heat, stirring constantly. Add light application of Parmesan or Romano cheese and garlic. Reduce to medium heat and stir in onions, butter, Lawry's salt and Madeira wine. Turn heat up to high. Add whipping cream and blend. Once blended, remove meat from pan and serve immediately. **Servings: 4**

Alternate Meats: Elk, moose, antelope, caribou, deer

"...Come gather 'round the table for this savory meal..."

Big Game Recipes...Steaks & Roasts

Fried game steaks are very simple to make. The meat hammer shaped these steaks to uniform thickness, which means they will be ready to eat at the same time.

Baked Vension Steaks Flamenco

For a special evening, serve with spinach salad, rice and a bottle of your favorite red wine.

2 lb. venison steaks
Salt and pepper
¼ cup flour
1 cup onions, thinly sliced
1 cup green pepper rings
2 cups fresh mushrooms, sliced
1 can Italian-style stewed tomatoes
¼ cup horseradish
2 Tbsp. Worcestershire sauce

Preheat oven to 350°. Season venison steaks with salt and pepper and coat with flour. Pound flour into both sides of steaks. Place steaks into large casserole dish. Cover with onions, green peppers and mushrooms. Drain stewed tomatoes and reserve juice. Pour tomatoes over vegetables and steaks. Mix reserve juice, horseradish and Worcestershire sauce in bowl and pour over above mixture. Bake 1 hour.   **Servings: 6**

Alternate Meats: Elk, moose, antelope, caribou, deer

Venison Birds

These "birds" won't fly away, but will melt in your mouth.
Serve with rice pilaf, Caesar salad and crusty bread.

2 lb. venison steak
2 cups commercial stuffing
¼ lb. sliced bacon
Flour
Salt and pepper
1 tsp. garlic powder
2 tsp. olive oil
1 cup water

Cut steaks into serving pieces and pound thin. Prepare stuffing according to package directions. Place stuffing in center of each steak. Roll steak and wrap bacon slice around each piece. Tie with string. Roll each "bird" in flour seasoned with salt, pepper and garlic powder. Heat pressure cooker and add oil. Brown meat on all sides and drain on paper towel. Return pieces to cooker and add water. Close lid securely and set pressure regulator. Cook 10 minutes with regulator rocking gently. Let pressure drop. Make gravy with liquid using 1 Tbsp. flour and ¼ cup water.

Servings: 4-6

Alternate Meats: Elk, moose, antelope, caribou, deer

"...Crisp on the outside, tender and juicy on the inside..."

Antelope Roast Chinese-Style

This roast is elegant served with vegetable stir-fry.

4 Tbsp. soy sauce
4 Tbsp. sherry
2 Tbsp. cornstarch
4 cloves garlic, minced
4-5 lb. antelope roast

Preheat oven to 300°. In bowl, mix soy sauce, sherry, cornstarch and garlic. Place roast in shallow pan and pour mixture over meat. Roast 4 hours or until desired doneness.   **Servings: 6**

"...Yankee pot roast lovers move over. This is for those who want the succulent taste of the wild game version..."

Soup Mix Venison Pot Roast

Serve with mixed green salad and fresh bread or Yorkshire pudding.

4-5 lb. venison roast	8 carrots, peeled and quartered
1 Tbsp. olive oil	6 large potatoes, peeled and quartered
1 pkg. dry onion/mushroom soup mix	2 Tbsp. flour or cornstarch
1 cup water	2 Tbsp. water

Preheat oven to 350°. Heat olive oil in roaster, add venison and brown on all sides. Add soup mix and water. Roast 2 hours, turning every 20 minutes. Add additional water if needed. Add carrots and potatoes, lower temperature to 325° and cook until vegetables are tender. Place meat and vegetables in separate baking dish and keep warm in oven. Skim fat from juices in roaster and heat in saucepan over medium flame. In small bowl, mix flour and water. Slowly add to liquid in saucepan. Bring to boil, reduce heat and let simmer until thickened. Serve with roast and vegetables.

Servings: 6-8

Alternate Meats: Elk, moose, antelope, caribou, deer

Glazed carrots top off this roast. Glazed carrots are easy to make in the pressure cooker.

Venison Pot Roast Italian-Style

Spoon sauce over angel hair pasta and serve with crusty bread.

5 lb. venison roast, boneless
Lawry's Seasoned Pepper, sprinkle
1 pkg. dry spaghetti sauce mix
1 can Italian-style stewed tomatoes

Place roast in crock pot. Sprinkle with Lawry's pepper and spaghetti mix. Add stewed tomatoes, cover and cook on low for 6 hours. **Servings: 6**

Alternate Meats: Elk, moose, antelope, caribou, deer

Rolled Venison Roast

Serve with a mixed green salad, boiled potatoes and steamed fresh vegetable.

1 pkg. dry onion soup mix
4 lb. venison roast, boneless
$1/4$ cup sherry

Preheat oven to 325°. Spread dry soup mix over roast and roll on double sheets of aluminum foil. Pour sherry over roast and seal foil edges carefully. Place on cookie sheet and bake 2-3 hours.

Servings: 4-6

Alternate Meats: Elk, moose, antelope, caribou, deer, buffalo

> ## "...These roasts are a piece of cake..."

> ## "...This recipe is a snap to prepare, especially after a day of hunting..."

Chow Down Venison Pot Roast

This "down home" pot roast is delicious with baked applesauce, biscuits and a spinach salad.

4 lb. venison roast	$1/2$ tsp. paprika
1 Tbsp. olive oil	1 bay leaf
Salt and pepper	1 tsp. dry minced onion
1 tsp. garlic powder	1 cup water

Heat pressure cooker and add oil. Brown meat on all sides. Season with salt, pepper, garlic and paprika. Add bay leaf, onion and water. Close lid securely and set pressure regulator. Pressure cook 45 minutes with regulator rocking gently. Let pressure drop. Remove roast and use juices to make gravy. **Servings: 4-6**

Alternate Meats: Elk, moose, antelope, caribou, deer

Big Game Recipes...Steaks & Roasts

Horseradish Venison Roast

Sliced and served with horseradish sauce, this savory roast presides over an assortment of fresh vegetable side dishes and a salad.

4-5 lb. venison roast
3 Tbsp. vinegar
4 Tbsp. brown sugar
Salt and pepper
1 can beef broth

4 cloves, whole
2 bay leaves
2 cloves garlic, sliced
6 stalks celery, chopped

Preheat oven to 350°. Place roast and all remaining ingredients in covered Dutch oven and roast 3-4 hours. Slice and serve with *Horseradish Sauce*. **Servings: 6**

Alternate Meats: Elk, moose, antelope, caribou, deer

Horseradish Sauce

$1/2$ cup horseradish
1 tsp. dry mustard
$1/2$ cup mayonnaise
$1/4$ tsp. paprika

Combine all ingredients in saucepan and heat through. Serve over sliced meat.

"...On a snowy winter evening, this dish will surely warm the coldest buckaroos..."

Chuckwagon Venison Roast with Vegetables

Serve with a tossed green salad and fresh rolls or sourdough bread.

4-5 lb. venison roast
Salt and pepper
1 Tbsp. olive oil
$1/4$ cup flour
$2^1/4$ cups buttermilk
2 Tbsp. beef bouillon, instant

$1/2$ tsp. sweet basil, rubbed
$1/2$ tsp. thyme, rubbed
6 medium red potatoes, quartered
6 carrots, peeled and cut into chunks
1 large Spanish onion, cut into wedges
2 cups broccoli flowerettes

Preheat oven to 350°. In roaster, salt and pepper meat and brown on all sides in olive oil. Remove meat and add flour to drippings. Cook and stir until brown. Add buttermilk, instant bouillon and remaining seasonings. Cook and stir until gravy thickens. Return roast to pan and spoon gravy over top. Cover and roast 1 hour. Add potatoes, carrots and onion and bake 45 minutes or until vegetables are tender. Add broccoli and bake 10 minutes. **Servings: 6**

Alternate Meats: Elk, moose, antelope, caribou, deer

"...This hunk of meat is absolutely delicious, and not difficult to make..."

Buffalo Roast Delight

Expecting a crowd? This hunk of meat is absolutely delicious, and not difficult to make. Serve with baked pears, boiled potatoes, broccoli and fresh bread.

6 cloves garlic, whole
$1/2$ cup canola oil
1 tsp. paprika
1 tsp. black pepper
$1/8$ tsp. sage, ground

$1/4$ tsp. oregano
10 lb. buffalo roast
Lawry's Mesquite Marinade
2 cans beef broth

Preheat oven to 350°. Press garlic cloves and save all meat and juice in small bowl. Add oil, paprika, pepper, sage and oregeno and stir well. Pour onto roast a little at a time and massage into meat vigorously. With long-bladed knife, poke holes in meat and massage with oil until all oil mixture is used. Place roast in large roaster and pour $1/2$ bottle Lawry's Mesquite Marinade over roast. Add beef broth to pan; do not pour over meat. Roast 1 hour. Turn roast and cook 2 more hours at 300°. Strain juice from pan, skim off fat and heat before serving with meat.

Servings: 12-14

Alternate Meats: Elk, moose

Wild West Roast Loin Supreme

Garnish with parsley and serve with mashed potatoes, tossed green salad and fresh-sliced tomatoes.

2 lb. antelope loin
Pepper, fresh ground, sprinkle
2 cans beef broth
2 cloves garlic, pressed
4 beef bouillon cubes

Preheat oven to 300°. Place meat in pan and sprinkle with pepper. Add 1 can beef broth. Marinate 4 hours in refrigerator, turning every hour. Remove meat. Add 1 can beef broth and pressed garlic and mix well. Return meat to dish and marinate for another 4 hours. Place meat and marinade in covered glass baking dish or roasting pan and cook 1 hour. Turn roast and cook 1 more hour until rare to medium-rare. Strain juice into saucepan. Add bouillon cubes and boil until cubes dissolve. Serve over meat and potatoes. **Servings: 4**

Alternate Meats: Elk, moose, caribou, deer

Cooking Tips: 2 cups stock may be used instead of second can of beef broth.

An excellent means of cooking wild game with domestic is slow-roasting it in a covered roasting pan with plenty of juices. Juices are strained afterward and semi-frozen to remove fats. See *Lamb What Am* for a delicious combination of lamb and antelope.

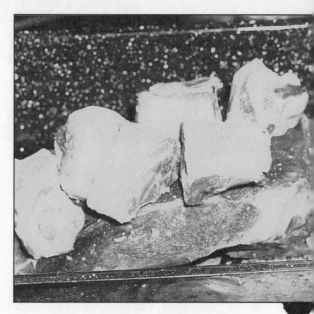

Lamb What Am

This is a succulent partnership of wild and tame meats. For a gourmet presentation, alternate thin slices of lamb and antelope on your favorite serving dish and garnish with parsley.

3-5 lb. lamb roast	Paprika, generous sprinkling
3-5 lb. antelope pieces	Pepper, dash
Salt, sprinkle	Teriyaki marinade
1 can beef broth	6-8 carrots, peeled and sliced in half crosswise
Garlic powder, generous sprinkling	6-8 small potatoes, peeled or scrubbed
Onion powder, light sprinkling	

Preheat oven to 325°. Wash and lightly salt lamb roast. Put in roaster with antelope pieces and top with beef broth, garlic powder, onion powder, paprika and pepper. Roast, uncovered, 1/2 hour. Apply several splashes of teriyaki marinade and ladle juices from pan over meat. To prevent meat from drying out, baste every 15 minutes and turn antelope. Roast 1 1/2 hours and add carrots and potatoes. If liquid level becomes low and antelope pieces are not sufficiently submerged in juices, add another can of beef broth or 2 cups water and 4 beef bouillon cubes. Dish is done when carrots are soft. Slice roast and antelope meat into serving pieces and serve with juice from roaster. **Servings: 6**

Cooking Tips: To remove fat from juice, strain juice into pot and put in freezer. The fat will rise and harden. Lift off disk of fat and discard. Reheat juice before serving.

Leg O'Lope

Mashed potatoes with gravy, buttered peas and a green salad with a light vinegar and oil dressing turn this dish into a feast.

1 antelope hind quarter	4 Tbsp. soy sauce
2 gallons cold water	1 cup teriyaki marinade
1/2 cup white vinegar	2-3 cloves garlic, sliced
2 lb. fresh beef fat	Paprika, sprinkle
3/4 cup sherry, port or Madeira wine	Pepper, sprinkle

Leave antelope hind quarter intact, but trim lower hock well into haunch area. Soak haunch in water and vinegar for 4 hours. Remove, rinse and dry with clean cloth. Remove all loose tissue. Lard meat by making deep incisions in haunch with long-bladed knife and inserting pieces of fresh beef fat. Place meat in roasting pan and slowly pour wine over haunch so it enters incisions; add soy sauce and teriyaki marinade. (Optional is the addition of 1/2 cup of beef broth to this marinade.) Season meat by forcing bits of garlic cloves into incisions or sprinkling with garlic powder. Dust with paprika and pepper and let sit for 6-24 hours. Cook haunch over low heat on gas grill or over coals. Make sure grill does not get too hot or outer layer of haunch may become overcooked. Spoon marinade left in roasting pan over roast as it cooks, but don't overdo this or marinade will run off roast and into coals. Turn roast and baste. **Servings: 8**

Alternate Meats: Deer

Cooking Tips: Larding meat will not cause it to become greasy or fatty because the grill will cook most of the fatty meat down. For those concerned with fat, the beef fat can be removed during last 10-20 minutes of cooking and discarded; otherwise it can be left intact. Lard or salt pork may be used in place of beef fat.

This meat should be served in relays. Slice off, lengthwise, a layer from haunch that is about medium and cut that layer into serving pieces. Turn roast so uncooked meat receives heat and slice off another cooked piece from exposed layer of haunch. Marinate top of haunch and let cook. Repeat entire process until whole haunch is cooked and served.

"...For a casual get-together with friends, keep this easy-to-prepare dish in mind..."

Barbecued Venison Roast

Sweet corn, coleslaw and fresh-baked bread complete this meal.

4-5 lb. venison roast
2 cups barbecue sauce
1 large onion, sliced
Salt and pepper

Preheat oven to 300°. Place roast in large roaster and top with 1 cup barbecue sauce. Sprinkle with onion, salt and pepper. Cover and roast 15 minutes. Spoon remaining sauce over meat. Cover and roast 2-3 hours until done.

Servings: 6

Alternate Meats: Elk, moose, antelope, caribou, deer

Big Game Recipes...Steaks & Roasts

Wild Boar Roast Sherwood Forest

This dish is complete as is, although French bread on the side is nice.

8-10 lb. wild boar roast, boned	1/4 tsp. Virginia Olson Savory
Pure lard	Seasonings Bake Blend
1 qt. stock or equivalent chicken broth	4 cubes beef bouillon
8 bay leaves	1-2 tsp. Lawry's Seasoned Pepper
8 cloves garlic	6 carrots, peeled and coined
1/8 tsp. marjoram	4 potatoes, peeled and cubed
1/8 tsp. tarragon	

Preheat oven to 300°. Brown meat in hot lard in large roasting pan. Lard may be wiped out before further cooking or left in pan. Add stock, bay leaves, garlic, marjoram, tarragon, savory seasonings and beef bouillon cubes to roast in roaster. Roast 3 hours. Turn oven down to 250°, add Lawry's Seasoned Pepper and cook until well done. When meat is done, pressure cook carrots and potatoes until tender. Add to roaster and cook only 15 minutes longer to marry vegetables with meat and juices. **Servings: Up to 12**

Cooking Tips: Turn roast every 1/2 hour to prevent it from drying out. Add stock or broth as needed.

Oven-Barbecued Javelina

Steamed broccoli and oven-roasted potatoes complete this tasty meal.

5 lb. javelina roast
2 qts. water
3 bouillon cubes
2 cans chicken broth
1 tsp. garlic powder
1 bottle commercial barbecue sauce

Preheat oven to 300°. Place meat in roasting pan with all ingredients except barbecue sauce. Cook 4 hours, basting often. Remove roast and strain liquid, saving 1 cup. Return roast to pan and top with barbecue sauce. Pour 1 cup of strained liquid around roast in pan. Reduce oven temperature to 250° and cook 1 hour.

Servings: 6

Alternate Meats: Wild boar, bear

> **"...Perhaps English cooks of three and four centuries ago never made a boar roast like this one, but it's good all the same..."**

This is a fine game meat roast. Note the lean cut of meat from this haunch. It will be served with mashed potatoes and green beans.

Buffalo Rump Roast

Use the gravy from this roast over mashed potatoes and serve with carrots and peas, a salad and fresh-baked rolls.

6-10 lb. buffalo roast, with or without bone	3-4 cloves garlic, sliced
Salt pork or beef fat or both	White or black pepper, sprinkle
3 cups water	Paprika, sprinkle
1 tsp. Worcestershire sauce	Onion salt, sprinkle
2 Tbsp. soy sauce	1/2 cup sherry
4 Tbsp. teriyaki marinade	1 can beef broth
2 beef bouillon cubes	

Preheat oven to 300°. If larded meat is desired, deeply score roast and insert strips of salt pork or beef fat. Soak roast in cold water for 1 hour. Rinse and dry. Check for final trim. Place water, Worcestershire sauce, soy sauce, teriyaki marinade, bouillon cubes and garlic in roaster. Add meat. Sprinkle with pepper, paprika and onion salt. Roast, covered, for 3 hours, basting every 1/2 hour. Pour sherry and broth on meat. Turn oven down to 250°. Cook until tender. **Servings: 8**

Alternate Meats: Bear, elk, moose, antelope, caribou, deer, mountain sheep, muskox

Cooking Tips: Remember to save and degrease gravy for sauce.

Far East Venison Roast

This roast can be served with wild rice, sautéd zucchini with grated Parmesan cheese and a fresh tossed salad.

5 lb. venison roast
2 cloves garlic, sliced
1 large onion, sliced
1 Tbsp. olive oil
2 cups strong black coffee
2 cups water
Salt and pepper
1/4 tsp. paprika

Preheat oven to 250°. Score venison roast and insert slivers of garlic and onion. Refrigerate overnight. Heat oil in roaster, add meat and brown all sides. Add coffee and water. Cover tightly and bake 5-6 hours. One hour before removing meat from oven, season with salt, pepper and paprika. **Servings: 6**

Alternate Meats: Elk, moose, antelope, caribou, deer, buffalo

Glazed carrots, mashed potatoes and game roast slices provide an "all-American" meal most people truly enjoy. A little game gravy will top off this dish just right.

Venison Blade Roast in Foil

Serve with boiled potatoes, cornbread and Italian salad.

2 onions	2 Tbsp. lemon juice
1 cup celery, diced	1 Tbsp. dry mustard
2 Tbsp. margarine or butter	4-6 lb. venison blade roast
3/4 cup catsup	Salt and pepper
2 Tbsp. vinegar	8 celery stalks, quartered
2 Tbsp. Worcestershire sauce	6 carrots, peeled and quartered
1 cup water	1 green pepper, thinly sliced
2 Tbsp. brown sugar	

Preheat oven to 325°. Dice 1 onion and sauté with diced celery in skillet with margarine until tender. Add catsup, vinegar, Worcestershire sauce, water, brown sugar, lemon juice and dry mustard and simmer 20 minutes. Pour 1/2 of mixture into center of double sheets of heavy foil, 3 ft. long. Place roast in center and add salt, pepper, 1 sliced onion, quartered celery stalks, carrots and green pepper. Pour remaining skillet mixture over roast and close foil around meat, sealing all edges. Bake on cookie sheet for 2-3 hours, depending on size of roast. **Servings: 6**

Alternate Meats: Elk, moose, antelope, caribou, deer, buffalo

> ## "...For special occasions with friends and family..."

Dutch Oven Boiled Game Meat

This recipe is especially popular throughout the Northeastern states. Serve with a wilted spinach salad and fresh-baked French bread.

2 lb. vension roast	8-10 carrots, peeled and halved
1 Tbsp. olive oil	1 cabbage head, quartered
Peppercorns	6-8 potatoes, peeled
Water	4 turnips, peeled
Beef broth or stock	1 lb. mushrooms, halved

Braise meat well in open Dutch oven with oil and peppercorns. Add 50/50 mixture of water and broth or water and stock. Liquid level should come halfway to meat. Cover and simmer 3 hours, turning meat at least four times. Remove meat and strain juices. Return meat and juices to pan. Add stock or broth if necessary. Add carrots, cabbage, potatoes, turnips. Cook until carrots are tender. Add mushrooms and cook until mushrooms are done. **Servings: 6**

Alternate Meats: Any red game meat.

Big Game Recipes...Gameburger

Venison-Filled Squash

Boiled red potatoes and a fresh fruit salad are a delicious addition to this dish.

2 acorn squash, medium	1/4 cup onion, diced
1 lb. ground venison	1/2 tsp. salt
Salt, sprinkle	2 Tbsp. brown sugar
Pepper, sprinkle	1/4 cup dry Italian bread crumbs
6 slices bacon, cut up	1 Tbsp. butter

Microwave whole acorn squash on high 8-10 minutes. Let stand 5 minutes. In skillet, season venison with salt and pepper and brown with bacon and onion. Drain on paper towel. Cut squash lengthwise and discard seeds and fibers. Scoop out squash from shells and set shells aside. In small bowl, whip squash with 1/2 tsp. salt and brown sugar until fluffy. Combine with vension mixture and spoon into squash shells. In small bowl, mix bread crumbs and butter and heat in microwave until melted. Microwave stuffed shells on medium 3 minutes. Top filled shells with bread crumbs and heat another 5 minutes.   Servings: 4

Alternate Meats: Elk, moose, antelope, caribou, deer

"...A delicious autumn meal..."

Spicy Venison-Stuffed Tomatoes

Cool off this spicy dish with a garden salad, fruit plate and toasted rolls.

6 tomatoes, large	1/2 tsp. oregano, rubbed
1 cup dry Italian bread crumbs	1/2 tsp. sweet basil, rubbed
1/2 cup chicken broth	2 Tbsp. parsley, chopped
Salt, sprinkle	1 lb. ground venison
Pepper, sprinkle	1/2 cup onion, minced
1/2 tsp. garlic powder	1/2 lb. fresh mushrooms

Preheat oven to 350°. Slice off tops of tomatoes. Carefully scoop out pulp and save. Invert shells to drain on paper towel. Mix bread crumbs, tomato pulp, chicken broth and herbs in small bowl. Brown venison, onion and mushrooms in skillet and drain on paper towel. Mix with bread crumb mixture and spoon into tomatoes. Don't pack tomatoes tightly; mound mixture slightly. Sprinkle with additional bread crumbs. Place in baking dish and bake 20-30 minutes.   Servings: 6

Alternate Meats: Elk, moose, antelope, caribou, deer

Venison Cabbage Rolls

This dish is sure to delight your family when served with twice-baked potatoes and garlic bread.

1 head cabbage, large
2 lb. ground venison
2 tsp. dry onion, minced
1 tsp. garlic powder
Salt, sprinkle
Pepper, sprinkle
1 tsp. horseradish
1 can tomato juice, large
1 can tomato soup
2 Tbsp. low-fat cottage cheese

Core cabbage and separate leaves. Heat large pot of water and blanch leaves until wilted. Place on paper towel to dry. In large bowl, mix venison, onion, garlic powder, salt, pepper and horseradish. Form a roll with 3-4 Tbsp. of meat mixture. Wrap each roll in a cabbage leaf. Pour tomato juice and soup into pressure cooker and stir. Place rolls into pressure cooker, leaving room for liquid to boil. Cover and cook 30 minutes with pressure regulator rocking gently. Let pressure drop. Serve cabbage rolls with cottage cheese spooned over top.   Servings: 4-6

Alternate Meats: Elk, moose, antelope, caribou, deer

Always microwave browned burger meat for a minute or two before using it in a recipe. Microwaving reduces leftover fats and expels some moisture.

Cooking sausage for any wild game dish demands care. It should first be fried and then microwaved briefly on a paper towel on high to further reduce fat content.

Venison-Stuffed Green Peppers

These are tasty with a side salad and hard rolls.

6 green peppers, large	1 tsp. onion powder
1 lb. ground venison	Salt, sprinkle
1 tsp. garlic powder	Pepper, sprinkle
2 tsp. mustard	2 tsp. horseradish
1/2 cup catsup	1/2 cup cheddar cheese, cubed
2 Tbsp. Worcestershire sauce	

Preheat oven to 325°. Slice off tops of peppers and scoop out insides. In large mixing bowl, mix venison with remaining ingredients. Stuff peppers with mixture. Stand peppers in shallow baking dish with 1/4-inch water. Bake 1 hour or until meat mixture is done.   Servings: 6

Alternate Meats: Elk, moose, antelope, caribou, deer

> **"...This is a simple dish that can be cooked in little time with little effort..."**

> **"...Stuff yourself with this hearty meal..."**

Stuffed Zucchini

This dish hits the spot when served with rice or potatoes and hot, fresh bread.

6 zucchini, medium	1 tsp. garlic powder
1 lb. ground venison	1 egg, beaten
1/2 cup dry Italian bread crumbs	1 tsp. dry onion, minced
1/2 cup milk	1 tsp. oregano
Salt, sprinkle	1 cup mozzarella cheese, shredded
Pepper, sprinkle	

Preheat oven to 350°. Parboil zucchini 8-10 minutes. Cool and cut lengthwise. Scoop out pulp, leaving 1/2-inch in shell. Coarsely chop pulp. In skillet, brown venison and drain on paper towel. In mixing bowl, mix pulp with all ingredients except cheese and spoon into shells. Bake 20-25 minutes. Sprinkle cheese over filled shells and bake until cheese is bubbly.   Servings: 6

Alternate Meats: Elk, moose, antelope, caribou, deer

"...This casserole is sure to become a favorite..."

Venison Goulash

Serve with hot garlic bread and a green salad.

3 cups elbow macaroni
2 lb. ground venison
1 onion, minced
2 cloves garlic, minced
1 green pepper, minced
2 cans Italian-stewed tomatoes
1 large can tomato juice
Salt, sprinkle
Pepper, sprinkle
1 cup catsup

Cook macaroni according to package directions and drain. In skillet, brown ground venison with onion and garlic. Drain on paper towel. In large Dutch oven, mix all ingredients and bring to a boil. Reduce heat and simmer 30 minutes, stirring frequently. **Servings: 6**

Alternate Meats: Elk, moose, antelope, caribou, deer

Baked Stuffed French Loaf

Enhance the flavors in this dish with a Caesar salad.

1 lb. ground venison	5 Tbsp. butter, melted
Salt, sprinkle	2 Tbsp. flour
Pepper, sprinkle	1½ cups milk
1 tsp. garlic powder	1 tsp. Worcestershire sauce
½ cup onion, diced	1 egg
2 cloves garlic (1 clove, minced)	2 cups cheddar cheese, shredded
1 loaf French bread	1 cup olives, chopped

Preheat oven to 375°. In skillet, sauté venison, salt, pepper, garlic powder, onion and minced garlic. Drain on paper towel. Break open French bread along seam or slice off top. Remove soft center and crumble. In skillet, melt 3 Tbsp. butter; sift in flour. Stir in milk slowly, cooking until smooth and thick. Remove from heat. Add Worcestershire sauce, egg, cheese, olives, meat mixture and crumbled bread crumbs. Mix well. Fill loaf and press edges together. Rub outside of loaf with garlic clove and brush with remaining 2 Tbsp. butter. Bake 30 minutes. **Servings: 2-4**

Alternate Meats: Elk, moose, antelope, caribou, deer

Mock Stroganoff

This delightful dish should be served over rice or noodles with a garden salad or fruit plate on the side.

2 lb. ground venison	Salt, sprinkle
1 cup onion, minced	Pepper, sprinkle
1 cup celery, minced	1 can cream of chicken soup
4 cloves garlic, minced	1 can cream of mushroom soup
1 lb. fresh mushrooms, sliced	2 cups sour cream
1 tsp. butter	

Brown venison in skillet and drain on paper towel. Sauté onion, celery, garlic and mushrooms in same skillet with butter; add venison. Season with salt and pepper. Stir in soups and simmer 5-10 minutes. Add sour cream. Stir and serve over pasta or rice. **Servings: 6**

Alternate Meats: Elk, moose, antelope, caribou, deer

"...Guaranteed to tickle your taste buds..."

Pepperoni and Venison Crusty Squares

Only a tossed salad is needed to make this meal complete.

1 lb. ground venison	2-3 tomatoes, thinly sliced
½ cup onion, minced	Salt, sprinkle
2 cups zucchini, sliced	Pepper, sprinkle
1 tsp. butter	1 tsp. oregano, rubbed
1 loaf frozen bread dough, thawed	1 cup cheddar cheese, grated
1 cup pepperoni, thinly sliced	

Preheat oven to 375°. Brown venison and onion in skillet. Drain on paper towel. In same skillet, sauté zucchini in butter. Drain on paper towel. Roll bread dough to ¼-inch thickness. Spoon venison mixture over dough. Top with zucchini. Add pepperoni slices. Top with tomatoes and sprinkle with salt, pepper and oregano. Bake 30 minutes or until dough is browned. Sprinkle with cheese and bake until cheese is melted and bubbly. **Servings: 6**

Alternate Meats: Elk, moose, antelope, caribou, deer

Green Chili Hamburgers

*Top with sliced tomato, onion and avocado
and serve on fresh hamburger buns.*

2 lb. ground venison
1 tsp. garlic powder
Salt, sprinkle
Pepper, sprinkle
1 small onion, minced
1 4-oz. can diced green chilies, drained

Mix all ingredients in large bowl and form into
patties. Broil on both sides until desired doneness. **Servings: 6**

Alternate Meats: Elk, moose, antelope, caribou, deer

Mock Venison Wellington

This meal is best served with a fruit salad.

1 lb. ground venison
1/2 cup green onions, sliced
1 clove garlic, minced
1 cup broccoli, steamed
1 cup low-fat mozzarella cheese, shredded
1/2 cup sour cream
Salt, sprinkle
Pepper, sprinkle
2 8-oz. cans crescent dinner rolls

Preheat oven to 350°. Brown ground venison, green onions and garlic in skillet.
Drain on paper towel and return to skillet. Add broccoli, cheese, sour cream, salt
and pepper. Simmer 5-10 minutes. Separate dough into 8 long rectangles. On
ungreased cookie sheet, overlap long sides of 2 rectangles 1/2-inch and press edges
to seal. Spoon meat mixture into center of dough. Bring long edges over filling and
seal. Repeat with all rectangles. Bake 20-25 minutes. **Servings: 4**

Alternate Meats: Elk, moose, antelope, caribou, deer

The great American cheeseburger is even greater when
made with rare gameburger.

"...American side dishes won't do for this meal..."

Korean-Style Venison Burgers

Serve with a rice dish and crusty bread.

2 lb. ground venison
4 Tbsp. brown sugar
2 Tbsp. sesame oil
4 Tbsp. soy sauce
2 Tbsp. toasted sesame seeds, crushed
1/2 cup green onions, sliced
2 cloves garlic, minced
Salt, sprinkle
Pepper, sprinkle

Combine all ingredients in bowl and form into
large patties. Grill, broil or fry until desired
doneness. **Servings: 6**

Alternate Meats: Elk, moose, antelope, caribou, deer

"...A burger by any other name is still a burger..."

Chinese-Style Hamburgers

For added zing, serve on onion rolls with coleslaw on the side.

2 lb. ground venison
1/2 lb. mushrooms, sliced
1 cup water chestnuts, minced
2 Tbsp. cornstarch
6 Tbsp. soy sauce
3 Tbsp. sherry
1/2 tsp. salt
1/2 tsp. pepper
2 Tbsp. brown sugar
3 cloves garlic, minced
1/4 tsp. ginger

In large bowl, mix meat, mushrooms, water chestnuts and cornstarch. In small
bowl, mix soy sauce, sherry, salt, pepper, brown sugar, garlic and ginger. Combine
meat and spice mixture and form into patties. Broil on both sides until desired
doneness. **Servings: 6**

Alternate Meats: Elk, moose, antelope, caribou, deer

Big Game Recipes...Gameburger

"...There's nothing to this little recipe..."

Lamburger/Lope on the Grate

For a tasty outdoor barbecue, serve on buns with a slice of onion and tomato.

1 lb. lamburger
1 lb. ground antelope
1/4 tsp. garlic powder
1/8 tsp. oregano
1/8 tsp. pepper
Paprika, dash

Mix all ingredients in large bowl and form into patties. Cook patties over hot coals until cooked through.   **Servings: 4**

Cooking Tips: Lamburger is very fatty, but when mixed with an equal amount of ground antelope, the combination is perfect. Cooking over hot coals reduces the fat content of the lamburger.

With only a touch of fat, these gameburgers are juicy and delicious. Cooked on a gas grill, they're a real treat.

Venison Hamburgers and Vegetables in Foil

This campfire dish can be eaten right out of the foil and served with bread and butter.

2 lb. ground venison
Salt, sprinkle
Pepper, sprinkle
1 tsp. garlic powder
1 large onion, sliced
6 carrots, peeled and quartered
4 potatoes, sliced thick

Preheat oven to 325°. Form venison into four patties. Place each patty on double sheets of aluminum foil. Sprinkle with salt, pepper and garlic powder. Layer onion, carrots and potatoes over each patty. Seal foil around meat. Bake on cookie sheet 1 hour.   **Servings: 4**

Alternate Meats: Elk, moose, antelope, caribou, deer, buffalo

Cooking Tips: 1-2 Tbsp. of Lawry's Lemon Pepper Marinade may be poured over stacked meat and vegetables before cooking as an alternative to spices.

These foil packages can be cooked in the campfire coals if turned every 10-15 minutes.

Venison-Roquefort Stuffed Hamburgers

Impress your family with this filling dish served with Caesar salad and scalloped potatoes.

2 lb. ground venison
Salt, sprinkle
Pepper, sprinkle
1 tsp. garlic powder
1 Tbsp. Worcestershire sauce
3 Tbsp. soy sauce
16 large fresh mushrooms, sliced
6 tsp. Roquefort cheese, crumbled

Preheat oven to 350°. Season venison with salt, pepper, garlic powder, Worcestershire sauce and soy sauce. Mix well. Divide into 12 patties. Top 6 patties with mushrooms and 1 tsp. cheese. Cover with remaining 6 patties and seal edges. Place patties on metal rack in baking pan. Bake 10 minutes. Turn patties over and bake 10 more minutes or until desired doneness.   **Servings: 6**

Alternate Meats: Elk, moose, antelope, caribou, deer

"...Set your mouth on fire with this dish..."

Louisiana Venison Burgers

Serve on toasted onion rolls with cold sliced tomatoes, onions and pickles.

1 1/4 lb. ground venison
1/4 cup green onions, sliced
1/2 tsp. Lawry's Seasoned Salt
1/4 tsp. oregano, rubbed
1 egg
1/2 tsp. Tabasco sauce
1/4 tsp. thyme, rubbed
1/2 tsp. Lawry's Garlic Powder
1/4 tsp. sweet basil, rubbed

In large mixing bowl, combine all ingredients. Shape into 4 patties. Broil 5-10 minutes on each side until desired doneness.   **Servings: 4**

Alternate Meats: Elk, moose, antelope, caribou, deer

Paprika Venison Burgers

With buttered noodles and a side salad, this dish is complete.

2 lb. ground venison	1 Tbsp. flour
1 egg	1 cup tomato juice
Salt, sprinkle	1 Tbsp. paprika
Pepper, sprinkle	1 tsp. garlic powder
1/2 cup dry Italian bread crumbs	1 tsp. Worcestershire sauce
1/2 cup milk	1 can cream of vegetable soup
1/4 cup onion, minced	1 cup sour cream
1 Tbsp. butter	

In large bowl, mix venison, egg, salt, pepper, bread crumbs, milk and onion. Shape into patties and brown on both sides in skillet. Remove patties and drain on paper towel. Melt butter in skillet and stir in flour, making a paste. Add tomato juice, paprika, garlic powder and Worcestershire sauce. Simmer 2-3 minutes, stirring. Return patties to skillet and simmer 11-20 minutes. Place patties on serving platter. Add soup and sour cream to mixture in skillet and heat, stirring constantly. Pour sauce over patties. **Servings: 6**

Alternate Meats: Elk, moose, antelope, caribou, deer

Crock Pot Venison Meatloaf

This dish is delicious served with a garden salad, corn and fresh rolls.

2 lb. ground venison
2 eggs
2 tsp. mustard
2 tsp. dry onion, minced
2 tsp. Lawry's Lemon Pepper Marinade
2 tsp. horseradish
1/2 cup catsup
1/2 cup celery, diced

Combine all ingredients in large bowl and shape into loaf. Place in crock pot and cover. Cook on low for 6 hours. **Servings: 6**

Alternate Meats: Elk, moose, antelope, caribou, deer

"...Let your crock pot do the work..."

"...This chopped steak is no 'chopped liver'..."

Game-Style Chopped Sirloin Steak

Serve this dish with classic American side dishes such as french fries, fried onions or potato salad.

2 lb. ground venison
Garlic powder, sprinkle
Paprika, sprinkle
1/4 oz. soy sauce

Spice meat with garlic powder, paprika and soy sauce. Shape into oblong steaks, not patties. Cook on gas grill or over hot coals with smoke chips until cooked through. **Servings: 4**

Alternate Meats: Elk, moose, antelope, caribou, deer

Cooking Tips: Meat may be finished with barbecue sauce.

Teriyaki Venison Burgers with Bacon

For an interesting change, serve on toasted buns with rice and a garden salad.

12 slices bacon	2 Tbsp. honey
2 lb. ground venison	2 Tbsp. lemon juice
Salt, sprinkle	2 Tbsp. white wine
Pepper, sprinkle	1 clove garlic, minced
1/4 cup soy sauce	1/4 tsp. ginger, ground

Preheat oven to 350°. Place bacon on metal rack in baking pan. Bake until bacon is almost crisp. Sprinkle venison with salt and pepper and form into 6 patties. Wrap each patty in 2 slices of bacon and secure with toothpicks. Place on metal rack in baking pan. Combine remaining ingredients in large bowl, pour over venison patties and refrigerate overnight. Drain and clean rack and pan. Return patties to metal rack in baking pan and bake 10 minutes or until desired doneness. **Servings: 6**

Alternate Meats: Elk, moose, antelope, caribou, deer

Bacon slices placed on a metal rack in a baking pan can be cooked in the oven. See *Teriyaki Venison Burgers with Bacon* for a delicious main dish.

Big Game Recipes...Gameburger

A meatloaf prepared in a ring-style microwave dish is simple to prepare. Here, hard-boiled eggs sliced in half were placed on top of the meat. It will be covered with another ring of meat.

Apple Meatloaf

Make a colorful fruit salad to enhance the flavor of this meatloaf.

2 lb. ground venison
2 cups dry stuffing mix
2 cups apple, minced
1 egg, beaten
1 Tbsp. dry mustard
1/4 cup onion, minced
1 Tbsp. horseradish
1/2 cup catsup

Preheat oven to 350°. Mix all ingredients in large bowl and place in loaf pan. Bake 45 minutes, draining when necessary. Meatloaf will pull away from edges when done.   **Servings: 6**

Alternate Meats: Elk, moose, antelope, caribou, deer

"...This may be *Just Another Meatloaf*, but it's quick and easy to make and is sure to find a number of fans at the dinner table..."

Just Another Meatloaf

Serve with baked potato and green beans.

2 lb. pre-spiced gameburger*
1 lb. ground pork
1 egg
1/4 cup fresh parsley, chopped
1/2 tsp. marjoram
1/2 cup dry milk

Preheat oven to 325°. In large bowl, mix gameburger and pork. Strip away majority of pork fat if grinding own. Add egg, parsley, marjoram and milk. Mix well using a potato masher. Bake 1 hour; reduce heat to 250° and continue cooking until done.   **Servings: 5**

*See Chapter 18 for information on pre-spiced gameburger.

Camper's Supper

This camper's meal is a tasty treat when served with vegetable soup and hot cornbread.

2 lb. ground venison
Salt, sprinkle
Pepper, sprinkle
1 tsp. garlic powder
1 head cabbage
3 cups carrots, peeled and shredded
4 cups potatoes, shredded
1 large onion, sliced
6 slices Velveeta cheese

Preheat oven to 350°. Season venison with salt, pepper and garlic powder. Mix well. Form 6 patties. Place each patty on one cabbage leaf on a double sheet of foil. Divide carrots, potatoes, onion and cheese slices evenly over patties and top each with another cabbage leaf. Seal foil around each patty and bake 30-45 minutes.

Servings: 6

"...This is a must for any camping trip..."

Alternate Meats: Elk, moose, antelope, caribou, deer

Cooking Tips: These can be cooked in the coals from a campfire. Cover the foil packages with coals and cook 15 minutes. Move coals and turn patties. Cook another 15 minutes. Remove and check for doneness.

Mixed Meatloaf

For variety, serve this dish with corn on the cob, baked potatoes and a tossed salad.

2 lb. non-fat gameburger*	Milk
1/4 lb. sausage, sliced	1 egg
1 lb. ground beef, lean	1/2 cup onion, diced
4-6 bacon strips, chopped	1/4 tsp. pepper
3 slices bread, white	1/2 bunch parsley, chopped

Preheat oven to 350°. In large bowl, mix all meats together. Moisten bread in milk. Add bread and egg to meat mixture. Add onion, pepper and parsley and mix well. Place in casserole dish and bake 30 minutes. Drain excess juices. Lower heat to 300° and bake until done. Do not overcook.   **Servings: 4-6**

Cooking Tips: 1/2 or 1 lb. of ground pork may be added to meat mixture.

*See Chapter 18 for information on preparing non-fat gameburger.

> ## "...Cold meatloaf makes excellent sandwich meat..."

Chinese-Style Meatloaf

Stir-fried vegetables are a delicious addition to this oriental-flavored dish.

2 lb. ground venison	1 can cream of mushroom soup
1 cup celery, chopped	1 can cream of chicken soup
1 cup apple juice	Salt, sprinkle
2 tsp. soy sauce	Pepper, sprinkle
1 onion, diced	1 can Chinese noodles
1 cup rice, uncooked	

Preheat oven to 375°. Combine all ingredients except Chinese noodles in casserole dish. Bake 30-45 minutes, draining liquid when necessary. Sprinkle on noodles and bake additional 20-25 minutes.   **Servings: 6-8**

Alternate Meats: Elk, moose, antelope, caribou, deer

Microwave Gameloaf

Serve with baked beans and a gelatin salad.

- 3 lb. non-fat gameburger*
- 1/3 cup Lawry's Mesquite Marinade
- 1/3 onion, diced
- 1 clove garlic, chopped
- 1/8 cup celery, chopped
- 1/8 cup parsley, chopped

In large bowl, thoroughly mix all ingredients. Shape into ring on microwave dish. Use ring-mold style microwave dish if available. Cook 20 minutes at 50% power. Turn dish after 10 minutes. Cut into meatloaf to check for doneness. If needed, microwave in 5-minute intervals at 50% power until meatloaf is cooked through. For an evenly cooked meatloaf, turn over after first 10 minutes of cooking, being careful not to break meatloaf apart.   **Servings: 6**

Cooking Tips: Instead of Lawry's Mesquite Marinade, mesquite-flavored barbecue sauce may be used.

*See Chapter 18 for information on preparing non-fat gameburger.

Venison Meatloaf

Serve with mixed vegetables, mashed potatoes and a garden salad.

- 2 lb. ground venison
- 1 tsp. garlic powder
- 1 tsp. lemon pepper
- 2 Tbsp. dry onion, minced
- 1 Tbsp. Worcestershire sauce
- 1/2 cup celery, diced
- 1/2 cup French salad dressing
- 2 Tbsp. horseradish
- 1 egg
- 1/2 cup barbecue sauce

Preheat oven to 375°. Mix all ingredients except barbecue sauce in casserole dish. Bake 1 hour, draining as necessary. Top with barbecue sauce and bake 15 minutes.   **Servings: 6**

Alternate Meats: Elk, moose, antelope, caribou, deer

Cooking Tips: For a variation, use 1/2 cup barbecue sauce and 1/2 cup diced green pepper instead of salad dressing. Form 6 individual meatloaves and bake at 350° for 30 minutes. Pour barbecue sauce over loaves and cook 10 more minutes.

A variety of meats can be used for meatloaf, including a venison and pork mix.

Big Game Recipes...Gameburger

Sweet and Sour Meatballs

*Served over rice, this is a hearty meal in itself,
but a tossed salad adds a nice touch.*

2 cups whole wheat bread crumbs
1 cup skim milk
1 tsp. garlic powder
Salt, sprinkle
Pepper, sprinkle
2 lb. ground venison

1 small onion, minced
1 cup grape jelly
2 12-oz. bottles chili sauce
$1/2$ cup water
1 cup sour cream

In large bowl, mix bread crumbs, skim milk and seasonings. Let stand 15 minutes. Add ground venison and onion. Form into meatballs the size of walnuts. Brown in skillet and drain on paper towel. In saucepan, mix grape jelly, chili sauce and water. Bring to a boil and then reduce heat to simmer. Drop meatballs into sauce and simmer 1 hour. Add sour cream and heat; do not boil.   **Servings: 6**

Alternate Meats: Elk, moose, antelope, caribou, deer

"...These saucy meatballs are a spicy taste treat..."

Venison Meatballs with Mushroom Noodles

Green beans and garlic bread complement this different-tasting dish.

1 can tomato soup
1 cup sour cream
2 lb. ground venison
1 cup dry Italian bread crumbs
Salt, sprinkle
Pepper, sprinkle
1 onion, minced
2 cloves garlic, minced

1 bay leaf
1 tsp. lemon juice
1 tsp. paprika
1 lb. pasta
$1/4$ cup almonds, slivered
1 lb. fresh mushrooms, sliced
1 tsp. butter

Mix soup and sour cream in small bowl. In large bowl, mix venison, bread crumbs, salt, pepper, onion, garlic and $1/4$ cup of soup/sour cream mixture. Mix well. Form into meatballs the size of walnuts. Brown in skillet and drain on paper towel. Return meatballs to skillet with remaining soup mixture and add bay leaf, lemon juice and paprika. Bring to a boil, cover and simmer 20 minutes, stirring occasionally. Cook and drain noodles according to package directions. Sauté almonds and mushrooms in skillet with butter until mushrooms are tender. Mix with noodles and pour onto serving platter. Pour meatballs and sauce over noodles.   **Servings: 6**

Alternate Meats: Elk, moose, antelope, caribou, deer

"...Meatballs, noodles and sauce make an excellent combination..."

Swedish Meatballs

*Served over noodles or rice,
this appetizing dish will leave you satisfied.*

2 lb. ground venison
1 tsp. lemon pepper
$1/4$ cup fresh parsley, minced
2 eggs
1 cup onion, minced
1 cup dry Italian bread crumbs
2 Tbsp. Worcestershire sauce
$1/2$ cup milk
See *Gravy for Swedish Meatballs*

Mix all ingredients in large bowl and form into meatballs the size of walnuts. Brown in skillet and drain on paper towel. Save drippings for gravy.   **Servings: 6**

Alternate Meats: Elk, moose, antelope, caribou, deer

Gravy for Swedish Meatballs

$1/4$ cup flour
Salt, sprinkle
Pepper, sprinkle
2 cups milk
$1^{1}/4$ cups sour cream

Add flour, salt and pepper to drippings left in skillet from browning *Swedish Meatballs*. Stir over medium heat 2-3 minutes. Add milk, stirring constantly until mixture begins to boil and thicken. Add sour cream and heat through. Serve over meatballs.

Venison Meatballs in Curried Tomato Sauce

These are filling when served over hot rice with steamed broccoli on the side.

1 can Italian-stewed tomatoes	Pepper, sprinkle
2 lb. ground venison	1 tsp. Lawry's Seasoned Salt
1/2 cup dry Italian bread crumbs	3 Tbsp. flour
1 onion, minced	1 Tbsp. brown sugar
Salt, sprinkle	1 tsp. curry powder

Drain 1/2 cup juice from tomatoes into large bowl and mix with meat, bread crumbs, onion, salt, pepper and seasoned salt. Form into meatballs the size of walnuts. Roll meatballs in flour. Brown in skillet and drain on paper towel. Add tomatoes, remaining juice, brown sugar and curry powder to skillet. Stir and simmer 3-5 minutes. Add meatballs and simmer 15-20 minutes, stirring occasionally.

Servings: 6

Alternate Meats: Elk, moose, antelope, caribou, deer

Barbecued Venison Meatballs

For variety, serve on Italian-style buns with condiments of your choice.

3 lb. ground venison
1 cup rice
2 eggs
3 cloves garlic, minced
1 cup onion, minced
Salt, sprinkle
Pepper, sprinkle
1 can evaporated milk
2 bottles barbecue sauce
3 onions, sliced
3 green peppers, sliced

Preheat oven to 350°. Cook rice according to package directions. In large bowl, mix first 8 ingredients. Form into meatballs the size of walnuts. Brown in skillet and drain on paper towel. Place meatballs into large baking dish and top with barbecue sauce. Add onions and green peppers. Cover and bake 1 hour. **Servings: 6**

Alternate Meats: Elk, moose, antelope, caribou, deer, buffalo

---

Venison Meatballs

This scrumptious dish is a real treat when served with rice or baked potatoes, tossed salad and bread.

2 lb. ground venison	1 egg
1 cup bread crumbs	1 tsp. garlic powder
Salt, sprinkle	1 tsp. horseradish
Pepper, sprinkle	1 Tbsp. Worcestershire sauce
2 Tbsp. dry onion, minced	1 cup tomato juice or water

Heat pressure cooker. In large bowl, mix venison, bread crumbs, salt, pepper, onion, egg, garlic powder, horseradish and Worcestershire sauce. Form into meatballs the size of walnuts. Place in pressure cooker and brown on all sides. Add tomato juice or water. Cover securely and cook 10 minutes with pressure regulator rocking gently. Remove from heat and let pressure drop. **Servings: 6**

Alternate Meats: Elk, moose, antelope, caribou, deer

Venison Porcupine Meatballs

For a well-balanced meal, serve with rice, green beans and buttered rolls.

2 lb. ground venison
1/2 cup rice, uncooked
Salt, sprinkle
Pepper, sprinkle
1 Tbsp. dry onion, minced
1 tsp. garlic powder
1 can tomato soup
1 cup tomato juice or water

In large bowl, mix venison, rice, salt, pepper, onion and garlic powder. Form into meatballs the size of walnuts. Brown in pressure cooker on all sides and drain on paper towel. Return meatballs to pressure cooker and add tomato soup and juice or water. Cover and cook 10 minutes with pressure regulator rocking gently. Remove from heat and let pressure drop. **Servings: 4-6**

Alternate Meats: Elk, moose, antelope, caribou, deer

"...Meatballs are always a hit at parties..."

When preparing gameburger for meatballs, adding a little fresh beef fat is fine, but only right before cooking. This gameburger was frozen fat-free. Fresh beef fat was added just before it was formed into meatballs.

Big Game Recipes...Ribs

Ribs can be sectioned before or after cooking, depending upon the cooking process. A meat cleaver like this one is ideal for the job.

Venison Short Ribs

These short ribs are big on taste when accompanied by a baked potato and fresh green salad.

2 lb. venison short ribs	¹/₂ tsp. paprika
2 cups flour	2 Tbsp. olive oil
Salt and pepper	1 cup water or tomato juice
1 tsp. garlic powder	1 beef bouillon cube

Cut ribs into serving pieces and soak in cold water for 15 minutes; dry on paper towel. Coat ribs with mixture of flour, salt, pepper, garlic powder and paprika. Heat pressure cooker, add olive oil and brown ribs on both sides. Drain browned ribs on paper towel. Add water or tomato juice to cooker and return ribs to cooker. Add bouillon cube, close lid securely and set pressure regulator. Cook 25 minutes with regulator rocking gently; let pressure drop. **Servings: 4**

Alternate Meats: Elk, moose, antelope, caribou, deer

> ## "...These short ribs are big on taste..."

Country Ribs For A Crowd

Coleslaw, baked beans and warm cornbread give these ribs a country flair.

10-15 lb. venison ribs	¹/₄ cup brown sugar
3 large onions, chopped	2 Tbsp. honey
3 bay leaves	1 Tbsp. celery seed
Hot water	3 cloves garlic, minced
2 cups catsup	1 tsp. oregano, rubbed
¹/₄ cup lemon juice	1 tsp. sweet basil, rubbed
¹/₄ cup orange juice	1 small can tomato sauce

Preheat oven to 300°. Cut ribs into serving pieces and soak in cold water 15 minutes; drain on paper towel. Place ribs on rack in large roasting pan. Add onions, bay leaves and enough hot water to cover ribs. Cover and roast 2¹/₂-3 hours or until meat is tender. While ribs are cooking, in saucepan combine catsup, lemon juice, orange juice, brown sugar, honey, celery seed, garlic, oregano, sweet basil and tomato sauce. Cover and simmer 1 hour or until sauce thickens and flavors are well blended. When tender, remove ribs from roasting pan and pour out water. Return ribs to roasting pan rack and cover with sauce. Roast 30 minutes to 1 hour or until sauce is set and edges begin to brown. **Servings: 8-10**

Alternate Meats: Elk, moose, antelope, caribou, deer

> ## "...Invite your friends and family over to share in this tasty treat..."

Big Game Recipes...Ribs

These ribs are being treated to a splash or two or Worcestershire sauce, an ideal pre-cooking condiment for ribs.

> "...These mouth-watering ribs are sure to stick to yours..."

Hawaiian Short Ribs

These ribs are tasty with baked beans, corn on the cob and cornbread.

3 lb. venison short ribs	2 Tbsp. white vinegar
2 Tbsp. olive oil	Salt and pepper
1 onion, thinly sliced	2 Tbsp. chopped parsley
1 tsp. garlic powder	2 Tbsp. soy sauce
1 tsp. ginger	4 Tbsp. brown sugar
2 tsp. dry mustard	1 cup water

Cut ribs into serving pieces and soak in cold water for 15 minutes; dry on paper towel. Heat pressure cooker, add olive oil and lightly sauté onions. Drain on paper towel. Brown ribs on and both sides; drain. Put remaining ingredients into cooker and add ribs and onions. Close cover securely, set pressure regulator and cook 25 minutes with pressure regulator rocking gently. Let pressure drop.   **Servings: 2-4**

Alternate Meats: Elk, moose, antelope, caribou, deer

Oven-Barbecued Ribs

Serve with coleslaw, sliced tomatoes and crusty bread for a delicious summer meal.

8-10 lb. venison ribs	1 tsp. fresh ginger root
3 cups water	1¼ cup chili sauce
2 pkgs. dry onion soup mix	⅔ cup brown sugar
⅔ cup honey	Salt and pepper
2 Tbsp. garlic, minced	2 Tbsp. molasses

Preheat oven to 375°. Cut ribs into serving pieces and soak in cold water for 30 minutes; drain on paper towel. Place ribs in large roasting pan and cover with water; boil until tender. Mix water, soup mix, honey, garlic, ginger root, chili sauce, brown sugar, salt, pepper and molasses in saucepan and simmer 10 to 20 minutes. When ribs are tender, drain and place on rack in roasting pan. Spoon or brush sauce over ribs and bake until ribs are glazed. Turn and baste ribs with remaining sauce until all sauce has been used.   **Servings: 4-6**

Alternate Meats: Elk, mooose, antelope, caribou, deer

Just Plain Deer Ribs

For a hearty meal, serve with potato salad and baked beans, the latter especially delicious with ribs.

4-5 lb. deer ribs
Teriyaki marinade
Garlic powder, sprinkle

Cut ribs into serving pieces and rub with teriyaki marinade. Sprinkle with garlic powder and let stand 4-8 hours. Cook ribs over medium coals until done. Hickory chips may be used for a smokey flavor.   **Servings: 4**

Cooking Tips: For a variation, baste ribs frequently with barbecue sauce during grilling. When grilling with barbecue sauce, keep the grill lid closed.

Whitetail buck ribs from a deer harvested in the fall are best by some standards. But for those closely watching fat intake, the fat should be trimmed from these ribs before marination.

Big Game Recipes...Ribs

Short Ribs with Noodles

Parmesan bread and a spinach salad complete this meal.

4 lb. venison short ribs
2 Tbsp. olive oil
Salt and pepper
1 tsp. garlic powder
1 onion, sliced
1 large can tomato juice
1 lb. pasta

Preheat oven to 350°. Cut ribs into serving pieces. Heat oil in skillet. Season ribs with salt, pepper and garlic powder and add to skillet with onion. Brown meat and onions and drain. Place ribs/onions in roasting pan and add tomato juice. Bake 3-4 hours or until ribs are tender. Cook pasta according to package directions and add to roaster. Bake 15-20 minutes longer. Serve liquid, ribs and pasta in soup dishes.

Servings: 6

Alternate Meats: Elk, moose, antelope, caribou, deer

Venison Ribs and Sauerkraut

Serve with fresh-steamed broccoli and warm rolls.

5-6 lb. venison ribs
Salt and pepper
2 Tbsp. olive oil
1 cup beef broth or apple cider
2 jars sauerkraut, drained
1 Tbsp. caraway seeds
1/4 cup brown sugar
4 apples, quartered

Preheat oven to 375°. Cut ribs into 4-inch pieces and soak in cold water for 30 minutes; drain on paper towel. Season ribs with salt and pepper and brown in heated skillet coated with light oil; place in roasting pan. Add beef broth or apple cider. Cover and bake 1 1/2 hours. Add sauerkraut, caraway seeds, brown sugar and apples. Cover and bake until apples are tender.

Servings: 6

Alternate Meats: Elk, moose, antelope, caribou, deer

Microwave Pork and Buck Ribs Over the Coals

These are mouth watering with hot, buttered corn on the cob and a fluffy baked potato.

2-3 lb. pork ribs
2-3 lb. deer ribs
3 Tbsp. olive or canola oil
Garlic powder, sprinkle
Oregano, sprinkle
Paprika, sprinkle
1 cup Lawry's Mesquite Marinade

Section pork and deer ribs and hand-rub with oil; dust with garlic powder and oregano. Place pork ribs in microwave dish on top of paper towels. Microwave 1 minute on high; turn ribs and repeat. Turn ribs and microwave 30 seconds on high; turn ribs and repeat. Put pork and deer ribs in one bowl and sprinkle with paprika. Add Lawry's Mesquite Marinade and mix by hand until all ribs are coated. Let sit 2 to 4 hours. Grill ribs over low heat until cooked through, turning often.

Servings: 4-6

Cooking Tips: Microwaving pork ribs reduces the fat content considerably, which prevents flare-ups during the cooking process.

"...Every year I work hard to get a buck whitetail because this is my favorite on-the-coals meal..."

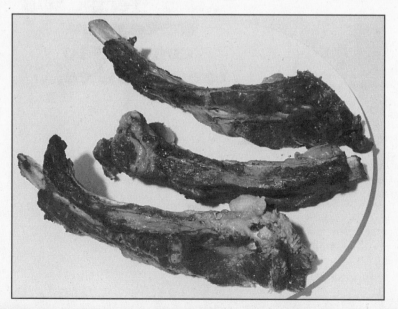

These ribs are ready to eat. All meaty game ribs will make a hearty dish when served with a potato and fresh vegetable.

Big Game Recipes...Heart, Tongue & Liver

Heart of Venison

Serve with mustard, mayonnaise or horseradish on French or Italian bread.

1 venison heart	4 bay leaves
2 qts. water	1/4 tsp. sweet basil
1/8 cup salt	1 small can tomatoes
2 cloves garlic, chopped	1/2 tsp. Worcestershire sauce
1/2 cup red wine	

Cut off top of heart and discard. Slice heart from top down to point so meat flattens out. Wash carefully. Soak in salt water 2 hours. Remove and rinse. Fill pressure cooker with water and add meat and remaining ingredients. Securely close lid and set pressure regulator. Cook 30 minutes. Allow pressure to drop. Remove heart and rinse. Allow meat to cool completely. Refrigerate. Slice thin for sandwich meat.

Servings: 4

Alternate Meats: Elk, moose, antelope, caribou, deer

Cooking Tips: The meat can also be cooked in a pot on the stove.

> "...This is delicious for lunch or dinner with a bowl of steaming soup..."

Stuffed Venison Heart

Serve with green salad, crusty bread and applesauce.

1-2 venison hearts	1 cup water or tomato juice
1 pkg. commercial stuffing mix	1 onion, whole or chopped
1 Tbsp. olive oil	1 beef bouillon cube
Salt and pepper	

Cut pocket in heart. Remove skin and soak in cold water for 15 minutes. Wipe dry. Prepare stuffing according to package directions. Stuff heart with dressing and fasten with toothpicks. Heat pressure cooker with olive oil. Brown heart lightly. Add remaining ingredients. Close lid securely and set regulator. Cook 45 minutes with regulator rocking gently. Remove from heat and let pressure drop.   **Servings: 2-4**

Alternate Meats: Elk, moose, antelope, caribou, deer

> "...This easy-does-it recipe is delicious..."

> "...This recipe will make many converts to tongue dishes..."

Tongue of Elk

Serve on French or Italian bread with condiments of your choice.

1 elk tongue	4 bay leaves
2 qts. water	1/4 tsp. sweet basil
1/8 cup salt	1 small can tomatoes
2 cloves garlic, chopped	1/2 tsp. Worcestershire sauce
1/2 cup red wine	

Slice tongue from top down to point so meat flattens out. Wash carefully. Soak in salt water 2 hours. Remove and rinse. Fill pressure cooker with water and add meat and remaining ingredients. Securely close lid and set pressure regulator. Cook 30 minutes. Allow pressure to drop. Remove tongue and rinse. Allow meat to cool completely. Refrigerate. Before serving, remove outer casing by slicing tongue longitudinally and peeling casing off; discard casing. Slice tongue crossways into thin pieces for sandwiches.   **Servings: 6-8**

Alternate Meats: Moose

Cooking Tips: In the field or in camp, the tongue must be removed immediately and washed well.

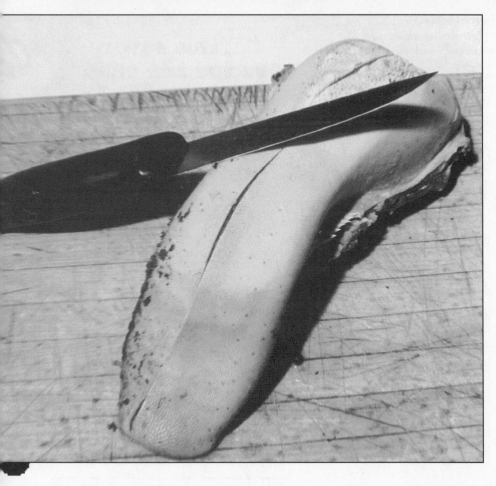

Tongue should be sliced down from top to point so the meat flattens out.

"...Sliced tongue makes excellent sandwich meat..."

Spiced Venison Tongue

Serve on crusty bread rolls with slices of tomatoes, onions and lettuce.

3-4 venison tongues	1 qt. water
Salt and pepper	2 Tbsp. pickling spices
1 lemon, sliced	1 tsp. garlic salt

Place all ingredients in large pot and cover. Simmer 1-2 hours or until tongue is done. Cool and remove connective tissue. Slice. **Servings: 6**

Alternate Meats: Elk, moose, antelope, caribou, deer

Chow Down Venison Tongue

Sliced vegetables, baked beans and Italian bread are delicious on the side.

1-2 venison tongues, washed	2 bay leaves
Salt and pepper	3 cloves garlic
1 onion, quartered	1 Tbsp. Worcestershire sauce
2 cups water	

Place washed tongues in pressure cooker with all ingredients. Close lid and set regulator. Cook 45 minutes with regulator rocking gently. Allow pressure to drop. Remove tongue from cooker and remove skin. Slice for sandwiches. Store tongue in strained liquid to keep moist. **Servings: 2-4**

Alternate Meats: Elk, moose, antelope, caribou, deer

"...Take this one along on your next picnic..."

Big Game Recipes...Heart, Tongue & Liver

Spanish-Style Venison Liver
Serve with rice and a cooked, in-season vegetable.

2 lb. venison liver, thinly sliced	8 slices bacon, cut into pieces
Lawry's Lemon Pepper	1 onion, sliced
1 can Spanish-style stewed tomatoes	1 bay leaf

Season liver with Lawry's Pepper and place in crock pot. Add remaining ingredients. Cover and cook on low 6 hours. Remove bay leaf before serving. **Servings: 4**

Alternate Meats: Elk, moose, antelope, caribou, deer

"...This savory recipe is a snap to prepare..."

Tongue can be considered an exotic dish because as good as it is, most elk, moose, and deer tongue is not used. Boiled in spices and sliced, tongue makes an excellent sandwich meat. Try it with a little horseradish.

Barbecued Venison Liver and Onions
You really don't need a barbecue for this succulant dish.
Serve with baked potatoes and a Caesar salad.

1 Tbsp. olive oil	4 Tbsp. vinegar
1 onion, sliced	4 Tbsp. brown sugar
2 cloves garlic, minced	1 Tbsp. Worcestershire sauce
1 lb. venison liver, sliced in thin strips	Salt and pepper
4 Tbsp. catsup	

In hot oiled skillet, sauté onion and garlic. Add liver and brown until red disappears. Mix in remaining ingredients and stir until liver is coated and mixture thickens into nice sauce. **Servings: 3-4**

Alternate Meats: Elk, moose, antelope, caribou, deer, buffalo

"...A delicacy not to be forgotten..."

"...For the light-weight camper, this easy-to-prepare meal does the trick..."

Moose Liver Over Coals
Serve with any in-season vegetable.

1 moose liver
Garlic powder, sprinkle
Paprika, sprinkle

Cube liver by slicing crosswise and lengthwise. Sprinkle meat with garlic and paprika. Place liver on skewers and hold over coals until just cooked through. **Servings: 4**

Cooking Tips: For a tasty alternative, place liver pieces in mixture of soy sauce, teriyaki glaze and garlic powder before barbecuing. Or dust each meat piece lightly with garlic powder and treat with teriyaki glaze before cooking.

Big Game Recipes...Heart, Tongue & Liver

Elk Liver with Wine Sauce

*Delicious with mashed potatoes
and sautéd zucchini.*

2 lb. elk liver
Bacon fat, butter, margarine or canola oil
See *Elk Liver Wine Sauce*
1 lb. bacon
1 large white onion, sliced

In skillet, cook liver in bacon fat, butter, margarine or oil. Prepare *Elk Liver Wine Sauce* and ladle directly over liver. In separate skillet, fry bacon to nearly tender. Add onion and sauté until done. Blot bacon and onion on paper towels. Serve with liver. **Servings: 4-5**

Alternate Meats: Moose, antelope, caribou, deer, buffalo

Cooking Tips: Liver can be marinated overnight in milk, paprika and garlic powder. Use enough milk to cover meat. Before cooking meat, drain and wipe dry, but do not wash.

Elk Liver Wine Sauce

1/2 cube butter or margarine
2 cups Madeira, sherry or port wine

Place butter and wine in hot skillet. Heat, stirring constantly for about 2 minutes. If strong wine aroma still persists, cook 1 minute more. Ladle over liver immediately.

Fried Venison Liver

*A hearty meat when served with sautéed onions,
green beans with bacon and mashed potatoes.*

1 venison liver	**1/8 tsp. tarragon**
1-2 cups white vinegar	**1/8 tsp. paprika**
1-2 qts. water	**1/8 tsp. garlic powder**
Milk	**Olive oil**
1/4 tsp. paprika	**Salt and pepper**
1 cup flour	

Soak liver for 2 hours in vinegar and water solution. Rinse well for 20 minutes. In bowl, mix milk and paprika. Use enough milk to cover liver. Refrigerate meat in milk mixture for 2-4 hours. Remove and drain meat, but do not blot. In small bowl, mix flour, tarragon, paprika and garlic powder. Dredge meat on both sides in flour mixture. In hot-oiled skillet over medium heat, fry meat until done. Season with salt and pepper. **Servings: 4**

Alternate Meats: Elk, moose, antelope, caribou, deer

Cooking Tips: Bacon grease can be used instead of olive oil to fry liver. Save bacon for a green bean side dish. Also, a mixture of canola oil and margarine (75/25) can be used to fry liver.

"...Wine sauce goes rather well with liver and onions..."

Never be afraid to experiment with wine. Liver and onions is not a dish normally considered a candidate for wine. However, deglazing the pan can produce a nice sauce that goes rather well with liver and onions.

Big Game Recipes...Soups & Stews

Simple Tomato-Game Meat Soup
Serve with oyster crackers and your favorite cheese.

1 lb. venison stew meat	1 can stewed tomatoes, diced
1/4 tsp. pepper	2 bay leaves
1 clove garlic, pressed	2 beef bouillon cubes
4 Tbsp. soy sauce	1/4 tsp. sweet basil
2 cans tomato soup	

Place meat in pressure cooker and cover with water. Add pepper, garlic and soy sauce. Cook 20 minutes. Let pressure drop. Add tomato soup, 1 soup can of water, stewed tomatoes, bay leaves, bouillon cubes and basil. Bring to boil. Reduce heat to simmer 5 minutes. **Servings: 4-5**

Alternate Meats: Elk, moose, antelope, caribou, deer

Cooking Tips: Out of meat? That's ok. This recipe without the meat is just good ol' tomato soup.

"...Nothing like a bowl of soup on a cold, rainy day..."

"...Soup's on..."

Simple Tomato-Game Meat Soup without the game meat!

Cabbage/Venison Soup
Delicious with a fresh tossed salad and breadsticks.

3 lb. meaty venison ribs
Salt and pepper
4 potatoes, peeled and cubed
1 onion, chopped
2 cans Italian-stewed tomatoes
2 Tbsp. brown sugar
2 cans beef broth
1/2 cup sherry
1 cabbage head, sliced in wedges
1 cup water

Preheat oven to 325°. Soak ribs in cold water for 30 minutes. Drain on paper towel. Place ribs in roasting pan and sprinkle with salt and pepper. Cover and bake 1 hour or until tender. Add remaining ingredients except cabbage. Cover and bake 3-4 hours. Add cabbage wedges and water if needed. Cover and cook 1 hour or until cabbage is tender. **Servings: 6**

Alternate Meats: Elk, moose, antelope, caribou, deer

Out-On-The-Range Venison Soup
Nothing like a homemade venison soup to keep you going. And so delicious with crusty bread sticks.

1 1/2 lb. venison, cubed	1 1/2 Tbsp. salt
1 Tbsp. fat	1/8 tsp. pepper
6-8 cups water	1/2 cup celery with leaves, chopped
1/2 cup onion, diced	2 Tbsp. fresh parsley
1 cup carrots, peeled and sliced	2 beef bouillon cubes
2 bay leaves	1/2 tsp. garlic powder

Heat pressure cooker and melt fat. Brown meat cubes. Add remaining ingredients. Close lid and set regulator. Cook 15 minutes with regulator rocking gently. Remove from heat and let pressure drop. **Servings: 4**

Alternate Meats: Elk, moose, antelope, caribou, deer

Cooking Tips: Add some chopped green onions or chives for additional color and flavor.

Big Game Recipes...Soups & Stews

Chicken Venison Soup

Planning a luncheon with family or friends? Prepare this savory soup ahead of time so you can have a good visit. Serve with crackers or crusty bread.

2 lb. boned venison, cubed
White or black pepper
Olive oil
1/8 cup soy sauce
2 cloves garlic, minced
1/2 cup Madeira or sherry wine
1/2 cup beef broth or stock
2 cans chicken broth
2 chicken bouillon cubes
3 cups water
2 Tbsp. dried onion

2 Tbsp. dried celery
1 clove garlic, chopped
1/4 cup parsley, chopped (optional)
1/4 tsp sweet basil
2 bay leaves
1/8 tsp. white or black pepper
1/2 - 1 lb. chicken, sectioned
8 carrots, peeled and sliced and cooked
2 cups barley, cooked (or)
2 cups rice, cooked

Dust venison with pepper. In hot-oiled skillet, braise venison. When venison is browned, add soy sauce and cook down. Add minced garlic and cook 1 minute. Add wine and let assimilate in broth. Add beef broth or stock and cook 1 minute on high heat. Transfer contents from skillet to pressure cooker. Stir in chicken broth, bouillon cubes and water and all seasonings. Treat chicken with olive oil and microwave on high 3 minutes on paper towel in microwave-safe dish. Turn pieces and cook 2 more minutes. Add chicken to pressure cooker. Close lid and set regulator. Cook 20 minutes. Let pressure drop. Add broth to increase liquid level and pressure cook 10-15 minutes. Remove from heat and let pressure drop. Strain all juices from cooker into large pot. Add boned chicken pieces and venison chunks to juices. Add cooked carrots and barley or rice. **Servings: 8**

Alternate Meats: Elk, moose, antelope, caribou, deer

Cooking Tips: Chicken broth can be replaced with 4 cups of stock; 1/2 chopped onion can be used instead of dried onion; 2 stalks chopped celery can replace dried celery.

"...Make this the soup-of-the-day..."

Barley Venison

Tasty with cornbread and fresh fruit platter.

2 lb. ground venison
1 onion, chopped
1 green pepper, chopped
1 cup celery, sliced
Salt and pepper
1/2 tsp. sweet basil
1/4 tsp. oregano
2 Tbsp. brown sugar
2 Tbsp. Worcestershire sauce
2 cans stewed tomatoes
3 cups beef broth
1 cup sherry
1 cup barley, uncooked

Sauté venison, onion, green pepper and celery in skillet. Drain on paper towel. Place meat mixture into large Dutch oven and add remaining ingredients. Bring to a boil and reduce heat to simmer. Cover and cook 1 hour. **Servings: 6**

Alternate Meats: Elk, moose, antelope, caribou, beer

"...Your guests will be 'game' to eat these soups..."

"...This is an encore dish, bar none..."

Gameburger Meatball Soup

A meal with crusty bread and a fruit plate.

2 1/2 lb. non-fat gameburger*
2 eggs
Parmesan cheese, sprinkle
1/4 tsp. sweet basil
1/2 cup parsley, chopped
1/4 tsp. pepper, fresh ground
Garlic powder, sprinkle

2 beef bouillon cubes
1 tsp. Worcestershire sauce
2 Tbsp. soy sauce
1 can chicken broth
Fresh vegetables, cooked
1 lb. macaroni, cooked and drained

Place gameburger in deep bowl. Add eggs. Sprinkle moderately with Parmesan cheese; add basil and parsley. Mix well. Add pepper and sprinkle of garlic powder and mix well. Form into meatballs the size of walnuts. In hot skillet, fry meatballs. Transfer to microwave dish with paper towels. Microwave 1 minute on high. Remove meatballs and place in large pot or Dutch oven. Cover with water; add bouillon cubes, Worcestershire sauce, soy sauce and chicken broth. Simmer 30 minutes. Add cooked vegetables and simmer for a few minutes. Add cooked macaroni and stir. **Servings: 5-6**

Alternate Meats: Elk, moose, antelope, caribou, deer

Cooking Tips: If desired, add 1/4 cup Madeira wine in the last 10 minutes of simmering. Simmer long enough for wine to assimilate into soup. Pinto beans can also be used. If this is desired, omit vegetables and wine and add diced stewed tomatoes with beans.

*See Chapter 18 for information on preparing non-fat gameburger.

Sometimes wine is added to soup just before eating, and sometimes it is cooked right into the soup.

Vegetable Soup in Super Stock
Serve with crackers or crusty bread.

Meat scraps, with bones	$^1/_2$ onion
2 cloves garlic, halved	$^1/_4$ cup soy sauce
$^1/_8$ tsp. Virginia Olson's Savory	$^1/_4$ cup teriyaki marinade
Seasonings Meat Blend	4 beef bouillon cubes
1 tsp. Virginia Olson's Savory	2 qts. water
Seasonings Garden Blend	1 can beef broth
Carrots, whole	Raw vegetables
Celery stalks, with tops	

Place meat scraps, bones, spices, carrots, celery, onion, soy sauce, teriyaki marinade and beef bouillon cubes in pressure cooker with 2 qts. water. Pressure cook 30 minutes. Let pressure drop. Add beef broth. Close lid and pressure cook 30 more minutes. Strain carefully; remove all bones. Add desired amounts of raw vegetables and pressure cook 3 minutes. **Servings: 6**

Alternate Meats: Elk, moose, antelope, caribou, deer

Cooking Tips: Frozen vegetables can also be used. Recommended vegetables include: carrots, peas, asparagus, broccoli, tomatoes, lima beans, onions, etc. Rice noodles or barley can be pre-cooked and added to stock with vegetables.

"...Be creative! The vegetables are entirely up to the one wearing the apron..."

"Veggie" Venison Soup
Serve with crackers and your favorite cheese.

1 Tbsp. fat	1 cup potatoes, peeled and diced
$1^1/_2$ lb. venison, cubed	1 cup carrots, peeled and diced
6 cups water	1 cup celery, diced
2 tsp. salt	2 Tbsp. fresh parsley, chopped
$^1/_4$ cup barley	1 tsp. garlic powder
2 cups tomatoes, whole	$^1/_8$ tsp. pepper
2 beef bouillon cubes	

Heat pressure cooker and melt fat. Brown venison cubes. Add remaining ingredients. Close lid and set regulator. Cook 15-20 minutes with regulator rocking gently. Remove from heat and let pressure drop. **Servings: 4-6**

Alternate Meats: Elk, moose, antelope, caribou, deer

"...Triple this recipe and freeze the leftovers to conserve time..."

"...This is fast and simple; however, the results speak of time spent and a gourmet approach..."

Wyoming Moose Stew

This is a complete meal with a mixed salad.

2 lb. moose meat, cubed
4 Tbsp. soy sauce
1 clove garlic, whole
Fresh ground pepper, dash
1 can beef broth
4 beef bouillon cubes

1 cup flour
Canola oil
Lard
1/4 cup sherry or port wine
6 carrots, peeled and diced
4 potatoes, peeled and cubed

Place meat in pressure cooker and cover with water. Meat should be under water by at least 2 cups. Add soy sauce, garlic, pepper, beef broth and bouillon cubes. Pressure cook 20 minutes. Let pressure drop. Open cooker and add more broth if liquid is too low. Cover and cook another 20 minutes. Let pressure drop. Remove meat and save liquid. Place meat in paper bag with flour. Shake to coat. Place meat in Dutch oven or skillet heated with canola oil and lard (75/25 mix) and brown. Add some of the liquid broth from pressure cooker and stir. Gravy will form automatically. Add more broth and wine and cook through, stirring. Pressure cook carrots and potatoes. Potatoes will take 4-5 minutes; carrots 3. Add cooked vegetables to stew, gently stirring. If stew is too thick, add more broth.   **Servings: 4**

Alternate Meats: Elk, antelope, caribou, deer, bear

Cooking Tips: To simplify preparation, add 1 package of frozen mixed vegetables directly to stew and let thaw while cooking. If camping, add canned vegetables.

"...Fresh crusty bread on the side will lend texture to any stew dish..."

Venison and Mushroom Stew

Serve over a bed of noodles with spinach and orange mandarin salad topped with a honey mustard dressing.

2 lb. venison stew meat
1 tsp. garlic powder
1 tsp. lemon pepper
1/4 cup flour
4 Tbsp. olive oil
1 can stewed tomatoes

1/2 can tomato paste
2 cans beef broth
3 bay leaves
1 onion, minced
1/2 lb. fresh mushrooms, sliced
Margarine

Soak stew meat in cold water for 30 minutes. Drain on paper towel. Season meat with garlic powder and lemon pepper. Dredge in flour and brown in hot-oiled skillet. Drain on paper towel. In same skillet, add stewed tomatoes, tomato paste, beef broth, bay leaves and onion. Bring to boil and add meat. Simmer 50-60 minutes, stirring occasionally. In separate skillet, sauté mushrooms in margarine. Add to stew and simmer 5-10 minutes. Remove bay leaves before serving.   **Servings: 6**

Alternate Meats: Elk, moose, antelope, caribou, deer

Country Venison Oven Stew

Serve with cornbread and honey-glazed carrots.

3 lb. vension steak, cubed
Olive oil
5 potatoes, peeled and quartered
1 large onion, sliced
2 beef bouillon cubes
Salt and pepper

Preheat oven to 250°. Heat large skillet and brown meat in olive oil. Drain on paper towel. Place cubes and remaining ingredients in oven-proof dish and cover. Bake 5-6 hours.

Servings: 4-6

Alternate Meats: Elk, moose, antelope, caribou, deer

Cooking Tips: This dish can also be prepared in a crock pot for the same amount of time.

"...Go a little bit country..."

Crock Pot Venison Stew

Serve this with a roll or two at the end of a long work day.

2 lb. venison stew meat
1 tsp. lemon pepper
Flour
2 tsp. olive oil
6 carrots, peeled and cut into chunks
8 stalks celery, cut into chunks
1 small onion, diced or sliced
4 potatoes, peeled and cut into chunks
2 cans beef broth

Season venison stew pieces with lemon pepper and coat in flour. Brown in skillet with olive oil. Drain on paper towel. Place venison in crock pot with vegetables and beef broth. Cover and cook on low 6 hours.   **Servings: 6**

Alternate Meats: Elk, moose, antelope, caribou, deer, buffalo

Venison and Bean Chili

Have a "Cinco de Mayo" feast with this meal.
Serve with warmed tortilla bread and salad.

2 lb. ground venison
1 medium onion, diced
1 tsp. garlic powder
1 large can tomato juice

3 15-oz. cans kidney beans, undrained
Salt and pepper
1 cup catsup
2-3 tsp. chili powder

In skillet, brown venison and onions. Drain on paper towel. Place meat and onions into large pot. Add remaining ingredients and simmer 2 hours.   **Servings: 6**

Alternate Meats: Elk, moose, antelope, caribou, deer

> **"...This meal practically cooks itself..."**

Crock Pot Barbecued Venison with Beans

Serve with boiled potatoes, hot cornbread and a fruit salad.

2 lb. venison stew meat
2 tsp. Lawry's Lemon Pepper
Flour
2 tsp. olive oil

1 cup barbecue sauce
1 cup beef broth
2 16-oz. cans dry lima beans, drained

Season stew meat with lemon pepper and dredge in flour. In hot-oiled skillet, brown meat. Drain on paper towel. Place meat in crock pot. Add barbecue sauce and beef broth. Cover and cook on low 6 hours. Add lima beans and cook on high 15 minutes.   **Servings: 6**

Alternate Meats: Elk, moose, antelope, caribou, deer

Texas-Style Venison Chili

Serve with taco chips and a fresh mixed green salad.

1 Tbsp. olive oil
3 lb. venison stew meat
1 onion, diced
1 cup green pepper, diced
4 cloves garlic, minced
1 tsp. oregano, rubbed
1 Tbsp. cumin

2 cans Mexican-style stewed tomatoes
1 large can tomato juice
2 beef bouillon cubes
2 Tbsp. chili powder
1 Tbsp. brown sugar
Salt and pepper

In hot-oiled skillet, brown meat. Drain on paper towel. In same skillet, sauté onion, green pepper and garlic. In large pot, combine sautéed mixture, meat and remaining ingredients. Cover and bring to boil; lower heat and simmer 2 hours.   **Servings: 6**

Alternate Meats: Elk, moose, antelope, caribou, deer

> **"...Don't forget the bread for sopping up the sauce..."**

This chili dish calls for canned beans and tomato juice to help keep it simple.

Border Country Ranch Beans

Serve with fresh bread and a salad.

1 Tbsp. olive oil
1-2 lb. boneless venison, cubed
4-5 cups pinto beans, sorted
1/8 tsp. sweet basil
1/2 onion, chopped
2 cloves garlic, chopped
3 bay leaves
1 large can tomatoes, whole

In skillet, brown venison in oil. In pot, combine beans, sweet basil, onion, garlic, bay leaves and venison. Add water to cover. Cover and simmer on low heat until beans are tender. When tender, add tomatoes and cook down. **Servings: 6-7**

Alternate Meats: Elk, moose, antelope, caribou, deer, buffalo

Cooking Tips: For a spicier version, replace tomatoes with Mexican-style stewed tomatoes.

This dish can also be prepared in the pressure cooker. Check for doneness every 20 minutes, adding liquid when necessary.

Aruba Cucumber Antelope Stew

Best if served with tomato wedges and cucumber slices.

3 Tbsp. olive oil
Salt and pepper
3 lb. antelope stew meat
1 cup celery, sliced
2 onions, sliced
1 green pepper, chopped
Fresh hot chilies, minced
2 cloves garlic, minced
2 cups beef broth
3 cucumbers, peeled, seeded and shredded

Coat skillet with oil and heat. Salt and pepper stew meat and brown in skillet. Drain on paper towel; wipe skillet down to remove remaining oil. Add 1 tsp. olive oil to skillet and sauté celery, onion, green pepper and chilies. Return meat to skillet and add garlic and beef broth. Cover and simmer 1 1/2-2 hours or until meat is tender. More chilies can be added if desired. Just before serving, stir in shredded cucumbers and heat through. **Servings: 6**

Alternate Meats: Elk, moose, caribou, deer

Cooking Tips: Crushed dried red peppers can be used in place of fresh hot chilies.

"...Hot, hot and hotter..."

Venison Bourguignon

Serve over noodles or rice with a Caesar salad and a glass of red wine.

6 strips bacon
Salt and pepper
2 lb. venison stew meat
Flour
1 can beef broth
1 onion, minced
3 cloves garlic, minced
2 Tbsp. catsup
1/2 tsp. oregano, rubbed
2 bay leaves
1 lb. fresh mushrooms, sliced and sautéed
1/2 cup red wine

Preheat oven to 325°. Fry bacon in skillet and drain on paper towel. Salt and pepper stew meat and coat in flour. Brown in skillet with bacon fat and drain on paper towel. Place all ingredients in baking dish except mushrooms and wine. Cover and bake 2 hours, stirring occasionally. Add mushrooms and wine and bake 20 minutes. **Servings: 6**

Alternate Meats: Elk, moose, antelope, caribou, deer

"...Moose meat is supreme in flavor, and if cooked properly, can be tender too..."

Tender Moose Stew

Serve over toast, or as a sit-down meal with mashed potatoes, salad and bread.

2 lb. moose meat, cubed
See *Tender Moose Marinade*
1/3 lb. salt pork
1 can beef broth
2 bay leaves
2 carrots, peeled and grated
2 stalks celery, diced
1 clove garlic, pressed
1/4 bunch fresh parsley, whole
1/8 tsp. black pepper
2 tomatoes, cubed

Prepare *Tender Moose Marinade*. Place meat and marinade in covered glass bowl and refrigerate 12 hours. Drain meat; save juice. Cube salt pork and sauté in skillet for 2 minutes. Add marinated moose to skillet and cook until well browned. Transfer entire contents of skillet to pressure cooker. Add beef broth and enough water to cover meat. Add bay leaves, carrots, celery, garlic, parsley, pepper and tomatoes. Cook 30 minutes. Cool pressure cooker and check meat for tenderness. If more cooking is required, add stock or broth to bring liquid to proper level. Pressure cook 10 more minutes if necessary. **Servings: 4**

Alternate Meats: Elk

Cooking Tips: Use a potato peeler to remove ribs from celery stalks before dicing.

Tender Moose Marinade

8-oz. port wine
3 Tbsp. olive oil
3 Tbsp. brandy

Thoroughly mix ingredients and refrigerate.

Big Game Recipes...Soups & Stews

"...The art of any stew lies in the blending and proportioning of the seasonings..."

Antelope Stew

Serve with dark rye bread and a glass of wine.

4 lb. antelope meat, boned and cubed
Pepper, dash
Paprika, dash
2 cloves garlic, crushed
1/2 cup flour
Canola oil

3/4 cup sherry drinking wine
8 cups stock (or 6 cans beef broth, 2 cans water)
5 potatoes, peeled and cubed
8 carrots, peeled and sliced
1 bunch green onions, chopped

Sprinkle meat with pepper and paprika. Stir in crushed garlic. Put meat in paper bag with flour and shake to coat. In skillet with oil, fry meat, stirring often, until cooked through. Don't allow flour coating to burn. Remove meat and deglaze frying pan with sherry. Bring stock to boil in large kettle. Place meat plus contents of deglazed frying pan into boiling stock and reduce heat. Broth will thicken immediately due to flour coating. If broth thickens too much, thin with more stock or broth. Cook potatoes and carrots until tender in pressure cooker. Add to kettle. Add green onions before serving; they should remain basically raw. **Servings: 6-7**

Alternate Meats: Elk, moose, caribou, deer

Cooking Tips: If serving leftover stew, check for thickness. It may have to be thinned with broth before reheating. Optional spices: oregano, sweet basil, tarragon and thyme. Add in moderation.

Old-Fashioned Venison Stew

Have a slice of apple pie after eating this stew, and you'll fondly remember mom.

2 lb. venison stew meat
1 tsp. garlic powder
Salt and pepper
Flour
4 tsp. olive oil

3 cans beef broth
8 carrots, peeled and sliced
3 large potatoes, peeled and cubed
2 cups celery, sliced
1 onion, diced

Soak venison in cold water for 1 hour. Drain on paper towel. Season meat with garlic powder, salt and pepper. Coat in flour and brown in skillet with hot olive oil. Drain on paper towel. Place venison in large Dutch oven. Pour in beef broth. Cover and simmer 2 to 3 hours or until meat is tender. Add vegetables and simmer until vegetables are done. **Servings: 6**

Alternate Meats: Elk, moose, antelope, caribou, deer

"...Have a fruit platter for dessert..."

Venison Curry

This meal is at its best served over rice with a green salad.

1 Tbsp. olive oil
1 onion, chopped
2 tsp. curry powder
2 lb. venison steak, cubed
1 clove garlic, minced
1 tsp. butter
1 lb. fresh mushrooms, sliced

1 tsp. salt
1 Tbsp. brown sugar
3 cups beef broth
2 tomatoes, peeled and quartered
2 Tbsp. cornstarch
2 Tbsp. water

Heat olive oil in skillet and sauté onion. Stir in curry powder and cook 1 minute. Add venison cubes and garlic. Brown quickly. In another skillet, melt butter and sauté mushrooms. Add salt, brown sugar and beef broth to browned venison cubes and onions. Cover and simmer 1 hour or until venison is tender. Add sautéed mushrooms and tomatoes. Cover and simmer 5 minutes or until tomatoes are tender, but not mushy. In small bowl, mix cornstarch and water to make a smooth paste. Add to venison mixture and simmer until thickened and clear. **Servings: 6**

Alternate Meats: Elk, moose, antelope, caribou, deer

"...This stew was meant for fine dining..."

French-Style Venison Stew

Serve with asparagus in a béarnaise sauce, french bread, a fresh green salad and a glass of Merlot.

2 lb. venison stew meat
1 Tbsp. olive oil
1 sachet bouque garni
2 cans chicken broth
Salt and pepper
1 tsp. garlic powder
2 cups celery, sliced
2 onions, quartered
2 cups turnips, cut into chunks
1/2 cup sherry

In skillet, brown stew meat in olive oil and drain on paper towel. Place all ingredients except sherry in large Dutch oven. Cover and bring to boil. Reduce heat and simmer 1 1/2 hours. Add sherry and heat through. **Servings: 6**

Alternate Meats: Elk, moose, antelope, caribou, deer

Crock Pot Venison Burgundy Stew

Serve with rice and sautéd zucchini with garlic and walnuts.

4 slices bacon, cut into pieces	2 cloves garlic, minced
2 lb. venison stew meat	1/4 tsp. thyme
Salt and pepper	2 beef bouillon cubes, crushed
1/4 cup flour	1 cup burgundy wine
1/4 tsp. marjoram	1/2 lb. mushrooms, sliced

In skillet, cook bacon until brown and crisp. Remove bacon; leave drippings. Season stew meat with salt and pepper. Dredge pieces in flour and brown in bacon fat. Drain on paper towels. Place meat, bacon, all seasonings, bouillon cubes and wine in crock pot. Cover and cook on low 6 hours. Add mushrooms and cook on high 15 minutes.   **Servings: 6**

Alternate Meats: Elk, moose, antelope, caribou, deer

Irish Stew

Served with a tankard of ale and some freshly baked dark bread, this makes a wonderful St. Patrick's Day meal.

2 lb. venison stew meat
4 large potatoes, peeled and cubed
2 onions, sliced
1/2 tsp. thyme
1 tsp. dried parsley
Salt and pepper
1 tsp. savory
2 cans beef broth

In Dutch oven, layer half of the potatoes, stew meat and onions. Sprinkle with spices. Layer remaining ingredients. Pour beef broth over entire mixture. Bring to boil and reduce to simmer 1 1/2 to 2 hours or until meat is tender.

Servings: 6

Alternate Meats: Elk, moose, antelope, caribou, deer

Dilled Venison Stew

Serve over rice or pasta with a cucumber and onion salad.

2 lb. venison stew meat	1/4 tsp. cloves
1 onion, chopped	2 tsp. dry dill weed
Salt and pepper	2 cans beef broth
2 cups carrots, peeled and sliced	2 Tbsp. cornstarch
1 cup celery, sliced	2 Tbsp. water
1 lemon, sliced	1/4 cup lemon juice

In large Dutch oven, combine venison, onion, salt and pepper, carrots, celery, lemon, cloves, dill weed and beef broth. Bring to boil and reduce heat to simmer for 1 hour. Remove meat to serving dish. Strain cooking liquid into saucepan. Remove vegetables and lemon slices. In small bowl, mix cornstarch and water. Stir into saucepan and cook until thickened. Blend vegetables and lemon in blender and add to sauce mixture. Add lemon juice and heat through. Pour over meat on serving platter.   **Servings: 6**

Alternate Meats: Elk, moose, antelope, caribou, deer

"...Whether on the range or at home, there is nothing like this dish to satisfy a large appetite..."

Canned pinto beans, Mexican salsa and a little fried venison produce a tasty meal at home or by the campfire.

Game stew is delicious, partly due to the fact that game meat is generally unmarbled and low in fat.

"...There's nothing like a stew to warm you up..."

Javelina Madeira Stew

So named because this tasty stew depends on Madeira wine.
Serve with biscuits or cornbread.

2 lb. javelina stew meat
2 qts. water
4 Tbsp. salt
2 tsp. baking soda
Canola oil
Fresh ground pepper, sprinkle
2 cloves garlic, diced
1/4 onion, diced
2 cans beef broth
8 carrots, peeled and diced
4 potatoes, peeled and cubed
1 cup Madeira wine

Marinate meat 1 hour in water, salt and baking soda mixture. Remove and rinse meat. Dry on paper towels. Braise meat in oiled Dutch oven or skillet, turning constantly. Add pepper, garlic, onion and 1 can beef broth. Bring to a boil and let boil 5 minutes. Add second can of broth and continue boiling for 5 more minutes. Reduce heat. Add carrots and potatoes. Cook 30 minutes. When vegetables are almost done, pour in wine. Cook until raw wine flavor is gone. **Servings: 4-6**

Alternate Meats: Elk, moose, antelope, caribou, deer

White Bean Venison Stew
Serve with biscuits or cornbread.

4 cups white beans	**White pepper, sprinkle**
4 bay leaves	**Garlic powder, sprinkle**
Oregano, pinch	**Olive oil**
1/8 tsp. sweet basil	**2 tsp. Worcestershire sauce**
1 clove garlic, uncut	**1/8 cup teriyaki marinade**
2 lb. venison stew meat	**1 medium can stewed tomatoes**

Place beans in pressure cooker and add water to cover, bay leaves, oregano, basil and garlic. Cook 20-30 minutes. Let pressure drop. Open cooker and add more water. Repeat process until beans are soft, but not breaking apart. If meat is tender, sprinkle with white pepper and garlic powder and fry in hot-oiled skillet. Toward end of frying, add Worcestershire sauce and teriyaki marinade. When pressure cooker has cooled, drain beans and save 1/2 qt. liquid. Return liquid and beans to pressure cooker. Add stewed tomatoes and bring to boil. Add cooked meat and stir well. **Servings: 6-8**

Alternate Meats: Elk, moose, antelope, caribou, deer

Cooking Tips: If meat is not tender, brown in skillet and then pressure cook in water with a little soy sauce for 10-20 minutes.

Sausage and Venison Stew
Serve with cornbread or freshly baked biscuits.

1 Tbsp. olive oil
2 lb. venison stew meat
1 lb. smoked sausage, sliced
2 bay leaves
4 cans beef broth
6 carrots, peeled and coined
1 large onion, quartered
2 cups celery, quartered
3 potatoes, peeled and quartered
Salt and pepper

In hot-oiled skillet, brown stew meat and sausage. Drain on paper towel. Place all ingredients into large Dutch oven or covered pot and simmer 2 hours. **Servings: 6**

Alternate Meats: Elk, moose, antelope, caribou, deer

Big Game Recipes...Soups & Stews

Venison Meatball Stew
Serve with rice and an Italian salad.

2 lb. ground venison	1 can Italian-style stewed tomatoes
1/4 cup milk	1 cup sherry
2 eggs	1/2 tsp. oregano, rubbed
Lawry's Lemon Pepper	1/2 tsp. sweet basil
1 cup beef broth	6 stalks celery, sliced
1 small can tomato paste	1 pkg. frozen Italian green beans, thawed
4 carrots, peeled and coined	

In bowl, mix venison, milk, eggs and lemon pepper. Form into meatballs the size of walnuts. Brown in skillet; drain on paper towel. Place meatballs in crock pot and add all ingredients except green beans. Cover and cook on low 6 hours. Add beans and cook on high 20 minutes or until beans are tender.   **Servings: 6**

Alternate Meats: Elk, moose, antelope, caribou, deer

Italian Stew with Game Meat
*Serve with Italian bread
and a fresh green salad.*

- 2 lb. red game meat, boned and cubed
- 1 can beef broth
- 1 clove garlic, crushed
  Black pepper, pinch
  1 onion, chopped
  2 large cans tomatoes, whole
  1/2 tsp. sweet basil
  Thyme, pinch
  2 bay leaves
  3 potatoes, peeled and cubed
  1 can green beans, drained

Place meat in pressure cooker and cover with water. Add beef broth, garlic, pepper and onion. Pressure cook 15 minutes; allow pressure to drop naturally. Add tomatoes, sweet basil, thyme and bay leaves. Pressure cook 5 minutes. Cool pressure cooker under water. Add potatoes and green beans. Pressure cook 3 minutes. Cool pressure cooker, remove lid and simmer until potatoes are cooked through.   **Servings: 6**

Alternate Meats: Red game meat; elk, moose, antelope, caribou, deer

Cooking Tips: This quick-to-make dish relies on red game meat. It was created with venison in mind, but other game meats also serve the purpose.

"...Serve over noodles, of course..."

"...Mouth watering..."

"...Excellent meals for watching your favorite football team on Sunday afternoons..."

Venison Ragout Stew
Cornbread is the perfect addition to this stew.

2 Tbsp. olive oil	Salt and pepper
2 lb. venison stew meat	1/2 tsp. thyme
2 cans kidney beans with juice	1/2 tsp. sweet basil
2 cans Italian-stewed tomatoes	3 bay leaves
1 1/2 cup dry red wine	4 potatoes, peeled and cubed
2 Tbsp. brown sugar	1 green pepper, chopped
2 cloves garlic, minced	2 onions, cut in wedges

In large Dutch oven, heat oil and brown meat. Drain on paper towel. Place meat, beans, tomatoes, wine, brown sugar, garlic, salt, pepper, thyme, basil and bay leaves in Dutch oven, bring to boil and reduce heat to simmer. Cook until meat is tender. Add potatoes, green peppers and onions. Simmer 30 minutes or until potatoes are done. Remove bay leaves before serving.   **Servings: 6**

Alternate Meats: Elk, moose, antelope, caribou, deer

Venison Stroganoff
*What a tasty meal. Serve over noodles;
add a salad and some fresh German bread.*

2 lb. venison stew meat	1 tsp. butter
Salt and pepper	2 lb. fresh mushrooms, sliced
1 tsp. garlic powder	2 bunches green onions, sliced
1/4 cup flour	2 cans beef broth
2 Tbsp. olive oil	2 cups sour cream

Soak stew meat in cold water for 30 minutes. Drain on paper towel. Season meat with salt, pepper and garlic powder. Dredge in flour and brown in hot-oiled skillet. Drain on paper towel. In same skillet, add butter and sauté mushrooms and green onions. In large pot, combine stew meat, mushrooms and green onions. Add beef broth and bring to boil. Reduce heat and simmer 15-20 minutes, stirring occasionally. Remove from heat and add sour cream.   **Servings: 6**

Alternate Meats: Elk, moose, antelope, caribou, deer

Big Game Recipes...Casseroles

"...Prepare ahead of time when you're on the go..."

Eggplant/Venison Bake
Steamed cauliflower, rolls and a gelatin salad finish this meal.

2 lb. ground venison
Salt and pepper
3 cloves garlic, minced
1 onion, minced
5-6 cups eggplant, cubed

1 lb. elbow macaroni
2 cans Italian-stewed tomatoes
1 can beef broth
1 pkg. hollandaise sauce mix

Preheat oven to 350°. Mix ground venison with salt, pepper, garlic and onion. Brown in skillet and drain on paper towel. Set aside. Sauté eggplant briefly. Add meat mixture and simmer for 5 minutes. Place entire mixture into casserole dish. Cook macaroni according to package directions and drain. Add stewed tomatoes and beef broth to noodles and mix. Pour into casserole dish. Prepare hollandaise mix according to package directions and pour over mixture in casserole dish. Bake for 15-20 minutes or until hot and bubbly.   **Servings: 6**

Alternate Meats: Elk, moose, antelope, caribou, deer

Ground Venison Casserole with Biscuits
Serve with any salad or fresh fruit plate.

2 lb. ground venison
1 onion, minced
2 cloves garlic, minced
Salt and pepper
1 can cream of chicken soup
1 can cream of mushroom soup
1 cup low-fat yogurt
1/2 cup milk
2 tomatoes, sliced
2 tubes refrigerated biscuits

Preheat oven to 375°. Brown venison with onion and garlic in skillet and drain on paper towel. Place meat mixture in baking dish and add all ingredients except tomatoes and biscuits. Mix well. Place sliced tomatoes on top of meat mixture. Place biscuits on top of tomato slices and bake for 20 minutes or until biscuits are golden brown.   **Servings: 6**

Alternate Meats: Elk, moose, antelope, caribou, deer

Venison Noodle Casserole
This can be served with hot, buttered garlic rolls and Italian-style green beans.

2 lb. ground venison
1 small onion, diced
1 cup celery, diced
Salt and pepper
1 tsp. garlic salt

1 lb. thin spaghetti
1 cup picante sauce
1 lb. cheddar cheese, grated
2 cans tomato soup

Preheat oven to 350°. Brown ground venison, onion, celery, salt, pepper and garlic salt in skillet; drain on paper towel. Cook spaghetti according to package directions and rinse in hot water. Place spaghetti in casserole dish and pour picante sauce over noodles. Add venison mixture and grated cheese. Top with tomato soup and bake 30 minutes.   **Servings: 6**

Alternate Meats: Elk, moose, antelope, caribou, deer

Venison Cabbage Casserole
Serve with a green salad and fresh rolls.

1 onion, diced
2 Tbsp. margarine
2 lb. ground venison
1 medium cabbage
2 cups cheddar cheese, grated
1 1/2 cups sour cream
Salt and pepper
1 cup dry Italian-style bread crumbs

Preheat oven to 350°. In skillet, sauté onion in margarine. Add ground venison and brown. Drain on paper towel. Cut cabbage into pieces and add to venison. Cover and cook over low heat until cabbage turns translucent. Add grated cheese, sour cream, salt and pepper. Mix thoroughly. Place in casserole dish and top with bread crumbs. Bake for 1 hour or until hot.   **Servings: 6**

Alternate Meats: Elk, moose, antelope, caribou, deer

"...What more could you ask for..."

Ground Venison and Zucchini Casserole
Serve with a gelatin salad and fresh rolls.

2 lb. ground venison
6 to 8 small zucchini, sliced
2 1/2 cups biscuit mix
3 1/2 cups canned spaghetti sauce
1 3/4 cups low-fat cottage cheese

3 egg whites
1 tsp. rubbed oregano
1/2 cup Parmesan cheese
1/2 cup grated Romano cheese

Preheat oven to 350°. Spray large baking pan with cooking spray. Brown ground venison in skillet and drain on paper towel. In baking dish, layer venison, zucchini slices and 1/2 cup biscuit mix. Top with spaghetti sauce. Mix 2 cups biscuit mix, cottage cheese, egg whites and oregano to form a soft dough. Spread over above mixture and sprinkle with Parmesan and Romano cheeses. Bake 45 minutes until bubbly. Let stand 20 to 30 minutes before serving.   **Servings: 6-8**

Alternate Meats: Elk, moose, antelope, caribou, deer

A large casserole, such as this one with green beans and gameburger, will feed a number of hungry guests.

Layered Venison Casserole
Cinnamon-spiced applesauce complements this casserole.

2 lb. ground venison
2 cups celery, diced
1 tsp. garlic powder
Salt and pepper
5 potatoes, sliced
2 cans green beans, drained
2 cans cream of celery soup

Preheat oven to 350°. Mix ground venison, celery and spices and brown in skillet. Place sliced potatoes in casserole dish followed by venison mix and green beans. Spread cream of celery soup over beans and bake for 1 hour or until potatoes are tender.   **Servings: 6**

Alternate Meats: Elk, moose, antelope, caribou, deer

"...Pizza in a crock pot?.."

Crock Pot Pizza Casserole
Hot garlic bread and a green leafy salad complete this meal.

2 lb. ground venison	$1/2$ cup beef broth
Salt and pepper	$1/2$ tsp. oregano, rubbed
$1/2$ tsp. garlic powder	$1/2$ tsp. sweet basil
1 pkg. scalloped potatoes	1 cup mozzarella cheese, cubed
1 can Italian-stewed tomatoes	$1/4$ cup Parmesan cheese, grated
1 can pizza sauce	$1/2$ cup Romano cheese, grated

Season ground venison with salt, pepper and garlic powder. Brown meat in skillet and drain on paper towels. Place browned venison in crock pot and add scalloped potatoes, Italian-stewed tomatoes, pizza sauce, beef broth and spices. Cover and cook on low for 4 hours. Stir in mozzarella cheese cubes, Parmesan and Romano grated cheeses. Turn control to high and cook for 15 minutes.   **Servings: 4**

Alternate Meats: Elk, moose, antelope, caribou, deer

Venison and Rice Casserole
Hard-crusted bread and a green lettuce salad finish this meal.

2 cups rice (white or brown), uncooked	Salt and pepper
4 cups chicken broth	1 tsp. oregano leaves
1 lb. ground venison	1 tsp. sweet basil
1 onion, chopped	4 Tbsp. brown sugar
2 16-oz. cans tomato sauce	3 cups low-fat cottage cheese
1 tsp. garlic powder	2 cups mozzarella cheese, shredded
2 tsp. parsley	

Preheat oven to 325°. Microwave rice in chicken broth for 10 minutes on high. Cover and microwave on simmer 15 to 20 minutes, or until rice is done. Brown venison and onion in skillet and drain on paper towel. Put meat back into skillet and add tomato sauce, spices and brown sugar. Cover and simmer 15 to 20 minutes, stirring occasionally. Combine cottage cheese and rice. Put $1/3$ rice mixture in bottom of casserole dish. Top with $1/3$ meat mixture. Alternate layers, ending with meat sauce. Sprinkle with cheese. Cover and bake for 30 minutes.   **Servings: 6**

Alternate Meats: Elk, moose, antelope, caribou, deer

"...Double this recipe and freeze the leftovers..."

Nowadays, crushing tomatoes through a colander is generally unnecessary because canned crushed tomatoes are available at the grocery store. But this method still works in a pinch.

Macaroni/Venison Casserole

Serve with a green leafy salad and lightly warmed french bread.

2 lb. ground venison
1 cup green pepper, minced
1 cup onion, minced
4 cups macaroni
2 cans cream of mushroom soup
2 cans Italian-stewed tomatoes
1 tsp. garlic powder
Salt and pepper
2 cups sharp cheddar cheese, shredded
1 8-oz. can Durkee French Fried
   Onion Rings

Preheat oven to 350°. Sauté venison, green pepper and onion in skillet and drain on paper towel. Cook macaroni according to package directions and drain. Combine all ingredients except onion rings in baking dish. Bake for 45 minutes; add onion rings and bake 15 minutes.

Servings: 6

Alternate Meats: Elk, moose, antelope, caribou, deer

Crock Pot Venison and Bean Casserole

Serve with fresh fruit and hard rolls.

2 lb. ground venison
1 cup green pepper, chopped
1 cup onion, diced
1 cup celery, diced
1 can kidney beans, drained
1 can garbanzo beans, drained
1 tsp. dry mustard
2 Tbsp. brown sugar
³/₄ cup catsup
1 tsp. garlic powder
Salt and pepper
3 tsp. vinegar
1 12-oz. can tomato juice

In skillet, brown ground venison and vegetables. Drain on paper towel. In separate bowl, mix beans, dry mustard, brown sugar, catsup, seasonings, vinegar and tomato juice. Place all ingredients in crock pot, mix and cook on low for 6 hours.

Servings: 6

Alternate Meats: Elk, moose, antelope, caribou, deer

"...Have your pie and eat it too..."

Venison Pie

Serve with a fresh onion and tomato salad.

2 lb. ground venison
1 onion, diced
Salt and pepper
¹/₄ tsp. garlic powder
1 tsp. chili powder
1 16-oz. can tomato sauce
1 can tomato soup
1 7-oz. can whole kernel corn, drained
¹/₂ lb. cheddar cheese, grated

Preheat oven to 350°. Brown venison and onion in skillet. Drain on paper towel. Return mixture to skillet and add seasonings, tomato sauce, tomato soup and corn. Bake 30 minutes or until hot and bubbly. Cover with grated cheese and bake until cheese is melted.

Servings: 6

Alternate Meats: Elk, moose, antelope, caribou, deer

"...Quick and easy...what a combination..."

Quick and Easy Venison/Scalloped Potato Casserole

This is best accompanied by a fresh fruit salad and lightly browned croissant rolls.

2 lb. ground venison	2 Tbsp. brown sugar
1 onion, minced	1 tsp. oregano, rubbed
1 green pepper, minced	1 16-oz. can Italian-stewed tomatoes
1 Tbsp. Worcestershire sauce	1 pkg. augratin scalloped potatoes
Salt and pepper	1 can beef broth

Preheat oven to 350°. Brown ground venison, onion and green pepper in skillet and drain on paper towel. Return to skillet and mix in Worcestershire sauce, salt, pepper, brown sugar, oregano, stewed tomatoes, potatoes and beef broth. Pour meat mixture into casserole dish and bake, covered, until potatoes are done, stirring occasionally. **Servings: 6**

Alternate Meats: Elk, moose, antelope, caribou, deer

Poppy Seed Venison Bake

This unusual dish can be served with rice or noodles, a salad and fresh rolls.

4 cups leftover venison roast, cubed
1 can cream of chicken soup
1 cup sour cream or low-fat yogurt
2 Tbsp. butter, melted
1½ cups Ritz crackers, crushed
Poppy seeds

Preheat oven to 375°. Place cubed meat in baking dish. Mix soup and sour cream or yogurt and pour over meat. Mix butter with crackers and sprinkle over meat. Sprinkle on desired amount of poppy seeds and bake for 45 minutes.

Servings: 6

Alternate Meats: Elk, moose, antelope, caribou, deer

Texas Venison Hash

This is delicious with biscuits for dipping.

2 red Spanish onions, sliced
2 green peppers, diced
2 lb. ground venison
1 cup beef broth
1 can Mexican-style stewed tomatoes
1 cup rice, uncooked
1 tsp. chili powder
Pepper

Preheat oven to 350°. Brown onion, green pepper and venison in skillet. Drain on paper towel. Stir in remaining ingredients and pour into casserole dish. Bake, covered, for 1 hour; uncover and bake 20 minutes. **Servings: 6**

Alternate Meats: Elk, moose, antelope, caribou, deer

"...This hearty hash is a meal all its own..."

Zucchini/Eggplant and Venison Bake

This tasty dish is best served over pasta with a side of garlic toast.

2 lb. ground venison
3 cups eggplant, cubed
3 cups zucchini, cubed
2 beef bouillon cubes
2 cans Italian-stewed tomatoes
1 tsp. garlic salt
1 small can tomato sauce
Salt and pepper

Preheat oven to 350°. Brown venison, eggplant and zucchini in skillet and drain. Mix bouillon cubes, stewed tomatoes, garlic salt, tomato sauce and salt and pepper in large casserole dish. Add meat mixture, stir, and bake for 30 minutes or until hot and bubbly. **Servings: 6**

Alternate Meats: Elk, moose, antelope, caribou, deer

"...Terrific when you're on the run..."

Fast Potato/Venison Casserole

This can be made into a quick meal with a side of fresh vegetables and dip and a cheese tray.

2 lb. ground venison	1 pkg. frozen Tater Tots
1 cup onion, minced	2 cans green beans, drained
2 cloves garlic, minced	2 cans cream of mushroom soup
1 cup celery, minced	Salt and pepper

Preheat oven to 350°. In skillet, sauté ground venison, onion, garlic and celery. Drain on paper towel. In large casserole dish, combine Tater Tots, meat mixture and green beans. Pour mushroom soup over casserole and add salt and pepper to taste. Bake 45-60 minutes or until hot and bubbly. **Servings: 6**

Alternate Meats: Elk, moose, antelope, caribou, deer

Many casseroles use beans as one or many of its ingredients. See *Mixed Bean and Venison Casserole* as an example.

Ground Venison Surprise
An artichoke salad and garlic rolls complement this dish.

2 lb. ground venison
1 onion, minced
2 cloves garlic, minced
Salt and pepper
1 lb. spaghetti noodles
1 can tomato soup
1 can cream of chicken soup
1 can cream of celery soup
1 can cheddar cheese soup
1 lb. mozzarella cheese, shredded

Preheat oven to 350°. Sauté venison, onion, garlic, salt and pepper in skillet and drain on paper towel. Cook spaghetti noodles according to package directions and drain. Layer spaghetti in bottom of casserole dish. Mix meat mixture with four cans of soup and spread over noodles. Bake for 25 minutes. Sprinkle with cheese and bake until bubbly. **Servings: 6**

Alternate Meats: Elk, moose, antelope, caribou, deer

Mixed Bean and Venison Casserole
Serve with a cracker and cheese tray and fresh-steamed broccoli.

2 lb. ground venison
1 cup green pepper, minced
1 cup onion, minced
2 cloves garlic, minced
1 cup brown sugar
1 cup catsup
4 Tbsp. vinegar
2 Tbsp. mustard
1 can lima beans, drained
1 can kidney beans, drained
1 can pinto beans, drained
1 can pork and beans
8 slices bacon, cooked and crumbled
Salt and pepper

Preheat oven to 300°. Brown venison, green pepper, onion and garlic in skillet and drain on paper towel. In large casserole dish, mix brown sugar, catsup, vinegar and mustard. Add beans and bacon and stir. Mix in meat and vegetables and add salt and pepper to taste. Bake 1½ to 2 hours. **Servings: 6**

Alternate Meats: Elk, moose, antelope, caribou, deer

Leftover Venison Roast and Macaroni Casserole
This dish is delicious with a spinach salad and bottle of red wine.

½ lb. mushrooms, sliced
1 cup green onions, diced
1 cup celery, diced
2 Tbsp. margarine
1 lb. macaroni
4 cups leftover venison roast, diced
1 can cream of celery soup
1 can cream of chicken soup
Salt and pepper
1 tsp. garlic powder
2 cups cheddar cheese, shredded
1 cup Swiss cheese, shredded

Preheat oven to 350°. In skillet, sauté mushrooms, green onions and celery in margarine. Cook macaroni according to package directions and drain. Combine all ingredients except cheeses and pour into large casserole dish. Bake for 1 hour. Top with cheeses and bake 15 minutes or until cheese is melted. **Servings: 6**

Alternate Meats: Elk, moose, antelope, caribou, deer

"...This noodle casserole gives leftovers a new reputation..."

Big Game Recipes...Sandwiches

Reuben Sandwich á La Venison

Serve with potato salad and garlic pickles.

12 slices rye bread	2 eggs, beaten
1-2 lb. leftover venison roast, sliced	1/2 cup milk
6 slices Swiss cheese	Salt and pepper
1 jar sauerkraut, drained	Olive oil, margarine or butter

On one slice of rye bread, layer sliced roast, cheese and sauerkraut. Top with another slice of bread. In small bowl, mix egg and milk. Dip each side of sandwich into mixture. In skillet with small amount of olive oil or margarine, brown each side of sandwich until golden brown.   **Servings: 6**

Alternate Meats: Elk, moose, antelope, caribou, deer

> ## "...There's nothing better to fill an empty stomach..."

Chopped Vension Sandwich

Serve this dish with pride and in-season fruit.

3 cups leftover venison roast, cubed	1 cup mayonnaise
1 1/2 cups celery, minced	Fresh onion buns
1/2 cup pickles, minced (sweet or dill)	1 cup sharp cheddar cheese, grated
Salt and pepper	

Preheat oven to broil. Combine venison, celery, pickles, salt, pepper and mayonnaise in bowl. Mix well. Toast each bun half. Spread with meat mixture and sprinkle with cheese. Place under broiler until cheese is bubbly. Top with remaining bun half.   **Servings: 6**

Alternate Meats: Elk, moose, antelope, caribou, deer

> ## "...It's amazing how much good eating is tucked away between two slices of bread..."

> ## "...Cook these up and feed the gang..."

Your Very Own Venison Sandwich

This is a very simple recipe that serves in making delicious cold cuts.

2-4 lb. game meat, boneless	1/8 tsp. onion salt
1 can beef broth	2 dashes Worcestershire sauce
1 can water	1/8 cup teriyaki marinade
1/4 tsp. garlic powder	

Preheat oven to 300°. Place all ingredients in roasting pan. Cover and cook for 30 minutes. Turn meat and cook for another 30 minutes. Check for doneness. If meat is still red in center, cook at 250° until meat is done. Remove and slice for sandwiches.   **Servings: 12**

Alternate Meats: Elk, moose, antelope, caribou, deer

Cooking Tips: Save juice for stock. Freeze in proper jar.

> ## "...And the sandwich stands alone..."

Earl of Venison Sandwich

Serve by itself or with a tossed salad.

6 English muffins	6 Tbsp. Thousand Island dressing
2 lb. leftover venison roast, sliced	1/4 cup olives, sliced
2 tomatoes, chopped	1 onion, thinly sliced
1 cucumber, minced	Salt and pepper
1 cup fresh sprouts	6 slices sharp cheddar cheese

Preheat oven to broil. Slice each muffin in half. Layer with meat, tomatoes, cucumbers, sprouts, salad dressing, olives, onions, salt and pepper. Top with cheese. Broil until cheese is bubbly. Top with other half of muffin.   **Servings: 6**

Alternate Meats: Elk, moose, antelope, caribou, deer

K.O. Venison Barbecue

*This is a Knock-Out dish for any occasion. Serve on fresh buns
with chunky baked applesauce and a tossed salad.*

2 Tbsp. olive oil	5 sticks celery, diced
4 lb. venison stew meat	1 bottle hickory barbecue sauce
4 cloves garlic, minced	Salt and pepper
2 onions, diced	2 Tbsp. Worcestershire sauce
Teaball filled with pickling spices	1 tsp. fine herbs
2 green peppers, diced	

In hot-oiled skillet, brown stew meat. Drain on paper towel. In heavy Dutch oven,
add meat, garlic, 1 diced onion and teaball with pickling spices. Add water to just
cover mixture. Simmer 2 hours or until meat can be shredded. Drain and shred
meat. Strain drained liquid and reserve half. Add green pepper, remaining onion
and celery to reserved liquid and boil 5 minutes to tenderize vegetables. Add barbecue sauce, return teaball and meat to pot and simmer 30 minutes, stirring often. Add
salt and pepper to taste. Blend in Worcestershire sauce and fine herbs. **Servings: 6**

Alternate Meats: Elk, moose, antelope, caribou, deer

"...A succulant dish under cover..."

"...This is poetry in venison..."

Ode to a Venison Sandwich

Potato chips and a pasta salad do justice to this sandwich.

1 lb. Velveeta cheese, cubed	2 onions, sliced
1/2 cup mayonnaise	2 cloves garlic, minced
1/2 cup milk	1 1/2 lb. leftover venison roast, sliced
1 tsp. dry mustard	6 8-inch French rolls, split
1 tsp. olive oil	

Combine cheese, mayonnaise, milk and mustard in microwave-safe bowl.
Microwave on high 3 minutes. Stir. Microwave 2 more minutes or until bubbly. In
hot oiled skillet, sauté onions and garlic. Drain on paper towel. Warm meat in
microwave for 2 minutes or less. Layer meat, onion/garlic and cheese mixture in
roll.   **Servings: 6**

Alternate Meats: Elk, moose, antelope, caribou, deer.

A buffet setting with wild and
domestic meats sliced for sandwiches. These meats can be
mixed or eaten separately.

An entire boneless game roast, sliced end to end, ideal for hot gamemeat sandwiches.

> **"...These recipes raise a sandwich from the routine to the spectacular..."**

Crock Pot Venison Sloppy Joe's

This hearty, hot sandwich is a complete meal when served with a tossed green salad.

5 lb. ground venison	1 Tbsp. lemon juice
1 onion, diced	1/2 cup catsup
Salt and pepper	1/2 cup green pepper, diced
2 cans tomato soup	1 cup celery, diced
1/2 cup water	1 tsp. dry mustard
1 Tbsp. vinegar	1 Tbsp. Worcestershire sauce
1/2 cup brown sugar	1 tsp. chili powder

In skillet, brown meat with onion, salt and pepper. Drain well. In crock pot, combine meat mixture with remaining ingredients. Cook on low for 4 hours. Serve on hamburger buns.   **Servings: 8-10**

Alternate Meats: Elk, moose, antelope, caribou, deer

Stuffed Venison Pockets

This tastes wonderful with a fresh fruit salad.

1 10-oz. pkg. frozen chopped spinach	1 small onion, sliced
1 1/2 lb. ground vension	1/2 tsp. dill weed
1/2 tsp. Lawry's Garlic Powder	1 cup cheddar cheese, grated
Salt and pepper	1 cup Monterey Jack cheese, grated
1/2 lb. fresh mushrooms, sliced	6-8 pita pockets

Slit spinach package and microwave on high 5 minutes. Rotate halfway through. Remove spinach from package and squeeze out liquid. Drain on paper towel. In skillet, sauté venison with garlic powder, salt and pepper. Drain on paper towel. In same skillet, sauté mushrooms, onions and dill. Drain on paper towel. In bowl, mix spinach, venison, mushrooms, onions and dill. Fold in cheeses. Open pita pockets and fill with meat mixture. Wrap each pocket with wax paper and microwave on high 2 minutes or until cheese is slightly melted.   **Servings: 6-8**

Alternate Meats: Elk, moose, antelope, caribou, deer

> **"...Definitely a pocketful of succulent taste..."**

Big Game Recipes...Sandwiches

Crescent Venison Pockets

These sandwiches are filling with coleslaw and a fresh fruit salad.

1 lb. ground venison
2 cloves garlic, minced
1/2 cup onion, minced
1 pkg. frozen chopped spinach
4 Tbsp. Parmesan cheese
1 cup mozzarella cheese, shredded
1 Tbsp. cornmeal
2 8-oz. cans crescent dinner rolls

Preheat oven to 350°. In skillet, sauté venison, garlic and onions. Drain on paper towel. Thaw spinach and drain on paper towel. In bowl, mix venison, garlic, onion, spinach, Parmesan and mozzarella cheeses. On baking sheet, sprinkle cornmeal. Separate crescent rolls into 8 rectangles. Spoon 1/2 cup mixture on each rectangle. Moisten edge of dough with water and bring unfilled half over filling. Pinch edges to seal. Bake 20 minutes or until golden brown.   **Servings: 4**

Alternate Meats: Elk, moose, antelope, caribou, deer

"...A tasty lunch or snack with very little effort..."

"...Or any other night of the week..."

Saturday Night Special

A green salad on the side will do nicely.

2 lb. ground venison
1 onion, minced
1-2 lb. jar sauerkraut, drained
1 Tbsp. caraway seeds
4 dozen frozen dinner roll dough, thawed
Salt and pepper
4 cups mozzarella cheese, shredded

Preheat oven to 400°. In skillet, sauté venison and onion until brown. Drain on paper towel. In small bowl, mix sauerkraut with caraway seeds. Roll out 6 dinner rolls, 1/4-inch thick. Place 2-3 Tbsp. venison mixture on roll. Top with 1-2 Tbsp. sauerkraut mixture. Add salt, pepper and 1-2 Tbsp. cheese. Roll out 6 more rolls and place on top of dough containing filling. Seal edges and place on baking sheet. Let set at room temperature for 15 minutes. Bake 15-20 minutes or until lightly browned. Repeat with remaining rolls/meat mixture.   **Servings: 6**

Alternate Meats: Elk, moose, antelope, caribou, deer

"...Make Texas-style your style..."

Texas-Style Hoagies

Good for lunch or dinner. Serve with baked applesauce and sweet corn.

2 lb. ground venison
1 onion, minced
1 can Mexican-style stewed tomatoes
1 4-oz. can green chilies, diced
4 Tbsp. brown sugar
Salt and pepper
1/2 cup catsup
6 fresh onion buns or 6 long hoagie buns

In skillet, brown meat and onions. Drain on paper towel. Add remaining ingredients except buns and simmer for 30 minutes until all flavors are blended. Spoon mixture onto toasted buns.

Servings: 6

Alternate Meats: Elk, moose, antelope, caribou, deer

"...A scrumptious pita magnifique..."

Venison-Packed Pita Pocket

A scrumptious pita magnifique...without the lamb. Serve with spinach salad.

2 lb. leftover venison roast, minced
1/8 tsp. cinnamon
1/8 tsp.nutmeg
3 Tbsp. lemon juice
2 cloves garlic, minced
2 tomatoes, chopped
2 Tbsp. fresh parsley, chopped
6 pita pockets
1 onion, thinly sliced
1 cup hamburger-style pickle slices
2 cups plain yogurt

In bowl, mix meat with all ingredients except onions, pickles and yogurt. Spoon mixture in pita bread and microwave on high 1 minute (per pocket). Open pocket and add onions, pickles and several spoonfuls of yogurt.   **Servings: 6**

Alternate Meats: Elk, moose, antelope, caribou, deer

Snowshoe Pot Roast

This is a self-contained meal; just add some freshly baked bread to soak up the juice.

2 young snowshoe hares
Marinade for Snowshoe Pot Roast
1/2 onion, sliced
Paprika, sprinkle
Garlic powder, sprinkle
1 cup stock or 1 can chicken broth
6 potatoes, peeled and cubed
12 carrots, peeled and sliced

Preheat oven to 275°. Marinate two hares in large sealable plastic bag for 24 hours. Place hares, with marinade, into roasting pot and add onion. Sprinkle meat with paprika and garlic powder. Add stock or chicken broth to pot. Roast, covered, for 1 1/2 hours. Turn hares and add more liquid if necessary. Re-cover and cook for another 1 1/2 hours. Add potatoes and carrots and continue to cook until vegetables are finished. Add more liquid, baste and turn hares as needed. Meat is finished when it falls off the bone. Place hares on serving dish surrounded by potatoes and carrots.   Servings: 4-6

Alternate Meats: [...] rabbit [...]

Cooking Tips: The marinade is vital to the success of this recipe. Hares taken in the winter can be very bitter tasting; hares of the early fall are best for this dish.

Marinade for Snowshoe Pot Roast

2 cups Burgundy wine
2 cups stock or 1 can chicken broth
1/4 tsp. nutmeg, ground
1/4 tsp. tarragon
1/2 onion, sectioned

Mix wine and stock or broth and transfer to large plastic storage bag. Add nutmeg, tarragon and onion. Shake to mix.

Rabbit in Tarragon Sauce

This dish can be served over pasta with a green, leafy salad.

2 rabbits, cut into serving pieces
Salt and pepper
4 Tbsp. olive oil
1 cup onion, chopped
1 cup carrot, chopped
1 cup celery, chopped
2 cans chicken broth
1/2 cup dry cooking sherry
2 tsp. tarragon
1 cup heavy whipping cream
2 Tbsp. Dijon mustard
1/2 cup parsley, minced

[...] with salt and pepper. [...] oil in skillet and brown rabbit. Remove meat and drain on paper towel. Add onion, carrot and celery to skillet. Sauté 5 minutes. Stir in enough flour to make a paste. Blend in broth, sherry and tarragon. Return rabbit to skillet. Bring sauce to a boil and reduce heat to simmer. Baste meat frequently for 45-60 minutes. Remove rabbit to serving platter and keep warm in oven. Strain and degrease sauce, discarding vegetables. Return remaining sauce to skillet and add cream. Simmer until thickened, stirring frequently. Remove from heat and add mustard and parsley. Pour sauce over rabbit and serve.

Servings: 6-8

Small Game Recipes...

Rabbit Filipino

This is truly tasty when served with boiled potatoes and a fresh garden salad.

2 rabbits
Special Marinade for Rabbit Filipino
2 Tbsp. cornstarch

Place marinade and meat in 3- to 4-quart with covered cooking pot or Dutch oven. Bring contents to a boil over medium heat. Reduce heat and simmer, stirring occasionally to keep meat from sticking. Simmer for 30 to 40 minutes, or until rabbit is tender. Remove meat and bay leaves from marinade and allow to cool. Place 1/2 cup marinade in shaker with cornstarch and shake to mix. Use only enough marinade/cornstarch to thicken the rest of the marinade. Discard what is not needed. Ladle marinade over the rabbit and serve.   Servings: 4-6

Alternate Meats: Squirrel, raccoon, muskrat

Cooking Tips: Rabbit meat may be deboned before ladling thickened marinade over meat.

"...This is a different-tasting dish liked by most who try it..."

Special Marinade for Rabbit Filipino

5 Tbsp. soy sauce
1/4 cup palm vinegar
3 cloves garlic, crushed or pressed
2 bay leaves
1/2 tsp. white pepper

In a stainless steel or glass bowl, combine soy sauce, palm vinegar, garlic, bay leaves and white pepper. Mix well.

Small Game Recipes...

Pressured Squirrel Marjoram

This is delicious with french fries, grilled mushrooms and onions, a green vegetable and fresh fruit salad.

4 squirrels, cut into serving pieces	1 onion, sliced
1 cup flour	1½ tsp. marjoram
⅛ tsp. salt	¼ cup soy sauce
¼ tsp. garlic powder	3 cans stock (optional)
¼ tsp. onion powder	3 potatoes, peeled and cubed
¼ cup sherry	6 carrots, peeled and sliced
1 Tbsp. olive oil	2 stalks celery, sliced
3 cans chicken broth (+1 can water)	

Coat squirrels in mixture of flour, salt, garlic powder and onion powder. Braise meat in skillet with olive oil and put in pressure cooker. Deglaze frying pan with sherry and pour contents of pan into pressure cooker. Add 2 cans chicken broth, onion, marjoram and soy sauce and cook for 20 minutes. Allow pressure to bleed off. Check liquid level and add stock alone or remaining can of broth and 1 can of water. Cook another 10 minutes. Allow pressure to bleed off, open cooker and add potatoes. Cook for 2 minutes. Remove pressure immediately under cool tap; add carrots and celery. Pressure cook for 2 more minutes. **Servings: 6-8**

Cooking Tips: Marjoram, a spice seldom used in this book, adds a special and unique flavor.

> **"...Marjoram adds a special and unique flavor to many recipes..."**

> **"...A real stick-to-the-ribs meal..."**

Royal Squirrel

Combined with mashed potatoes and a broccoli and cauliflower mix, this is a real stick-to-the-ribs meal.

4 squirrels, sectioned
Universal Marinade (See p. 279)
1 cup flour
1 cup cracker meal
2 Tbsp. margarine
¼ tsp. Worcestershire sauce
½ tsp. soy sauce
½ cup sherry
Garlic powder, sprinkle

Marinate meat in *Universal Marinade* for 2-6 hours, depending on desired flavor. Bread meat in flour and cracker meal mix. Cook over low heat for 20-30 minutes in covered pan using margarine to prevent sticking. Turn meat and add Worcestershire and soy sauces; re-cover and let cook. Turn meat, add sherry and garlic powder and finish cooking. **Servings: 4-6**

Alternate Meats: Rabbit

Cooking Tips: Parboiling or pressure cooking the meat tenderizes it before marination. For browner meat pieces, do not add wine to the pan until the meat is cooked. The meat may be sprinkled with pepper and garlic powder before breading.

Brandied Squirrel

It's important to balance this rich meat dish with a green vegetable and salad rather then potatoes or pasta.

4 squirrels, sectioned	1-2 lb. mushrooms, sliced
4 Tbsp. olive oil	2 Tbsp. butter
4-6 green onions, chopped	1½ cups heavy cream
2 cloves garlic, whole	3 egg yolks
1 cup brandy	¼ cup port wine
½ cup dry vermouth	

Pressure cook squirrel covered with water for 10-15 minutes. Brown squirrel pieces in skillet with olive oil. Add onions and garlic and cook for 5 minutes over low heat. Add brandy and vermouth. Caution: vermouth may flame. Simmer for 30 minutes. In separate skillet, sauté mushrooms in light butter and add to meat; cook 5 minutes more. Warm cream in saucepan; beat egg yolks in bowl. Place rabbit pieces on a platter. Stir warm cream into the juices left in skillet. Remove ½ cup of this mixture and blend with eggs. Return mixture to skillet and add port wine. Simmer on low for 5 minutes; do not let boil. Pour over meat. **Servings: 4-6**

Alternate Meats: Rabbit

Cooking Tips: Do not use a lightweight or non-stick frying pan to prepare this dish. Instead, use a heavy cast-iron skillet or Dutch oven.

This meal is not low in fat like many of the other recipes found here.

> **"...Experiment with different spices to find your favorite flavor..."**

Small Game Recipes...

Old-Fashioned Squirrel Stew
Serve with buttered cornbread for a good country taste.

3-4 squirrels, sectioned
1 Tbsp. olive oil
1 tsp. Worcestershire sauce
2 Tbsp. soy sauce
1 cup sherry or Burgundy wine
2 cups stock or 1 can chicken broth
1 qt. water

1 clove garlic, pressed or crushed
$1/8$ tsp. white or black pepper
$1/2$ onion, whole
6-8 carrots, peeled and diced
1 large can tomatoes
4 potatoes, cubed

Braise sectioned meat in frying pan with oil over medium heat. Add Worcestershire sauce and turn meat rapidly for 2 minutes. Add soy sauce and stir meat vigorously. Turn heat up to high and add wine. Stir vigorously for 2 minutes. Lower heat to medium and add stock or chicken broth. Cook for 5 minutes. Pour contents of pan into large pot or pressure cooker. Add water, garlic, pepper and onion and pressure cook for 20 minutes. Remove meat and juices from pressure cooker and put in crock pot. (If standard pot is used instead of pressure cooker, use more liquid and cook for at least 2 hours over low heat.) Add carrots and tomatoes to the crock pot. Set crock pot on low and simmer for 2 hours. Add potatoes and cook until potatoes are done. **Servings: 4-5**

Cooking Tips: This is a hearty meal and many variations are possible; experiment with different spices. For a variation, 1 can of green beans can be added.

"...All you need is a skillet and a large appetite..."

Bouillon Squirrel
Peas and mashed potatoes are excellent side dishes for this recipe.

4 squirrels, sectioned
Pepper, sprinkle
Lemon pepper, sprinkle
Paprika, sprinkle
Garlic powder, sprinkle
Canola or peanut oil
6 Tbsp. soy sauce
2 Tbsp. water
8 chicken bouillon cubes

Sprinkle meat with pepper, lemon pepper, paprika and garlic powder. Fry in pan coated with canola or peanut oil over low heat for about 10 minutes, turning often. Add soy sauce, water and chicken bouillon cubes. Cook over low heat, adding water to maintain plenty of juice. **Servings: 4-6**

Alternate Meats: Rabbit

Cooking Tips: Don't let the meat dry out—cook it slowly in a covered frying pan after all ingredients are added. If more soy sauce is desired, add a 50/50 soy and water mixture.

"...Wine adds a richness to any bland dish..."

Pressure Squirrel
Add corn on the cob and a fresh green salad for a wonderful low-fat dinner.

4 squirrels, sectioned
$1/4$ tsp. garlic salt or powder
4 chicken bouillon cubes
$1/4$ cup soy sauce
$1/8$ cup teriyaki sauce
Oil or margarine

Place all ingredients in pressure cooker. Add water to cover. Cook for 20-30 minutes. Remove meat from pressure cooker and drain off all water. Fry squirrel in skillet with oil or margarine until thoroughly cooked and browned. **Servings: 4-6**

Alternate Meats: Rabbit

Cooking Tips: Paprika, sweet basil and wine can be added when frying for a little extra flavor. The meat can be cooked in a pressure cooker and then finished in a frying pan several hours or even a day later.

Squirrel Stew
This is a self-contained meal that requires little more than a bit of freshly baked bread to soak up those last few morsels.

4 squirrels, cut into serving pieces
Canola or peanut oil
1 white onion, chopped
2 cloves garlic, minced
$1/8$ tsp. paprika
$1/8$ tsp. pepper
Thyme, pinch

1 cup Madeira wine
$4 1/4$ qts. stock
$2 1/2$ Tbsp. cornstarch
7 carrots, peeled and sliced
5 stalks celery, sliced
5 potatoes, cubed

Brown squirrel in frying pan coated with canola or peanut oil for 2 to 3 minutes over medium heat. Add onion, garlic, paprika, pepper and thyme. Keep stirring to avoid burning the onion. When onion is cooked, add Madeira and heat through. Remove squirrel and place in large Dutch oven, cooking pot or pressure cooker. Pour 3 qts. stock over meat. (If using pressure cooker, make sure the stock is a couple of inches over the top of meat.) Cook over low heat for 1 hour in Dutch oven or pot, 20 to 30 minutes in a pressure cooker, until meat and juices are well mixed. Thicken with $1 1/4$ cups stock and cornstarch. Mix well. Cook carrots, celery and potatoes until done; add to stew. **Servings: 4-6**

Alternate Meats: Rabbit

Cooking Tips: $1/2$ cup teriyaki marinade and $1/4$ cup soy sauce or 1 cup Lawry's Mesquite Marinade and $1/2$ cup chicken broth may be substituted for wine. A 50/50 combination of chicken broth and water may be substituted for stock.

Small Game Recipes...

Young Jackrabbit in Marinade

This rabbit is tasty with a side of baked beans.

2 jackrabbits, sectioned
See *Marinade for Young Jackrabbit*
1 cup flour
1/8 tsp. garlic salt
1/8 tsp. onion salt or powder
1/8 tsp. black or white pepper
3/4 cup cracker crumbs
Canola oil or margarine

Marinate sectioned rabbits for 24 hours in a sealable plastic bag. Discard marinade. Add flour, garlic salt, onion salt, pepper and cracker crumbs to sectioned meat in bag. Seal bag and shake to coat meat. Fry meat over low to medium heat in skillet with canola oil or margarine. **Servings: 6-8**

Alternate Meats: Young snowshoe hare

Cooking Tips: Special care is needed with all hares. Save only the back legs and saddle of the animal; the front legs and chest region are of no value.

For a variation to this recipe, pre-cook the jackrabbits in a pressure cooker with water for 20 minutes with 1/2 tsp. soy sauce, 1/4 tsp. Worcestershire sauce, 2 bouillon cubes and a dash of garlic powder. Remove pieces and begin marinating as above.

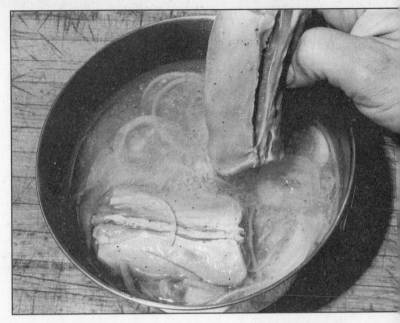

Rabbit can be marinated in beer and spices to prepare it for cooking.

Marinade for Young Jackrabbit

1 can beer
2 onions, sliced
Garlic powder, sprinkle
Paprika, sprinkle
1/4 tsp. ground clove
1/4 tsp. nutmeg
2 large bay leaves
Tarragon, pinch

Mix all ingredients together for a marinade that will help "tame" jackrabbit, which is a strong-flavored dark meat.

Cooking Tips: This marinade may be cooked separately and served on top of the meat.

Colonial Rabbit

Served with boiled potatoes, a green bean casserole, dinner rolls and a leafy salad, this makes a perfect meal for the holidays.

2 cottontail rabbits, sectioned
Flour
1 Tbsp. olive oil
1 can chicken broth or stock
1/2 onion, diced
3 carrots, peeled and coined
3 bay leaves
1 clove garlic, pressed
1 small can tomato puree
1/4 cup very cold water
2 Tbsp. flour
1/2 cup port or sherry wine
4 Tbsp. currant jelly
1/2 lb. mushrooms, sliced

Flour meat and brown in skillet with oil. Remove meat from pan. Add chicken broth and bring to a boil. Stir in onion, carrots, bay leaves and garlic and simmer for 20-30 minutes. Add tomato puree and continue to simmer. Remove 1/4 cup broth from pan and combine with water and flour, mixing until smooth. Return mixture to pan and continue simmering; add wine and currant jelly. Return rabbit to pan. When rabbit is cooked through, remove from mixture. Strain the mixture to catch bones. Sauté mushrooms and add to broth or serve on the side. **Servings: 4-6**

Alternate Meats: Squirrel

Cooking Tips: The meat can be pressure cooked for 5-10 minutes to speed up the preparation of this dish. This recipe was originally Early American; easy-to-find ingredients are used to simplify the cooking.

"...Gourmet quality; simple preparation..."

Small Game Recipes...

"...The marinade is vital to this recipe's success..."

Snowshoe Pot Roast

This is a self-contained meal; just add some freshly baked bread to soak up the juice.

2 young showshoe hares
See *Marinade for Showshoe Pot Roast*
1/2 onion, sliced
Paprika, sprinkle
Garlic powder, sprinkle
1 cup stock or 1 can chicken broth
6 potatoes, peeled and cubed
12 carrots, peeled and sliced

Preheat oven to 275°. Marinate two hares in large sealable plastic bag for 24 hours. Place hares, with marinade, into roasting pot and add onion. Sprinkle meat with paprika and garlic powder. Add stock or chicken broth to pot. Roast, covered, for 1 1/2 hours. Turn hares and add more liquid if necessary. Re-cover and cook for another 1 1/2 hours. Add potatoes and carrots and continue to cook until vegetables are finished. Add more liquid, baste and turn hares as needed. Meat is finished when it falls off the bone. Place hares on serving dish surrounded by potatoes and carrots. **Servings: 4-6**

Alternate Meats: Very young jackrabbits taken in the spring.

Cooking Tips: Hares taken in the winter can be very bitter tasting; hares of the early fall are best.

Marinade for Snowshoe Pot Roast

2 cups Burgundy wine
2 cups stock or 1 can chicken broth
1/4 tsp. nutmeg, ground
1/4 tsp. tarragon
1/2 onion, sectioned

Mix wine and stock or broth and transfer to large plastic storage bag. Add nutmeg, tarragon and onion. Shake to mix.

Rabbit in Tarragon Sauce

This dish can be served over pasta with a green leafy salad.

2 rabbits, cut into serving pieces
Salt and pepper
4 Tbsp. olive oil
1 cup onion, chopped
1 cup carrot, peeled and chopped
1 cup celery, chopped
Flour
2 cans chicken broth
1/2 cup sherry
2 tsp. tarragon
1 cup heavy whipping cream
2 Tbsp. Dijon mustard
1/4 cup parsley, minced

Season rabbit with salt and pepper. Place olive oil in skillet and brown rabbit. Remove meat and drain on paper towel. Add onion, carrot and celery to skillet. Sauté 5 minutes. Stir in enough flour to make a paste. Blend in broth, sherry and tarragon. Return rabbit to skillet. Bring sauce to a boil and reduce heat to simmer. Baste meat frequently for 45-60 minutes. Remove rabbit to serving platter and keep warm in oven. Strain and degrease sauce, discarding vegetables. Return remaining sauce to skillet and add cream. Simmer until thickened, stirring frequently. Remove from heat and add mustard and parsley. Pour sauce over rabbit and serve.
Servings: 6-8

Rabbit Filipino

Serve with boiled potatoes and a garden salad.

2 rabbits, sectioned
See *Special Marinade for Rabbit Filipino*
2 Tbsp. cornstarch

Marinate in *Special Marinade for Rabbit Filipino* 4 hours in refrigerator. Place marinade and meat in 3-4 qt. uncovered cooking pot or Dutch oven. Bring contents to a boil over medium heat. Reduce heat and simmer, stirring occasionally to keep meat from sticking. Simmer for 30 to 40 minutes, or until rabbit is tender. Remove meat and bay leaves from marinade and allow to cool. Place 1/2 cup marinade in shaker with cornstarch and shake to mix. Use only enough marinade/cornstarch to thicken the rest of the marinade. Discard what is not needed. Ladle marinade over the rabbit and serve. **Servings: 4-6**

Alternate Meats: Squirrel, raccoon, muskrat

Cooking Tips: Rabbit meat may be boned before ladling thickened marinade over meat.

"...This is a different-tasting dish liked by most who try it..."

Special Marinade for Rabbit Filipino

5 Tbsp. soy sauce
1/4 cup palm vinegar
3 cloves garlic, crushed or pressed
2 bay leaves
1/2 tsp. white pepper

In a stainless steel or glass bowl, combine soy sauce, palm vinegar, garlic, bay leaves and white pepper. Mix well.

Small Game Recipes...

Snowshoe in Sour Cream Sauce
Pasta can be served on the side or as a base for this dish.

4 snowshoe hares, sectioned
¼ cup soy sauce
⅛ cup teriyaki marinade
¼ tsp. black pepper
¼ tsp. garlic powder
¼ tsp. onion salt
2 cups flour

1 Tbsp. olive oil
1 onion, chopped
2 cup mushrooms, sliced
¼ bunch fresh parsley, chopped
½ cup whipping cream
½ cup sour cream

Preheat oven to 350°. Pressure cook hares for 20 minutes with the following spices in the water: soy sauce, teriyaki marinade, black pepper. Remove meat and let cool. Mix garlic powder and onion salt with flour and flour the meat. Brown floured meat in frying pan with oil over medium heat. Leave meat in skillet. Stir in onion and mushrooms and brown. Add parsley and mix well. Stir in whipping cream and sour cream. Pour into a glass cooking dish and bake for 5 minutes.   **Servings: 6-8**

Alternate Meats: Very young jackrabbits taken in the spring.

Curried Rabbit
Served over rice with an oriental mixed vegetable,
this has a nice sweet-and-sour flavor.

2 onions, sliced
2 Tbsp. olive oil
2 rabbits, cut into serving pieces
2 cloves garlic, minced
½ cup honey
Salt and pepper

3 cups grapefruit juice
2 tsp. cinnamon
3 tsp. curry powder (more if desired)
2 zucchini, sliced
2 green peppers, sliced
2 cups crushed pineapple with juice

In large skillet, sauté onions in olive oil. Add rabbit and garlic and continue to sauté until rabbit is browned. Mix honey, salt, pepper, grapefruit juice and spices in separate bowl. Pour over simmering rabbit. Cover and continue to simmer for 45 minutes. Add sliced vegetables and pineapple and simmer until vegetables are tender.
Servings: 6-8

Cooking Tips: For a thicker sauce, add cornstarch to the honey, salt, pepper, grapefruit juice and spice mix.

Mesquite Rabbit
Serve with baked beans, corn on the cob
and french fries.

2 rabbits, sectioned
See *Spiced Oil Marinade*
Lawry's Mesquite Marinade

Preheat oven to 200°. Rub *Spiced Oil Marinade* into sectioned meat and place meat on grill over very low heat. (Use low setting on gas grill, or allow coals to burn well down if using charcoal grill.) If using a gas grill, place one can of Bar-B-Q Smoke Pot on the lava rock and allow can to emit smoke. If using a charcoal grill, lay bits of mesquite wood or any kind of wood chips on coals to make smoke.

Smoke rabbit pieces well, but do not allow them to dry out. Frequently baste rabbit with *Spiced Oil* during cooking. Remove smoked rabbit pieces from grill and place in roasting pan. Do not allow pieces to touch. Pour Lawry's Mesquite Marinade over pieces and bake until rabbit is finished. Turn often and add marinade when needed.   **Servings: 6-8**

Cooking Tips: Because the smoking process can cause the meat to dry out, it is extremely important to keep it moist by basting.

Spiced Oil Marinade
1 cup canola oil
2 garlic cloves, crushed
¼ tsp. paprika
1 Tbsp. teriyaki marinade

Mix all ingredients well.

Cottontail rabbits fry nicely into a dish fit for a king.

Small Game Recipes...

The rabbit pieces are being soaked in salt water and will emerge white and clean and ready for cooking.

"...Excellent in camp—it's fast and simple..."

Pan-Fried Rabbit

This can be made into a wonderful low-fat dinner if served with steamed green beans, rice and a fresh fruit salad for dessert.

2 rabbits, sectioned
Canola oil
Pepper, sprinkle
Garlic powder, sprinkle
Paprika, sprinkle
Onion salt, sprinkle

Place meat in frying pan coated with light canola oil and cook over low heat. Season both sides of meat to taste and cook until almost done. Turn heat up to medium to brown rabbit. Cook meat until well-done, not rare. **Servings: 4-6**

Cooking Tips: This dish is best with tender rabbit; for more mature rabbits, see *Pressure Squirrel* (p. 223). Pure lard or butter may be used instead of oil for more flavor and more fat.

Rabbit Madeira

This makes a wonderful summer dinner when served with a rice dish and fresh fruit platter.

1¹/₂ cups dry bread crumbs	Rind of 2 oranges
1 tsp. garlic powder	2 cups orange juice
1 tsp. rosemary	¹/₄ cup lemon juice
2 rabbits, cut into serving pieces	1 cup Madeira or sherry wine
2 eggs, beaten	1 lb. fresh mushrooms, sliced
4 Tbsp. cornstarch	

Preheat oven to 350°. Mix bread crumbs, garlic powder and rosemary. Dip rabbit in eggs and coat thoroughly in bread crumb mixture. Brown rabbit under broiler and place in baking dish. Combine cornstarch, orange rind, juices and Madeira wine or sherry to make sauce. Pour sauce over browned rabbit and cover. Bake 1 hour or until rabbit is tender. Stir often to completely cover rabbit. Add mushrooms and cook until tender. **Servings: 6-8**

Rabbit Nepal

Served over rice with a glass of white wine and a fresh green salad with creamy garlic dressing, this is a gourmet treat.

2 Tbsp. coriander, ground	2 Tbsp. olive oil
1 tsp. tumeric	2 cloves garlic, minced
1 tsp. ginger, ground	1 onion, minced
2 Tbsp. cornstarch	2 cans stewed tomatoes, drained
2 cups plain low-fat yogurt	2 cups frozen peas
2 rabbits, cut into serving pieces	Salt and pepper

Combine spices, cornstarch and yogurt. Coat rabbit well with this mixture and refrigerate overnight. In large skillet, heat oil and add garlic, onion, marinated rabbit and yogurt sauce. Cover, simmer and stir often until rabbit is browned and tender (about 1 hour). Add stewed tomatoes, peas, salt and pepper during last 10 minutes of cooking. **Servings: 6-8**

"...A gourmet treat..."

Small Game Recipes...

"...Perfect meat for experimentation with ingredients..."

Small Game Hash
Serve with dinner rolls and a fresh green salad.

Potatoes, peeled and cubed
3 carrots, peeled and diced
Leftover rabbit, cubed
1-2 cups stock or beef broth
Salt and pepper
Onion salt

Boil potatoes and carrots until slightly undercooked. Combine cooked leftover meat, potatoes, carrots, stock or broth in skillet and simmer for 1/2 hour. Season to taste. **Servings: 4**

Alternate Meats: Squirrel, possum, raccoon, muskrat.

Cooking Tips: Do not overcook potatoes or they will turn mushy later. Optional ingredients that will spice up this dish are salsa, white pepper (added at the end of cooking time) and diced onion (added with the potatoes and carrots).

Use 1 lb. potatoes for every 1 lb. rabbit meat.

Rabbit Fricassee
Serve with a carrot or sweet potato dish and a heavy, thick-crusted bread.

2 cups red wine
2 Tbsp. lemon juice
2 bay leaves
1 tsp. thyme
1/4 tsp. marjoram
Salt and pepper
1 tsp. garlic powder
2 rabbits, cut into serving pieces
2 Tbsp. olive oil
1 onion, chopped
2 cloves garlic, minced
2 Tbsp. cornstarch

Mix wine, lemon juice, bay leaves, thyme, marjoram, salt, pepper and garlic powder to make a marinade. Place rabbit in large baking dish and pour marinade over rabbit. Cover and refrigerate overnight. Remove rabbit from marinade when ready to cook and dry well. Strain marinade and save. Heat oil in a large skillet. Sauté onions and garlic. Add rabbit and brown. Add cornstarch to marinade and pour over rabbit. Cover and simmer 1-1 1/2 hours or until tender. **Servings: 6-8**

Rabbit Braised in Wine
Serve with a side of fettucine, garlic bread and a fresh salad.

2 rabbits, cut into serving pieces
Salt and pepper
Flour
2 Tbsp. olive oil
2 onions, sliced
2 cloves garlic, minced
6 carrots, peeled and sliced
1 lb. fresh mushrooms, sliced
2 Tbsp. fresh parsley, minced
1/4 tsp. thyme
1/2 tsp. oregano, rubbed
4 bay leaves
2 cups dry white wine

Preheat oven to 350°. Salt and pepper rabbit and coat with flour. Place oil, onions, garlic, carrots and mushrooms in large casserole dish. Place rabbit on top of vegetables. Sprinkle with parsley, thyme and oregano. Add bay leaves and wine. Cover and bake 1 hour or until rabbit is tender. Remove bay leaves before serving.

Servings: 6-8

Rabbit Sauté
Serve over a bed of rice and garnish with fresh parsley for a splash of color.

3 Tbsp. olive oil
2 rabbits, cut into serving pieces
4 cloves garlic, minced
2 large onions, minced
1 cup white wine
2 16-oz. cans tomato sauce
1 tsp. thyme
4 bay leaves
1 tsp. sweet basil, rubbed
1 tsp. dry parsley
1 can black olives

Heat olive oil in large skillet and brown rabbit, garlic and onions. Remove rabbit and drain on paper towel. Pour in wine and bring to a boil. Add tomato sauce, thyme, bay leaves, sweet basil and parsley. Stir well; return rabbit to skillet. Cover and simmer 30 minutes. Add olives and simmer 10 additional minutes. **Servings: 6**

"...This dish practically cooks itself..."

Crock Pot Rabbit
This dish is at its best served over rice with a fresh green salad.

2 rabbits, cut into serving pieces
1 cup celery, sliced
1 cup carrots, peeled and sliced
1 onion, chopped
1 can water chestnuts, sliced
2 cups fresh mushrooms, sliced
3 cups chicken broth
Salt and pepper
2 Tbsp. cornstarch
1/2 cup sherry

Place all ingredients except cornstarch and sherry in crock pot and cook on low for 6 hours. Remove rabbit from pot. In a separate bowl, combine sherry and cornstarch. Pour into crock pot to thicken the sauce. Return rabbit to the crock pot and mix. **Servings: 6-8**

Upland Game Recipes...

Skillet Quail

Garden vegetables and pinto beans add a splash of color to this meal.

8 quail
Garlic powder, dusting
Paprika, dusting
White pepper, dusting
Canola oil

Soak quail in lightly-salted water for 2 hours. Remove and dry birds. Dust birds inside and out with garlic powder, paprika and white pepper. Fry birds in covered skillet coated with canola oil over medium heat for 20 minutes; uncover for 10 more minutes. Make sure the quail are cooked thoroughly and properly. Test the meat near the bone with a covered knife to gauge doneness. **Servings: 4**

Alternate Meats: Young dove, young partridge

Cooking Tips: For additional flavor, place a few flakes of oregano and tarragon leaves inside cavity before frying.

Stuffed Quail

This gourmet meal is excellent with a salad, green beans and crusty bread.

8 quail	2 cups water
Lard	2 cups broth or stock
White pepper, sprinkle	4 Tbsp. soy sauce
Paprika, sprinkle	4 drops sesame oil
Garlic powder, sprinkle	6 beef bouillon cubes
1 pkg. prepared stuffing, chicken flavor	Lawry's Mesquite Marinade

Preheat oven to 300°. Skin or pluck quail. Soak birds 1 hour in salt water and then 10 minutes in clear water. Drain birds and dry on paper towels. Rub each bird sparingly with lard, massaging it into the meat. Sprinkle each bird with white pepper, paprika and garlic powder. Prepare stuffing according to package directions and stuff each bird, place in roasting pan. Add water, broth or stock, soy sauce, sesame oil and bouillon cubes. Cover and cook two hours. Make an incision in birds to check doneness. If needed, continue cooking for another 30 minutes. When done, evenly coat birds with marinade and cook, uncovered, until marinade is hot.

Servings: 4

Alternate Meats: Partridge

Cooking Tips: If Lawry's Mesquite Marinade is not available, teriyaki glaze (not teriyaki marinade) may be used.

Marinated Dove

Create a nutritious meal by serving baked beans and corn with this dish.

16 mourning or whitewing dove breasts
Universal Marinade (See p. 000)
Flour
Margarine
Canola oil

Marinate dove breasts all day in *Universal Marinade*. Flour each section of meat and place in skillet with equal mixture of margarine and canola oil. Cover and fry over medium heat until cooked through. **Servings: 4**

Cooking Tips: Instead of canola oil, an equal amount of lard may be mixed with margarine.

Marinated Fried Quail

Enhance the flavor of this dish by serving it with corn and a side salad.

8 quail
1 qt. water
¼ cup soy sauce
Universal Marinade (See p. 000)
Canola oil

Parboil quail slowly for 1 hour (or pressure cook 10 minutes) in water with soy sauce. Rinse and dry birds. Marinate meat for 2-6 hours in *Universal Marinade*. Remove birds and let stand for ½ hour to drain. Dry birds to remove remaining marinade. Fry birds over medium heat in skillet with canola oil until golden brown. **Servings: 4**

Alternate Meats: Partridge

Cooking Tips: A light dusting with white pepper during frying adds a bit of zest to the finished product.

Upland Game Recipes...

"...A fast and easy basic recipe that results in a fine meal..."

Wild Turkey Fiesta Casserole

This wild casserole is a real fiesta when served with a fresh fruit salad.

2 frozen pie crusts	¹/₂ cup onion, minced
1 cup low-fat yogurt	¹/₂ cup celery, minced
¹/₄ cup low-fat milk	1 tsp. olive oil
¹/₄ tsp. cumin	2 cups fresh spinach, chopped
4-oz. diced green chilies, drained	2 cups leftover wild turkey, cubed
1 can cream of chicken soup	1 cup Monterey Jack cheese, shredded
1 clove garlic, minced	1 cup sharp cheddar cheese, shredded

Preheat oven to 375°. Thaw pie crusts and cut slits in several places. Place bottom crust in pie pan. In large mixing bowl, combine yogurt, milk, cumin, green chilies and soup. Sauté garlic, onion and celery in skillet with olive oil. Add spinach and continue to sauté. Add to large mixing bowl. In another bowl, mix turkey and cheeses. Layer the two mixtures in pie crust, alternating until all is used. Place second pie crust over last layer. Seal and flute. Bake 1 hour.   **Servings: 4**

Alternate Meats: Any leftover game bird meat.

"....A real time saver!.."

Wild Turkey and Biscuit Bake

Eating a well-balanced meal is easy. Serve this dish with a crisp garden salad and fresh fruit.

- 1 cup fresh mushrooms, sliced
- ¹/₄ cup green onions, sliced
- 1 tsp. olive oil
- 2 cups leftover wild turkey, cubed
- 1 cup chili sauce
- ¹/₄ cup brown sugar
- 2 Tbsp. mustard
- 2 cups biscuit mix

Preheat oven to 375°. Sauté mushrooms and green onions in skillet with olive oil. Drain on paper towel. Mix turkey, chili sauce, brown sugar and mustard in large bowl. Stir in mushrooms and onions and pour into casserole dish. Prepare biscuit mix according to package directions and spoon onto mixture in casserole dish. Bake 30 minutes until biscuit topping is lightly browned.

Servings: 6

Alternate Meats: Any wild bird meat.

Fruited Wild Turkey Pot Pie is delicious; there are few better ways to use leftover turkey.

"...Absolutely gourmet!.."

Wild Turkey Pot Pie

This dish is excellent with a gelatin salad and mashed potatoes.

3 cups leftover wild turkey, cubed	3 cups leftover gravy
3 potatoes, peeled, cubed and boiled	Salt
1 can green beans, drained	Pepper
1 cup celery, chopped	1 tsp. garlic powder
2 cups frozen peas	3 cups biscuit dough

Preheat oven to 400°. Mix turkey, cooked potatoes, green beans, celery, peas and gravy in large baking dish. Sprinkle with salt, pepper and garlic powder. Follow biscuit dough directions on package to prepare top crust. Roll out dough and place over mixture in baking dish. Flute edges and cut slits in top. Bake 1 hour.

Servings: 6

Cooking Tips: Any prepared chicken/turkey gravy will work if you do not have leftovers.

Upland Game Recipes...

Wild turkey, well-cooked and ready to serve.

Wild Turkey Pilaf

This delightful dish is tasty with creamed carrots and hot rolls.

2 Tbsp. butter
1 onion, diced
$^1/_2$ cup green pepper, diced
2 cups rice, uncooked
5 cups chicken broth
4 cups leftover wild turkey, diced
Salt, sprinkle
Pepper, sprinkle
1 cup cheddar cheese, shredded

Melt butter in large saucepan. Sauté onion and green pepper. Add rice and continue sautéing. Add broth, turkey, salt and pepper. Bring to a boil and then reduce heat to simmer. Cover and cook 20-30 minutes. Fluff mixture and pour into serving dish. Sprinkle with cheese. **Servings: 6**

Wild Turkey Stuffed Pie

To enhance the flavor of this dish, serve with mashed potatoes and baked squash.

2 cups leftover wild turkey, cubed
$^1/_2$ tsp. salt
$^1/_2$ tsp. pepper
1 cup leftover turkey stuffing
$^1/_2$ cup green onions, sliced
1 clove garlic, minced
$^1/_2$ cup peas
1 cup milk
2 eggs
$^1/_2$ cup biscuit mix

Preheat oven to 375°. Mix turkey, salt, pepper, stuffing, green onions, garlic and peas in large bowl. Spoon into baking dish. In separate bowl, mix milk, eggs and biscuit mix and pour over turkey mixture. Bake 30 minutes or until knife inserted into center comes out clean. **Servings: 4**

Cooking Tips: Any prepared turkey stuffing will work if you do not have leftovers.

Old-Fashioned Roast Wild Turkey

For a hearty meal, serve with a green salad, broccoli, cranberry sauce or whole cranberries and mashed potatoes and gravy.

1 turkey
Lard
Garlic salt, sprinkle
Onion salt, sprinkle
Black pepper, sprinkle
Paprika, sprinkle
1 pkg. commercial stuffing, chicken flavor

Stock
1 can chicken broth
6 chicken bouillon cubes
1 can water
Garlic powder, sprinkle
1 Tbsp. margarine

Preheat oven to 275°. Wash and dry bird completely. Rub turkey vigorously with lard to prepare skin for browning and help prevent drying. Sprinkle garlic salt, onion salt, black pepper and paprika all over bird, inside and out. Prepare stuffing according to package directions. Stuff bird by forcing stuffing into crop area first, and then folding skin back to hold stuffing in place. Stuff cavity full. Place extra stuffing into bread pan, cover with aluminum foil and set aside. Coat bottom of roasting pan with lard and add turkey, breast up. Add stock, chicken broth, bouillon cubes and water to roasting pan. Sprinkle breast of bird with garlic powder and paprika. Place margarine on top of breast and press down on bird to hold in place so it bastes the bird at it cooks. Cook younger birds 3-4 hours and older birds as long as 7 hours. Baste every $^1/_2$ hour with liquid from bottom of pan. Place extra stuffing in oven during last 2 hours of cooking. Mix this stuffing with stuffing from turkey before serving to obtain the proper moisture level.

Servings: 6

Cooking Tips: To retain moisture, cover bird with aluminum foil before covering with roasting pan lid. Optional: add $^1/_2$ cup sherry to broth in pan toward end of cooking cycle.

Instead of using commercial stuffing, see *Side Dish Recipes* for homemade stuffing recipes.

> **"...Very little effort is required to produce a gourmet meal with this recipe..."**

Upland Game Recipes...

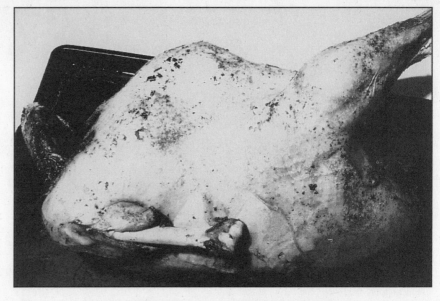

This wild turkey will be roasted in a covered pan to keep it tender.

Wild Turkey and Biscuit Casserole

A tomato and onion salad and warm croissants finish off this dish.

4 eggs
2 cups milk
2 cups biscuit mix
1/2 tsp. sage
2 pkgs. dry chicken gravy mix
4-6 cups leftover wild turkey, chopped
1/2 cup celery, diced
1/2 cup onion, diced
1 cup cheddar cheese, shredded

Preheat oven to 350°. Beat eggs, milk, biscuit mix, sage and gravy mix in large bowl. Add turkey, celery, onion and cheese. Pour into baking dish. Bake 1 hour until lightly browned and knife inserted in center comes out clean.

Servings: 6

Wild Turkey and Wild Rice Casserole

This holiday meal would be best served with cranberries and a relish tray.

2 cups wild rice
1 cup brown rice
5 cups chicken broth
4 cups leftover wild turkey, diced
1 lb. mushrooms, sliced
1 pint heavy cream
1 tsp. butter
2 cups celery, diced
1 can water chestnuts, sliced
2 cans chicken broth
4 Tbsp. onion, chopped
1 tsp. garlic, chopped
Salt
Pepper
4 Tbsp. Parmesan cheese, grated

Preheat oven to 350°. Combine wild rice, brown rice and 5 cups chicken broth in microwave dish. Microwave on high 15 minutes. Cover and microwave on simmer 15 minutes. In mixing bowl, toss rice with turkey and mushrooms. Add cream, butter, celery, water chestnuts, 2 cans chicken broth, onion, garlic, salt and pepper. Pour into baking dish and sprinkle with Parmesan cheese. Bake 1 hour.

Servings: 6

Fruited Wild Turkey Pot Pie

Liven up this fruity pie with a fresh garden salad served on the side.

2 frozen pie crusts
1 tsp. butter
1 Tbsp. cornstarch
1/2 tsp. ginger
1 Tbsp. soy sauce
1 Tbsp. Worcestershire sauce
1 tsp. mustard
1/2 cup orange juice
2 cups leftover wild turkey, cubed
1/2 cup celery, minced
1/4 cup seedless raisins
1/4 cup apple, minced
1/4 cup onion, minced
1/4 cup green pepper, minced
2 cloves garlic, minced
1 tsp. olive oil

Preheat oven to 400°. Thaw pie crusts and place one pie crust into pie pan. In saucepan, melt butter and add cornstarch, ginger, soy sauce, Worcestershire sauce and mustard. Slowly add orange juice and cook over medium heat, stirring constantly. When mixture begins to thicken, remove from heat. Stir in turkey, celery, raisins and apples. In skillet, sauté onion, green pepper and garlic in olive oil. Drain on paper towel and add to above mixture. Pour into pie shell. Cut slits in second pie shell and place on top of mixture. Seal and flute. Bake 1 hour or until golden brown. Let stand 15 minutes before serving.   **Servings: 4**

Alternate Meats: Any leftover game bird meat.

"...A hearty meal for a hearty appetite..."

Upland Game Recipes...

Wild Turkey Asparagus Pie
A green leafy salad will liven up this meal.

1/2 cup green onions, sliced	1 cup Half and Half
1 cup fresh mushrooms, sliced	1/2 tsp. garlic powder
1 tsp. butter	Salt
1 lb. fresh asparagus spears	Pepper
1 8-oz. can crescent dinner rolls	2 cups leftover wild turkey, cubed
2 Tbsp. butter	2 Tbsp. sherry
2 Tbsp. flour	

Preheat oven to 375°. Sauté green onions and mushrooms in skillet with 1 tsp. butter. Drain on paper towel. Steam asparagus until barely tender. Drain on paper towel. Separate dough and place in ungreased pie pan in spoke fashion, letting tips overlap rim by about 3 inches. Press dough in bottom of pan and sides to form crust. In saucepan, melt 2 Tbsp. butter and add flour. Stir to make paste. Add cream and stir until smooth. Add garlic powder, salt and pepper. Continue cooking and stirring until thickened. Stir in turkey, onions, mushrooms and sherry. Pour into crust. Layer asparagus over mixture. Bring tips of dough over filling to center. Do not overlap crust. Bake 30 minutes or until golden brown. **Servings: 6**

Wild Turkey Taboule
To complete this meal, serve with a cheese and cracker tray or hot buttered rolls.

1 7-oz. pkg. Taboule wheat salad mix	2 Tbsp. parsley, chopped
1 1/2 cups chicken broth	2 Tbsp. onion, minced
1/3 cup olive oil	2 Tbsp. lemon juice
2 cups leftover wild turkey, cubed	1 Tbsp. wine vinegar
1/2 cup tomato, chopped	

In large bowl, combine wheat salad mix with chicken broth and oil. Stir and let stand 30 minutes. Blend in turkey, tomato, parsley, onion, lemon juice and wine vinegar. Chill. Fluff and serve on lettuce leaves. **Servings: 4**

"...The marinade makes this dish..."

Sage Hen Supreme
Delicious when served with baked beans, french fries and fresh vegetables.

1 large sage hen
Universal Marinade *(See p. 279)*
Flour

Bone sage hen, removing breast meat from keel and leaving legs intact. Discard backplate. Slice breasts into thin steaks using thin-bladed knife. Marinate steaks in *Universal Marinade* for several hours. Remove meat and discard marinade. Flour meat generously and cook slowly in skillet over low to medium heat until brown and cooked through. **Servings: 3**

Alternate Meats: Grouse, chukar

Cooking Tips: Since sage hen is a very dark meat, it's best marinated to lighten the color, impart flavor and reduce an overly "sagey" taste.

"...A gourmet dinner; ideal to impress friends..."

Grouse and Dumplings
This hearty meal should be served with warm rolls and a dinner salad.

4 large or 6 small grouse	See *Dumplings*
1 cup flour	2 pinches sweet basil, ground
Cooking oil	1/4 tsp. garlic clove, minced
White pepper, dusting	Stock or chicken broth
Onion salt, dusting	See *Gravy for Grouse and Dumplings*

Bone grouse by removing breast meat from keel. Cut legs away from bony backplate with game shears and discard backplate. Parboil breasts and legs for 1 hour in large pot or pressure cook 10 minutes. Coat meat with flour and place in deep Dutch oven heated with oil. Lower heat and dust meat with white pepper, onion salt, basil and garlic. Distribute garlic evenly over meat. Add stock or chicken broth to fully cover meat. (This stock will be used to cook the dumplings and make the gravy.) Cover and simmer until tender. Remove meat and set aside. When dumplings and gravy are complete, place meat and dumplings on a dish and smother with gravy. **Servings: 8**

Alternate Meats: Partridge, pheasant, chukar; this recipe works well with all grouse except sage grouse.

Cooking Tips: Bacon drippings or olive oil may be used to fry meat instead of cooking oil.

Dumplings

1 1/2 cups flour, sifted
3 tsp. baking powder
1/4 tsp. salt
1 tsp. sugar
Lukewarm water

In large bowl, sift together flour, baking powder, salt and sugar. Make a dough by adding lukewarm water slowly until proper consistency is reached. Bring stock used to cook grouse to gentle boil and drop dumpling dough into liquid using a tablespoon. Remove finished dumplings and set aside.

Gravy for Grouse and Dumplings

Stock
3-5 Tbsp. cornstarch
1/8 cup margarine
1/4 cup milk

Remove 1 cup of stock from Dutch oven used to cook grouse and add cornstarch to make a thickener the consistency of whole milk. Add margarine and milk to remaining juice in Dutch oven. Stir. Bring to low boil and add thickener until gravy is smooth. Pour gravy over meat and dumplings.

Upland Game Recipes...

Just Plain Dove

Certainly not plain when served with rice and a fresh steamed vegetable.

16 dove breasts
1¹/₂ gallons water
³/₄ cup white vinegar
Garlic powder, sprinkle
Paprika, sprinkle
Onion powder, sprinkle
White pepper, sprinkle
Canola oil or peanut oil

Soak dove breasts for 2 hours in water/vinegar mixture. Wash each breast and dry on paper towel. Spice top side of each breast with garlic powder, paprika, onion powder and white pepper. Place each breast, bone-side down, in skillet with canola oil or peanut oil. Cover and cook 5-10 minutes over medium heat. Turn meat, cover and cook until done. **Servings: 4**

"...A quick, easy and tasty way to cook dove breasts..."

Marsala Breast of Dove in Rice

Impress your friends with this gourmet meal served with hot fresh bread and a green leafy salad.

4 cups rice, uncooked	**Pepper, sprinkle**
4 Tbsp. margarine	**¹/₂ tsp. rosemary, hard rubbed**
16 dove breasts	**1 lb. mushrooms, whole**
Lemon juice	**1 medium onion, chopped**
Salt, sprinkle	**1 cup Marsala wine**

Preheat oven to 350°. Sauté rice in skillet with margarine over medium heat. Cook until light brown in color. Place rice in bottom of casserole dish. Rest dove breasts, meat-side up, on rice. Sprinkle with lemon juice, salt, pepper and rosemary. Surround breasts with mushrooms and onions. Pour wine over meat and rice. Cover and bake 30 minutes or until rice is fluffy and breasts are tender and cooked through. Make small incision in dove to check for doneness. **Servings: 4**

Quail Breasts with Fruited Rice

For a complete meal, serve with buttered croissants and a green leafy salad.

¹/₂ cup celery, minced	**¹/₂ tsp. poultry seasoning**
¹/₄ cup onion, minced	**1 cup apple, diced**
1 tsp. olive oil	**¹/₂ cup seedless golden raisins**
2 cups chicken broth	**6 quail breasts**
1 7-oz. pkg. rice pilaf, chicken flavored	**6 slices bacon**

Preheat oven to 350°. In skillet, sauté celery and onion in olive oil. Add chicken broth and bring to boil. Stir in rice pilaf contents and poultry seasoning. Cover and simmer until rice is tender and liquid is absorbed. Add apples and raisins. Spoon mixture into baking dish. Arrange quail breasts on top of rice mixture and top each breast with one slice of bacon. Cover and bake 15 minutes. Remove cover and bake 30-45 minutes or until quail breasts are tender. **Servings: 6**

"...Quail are tasty birds demanding very little attention to make them excellent..."

Wild turkey can be used in a variety of different dishes—the leftovers especially good in casseroles.

234

Upland Game Recipes...

Skillet Quail

Garden vegetables and pinto beans add a splash of color to this meal.

8 quail
Garlic powder, dusting
Paprika, dusting
White pepper, dusting
Canola oil

Soak quail in lightly-salted water for 2 hours. Remove and dry birds. Dust birds inside and out with garlic powder, paprika and white pepper. Fry birds in covered skillet coated with canola oil over medium heat for 20 minutes; uncover and fry 10 more minutes. Make sure the quail are cooked through, but not overcooked. Test for red juices in breast area with sharp-pointed knife to gauge doneness. **Servings: 4**

Alternate Meats: Young dove, young partridge

Cooking Tips: For additional flavor, place a few flakes of oregano and tarragon leaves inside cavity before frying.

Marinated Fried Quail

Enhance the flavor of this dish by serving it with corn and a side salad.

8 quail
1 qt. water
1/4 cup soy sauce
Universal Marinade *(See p. 279)*
Canola oil

Parboil quail slowly for 1 hour (or pressure cook 10 minutes) in water with soy sauce. Rinse and dry birds. Marinate meat for 2-6 hours in *Universal Marinade*. Remove birds and let stand for 1/2-hour to drain. Dry birds to remove remaining marinade. Fry birds over medium heat in skillet with canola oil until golden brown. **Servings: 4**

Alternate Meats: Partridge

Cooking Tips: A light dusting with white pepper during frying adds a bit of zest to the finished product.

Stuffed Quail

This gourmet meal is excellent with a salad, green beans and crusty bread.

8 quail	2 cups water
Lard	2 cups broth or stock
White pepper, sprinkle	4 Tbsp. soy sauce
Paprika, sprinkle	4 drops sesame oil
Garlic powder, sprinkle	6 beef bouillon cubes
1 pkg. commercial stuffing, chicken flavor	Lawry's Mesquite Marinade

Preheat oven to 300°. Skin or pluck quail. Soak birds 1 hour in salt water and then 10 minutes in clear water. Drain birds and dry on paper towels. Rub each bird sparingly with lard, massaging it into the meat. Sprinkle each bird with white pepper, paprika and garlic powder. Prepare stuffing according to package directions and stuff each bird. Place in roasting pan and add water, broth or stock, soy sauce, sesame oil and bouillon cubes. Cover and cook 2 hours. Make an incision in birds to check doneness. If needed, continue cooking for another 30 minutes. When done, evenly coat birds with marinade and cook, uncovered, until marinade is hot.

Servings: 4

Alternate Meats: Partridge

Cooking Tips: If Lawry's Mesquite Marinade is not available, teriyaki glaze (not teriyaki marinade) may be used.

Marinated Dove

Create an exciting meal with a salad, baked beans, white rice and bread and butter.

16 mourning or whitewing dove breasts
Universal Marinade *(See p. 279)*
Flour
Margarine
Canola oil

Marinate dove breasts all day in *Universal Marinade*. Flour each section of meat and place in skillet with equal mixture of margarine and canola oil. Cover and fry over medium heat until cooked through. **Servings: 4**

Cooking Tips: Instead of canola oil, an equal amount of lard may be mixed with margarine.

Upland Game Recipes...

Quail On Coals with Flavored Oil

This fireside dish is excellent served with baked potatoes, baked beans and bread.

2 cups canola oil	$\frac{1}{8}$ tsp. sweet basil
$\frac{1}{2}$ onion, chopped	2-3 drops sesame oil
Tarragon, pinch	$\frac{1}{8}$ tsp. garlic powder or salt
White pepper, pinch	12 quail

Mix oil, onion, tarragon, pepper, sweet basil, sesame oil and garlic powder or salt in large bowl. Allow mixture to stand 2 to 3 hours. Rub each quail thoroughly with oil mixture, working oil into the meat. Cook each bird on grate over medium-hot coals. Watch birds carefully, turning often to prevent overcooking in any one spot.

Servings: 6

Alternate Meats: Partridge

Cooking Tips: Quail may be rubbed with oil mixture 2 hours before cooking. Apply oil several times, before and during the cooking process. Without this oil mixture, quail tend to dry out badly over the coals.

"...The heart of this recipe is the oil mixture..."

"...Gourmet, all the way..."

Tender Fried Quail

This gourmet dish is best served with a baked potato topped with sour cream and chives, green beans and a glass of wine.

8 quail	$\frac{1}{8}$ tsp. garlic powder
$\frac{1}{4}$ cup soy sauce	$\frac{1}{8}$ tsp. onion powder
$\frac{1}{8}$ tsp. Lawry's Seasoned Salt	$\frac{1}{8}$ tsp. pepper, white or black
$\frac{1}{8}$ tsp. Lawry's Seasoned Pepper	Canola oil

Pre-cook quail for 10 minutes in pressure cooker (or parboil slowly 1 hour) in water treated with soy sauce, seasoned salt, seasoned pepper, garlic powder, onion powder and pepper. Remove birds from water, drain and dry. Fry birds in skillet with canola oil over medium heat until golden brown, turning often to ensure even cooking. Since birds are partially cooked, they will finish rapidly. Cook through, but do not overcook or they will be dried out.

Servings: 4

Alternate Meats: Partridge

Cooking Tips: During the last 5 minutes of cooking, $\frac{1}{2}$ cup of port wine may be added.

"...If not smoked too long, quail will remain moist..."

Smoked Quail

This is often taken on hiking trips and eaten for lunch without anything else.

8 quail
$\frac{1}{8}$ cup salt
2 qts. water
Lawry's Mesquite Marinade
Lard
White pepper, sprinkle
Garlic powder, sprinkle

Soak quail in salt water 1 hour. Vigorously rub down meat with marinade, but do not over-apply. Let birds stand 10 minutes. Lightly rub down with lard. Dust with pepper and garlic powder. Smoke or grill birds until done.

Servings: 4

Quick Campsite Game Bird Soup

This tasty soup is best served with crackers, bread or croutons.

2 qts. water
1 clove garlic, chopped
$\frac{1}{4}$ cup soy sauce
4 chicken bouillon cubes
2 lb. game birds, sectioned
2 pkgs. dry soup mix, chicken flavor

In large pot or pressure cooker, mix water, garlic, soy sauce and bouillon cubes. Add meat and boil or pressure cook until tender. Strain liquid and bone meat. Return meat to liquid and add soup mix. Heat through.

Servings: 5-6

Alternate Meats: Quail, pheasant, dove, chukar, grouse, turkey, partridge

Cooking Tips: Frozen or canned vegetables, such as green beans, cauliflower or corn, can be added for flavor.

"...There's nothing like a bowl of soup after a long day of hunting..."

Upland Game Recipes...

Not So Fancy Pheasant

*A baked potato and green beans are
"not so fancy" asides to this dish.*

2 Tbsp. margarine
1 cup canola oil
2 pheasant, refrigerated
3 cups water
12 chicken bouillon cubes
1/4 cup soy sauce
Stock or broth

Preheat oven to 300°. Melt margarine in skillet
and mix with canola oil. Remove birds from
refrigerator and paint with margarine/oil mixture. Place birds in roasting pan and add water,
bouillon cubes and soy sauce. Cook 1 hour.
Turn birds in pan and reduce heat to 250°. Add
stock or broth as needed. Cook until tender.

Servings: 4

Alternate Meats: Grouse, chukar

Cooking Tips: Orange, lemon and apple slices,
with peels, may be inserted into each pheasant
cavity before cooking.

For a superb gravy base, add 1/2 cup of sherry
3 hours into the cooking process.

This boned, cooked pheasant is smothered in a
sauce thickened with whole wheat flour. A rice dish
and fresh vegetable would complete this meal.

Roast Pheasant with Wine Sauce

Delicious with mashed potatoes and gravy, cranberry sauce and broccoli.

2 pheasant
Olive oil
Garlic salt or powder, sprinkle
Onion powder, sprinkle
Ground sage, trace
White pepper, dusting

1 can chicken broth
4 slices bacon
1 cup sauterne wine
1/2 bunch parsley, chopped
2 chicken bouillon cubes
1/2 cup green onions, diced

Preheat oven to 275°. Using heavy knife, split birds down keel, halving each one.
Rub olive oil vigorously into birds on all sides. Sprinkle garlic salt or powder and
onion powder on birds; rub trace of ground sage into breast meat only. Dust with
white pepper. Set aside. Pour chicken broth into large roasting pan and add pheasant halves, breast-side up. Lay 1 slice of bacon lengthwise over each breast half.
Cover and cook 2 hours. Uncover and turn birds breast-side down, adding more
broth if needed. Add wine, parsley, bouillon cubes and green onion to broth in pan.
Cook 2 more hours or until tender and cooked through.   **Servings: 4**

Alternate Meats: Grouse, chukar

Cooking Tips: Two cups of stock may be used instead of chicken broth. If cover of
roasting pot does not seal well, use aluminum foil to create a better seal.

"...When cooked slowly, the meat in this dish is very tender..."

"...Easy to do!.."

Marsala Pheasant

*Add a splash of color to this meal with a green salad and
white rice or a potato dish.*

1 cup green onions, sliced
2 lb. fresh mushrooms, sliced
1 Tbsp. butter
2 pheasant
2 apples
2 potatoes

1 Tbsp. lard
Salt, sprinkle
Pepper, sprinkle
1 cup chicken broth
1/2 cup Marsala wine

Preheat oven to 350°. Sauté green onions and mushrooms in skillet with butter.
Stuff each pheasant with 1 apple and 1 potato. Rub lard over breasts and sprinkle
with salt and pepper. Place birds in roasting pan and add broth and wine. Cover and
bake 45 minutes, basting every 15 minutes with juices from pan. Add mushrooms
and green onions. Bake another 45 minutes, continuing to baste.   **Servings: 6**

Upland Game Recipes...

"...This is a tasty one-dish meal..."

Micro/Oven Tender Pheasant

Complete with meat, noodles and vegetables, this is a lovely dinner for two.

1 pheasant
Garlic powder, sprinkle
White pepper, sprinkle
Onion salt, sprinkle

1/2 tsp. Worcestershire sauce
1 cup Madeira wine
2 cups stock or broth
1/4 cup soy sauce

Preheat oven to 250°. Section pheasant by boning breast meat from keel and cutting away legs and thighs. Place pieces in microwave dish and sprinkle with garlic powder, white pepper, onion salt and Worcestershire sauce. Add wine, 1 cup stock or broth and soy sauce. Microwave 5 minutes on full power and 5 minutes on 50% power. Add remaining stock or broth and turn meat. Cook in oven for 3 hours.

Servings: 2

Alternate Meats: Grouse, chukar

Cooking Tips: Mixed frozen vegetables can be added during the last 30 minutes of oven cooking. Stir vegetables in with broth and meat. Cooked noodles can also be added during last 5-10 minutes.

Fast & Easy Fried Pheasant

Spice up this quick meal with a basket of hot french fries.

1 pheasant
Garlic powder, sprinkle
Onion powder, sprinkle
White pepper, sprinkle
Canola oil
1/4 cup teriyaki marinade

Bone breast and thigh meat, leaving lower legs intact. Thinly slice meat with filet knife. If using older birds, pressure cook 10 minutes. Younger birds will already be tender. Sprinkle meat with garlic powder, onion powder and white pepper. Fry in skillet with canola oil over medium-high heat, turning often. After 2 minutes, add teriyaki marinade to pan and stir constantly. **Servings: 2**

Alternate Meats: Grouse, chukar

Cooking Tips: Once meat is pressure cooked, it can be put in refrigerator and finished at a later time.

At end of frying cycle, 1/4 stick of margarine may be added to pan. Turn up heat and blend with teriyaki marinade. This may be thickened with 1 tsp. of cornstarch dissolved in stock.

Pheasant Breasts with Orange Sauce

Serve this citrus dish with white rice and a crisp garden salad.

1 cup apricot jam
1 cup orange marmalade
1/4 cup orange juice concentrate
4 pheasant breasts
Salt, sprinkle
Pepper, sprinkle

Preheat oven to 350°. Mix jam, marmalade and concentrate in shallow baking dish. Place pheasant breasts on mixture. Sprinkle with salt and pepper. Bake 45-60 minutes, turning breasts every 15 minutes. **Servings: 2-4**

Pheasant Casserole

This hearty meal only needs rolls or bread and butter to make it complete.

2 pheasant
Salt, sprinkle
Pepper, sprinkle
Flour
2-4 Tbsp. olive oil
1 cup green onions, sliced

2 lb. fresh mushrooms, sliced
2 cloves garlic, minced
1/2 tsp. thyme
1/2 tsp. rosemary
2 bay leaves
1 cup sherry

Preheat oven to 350°. Cut pheasant into serving pieces and sprinkle with salt and pepper. Coat pieces with flour and brown in skillet with oil. Drain on paper towel. Sauté green onions, mushrooms and garlic in skillet. Place pieces in baking dish and add mushrooms and onions. Add spices and bay leaves. Pour sherry over birds and cover. Bake 25-30 minutes or until tender. Remove bay leaves before serving.

Servings: 6

"...You'll go wild over this dish..."

Wild Rice Pheasant

Cool off this dish with a crisp garden salad and fresh fruit plate.

1/2 cup wild rice
1/2 cup brown rice
1 can chicken broth
2 lb. fresh mushrooms, sliced
1/2 cup green onions, sliced
1 Tbsp. butter

2 pheasant
1 Tbsp. lard
Salt, sprinkle
Pepper, sprinkle
Paprika, sprinkle

Preheat oven to 350°. Place wild rice, brown rice and broth into microwave dish. Cover and cook on simmer until tender. Sauté mushrooms and green onions in skillet with butter and mix with cooked rice. Stuff birds with rice and mushroom mixture. Place in roasting pan and smooth lard over pheasant breasts. Sprinkle with salt, pepper and paprika. Cover and roast 1 1/2 hours, basting frequently. **Servings: 6**

Game Birds Over Coals

For a change of pace, serve these birds with rice pilaf and a fruit salad.

2 game birds
3/4 cup teriyaki marinade
1/4 cup water
Margarine or canola oil
1 bottle prepared barbecue sauce

Breast-out game birds and marinate in teriyaki marinade and water for 30 minutes. Grill over low heat until almost done, basting with margarine or cooking oil to retain juices. Baste meat with barbecue sauce and grill for a few minutes; turn pieces and baste again. **Servings: 4**

Alternate Meats: Quail, pheasant, dove, chukar, grouse, turkey, partridge

Waterfowl Recipes...

Pineapple Duck Stew
Serve with fresh vegetables and cornbread.

3 ducks, sectioned
Salt and pepper
Flour
2 Tbsp. olive oil
1/2 cup pineapple juice
1 cup chicken broth

1 Tbsp. soy sauce
1/2 tsp. ginger
1 can water chestnuts, sliced
1 green pepper, sliced
1 can pineapple chunks
1-2 Tbsp. cornstarch

Preheat oven to 350°. Salt and pepper duck pieces and dredge in flour. Heat skillet with oil, brown meat and drain on paper towel. Place duck, pineapple juice, broth, soy sauce, ginger and water chestnuts in large Dutch oven. Cover and bake 1 hour. Add green pepper and pineapple chunks. Cover and bake 15-20 minutes. In small bowl, mix cornstarch and small amount of water. Pour over duck; stir until thickened.

Servings: 6

"...A savory meal, Hawaiian style..."

Duck with Rice Madeira
Serve with Scotch bread and a mixed green salad.

4 duck breasts
1 cup rice mix
2 Tbsp. olive oil
1 cup chicken broth
1 cup mushrooms
1 tsp. sweet basil
1 cup Madeira wine
1/2 cup green onions, sliced

Preheat oven to 350°. Blend rice mix, chicken broth and wine in casserole dish. Sprinkle duck breasts with salt, pepper and basil. Heat skillet with oil and sauté mushrooms and green onions. Pour in casserole dish and top with meat. Cover and bake 45 minutes or until breasts are tender.

Servings: 2-4

Cooking Tips: The rice mixture consists of 1/4 cup wild rice, 3/4 cup brown or white rice.

Fried Goose Breast
For an intimate evening with your spouse or a friend, this is the meal. Serve with rice or baked potatoes and a fruit salad.

1 goose breast, sliced
Salt and pepper
3 Tbsp. flour
2 Tbsp. olive oil

2 onions, sliced
1 1/4 cups Burgandy wine
1 cup chicken broth

Salt and pepper goose breast and dredge in flour. Heat skillet with oil and sauté onions. Remove and set aside. In same pan, brown meat. Remove and set aside. Add flour and stir until bubbly. Slowly add Burgandy and broth. Add salt and pepper and stir until thickened. Return goose, onions and simmer, covered, 1-2 hours.

Servings: 2

Apricot and Apple Stuffed Duck
A sweet potato dish and a green salad complete this dish.

2 ducks
Salt and pepper
Lard or butter
2 cups bread crumbs
1/2 cup golden raisins

1 cup dried apricots, diced
2 apples, diced
3 Tbsp. red current jelly
1 cup chicken broth
1/4 cup sherry

Preheat oven to 350°. Salt and pepper ducks. Rub with lard or butter. In bowl, combine remaining ingredients and stuff duck. Place on rack in roasting pan and cover. Roast 1 1/2 - 2 hours or until ducks are golden brown.

Servings: 6

Duck a la Skillet
Serve with a salad and crusty bread.

4 cups duck meat, cubed
1 tsp. Lawry's Lemon Pepper
1/3 cup flour
2 tsp. olive oil

4 potatoes, peeled and quartered
1 onion, sliced
1 green pepper, sliced
1 can cream of mushroom soup

Season duck with lemon pepper and dredge in flour. In heated skillet, brown duck in oil and drain on paper towel. Clean skillet, return duck and add remaining ingredients. Simmer 1 hour, stirring occasionally until done.

Servings: 4-6

"...On a crisp fall day, think about this easy dish to make..."

Waterfowl Recipes...

Down Home Roast Goose

Delicious when served with an orange sauce, broccoli and tossed salad.

5-8 lb. goose	1/8 cup teriyaki marinade
2 cloves garlic, crushed	1/8 cup sherry or port wine
Virginia Olson's Savory Seasonings Poultry Blend, sprinkle	1 pkg. commercial stuffing
	2 cups water
Paprika, sprinkle	2 cups stock or chicken broth
White pepper, sprinkle	6 chicken bouillon cubes
1 qt. water	

Preheat oven to 350°. Season goose with garlic, poultry blend, paprika and white pepper. Add 1 qt. water to roaster and place goose on rack in roaster, breast down. Pour teriyaki marinade and wine into cavity and cook 1 hour. Discard liquid, stuff goose with any prepared stuffing and return to roaster. Add 2 cups water, stock and bouillon cubes. Reduce heat to 300° and roast 2 hours or until desired doneness.

Servings: 4-6

Cooking Tips: As with any game meat taken with shotgun, ensure all shot is removed before cooking.

Goose can be roasted like wild turkey; the difference is the level of moisture. Turkey can dry out easily, whereas goose has more oils under its skin.

Goose Stew

An instant success with families, especially those with young children. Serve with baked applesauce, a tossed salad and fresh Italian bread.

5-8 lb. goose	3 Tbsp. butter
3 cups water	3 onions, minced
Virginia Olson's Savory Seasonings Poultry Blend, sprinkle	1 cup celery, chopped
	1/2 cup green pepper, chopped
Celery salt, sprinkle	1/2 cup wild rice, cooked

Preheat oven to 350°. Place goose in kettle with water, poultry blend and celery salt. Cover and simmer 1 1/2 hours; do not boil. Reserve broth and place in refrigerator. Remove skin and gristle from goose, bone, dice and set aside. In large skillet with butter, sauté onions, celery and green pepper. Stir in reserved, degreased broth. Cover and simmer 5 minutes. In large kettle, combine goose, cooked rice and contents of skillet. Heat through.

Servings: 6

Cooking Tips: Make sure muscle and stringy tissues are removed from goose before dicing.

"...An excellent meal for the holidays..."

Goose Over Coals

Serve with an orange sauce, rice, in-season fresh vegetable and tossed salad.

- 5-8 lb. goose
- Margarine or lard
- 1/4 cup lemon juice
- 1/8 cup canola oil
- 1 clove garlic, pressed

Wash and dry goose with paper towel or clean cloth. Cut goose in half, directly down breastbone, and rub breast with margarine or lard. In small bowl, mix lemon juice, oil and garlic. Brush meat cavity generously with mixture. Goose halves can be spitted over low coals or gas grill, or placed directly on grate. Cook over low heat until done.

Servings: 6-8

Cooking Tips: See *Sauces, Marinades & Gravies* for several orange sauce recipes.

"...Quick and easy to prepare, this dish has class and is very tasty, too...

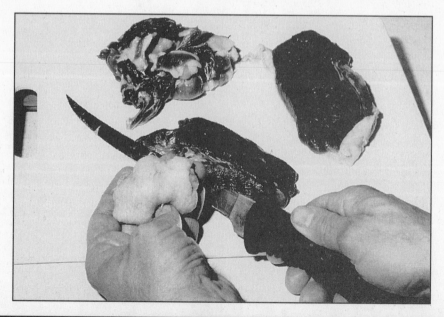

Fat must be removed from a boneless chunk of waterfowl meat before it can be cubed for duck soup.

Waterfowl Recipes...

Duck pieces are being marinated in a special vacuum food saver before being added to a recipe.

Aluminum Foil Duck

*A quick and easy recipe for camp
or backyard barbecue.*

2 ducks, cooked and boned
4 potatoes, peeled and sliced
6 carrots, peeled and sliced
1 large onion, quartered or sliced
Salt and pepper

In long piece of aluminum foil, place meat and vegetables; add salt and pepper. Double wrap foil around meal and close securely. Place on medium-hot coal bed and cook until vegetables are soft.   Servings: 4-6

Cooking Tips: Refer to *Quack and Cluck Soup* for duck cooking and boning instructions.

Coal bed should not be too hot or dinner will burn.

Wild Goose Noodle Casserole

For hunters with young children who are a little leary of wild game, this is the dish for them. Serve with green vegetables, a tossed salad and rolls.

5-8 lb. goose	Celery salt, sprinkle
3 cups water	1 8-oz. pkg. noodles
Virginia Olson's Savory Seasonings	1 large bag potato chips, crushed
Poultry Blend, sprinkle	2 cans cream of celery or mushroom soup

Preheat oven to 350°. Place goose in kettle with water, poultry blend and celery salt. Cover and simmer 1½ hours; do not boil. Reserve broth and place in refrigerator. Remove skin and gristle from goose, bone, dice and set aside. Prepare noodles as directed on package. Place one layer in bottom of casserole dish. Add layer of diced meat and layer of chips. Repeat process until meat is used. In small bowl, blend 1 can soup and 1 can reserved, degreased broth. Pour ⅔ over casserole, cover and bake 25 minutes. Add remaining liquid, cover and cook 20 minutes.

Servings: 6

Cooking Tips: Make sure muscle and stringy tissues are removed from goose before dicing.

"...Hold onto your appetites..."

Sauerkraut Duck

Serve with boiled potatoes and a tossed green salad.

¼ lb. bacon	2 cups beer
1 onion, diced	2 ducks
2 cloves garlic, minced	Salt and pepper
1 large can sauerkraut, drained	¼ cup red currant jelly
1½ tsp. caraway seed	

Preheat oven to 350°. In skillet, cook bacon until soft and drain on paper towel. In same skillet, sauté onion and garlic and drain on paper towel. Combine bacon, onion, garlic, sauerkraut, caraway seed and 1 cup beer in skillet. Simmer 5-10 minutes. Pour skillet mixture into roasting pan and place ducks on top. Add salt and pepper to taste. Cover and bake 1½ to 2 hours or until ducks are done. Baste every 15 minutes with remaining beer. Glaze ducks with jelly 15 minutes before end of cooking time.

Servings: 6

"...No doubt, a winning recipe for any occasion..."

Waterfowl Recipes...

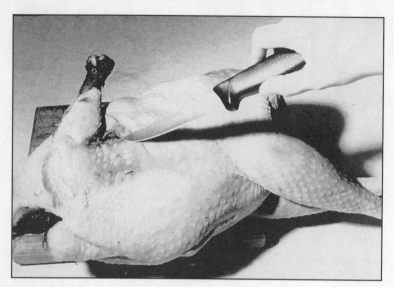

As with any game meat taken with shotgun, make sure all shot is removed before cooking.

"...This is a meal fit for royalty..."

Sherried Duck Casserole

Serve over noodles and accompany with a spinach salad and fresh Italian bread.

4 cups leftover duck meat, cubed
1 can cream of mushroom soup
$^3/_4$ cup sherry
$^1/_2$ pkg. dry onion soup mix

Preheat oven to 350°. Combine all ingredients in casserole dish. Cover and bake 2-2$^1/_2$ hours or until duck is completely done.   **Servings: 4**

"...An elegant meal that is easy to fix and so good to eat..."

Sour Cream Duck

Serve with sweet potatoes and a tossed salad.

2-3 ducks, sectioned	3 cloves garlic, minced
Salt and pepper	2 cups sour cream
Flour	1 cup chicken broth
4 Tbsp. olive oil	$^1/_4$ cup red currant jelly
1 tsp. butter	1 tsp. thyme
1-2 lb. fresh mushrooms, sliced	$^1/_2$ tsp. rosemary
1 cup green onions, sliced	

Preheat oven to 350°. Salt and pepper ducks and dredge in flour. In heated skillet, brown ducks in oil and drain on paper towel. Using same skillet, heat butter and sauté mushrooms, green onions and garlic. Place ducks in baking dish and top with sautéed mixture. In small bowl, mix sour cream, chicken broth and jelly. Pour over ducks. Sprinkle with thyme and rosemary. Cover and bake 1 hour.   **Servings: 4-6**

Cooking Tips: Low-fat yogurt can be substituted for sour cream.

Country-Style Duck Soup

Serve with crackers or crusty bread.

2 large or 3 small ducks	1 tsp. Worcestershire sauce
2 cloves garlic, crushed	$^1/_4$ cup teriyaki marinade
$^1/_4$ tsp. paprika	1-2 cans beef broth
2 bay leaves	6-8 carrots, peeled and sliced
$^1/_8$ tsp. pepper	4-6 celery ribs, peeled and sliced
4 beef bouillon cubes	$^1/_2$ cup Madeira or cream sherry wine
Celery salt, sprinkle	1 cup barley
2 Tbsp. soy sauce	

Skin ducks and wash in cold water. Place in pressure cooker with water and add garlic, paprika, bay leaves, pepper, bouillon cubes, celery salt, soy sauce, Worcestershire sauce and teriyaki marinade. Close lid securely and set regulator. Pressure cook 20-30 minutes. Allow pressure to drop. Bone meat and strain juices. Return meat and juices to pressure cooker. Add beef broth, carrots, celery ribs and wine and pressure cook 3 minutes. Let pressure drop immediately. In separate pan, cook barley per directions on package, strain juice and transfer to soup. Continue simmering until vegetables are tender. If liquid is low, add 1 cup of barley juice.

Servings: 4-5

Cooking Tips: This can also be prepared in a covered Dutch oven, but will cook for a longer period of time.

"...Simple as duck soup..."

Waterfowl Recipes...

Spiced Duck
Serve with sweet potatoes and a spinach salad.

4 cups duck meat, diced
2 tsp. olive oil
1 onion, diced
2 allspice, whole
2 cloves garlic, whole

1 bay leaf
4 cups chicken broth
Salt and pepper
Flour

In skillet heated with oil, brown duck and onion thoroughly. Add remaining ingredients and simmer 1½-2 hours. Remove bay leaf, cloves and allspice. Add flour to thicken gravy.   **Servings: 4-6**

> ## "...Any season is open season with this dish..."

> ## "...You can have your duck and eat it too..."

Duck Creole
Serve with Spanish rice and a tossed salad.

3 ducks, sectioned
Olive oil
2 lb. fresh mushrooms, sliced
1 bunch green onions, sliced
3 cloves garlic, minced
1 green pepper, diced
1 can Italian-style stewed tomatoes
1 cup chicken broth

3 bay leaves
¼ tsp. thyme
¼ tsp. rosemary
½ tsp. cumin
¼ cup sherry
1-2 tsp. chili powder
¼ tsp. allspice
Salt and pepper

Preheat oven to 325°. Heat skillet with oil and brown duck pieces. Drain on paper towel. Place meat in baking dish and add remaining ingredients. Cover and bake 1½-2 hours.   **Servings: 6**

> ## "...It's nourishment for body and spirit..."

Quack and Cluck Soup
Good accompaniments to this meal are an assortment of crackers and cheeses.

1 chicken, sectioned
Olive oil
Virginia Olson's Savory
   Seasonings Poultry Blend or
   Lawry's Seasoned Salt
Garlic powder, sprinkle
Paprika, sprinkle

Pepper, sprinkle
2 large ducks, sectioned
⅛ cup soy sauce or teriyaki marinade
1 can chicken broth
1 can beef broth
Fresh or frozen vegetables, sliced

Skin chicken if desired. Rub with olive oil and place on plate with paper towel. Microwave on 70% power for 10 minutes. Season with poultry blend or Lawry's salt, garlic powder, paprika and pepper. Place in skillet heated with oil and fry until brown. Allow to cool; bone and set aside. Place duck in pressure cooker with water. Add poultry blend or Lawry's salt, garlic powder, paprika, pepper, soy sauce or teriyaki marinade. Close lid securely and set pressure regulator. Cook 20-40 minutes, depending on size of ducks, with regulator rocking gently. Allow pressure to drop. Cool meat; bone and set aside. Strain and save juices. In large cooking pot, add juices from duck, chicken broth, beef broth and both meats. Bring to boil and add choice of sliced vegetables. Continue boiling slowly until vegetables are soft.
                    Servings: 6

Cooking Tips: The chicken can also be pressure cooked and juices used for stock. Degreasing the broth before adding it to the cooking pot makes a much nicer soup. Put broth into refrigerator until grease solidifies; remove from top and discard.

Boned Duck Á L'Orange
Serve over a bed of rice along with broccoli and fresh bread.

2 lb. duck meat, cooked and boned
2 qts. stock or stock/broth mixture
4 beef bouillon cubes
Orange Sauce I *(See p. 276)*

In pressure cooker, combine duck, stock and bouillon cubes. Close lid securely and set pressure regulator. Cook 10 minutes with regulator rocking gently. Allow pressure to drop. Prepare *Orange Sauce I*. In large bowl, strain duck meat, saving juice. Place meat in deep serving dish. Blend strained juice and orange sauce. Pour over duck.   **Servings: 2-3**

Cooking Tips: Use boned duck meat as described in *Quack and Cluck Soup* recipe.

> ## "...A very easy and tasty recipe for busy hunters..."

Waterfowl Recipes...

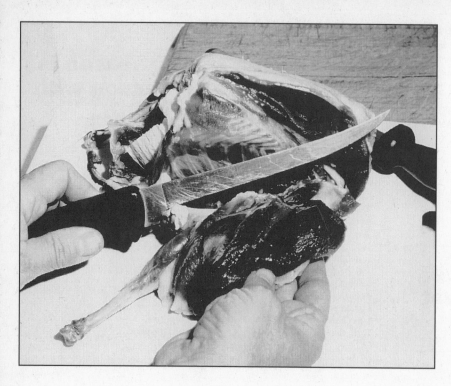

One-half of a goose breast completely removed from the carcass.

Royal Crispy Duck Basting

2 qts. stock or broth
2 green onions, sliced
1/2 bunch parsley
1 apple, peeled and quartered
6 juniper berries
2 cups Madeira, sherry or port wine

Combine all ingredients except wine in cooking pan. Boil liquid rapidly for 15 minutes. Reduce heat and boil gently for 45 minutes. Add wine and boil gently for 30 minutes. Strain liquid in fine strainer; retain only clear broth. Set aside.

Cooking Tips: This basting can be made the day before the ducks are roasted. Also, to ensure the parsley flavor, rinse bunch under cold water and squeeze out by hand.

Royal Crispy Duck Roast

Serve with soup, sweet potatoes and spinach salad.

8 large ducks	**Olive oil or melted lard**
4 cloves garlic, crushed	**Margarine**
Tarragon, trace	**See *Royal Crispy Duck Basting***
White pepper, sprinkle	**1 pkg. commercial stuffing**
Unbleached cloth	

Preheat oven to 250°. Clean, wash and dry ducks. Press crushed garlic into duck breasts with fingers. Sprinkle with tarragon and white pepper. Wipe unbleached cloth with oil or lard. Wrap each breast with cloth and coat with margarine using fingers. Place in roaster, breast down and baste with *Royal Crispy Duck Basting*. Cover and cook 3 hours, basting every 1/2 hour. Remove meat to cool. Stuff each duck with any prepared stuffing and return to roaster, breast up. Cook until tender. Strain broth from roasting pan into saucepan. Place in refrigerator to solidify grease; remove from top of pan. Heat remaining broth and serve as juice. Remove cloth from ducks before serving.

Servings: 12-16

Cooking Tips: Any leftover stuffing can be covered in aluminum foil and cooked alongside ducks. Mix with stuffing from birds before serving.

Unbleached cloth can be obtained from restaurant supply houses or fabric stores.

Duck Ragout

You can be out hunting while this savory dish is cooking.
Serve with noodles or rice and a green salad.

4 cups duck meat, cubed	**1 tsp. bouquet garni**
1 can chicken broth	**1/2 cup sherry**
1/2 cup commercial stuffing	**Salt and pepper**
1 onion, diced	**1 can mushrooms, sliced**

Preheat oven to 325°. Combine all ingredients in baking dish. Cover and bake 2 1/2 hours or until duck is completely done and mixture is browned.

Servings: 6

"...This dish requires a lot of cooking time, but not a lot of kitchen time..."

Waterfowl Recipes...

Pineapple Duck Stew

Serve with fresh vegetables and cornbread.

3 ducks, sectioned
Salt and pepper
Flour
2 Tbsp. olive oil
1/2 cup pineapple juice
1 cup chicken broth
1 Tbsp. soy sauce

1/2 tsp. ginger
1 can water chestnuts, sliced
1 green pepper, sliced
1 can pineapple chunks
1-2 Tbsp. cornstarch
Water

Preheat oven to 350°. Salt and pepper duck pieces and dredge in flour. Heat skillet with oil, brown meat and drain on paper towel. Place ducks, pineapple juice, chicken broth, soy sauce, ginger and water chestnuts in large Dutch oven. Cover and bake 1 hour. Add green pepper and pineapple chunks. Cover and bake 15-20 minutes. In small bowl, mix cornstarch and small amount of water. Pour over ducks; stir until thickened.

Servings: 6

"...A savory meal, Hawaiian-style..."

Duck with Rice Madeira

Serve with Scotch bread and a mixed green salad.

1/4 cup wild rice
3/4 cup brown or white rice
2 cups chicken broth
1 cup Madeira wine
4 duck breasts
Salt and pepper
1 tsp. sweet basil
2 Tbsp. olive oil
1 lb. fresh mushrooms, sliced
1/2 cup green onions, sliced

Preheat oven to 350°. Blend rices, chicken broth and wine in casserole dish. Sprinkle duck breasts with salt, pepper and basil. Heat skillet with oil and sauté mushrooms and green onions. Pour in casserole dish and top with meat. Cover and bake 45 minutes or until breasts are tender.

Servings: 2-4

Fried Goose Breast

For an intimate evening with your spouse or a friend, this is the meal. Serve with rice or baked potatoes and a fruit salad.

1 goose breast, sliced
Salt and pepper
3 Tbsp. flour
2 Tbsp. olive oil

2 onions, sliced
1 1/4 cups Burgundy wine
1 cup chicken broth

Salt and pepper goose breast and dredge in flour. Heat skillet with oil and sauté onions. Remove and set aside. In same pan, brown meat. Remove and set aside. Add flour and stir until bubbly. Slowly add Burgundy and broth. Add salt and pepper and simmer, stirring until a nice gravy forms. Add goose and onions and simmer, covered, 15-20 minutes or until desired doneness.

Servings: 2

Apricot and Apple Stuffed Duck

A sweet potato dish and a green salad complete this dish.

2 ducks
Salt and pepper
Lard or butter
2 cups bread crumbs
1/2 cup golden raisins

1 cup dried apricots, diced
2 apples, diced
3 Tbsp. red currant jelly
1 cup chicken broth
1/4 cup sherry

Preheat oven to 350°. Salt and pepper ducks. Rub with lard or butter. In bowl, combine remaining ingredients and stuff ducks. Place on rack in roasting pan and cover. Roast 1 1/2-2 hours or until ducks are golden brown.

Servings: 6

Duck á la Skillet

Serve with a salad and crusty bread.

4 cups duck meat, cubed
1 tsp. Lawry's Lemon Pepper
1/3 cup flour
2 tsp. olive oil

4 potatoes, peeled and quartered
1 onion, sliced
1 green pepper, sliced
1 can cream of mushroom soup

Season duck with lemon pepper and dredge in flour. In heated skillet, brown duck in oil and drain on paper towel. Clean skillet, return duck and add remaining ingredients. Simmer 1 hour, stirring occasionally until done.

Servings: 4-6

"...On a crisp fall day, think about this easy dish to make..."

Waterfowl Recipes...

Roast Duck Elegant

Serve with stuffing or wild rice, a green vegetable, salad and rolls.

3 ducks	³/₄ bunch parsley
1-2 qts. water	6 beef bouillon cubes
¹/₈ cup baking soda (per qt. of water)	3 cloves garlic, crushed
Lard	Paprika, sprinkle
3 apples, whole or sliced	1 can chicken broth or 2 cups stock
1¹/₂ onions, sliced	¹/₂ cup claret or sherry

Preheat oven to 300°. In large bowl, submerse cleaned and skinned ducks in water and baking soda for 2 hours. Rinse and dry meat and rub with lard. Stuff cavities with apples, onions and parsley. Place ducks in roasting pan filled halfway with water. Add bouillon cubes and garlic and sprinkle with paprika. Cover and roast 1 hour. Turn birds over and add chicken broth or stock. Roast, covered, 1 hour. Turn birds breast-side up, add wine and re-cover. Reduce heat to 250° and roast until meat is tender. Discard contents of cavities before serving. **Servings: 6**

Cooking Tips: Wine may be added to duck cavity after first hour of cooking. Use ¹/₈ cup per bird. Try different wines and spices for variety. Ducks may also be stuffed with wild turkey or bread stuffing.

Remember to "burst" parsley before using by rinsing under warm water and squeezing out by hand. This brings out the flavor.

Duck Breasts in Bordeaux

Juices from the roasting pan and the marinade make delicious toppings for the meat.

2 Tbsp. olive oil	6 duck breasts
2 cups Bordeaux wine	Lard
2 cloves garlic, minced	Margarine
Thyme, sprinkle	Sherry
2 carrots, peeled and thinly sliced	2 cups stock or 1 can chicken broth
1 small onion, sliced	4 Tbsp. margarine

In glass dish, mix olive oil, wine, garlic and thyme. Add carrots, onion and duck breasts. Marinate 24 hours in refrigerator. Preheat oven to 250°. Strain and save marinade in small bowl. In skillet, sauté meat in lard and margarine (50/50 mix) for 5 minutes. Transfer meat to roasting pan. Pour off ²/₃ of fat left in skillet. Deglaze skillet with sherry. Add skillet contents to roasting pan. Add stock or broth, cover and roast until ducks are tender. In saucepan, cook strained marinade over low heat until reduced to roughly ¹/₃ of original volume. Add margarine and mix well and serve with meat. Remove duck breasts and strain juices; serve with meat.

Servings: 6-8

Alternate Meats: Goose

Cooking Tips: This is an excellent recipe for smaller ducks. As this recipe only calls for breast meat, save rest of duck for stock.

"...This is as elegant as it gets..."

"...An absolutely wonderful meal, and so simple to make..."

Sweet and Sour Duck

Serve over a bed of rice with a fruit salad.

2 cups cold roast duck, cubed
2 tsp. butter
2 tsp. flour
¹/₂ cup brown sugar
1 pkg. dry onion soup mix
1 tsp. dry mustard
¹/₂ cup vinegar
1¹/₂ cups hot water

In skillet heated with butter, sauté duck until brown. Add flour. Stir until mixture is blended and creamy. Add remaining ingredients and simmer 15-20 minutes. **Servings: 2-4**

"...A great lunch on a cold day, after an early hunt..."

Hot Duck Sandwich

Must serve with mashed potatoes and green beans, all smothered in gravy.

1 qt. Standard Game Gravy *(See p. 283)*
12-18 bread slices
1 duck, cooked, boned and sliced

Make game gravy according to recipe. Toast bread. Place duck slices on toast and cover with gravy. **Servings: 6-8**

Cooking Tips: Refer to *Quack and Cluck Soup* recipe for duck cooking and boning instructions.

No Bull Frog Legs
Serve with french fries and a mixed green salad.

16 frog legs
1/4 cup salt
1 qt. water
Garlic powder, sprinkle
Onion powder, sprinkle
White pepper, sprinkle
Virgina Olson Savory Seasonings
    Fish Blend, sprinkle
2 eggs, beaten
1-2 cups buttermilk
1-2 cups canned milk or whole milk
1/4 tsp. salt
Flour or flour/cracker crumbs mixture
1 Tbsp. canola oil
2-3 tsp. margarine

Soak legs in salt and water for 1-2 hours. Soak in clear water for 1/2 hour. Rinse and blot dry. Sprinkle with garlic powder, onion powder, white pepper and Virginia Olson's seasoning. In bowl, mix eggs, milk and 1/4 tsp. salt. Add meat and soak 1 hour. Coat legs with flour or flour/cracker crumbs mixture. Fry in heated skillet with canola oil. Turn meat often so it does not burn. When golden brown, reduce heat to very low and add margarine.   **Servings: 2**

Cooking Tips: The grease in pan may have to be changed in middle of cooking process to prevent legs from becoming too dark. Remove frog legs to dish and pour off oil. Wipe pan and add margarine. Return legs to pan and continue to fry until done.

> **"...Frog legs are as tasty as fried chicken..."**

Twice-Fried Old-Time Turtle Soup
Delicious with crackers or crusty bread.

2 lb. turtle meat, cubed
1 qt. cold water
1 tsp. baking soda
Flour
1 tsp. baking powder
1/4 tsp. salt
2 qts. chicken stock or broth
Garlic powder, sprinkle
Ground pepper, sprinkle
1/2 onion, diced
Paprika, sprinkle
Virginia Olson Savory Seasonings Fish Blend
4 celery stalks, diced

Exotic Meat Recipes...

> **"...The turtle is an exotic dish worth trying if turtle meat is available..."**

Soak turtle chunks in cold water and baking soda overnight. Transfer meat to pressure cooker and cover with water. Close lid securely and set regulator. Pressure cook 10-15 minutes. Let pressure drop. Coat meat with flour and fry in skillet over medium heat. Dry on paper towel. In large bowl, combine 2 cups flour, baking powder, eggs, milk and salt. Use enough milk to create a dough-like batter. Coat each piece of meat with batter and fry again until golden brown. In large kettle, combine meat with stock or broth. Add garlic powder, pepper, onion, paprika and Virginia Olson Savory Seasonings Fish Blend. Bring to boil and then reduce heat. Boil soup slowly for 1/2 hour. Precook potatoes and celery in pressure cooker and add to soup.   **Servings: 4**

Cooking Tips: When pressure cooking, some people prefer to add chile powder to the water. Use 1 Tbsp. of mild, medium or hot chile powder for every 2 pounds of turtle. See Chapter 15 for information on preparing meat for cooking.

Mountain Man Beaver
Serve with tossed salad and Italian bread.

1 beaver carcass
2 Tbsp. lard
2 Tbsp. canola oil
White pepper, dash
Paprika, dash
1/8 cup teriyaki marinade
Water
Beef stock or broth
1/2 lb. fresh green beans
10 carrots, peeled, center cut
2 onions, squared

Bone meat and cut into bite-size squares. In heated Dutch oven, melt lard and canola oil and braise meat. Add white pepper, paprika and teriyaki marinade while stirring. Transfer meat to pressure cooker and cover with 50/50 mixture of water and stock or broth. Close lid securely and set regulator. Pressure cook 15 minutes. Let pressure drop and add green beans, carrots and onions. Pressure cook 3 minutes. Let pressure drop and simmer in open cooker 5-10 minutes.   **Servings:4-6**

> **"...The mountain men in your family will love this one..."**

Exotic Meat Recipes...

"...After tasting mountain lion, you're sure to 'pitch in greedily' to finish off this dish..."

Mountain Lion Steaks

Serve with baked potatoes and a tossed salad.

1 lb. mountain lion loin
Universal Marinade *(See p. 279)*
Flour
2 Tbsp. canola oil
1 tsp. bacon fat

Cut loin crosswise into 1-inch thick portions. Marinate in *Universal Marinade* 4-6 hours. Flour both sides of meat and fry in skillet with oil and bacon fat over medium heat until cooked through; do not overcook. **Servings: 2**

Cooking Tips: There is no reason to age cougar meat; it is tender even from the mature cat. For prime steaks, it is recommended that the cavity of the cat be cleaned and washed as soon as it is harvested. Special care should be taken when rendering the hind quarters into steak meat. The front quarters might serve for cubed meat.

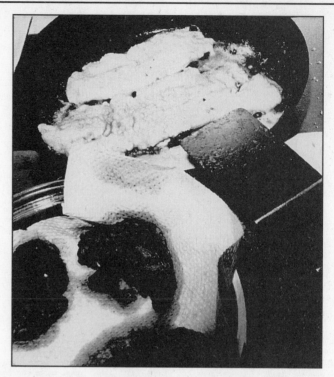

Mountain lion meat is always tender, especially when marinated in *Universal Marinade* and fried.

"...It looks like pork loin, but tastes better..."

"...Celebrate Groundhog Day at your house..."

Baked Groundhog Deluxe

Serve with mashed potatoes, a spinach salad and fresh Italian bread.

1 ground hog	1/4 tsp. paprika
2 qts. water	1/4 bunch parsley, whole
1/4 cup salt	4 beef bouillon cubes
1/2 cup soy sauce	1/4 tsp. white pepper
2 cloves garlic, whole	1 cup stock or beef broth
1/4 onion	Teriyaki glaze (optional)

Preheat oven to 325°. Cut meat into serving pieces and soak in 1 qt. water and salt for 4 hours. Transfer meat to 1 qt. clear water and soak 4 hours. Drain and dry meat. In pressure cooker, submerse meat in water and add soy sauce, garlic cloves, onion, paprika, parsley, bouillon cubes and white pepper. Cover lid securely and set regulator. Cook 20 minutes with regulator rocking gently. Allow pressure to drop. Rinse and dry meat; discard juices. Place meat in open roaster and add stock or broth. Roast 30 minutes, turning meat often. If desired, brush with teriyaki glaze while cooking. **Servings: 4**

Alternate Meats: Prairie dog, marmot, woodchuck, rockchuck

Cooking Tips: Only young, half-grown specimens are recommended for this recipe. Be certain to remove glands from undersides of legs before soaking meat.

Exotic Meat Recipes...

No Bull Frog Legs

Serve with french fries and a mixed green salad.

16 frog legs	2 eggs, beaten
1/4 cup salt	1-2 cups buttermilk
1 qt. water	1-2 cups canned or whole milk
Garlic powder, sprinkle	1/4 tsp. salt
Onion powder, sprinkle	Flour or flour/cracker crumb mixture
White pepper, sprinkle	1 Tbsp. canola oil
Virgina Olson's Savory Seasonings	2-3 tsp. margarine
Fish Blend, sprinkle	

Soak legs in salt water 1-2 hours. Soak in clear water 1/2-hour. Rinse and blot dry. Sprinkle with garlic powder, onion powder, white pepper and Virginia Olson's seasoning. In bowl, mix eggs, buttermilk, milk and 1/4 tsp. salt. Add meat and soak 1 hour. Coat legs with flour or flour/cracker crumb mixture. Fry in skillet heated with canola oil. Turn meat often so it does not burn. When golden brown, reduce heat to very low and add margarine. Toss to mix. **Servings: 2**

Cooking Tips: The pan grease may have to be changed in the middle of the cooking process to prevent legs from becoming too dark. Remove frog legs to dish and pour off oil. Wipe pan and add margarine. Return legs to pan and continue to fry until done.

> **"...Frog legs are as tasty as fried chicken..."**

Twice-Fried Old-Time Turtle Soup

Delicious with crackers or crusty bread.

2 lb. turtle meat, cubed	2 qts. chicken stock or broth
1 qt. cold water	Garlic powder, sprinkle
1 tsp. baking soda	Ground pepper, sprinkle
Flour	1/2 onion, diced
1 tsp. baking powder	Paprika, sprinkle
2 eggs	1/8 tsp. Virginia Olson's Savory Seasonings Fish Blend
Milk	2 large potatoes, peeled and diced
1/4 tsp. salt	4 celery stalks, diced

Soak turtle chunks in cold water and baking soda overnight. Transfer meat to pressure cooker and cover with water. Close lid securely and set regulator. Pressure cook 10-15 minutes. Let pressure drop. Coat meat with flour and fry in skillet over medium heat. Dry on paper towel. In large bowl, combine 2 cups flour, baking powder, eggs, milk and salt. Use enough milk to create a dough-like batter. Coat each piece of meat with batter and fry again until golden brown. In large kettle, combine meat with stock or broth. Add garlic powder, pepper, onion, paprika and Virginia Olson's Savory Seasonings Fish Blend. Bring to boil and then reduce heat. Boil soup slowly for 1/2 hour. Pre-cook potatoes and celery in pressure cooker and add to soup. **Servings: 4**

Cooking Tips: When pressure cooking, some people prefer to add chili powder to the water. Use 1 Tbsp. of mild, medium or hot chili powder for every 2 lbs. of turtle.
See Chapter 15 for information on preparing meat for cooking.

> **"...This is an exotic dish worth trying if turtle meat is available..."**

Mountain Man Beaver

Serve with tossed salad and Italian bread.

1 beaver carcass	Water
2 Tbsp. lard	Beef stock or broth
2 Tbsp. canola oil	1/2 lb. fresh green beans
White pepper, dash	10 carrots, peeled and center cut
Paprika, dash	2 onions, squared
1/8 cup teriyaki marinade	

Bone meat and cut into bite-sized squares. In heated Dutch oven, melt lard and canola oil and braise meat. Add white pepper, paprika and teriyaki marinade while stirring. Transfer meat to pressure cooker and cover with 50/50 mixture of water and stock or broth. Close lid securely and set regulator. Pressure cook 15 minutes. Let pressure drop and add green beans, carrots and onions. Pressure cook 3 minutes. Let pressure drop and simmer in open cooker 5-10 minutes. **Servings:4-6**

> **"...The mountain men in your family will love this one..."**

Exotic Meat Recipes...

Appalachian Possum

This is a modified version of an old Appalachian recipe. Serve with honey-spiced acorn squash, tossed salad and crusty bread.

1 possum, whole
2 qts. cold water
1/8 cup salt
See *Possum Stuffing*
6 beef bouillon cubes
4 bay leaves
2 celery stalks, chopped
1 medium onion, chopped

Preheat oven to 375°. Soak possum in cold salt water for 8 hours. Rinse meat in cold water and refrigerate 2-4 hours. Prepare *Possum Stuffing*. Stuff possum cavity with *Possum Stuffing* and close cavity with string or skewer. In roasting pan, submerse meat halfway in water and add bouillon cubes, bay leaves, celery and onion. Place extra stuffing around meat. Roast 2 hours; turn meat, reduce heat to 300° and roast 1 hour. Meat should be tender; if not, reduce heat to 250° and roast 1 more hour. Remove bay leaves before serving. **Servings: 4**

Prairie Dog Chili

Serve with corn or flour tortillas and refried beans for a south-of-the-border taste.

4 prairie dogs
2 qts. water
1/4 cup salt
4 Tbsp. red chili powder
2 beef bouillon cubes
2 Tbsp. cornstarch
1/2 pt. beef broth

Cut meat into serving pieces and soak in 1 qt. salt water for 4 hours. Transfer meat to 1 qt. clear water and soak for 4 hours. Drain, dry and bone meat. In pressure cooker, submerse meat in water and add chili powder and bouillon cubes. Cover lid securely and set pressure regulator. Cook for 20 minutes with regulator rocking gently. Allow pressure to drop and thicken juice with cornstarch and broth mixture. **Servings: 2**

Alternate Meat: Groundhog

Cooking Tips: Tortillas should be served warm to eliminate doughy taste. They should be heated on top of the stove, directly on the heat source.

Possum Stuffing

1 lb. Italian sausage, cut into pieces
4 cups bread, cubed
1/2 onion, chopped
1/4 tsp. white pepper

Fry sausage in skillet and drain. Place on microwave-safe dish on top of 4 paper towels and microwave on high 1 1/2 minutes. In bowl, combine sausage, bread, onion and white pepper.

This rattler is ready to be sectioned and fried. Delicious when served with french fries and baked beans.

Fried Rattler

Serve with french fries, baked beans and a tossed salad.

1 large rattler	**1/8 tsp. pepper**
1 qt. water	**Tarragon, pinch**
4 Tbsp. salt	**Thyme, pinch**
Universal Marinade (See p.279)	**Lard or canola oil**
1 cup flour	**Margarine**
1/8 tsp. paprika	

Wash carcass under running water and soak 2 hours in salt water. Rinse and dry meat well. Cut and section meat into pieces that will fit fry pan. In large bowl, marinate meat in *Universal Marinade* 4-8 hours. Coat each piece with mixture of flour, paprika, pepper, tarragon and thyme. In skillet heated with 50/50 lard and margarine or canola oil and margarine, fry rattler until done. **Servings: 2**

Cooking Tips: See Chapter 15 for information on preparing meat for cooking.

> **"...Capture the tantalizing flavor of rattlesnake with this exciting dish..."**

Special Quesadillas
This savory dish is topped with salsa, sour cream and guacamole.

2 tsp. olive oil	1 can refried beans
1 large onion, sliced	1/4 cup milk
2 cups mushrooms, sliced	1 lb. Monterey Jack cheese, shredded
1 green pepper, sliced	1 lb. sharp cheddar cheese, shredded
1 red pepper, sliced	4 tomatoes, chopped
2 lb. ground venison	1 can olives, sliced
Salt and pepper, sprinkle	Jalapeno pepper, seeded and chopped
12 large flour tortillas	

In wok or large skillet with oil, stir-fry onion, mushrooms and green and red peppers until just tender. Drain on paper towels and set aside. In same skillet, sprinkle meat with salt and pepper and sauté; drain on paper towels and set aside. Heat tortillas in microwave 30 seconds on high. Place on serving plate. In skillet, combine refried beans, milk and 1/4 cup of each cheese. Simmer and stir until creamy. Spread 1/4-1/2 cup beans on each tortilla and add desired amounts of meat, vegetables, tomatoes, olives and jalapeno peppers. Fold in half. **Servings: 6**

Alternate Meats: Elk, moose, antelope, caribou, deer

> "...Have your appetite fortune come true with this dish..."

Enchilada Excitement
Serve with refried beans and taco chips.

2 lb. ground venison	36 corn tortillas
1 large onion, minced	1/2 cup olive oil
See *Enchilada Sauce*	4-6 cups cheddar cheese, shredded

Preheat oven to 325°. Brown venison and onion in skillet and drain on paper towels. Prepare *Enchilada Sauce*. In separate skillet heat olive oil; dip tortillas in oil and meat mixture. Roll tortilla and place seam side down in baking dish. Add layer, cover with sauce and bake 20-25 minutes or until bubbly. **Servings: 6-10**

Alternate Meats: Elk, moose, antelope, caribou, deer

Enchilada Sauce

1 cup olive oil
1 tsp. garlic powder
1 tsp. onion salt
1 cup flour
1 tsp. sugar
2-4 tsp. red Mexican chili powder
1 can tomato soup
1 can cheddar cheese soup
1 large can tomato juice
1 1/2 qts. hot water

In large saucepan, heat olive oil. Add garlic powder, onion salt, flour, sugar and chili powder. Cook over medium heat until mixture bubbles. Add soups and tomato juice and bring to boil. Add hot water and simmer 15 minutes stirring constantly.

Mexican-Style Venison Steak with Beans
Zap your taste buds with this dish; best served with white rice.

2 lb. venison steak	4 Tbsp. green chili, diced
Salt and pepper, sprinkle	1-2 tsp. chili powder
1 onion, diced	1 clove garlic, minced
1 beef bouillon cube, crushed	1/2 tsp. cumin
1 16-oz. can stewed tomatoes	1 16-oz. can kidney beans, drained

Season steak with salt and pepper. Cut into 1/2-inch wide strips and place in crock pot. Add onion, bouillon cube, stewed tomatoes, diced chili, chili powder, garlic and cumin. Cover and cook on low 6 hours. Turn control to high and add beans. Cook, covered, 30 minutes. **Servings: 6**

Alternate Meats: Elk, moose, antelope, caribou, deer

> "...Have a fiesta with this dish..."

Spanish Rice
This dish is a delightful extender to any main course.

12 slices bacon	2 cans Mexican-style stewed tomatoes
1 bunch green onions, sliced	Salt and pepper, sprinkle
1 green pepper, diced	1/4 lb. cheddar cheese, grated
6 cups rice, cooked	

Fry bacon in skillet; dry and crumble. In same skillet, sauté onion and green pepper in bacon fat and drain on paper towel. Discard grease, return bacon and onion mixture to skillet and add all remaining ingredients except cheese. Simmer 25-30 minutes; top with cheese before serving. **Servings: 6**

> "...This is a testimony to good eating..."

Ethnic Recipes...

"...This savory dish deserves three olés..."

Red Chili Mexicana

Accent this tasty meal with refried beans and warmed flour tortillas.

4-5 lb. boned game meat, cubed	1 can beef broth
Lard	$1/4$ tsp. Worcestershire sauce
4-6 Tbsp. red chili powder	Cornstarch
$1/8$ tsp. paprika	Cold broth
$1/4$ tsp. black pepper	

Braise meat in heated skillet with small amount of lard. Drain on paper towel. Place in pressure cooker; cover with water and add chili powder. Cover lid securely; set regulator and cook 20 minutes with regulator rocking gently. Allow pressure to drop; add paprika, black pepper, beef broth and Worcestershire sauce. Pressure cook 20 minutes. Allow pressure to drop. In separate bowl, mix cornstarch and cold broth to form paste. Mix with juices in pressure cooker to thicken.   **Servings: 8-9**

Alternate Meats: Elk, moose, antelope, caribou, deer, bear, javelina, buffalo

Cooking Tips: Prepared salsa can be added when spices are mixed in for additional flavor. Also, 1 lb. cubed chuck beef steak with fat can be added when braising game meat for more familiar flavor.

Flautas with Venison Flair

These can be made ahead of time and refrigerated until ready to bake.

$1^1/_2$ lb. ground venison	8 large flour tortillas
1 lb. chorizo sausage	1 cup picante sauce
2 8-oz. cans green chili salsa, diced	$1/2$ cup green onion tops, chopped
1 16-oz. can refried beans	2 large tomatoes, chopped
$1/2$ tsp. cumin	3 cups cheddar cheese, grated
1 tsp. Lawry's Garlic Salt	4 cups lettuce, shredded
1 cup Monterey Jack cheese, shredded	1 cup sour cream

Preheat oven to 350°. In skillet, brown venison and sausage and drain on paper towels. Return meat to skillet and add salsa. Simmer until most liquid has evaporated. Combine beans, cumin, garlic salt and Monterey Jack cheese in dish; microwave 2 minutes on high and stir. Microwave again until cheese is melted. Heat tortillas in microwave 30 seconds on high. Spread each with bean mixture followed by meat mixture; roll up and place seam-side down in baking dish. Top with picante sauce and add green onions, tomatoes and cheddar cheese. Bake, uncovered, 20-30 minutes or until bubbly. Place each flauta on a lettuce bed and top with sour cream.   **Servings: 6-8**

Alternate Meats: Elk, moose, antelope, caribou, deer

"...This is a favorite with the kids..."

Guacamole Olé

Serve as an appetizer with taco or tortilla chips or as a complement to any Mexican dish.

- **4 ripe avocados, peeled**
- **1 small can roasted diced green chilies, drained**
- **2 ripe tomatoes, peeled and diced**
- **$1/4$ bunch green onions, diced**
- **1 tsp. lemon juice**

In medium bowl, mash avocados into paste and add green chilies. Mix well; add tomatoes, green onions and lemon juice. Stir well.

Servings: 8-10

Cooking Tips: Keeping one or two avocado seeds under the dip helps maintain its green color. Otherwise, if dip turns brown, stir and green color will surface.

Flour tortillas can be warmed right on the coils of an electric stove to remove their "doughy" taste.

Ethnic Recipes...

"...Have your appetite fortune come true with this dish..."

Special Quesadillas
This savory dish is topped with salsa, sour cream and guacamole.

2 tsp. olive oil
1 large onion, sliced
2 cups mushrooms, sliced
1 green pepper, sliced
1 red pepper, sliced
2 lb. ground venison
Salt and pepper, sprinkle
12 large flour tortillas

1 can refried beans
1/4 cup milk
1 lb. Monterey Jack cheese, shredded
1 lb. sharp cheddar cheese, shredded
4 tomatoes, chopped
1 can olives, sliced
Jalapeño peppers, seeded and chopped

In wok or large skillet with oil, stir-fry onions, mushrooms and green and red peppers until just tender. Drain on paper towels and set aside. In same skillet, sprinkle meat with salt and pepper and sauté; drain on paper towels and set aside. Heat tortillas in microwave 30 seconds on high. Place on serving plate. In skillet, combine refried beans, milk and 1/4 cup of each cheese. Simmer and stir until creamy. Spread 1/4-1/2 cup beans on each tortilla and add desired amounts of meat, vegetables, tomatoes, olives and jalapeño peppers. Fold in half. **Servings: 6**

Alternate Meats: Elk, moose, antelope, caribou, deer

Enchilada Excitement
Serve with refried beans and taco chips.

2 lb. ground venison
1 large onion, minced
See *Enchilada Sauce*

1/2 cup olive oil
36 corn tortillas
4-6 cups cheddar cheese, shredded

Preheat oven to 325°. Brown venison and onion in skillet and drain on paper towels. Prepare *Enchilada Sauce*. In separate pan, heat olive oil; dip tortillas in oil and drain on paper towels. Fill each tortilla with 2 Tbsp. meat; cover meat with cheese and 2 Tbsp. sauce. Roll and arrange side-by-side in baking dish. When dish is full, cover with remaining sauce and bake 20-25 minutes or until bubbly. **Servings: 6-10**

Alternate Meats: Elk, moose, antelope, caribou, deer

Enchilada Sauce

1 cup olive oil
1 tsp. garlic powder
1 tsp. onion salt
1 cup flour
1 tsp. sugar
2-4 tsp. red Mexican chili powder
1 can tomato soup
1 can cheddar cheese soup
1 large can tomato juice
1 1/2 qts. hot water

In large saucepan, heat olive oil. Add garlic powder, onion salt, flour, sugar and chili powder. Cook over medium heat until mixture bubbles. Add soups and tomato juice and bring to boil. Add hot water and simmer 15 minutes, stirring constantly.

"...Have a fiesta with this dish..."

Mexican-Style Vension Steak with Beans
Zap your taste buds with this dish, best served with white rice.

2 lb. vension steak
Salt and pepper, sprinkle
1 onion, diced
1 beef bouillon cube, crushed
1 16-oz. can stewed tomatoes

4 Tbsp. diced green chilies, drained
1-2 tsp. chili powder
1 clove garlic, minced
1/2 tsp. cumin
1 16-oz. can kidney beans, drained

Season steak with salt and pepper. Cut into 1/2-inch wide strips and place in crock pot. Add onion, bouillon cube, stewed tomatoes, green chilies, chili powder, garlic and cumin. Cover and cook on low 6 hours. Turn control to high and add beans. Cook, covered, 30 minutes. **Servings: 6**

Alternate Meats: Elk, moose, antelope, caribou, deer

Spanish Rice
This dish is a delightful extender to any main course.

12 slices bacon
1 bunch green onions, sliced
1 green pepper, diced
6 cups rice, cooked

2 cans Mexican-style stewed tomatoes
Salt and pepper, sprinkle
1/4 lb. cheddar cheese, grated

Fry bacon in skillet; dry and crumble. In same skillet, sauté green onions and green peppers in bacon fat and drain on paper towel. Prepare rice according to package directions. Discard grease from skillet, return bacon and onion mixture to skillet and add all remaining ingredients except cheese. Simmer 25-30 minutes; top with cheese before serving. **Servings: 6**

"...This is a testimony to good eating..."

Ethnic Recipes...

Refried beans are a healthy addition to a variety of Mexican dishes. They can also be eaten separately as a side dish.

Refried Beans El Scratcho
Accent your fried venison dinner with this Mexican side dish.

4 cups pinto beans	1/2 cup milk (optional)
1/8 tsp. garlic salt	1/2 lb. white cheese
1/8 tsp. onion salt	1/2 lb. yellow cheese
10 Tbsp. lard or 2 Tbsp. canola oil	

In pressure cooker, combine beans, garlic salt and onion salt and fill with water. Close lid securely and set regulator. Pressure cook 20 minutes. Let pressure drop and add more water if necessary. Pressure cook 20 more minutes. Allow steam to escape; add more water and 6 Tbsp. lard or 1 Tbsp. oil. Pressure cook again until beans are very soft. Transfer beans with water to open Dutch oven. Boil slowly 10 minutes and add 4 Tbsp. lard or 1 Tbsp. oil. Mash beans until creamy. Stir in milk. Cut cheeses into small squares and add to beans. **Servings: 10**

Cooking Tips: Cooking beans in pressure cooker saves time, but they can also be pot-cooked. Be sure all rocks are removed and beans are rinsed before starting recipe.

If watching cholesterol levels, substitute lard with canola oil.

If smoother beans are desired, add 3/4 cup milk and stir before adding cheese.

"...This is one ethnic dish sure to become a standard in your home..."

Mexican Chili Relleno Casserole
This goes nicely with a venison roast or upland game dish.

2 eggs, beaten
1 cup milk
1/4 cup flour
1 lb. Monterey Jack cheese, shredded
1 8-oz. can diced green chilies, drained
1 cup cracker crumbs

Preheat oven to 350°. In small bowl, mix eggs, milk and flour. Pour small amount into bottom of baking dish. Layer cheese and green chilies; repeat until all is used. Top with cracker crumbs. Pour remaining egg mixture over layers. Bake 30-45 minutes or until inserted knife comes out clean. **Servings: 6**

"...Dress up your venison roast with *Green Chili Corn Pudding* and serve it on St. Patrick's Day..."

Green Chili Corn Pudding
Looking for something more interesting than canned green beans? Try this tasty dish.

2 lb. frozen corn, thawed	2 cups Half and Half
1 4-oz. can diced green chilies, drained	2 tsp. sugar
1 tsp. salt	1/2 tsp. garlic powder
1/4 tsp. pepper	1 cup Monterey Jack cheese, shredded
3 eggs, beaten	1/2 cup dry Italian-style bread crumbs

Preheat oven to 350°. Combine all ingredients except bread crumbs in casserole dish. Set dish in pan with 1-inch of water. Top with bread crumbs. Cover and bake 1 hour 15 minutes or until inserted butter knife comes out clean. **Servings: 6**

Ethnic Recipes...

Gameburger Chili Beans and Tortillas

Serve with shredded lettuce, sour cream and guacamole.

2 lb. non-fat gameburger*
1 can pinto beans
1 jar Mexican salsa
1 pkg. flour tortillas

Brown meat in skillet. Add beans and desired amount of salsa. Stir. Spoon over warmed flour tortillas. **Servings: 4**

Alternate Meats: Elk, moose, antelope, caribou, deer

Cooking Tips: Tortillas can be warmed directly over open flame or on electric stove grill.

*See Chapter 18 for tips on preparing non-fat gameburger.

Mexican Green Chili Venison Roll-Ups

Garnish with sliced avocados and salsa.

1 lb. ground venison	1 can sliced olives, drained
1/2 cup onion, minced	1/2 cup sour cream
2 cloves garlic, minced	Salt and pepper, sprinkle
1 4-oz. can diced green chilies, drained	1 Tbsp. cornmeal
1 cup Monterey Jack cheese, shredded	2 8-oz. cans crescent rolls

Preheat oven to 350°. Sauté venison, onion and garlic in skillet and drain on paper towels. In bowl, blend meat mixture with chilies, cheese, olives, sour cream, salt and pepper. Sprinkle cornmeal on baking sheet. Separate rolls into 8 rectangles and press perforations to seal. Spoon 1/2 cup meat mixture over each rectangle. Roll lengthwise, pinch edges to seal and place seam-side down on baking sheet. Bake 25-30 minutes or until golden brown. **Servings: 4**

Alternate Meats: Elk, moose, antelope, caribou, deer

Venison Tacos

Picnic in your backyard with this dish. Serve with an avocado salad.

2 lb. ground venison	2 cups sharp cheddar cheese, shredded
1 small onion, minced	2 cups lettuce, shredded
1 clove garlic, minced	1 can olives, sliced and drained
1 16-oz. can Italian-style tomato sauce	4 tomatoes, chopped
1 pkg. Lawry's Taco Spices & Seasonings Mix	1 jar taco sauce
2 pkgs. taco shells	1 cup sour cream

Preheat oven to 350°. Brown meat in skillet with onion and garlic and drain on paper towels. Return mixture to skillet and add tomato sauce and Lawry's Taco Seasoning and simmer 15-20 minutes. Heat taco shells in oven and place on paper towels to absorb oil. Fill each shell with meat mixture, cheese, lettuce, olives, tomatoes, taco sauce and sour cream. **Servings: 6**

Alternate Meats: Elk, moose, antelope, caribou, deer

Burrito Venison Casserole

Serve this burrito delight with salsa, chopped tomatoes and shredded lettuce.

2 lb. ground venison	1 can cream of mushroom soup
1 cup onion, minced	1 16-oz. can refried beans
2 cloves garlic, minced	1/4 cup milk
2 pkgs. Lawry's Taco Spices & Seasonings Mix	Flour tortillas
2 cups low-fat sour cream	2 cups Monterey Jack cheese, shredded
	1 cup sharp cheddar cheese, shredded

Preheat oven to 350°. Brown meat in skillet with onion, garlic and Lawry's Taco Seasoning and drain on paper towels. In bowl, mix sour cream and mushroom soup. In separate bowl, mix beans and milk. In casserole dish, layer meat, beans, soup mixture, tortillas and cheeses. Continue layering, omitting final layer of cheeses. Bake 45 minutes until bubbly. Sprinkle with remaining cheeses and bake until bubbly. **Servings: 6**

Alternate Meats: Elk, moose, antelope, caribou, deer, buffalo

Easy Chili Rellenos

This winning combination of cheese and eggs will zap new life into a breakfast or lunch.

1 small can whole roasted green chilies, peeled
1/2 lb. white or yellow cheese, sliced
1 Tbsp. olive oil
4 eggs

Rinse chilies and dry on paper towels. Insert 1 slice of cheese inside each chili. Heat skillet with oil and fry chilies 30 to 45 seconds per side. In seperate skillet, scramble eggs. Ladle scrambled eggs over top of chilies as they continue to cook. Using spatula, turn rellenos over and cook until done. Place on plate and microwave on high 20-30 seconds. **Servings: 4**

Ethnic Recipes...

Mexican Salsa

*Serve as an appetizer with corn chips
before bringing out one of those great
Mexican-style game dinners.*

1 can roasted chopped green chilies,
   drained
4 tomatoes, chopped
1/4 tsp. oregano
1/8 tsp. peanut oil
Garlic powder, dash
1 green onion, chopped

In small bowl, mix chilies with tomatoes and
add oregano, peanut oil, garlic powder and green
onion. Serve cold or at room temperature.

Servings: 6

Mexican Venison Casserole

*This is a delicious Mexican medley.
Serve with a tossed green salad and hot garlic bread.*

2 lb. ground venison
1 tsp. Lawry's Seasoned Pepper
1 pkg. Lawry's Taco
   Spices & Seasonings Mix
1 can stewed tomatoes
2 8-oz. cans tomato sauce

1 4-oz. can diced green chilies, drained
12-15 corn tortillas
1/4 cup fresh parsley, chopped
1 cup low-fat ricotta cheese
1/4 cup Parmesan cheese, grated
3 cups Monterey Jack cheese, grated

Preheat oven to 350°. Brown meat in skillet with Lawry's Seasoned Pepper and
drain on paper towels. Return meat to skillet and add Lawry's Taco Seasoning,
stewed tomatoes, tomato sauce and chilies. Bring to boil and reduce heat to simmer
10-15 minutes. Place 1/2 meat mixture in large casserole dish and top with tortillas.
Sprinkle with parsley and 1/2 cup each of ricotta, Parmesan and Monterey Jack
cheeses. Repeat layers, ending with Monterey Jack cheese. Bake, uncovered, 30-45
minutes or until bubbly. Let stand 20 minutes before serving.   **Servings: 6**

Alternate Meats: Elk, moose, antelope, caribou, deer

Venison Taco Salad

This luncheon meal tastes great with in-season fruit.

1 1/4 lb. ground venison
1 8-oz. can tomato sauce
1 can ranch beans, undrained
1/4 cup green chilies, diced
1/2 tsp. cumin
2 Tbsp. cilantro, chopped

1 small bag tortilla chips, lime
1/2 cup olives, sliced
6 cups lettuce, shredded
1/2 cup green onion, chopped
2 cups cheddar cheese, grated
1/2 cup sour cream

Brown venison in skillet and drain on paper towels. Return meat to skillet and add
tomato sauce, ranch beans with juice, chilies and cumin. Bring to boil; reduce heat
and simmer 10-15 minutes. Stir in cilantro. Place tortilla chips on serving plate and
spoon meat mixture into center. Sprinkle with olives, lettuce and green onions. Top
with cheese and sour cream.   **Servings: 6**

Alternate Meats: Elk, moose, antelope, caribou, deer

"...This makes a great meal-on-the-run..."

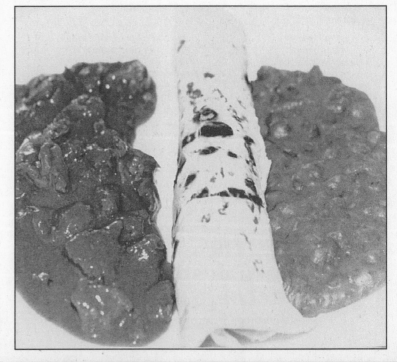

Chili Con Carne with tortilla and refried
beans. The *Chili Con Carne* was made
with game meat, of course.

Ethnic Recipes...

Mexican Sloppy Joes with Corn Dumplings
Sloppy Joes never had it so good. Serve with a mixed green salad.

2 lb. ground venison
1 cup onion, diced
1 cup green pepper, diced
1 pkg. Lawry's Taco
   Spices & Seasonings Mix
1/4 cup brown sugar
1/4 cup diced green chilies, drained

1 8-oz. jar picante sauce, mild
1/4 cup white vinegar
2 cups biscuit mix
1 cup milk, skim
1/2 tsp. oregano, rubbed
2/3 cup cornmeal
1 7-oz. can whole kernel corn, drained

Brown venison in skillet with onion and drain on paper towels. Return mixture to skillet and add green pepper, Lawry's Taco Seasoning, brown sugar, chilies, picante sauce and white vinegar. Cover and simmer 1 hour until thickened. In bowl, combine biscuit mix, milk, oregano, cornmeal and corn. Using soup spoon, drop dumpling mixture over venison mixture. Cook, uncovered, 10-15 minutes. Cover and cook 10-15 minutes until dumplings are done. **Servings: 6**

Alternate Meats: Elk, moose, antelope, caribou, deer

"...One of the more delicious meals in our lineup..."

"...Fast and tasty..."

Mexican Stir-Fry
Serve this stir-fry with Spanish Rice and warmed tortillas.

1 1/2 lb. game meat, boned and cubed
1 clove garlic, sliced
1/2 tsp. Worcestershire sauce
3 Tbsp. soy sauce
2 Tbsp. lard or canola oil
4-oz. diced green chilies, drained
1 jar Mexican salsa

Place meat in pressure cooker with garlic, Worcestershire and soy sauces. Fill with water. Close lid securely, set regulator and pressure cook 15 minutes. Let pressure drop and discard liquids. Heat skillet with lard or canola oil and stir-fry meat while adding chilies and salsa. Cook until blended. **Servings: 4-6**

Alternate Meats: Elk, moose, antelope, caribou, deer

Busy Day Venison Enchiladas
Brighten any busy day with this dish. Serve with nacho chips and salsa.

2 lb. ground venison
1 16-oz. jar picante sauce
1 4-oz. can diced green chilies, drained
1 16-oz. can pinto beans, drained
1 lb. Mexican-style Velveeta cheese, cubed

1/2 cup olive oil
16-20 corn tortillas
1 cup sour cream
1 cup tomato, chopped
1 cup olives, sliced

Preheat oven to 350°. Brown meat in skillet and drain on paper towels. Return meat to skillet and add picante sauce and chilies. Simmer 10 minutes; add beans and 1/4 of cheese cubes and simmer until cheese is melted. In saucepan, heat olive oil; dip tortillas in oil and drain on paper towels. Fill each tortilla with 1/4 cup meat mixture, roll and place in baking dish seam-side down. Bake 25 minutes; top with remaining cheese cubes. Bake 10-12 minutes or until cheese is melted. Top with sour cream, tomatoes and olives. **Servings: 6**

Alternate Meats: Elk, moose, antelope, caribou, deer

Antelope Fajitas
Serve with guacamole and refried beans. You may want to add a spoonful of guacamole inside the tortillas.

2 lb. antelope meat, boned
Soy sauce, dash
Garlic powder, sprinkle
2 tsp. olive oil
1/4 cup teriyaki marinade

1/4 cup Madeira wine
2 bunches green onions, whole
4-5 flour tortillas
Monterey Jack cheese, sliced

Slice meat into thin strips. Rub meat with soy sauce and garlic powder and marinate overnight. Heat skillet with oil and teriyaki marinade and sauté meat. When marinade has assimilated, add wine and cook until blended; set aside. In same skillet, sauté green onions with bulbs. Heat tortillas over open flame or on electric stove grate. On each tortilla, layer 1 slice of cheese, 1 green onion, 2 meat strips and a small amount of pan drippings. Fold and microwave 15-20 seconds or until cheese is melted. **Servings: 4-5**

Alternate Meats: Elk, moose, caribou, deer

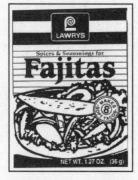

"...Spice up your menu with these hot meals..."

Ethnic Recipes...

Wild Turkey Enchilada Pie

This delicious meal can be topped with salsa, sour cream and avocado.

1 frozen pie crust, thawed	3 eggs
2 tsp. olive oil	1/2 cup milk, skim
1/2 cup onion, minced	1/2 tsp. garlic powder
1 1/2 cups leftover wild turkey, cubed	1 tsp. Worcestershire sauce
1/4 cup diced green chilies, drained	1/4 tsp. cumin
1 cup Monterey Jack cheese, shredded	2 drops Tabasco sauce
1/2 cup olives, sliced	

Preheat oven to 400°. Place crust in pie pan, flute and bake 10-12 minutes or until lightly browned. Heat skillet with oil, sauté onions and drain on paper towel. In pie crust, layer turkey, onions, chilies, cheese and olives. In bowl, mix eggs, milk, garlic powder, Worcestershire sauce, cumin and Tabasco sauce. Pour over layers in pie crust and bake 45-60 minutes or until inserted knife comes out clean. Let stand 20 minutes before serving. **Servings: 4-6**

Jalapeño Pepper Muffins

Enliven any venison dish with this exciting bread recipe.

2 cups flour
2 Tbsp. brown sugar
3 tsp. baking powder
1 tsp. baking soda
1/2 tsp. salt
1 cup sharp cheddar cheese, shredded
4 Tbsp. jalapeño peppers, diced
1 cup low-fat milk
1/4 cup canola oil
1 egg, beaten

Preheat oven to 375°. Blend flour, brown sugar, baking powder, baking soda and salt in bowl. Stir in cheese, jalapeño peppers, milk, oil and egg. Line muffin pan with paper cups. Fill each cup 2/3 full. Bake 20-25 minutes or until muffins are lightly browned. **Servings: 6**

> ## "...This dish is music to your palate; each bite is the high note of flavor..."

Mexican food prepared with game meat is delicious! There are a great variety of dishes that can be made.

> ## "...So good, they'll vanish before your eyes..."

Vanishing Venison Nachos

Serve as a spicy snack or appetizer.

1 lb. ground venison	1 lb. Mexican Velveeta cheese, cubed
1 tsp. garlic powder	1 cup picante sauce, medium hot
Salt and pepper, sprinkle	1 4-oz. can diced green chilies, drained
1/2 tsp. cumin	1 pkg. tortilla chips, lime
1 Tbsp. lard	1/2 cup sour cream
1 16-oz. can refried beans	1 cup cheddar cheese, shredded
1/2 cup Monterey Jack cheese, shredded	1 cup olives, sliced
1/4 cup skim milk	

Brown meat in skillet with garlic powder, salt, pepper and cumin and drain on paper towels. In same skillet, melt lard; add beans and bring to boil. Stir in Monterey Jack cheese and milk and simmer 5 minutes. Place Velveeta cheese into dish; microwave on high 2 minutes and stir. Add picante sauce and chilies; microwave on high 2-4 minutes or until bubbly. Place tortilla chips on large serving platter, layer with melted cheese mix, meat and refried beans. Top with additional picante sauce and sour cream. Sprinkle with cheddar cheese and olives. **Servings: 6**

Alternate Meats: Elk, moose, antelope, caribou, deer

Ethnic Recipes...

Titan Tostadas

A scrumptious lunch dish or snack.

2 lb. ground venison	1-2 pkgs. tostada shells
Salt and pepper, sprinkle	1 cup sour cream
1 can refried beans	1 4-oz. can diced green chilies, drained
1/4 cup milk	2 cups tomatoes, chopped
2 1/4 cups cheddar cheese, shredded	1 can olives, sliced
1/4 cup Monterey Jack cheese, shredded	1 head lettuce, shredded

Preheat oven to 350°. Salt and pepper meat; brown in skillet and drain on paper towels. In same skillet, combine beans, milk, 1/4 cup cheddar and Monterey Jack cheeses. Heat until bubbly. Place tostada shells on cookie sheet and heat both sides. Spread 2-3 Tbsp. bean mixture and 1/4 cup meat over each tostada shell. Layer with sour cream, chilies, tomatoes, olives, lettuce and remaining cheddar cheese. Serve immediately.   **Servings: 6**

Alternate Meats: Elk, moose, antelope, caribou, deer

Crusty Mexican Venison-Bean Bake

At your next block party, surprise your neighbors with this. Tomato slices with avocado-lime dressing will help cool this fire.

2 lb. ground venison	2 eggs, beaten
1 onion, minced	2 cans pinto beans, undrained
2 cloves garlic, minced	1 tsp. Lawry's Lemon Pepper
1 cup flour	2-4 tsp. chili powder
1 cup sour cream	1 4-oz. can diced green chilies, drained
1 tsp. baking powder	1 jar picante sauce
1/2 tsp. baking soda	1-2 cups Monterey Jack cheese, shredded

Preheat oven to 350°. Brown meat in skillet with onion and garlic and drain on paper towels. In large bowl, mix flour, sour cream, baking powder, baking soda and eggs. Spread thinly in bottom and sides of baking dish. In mixing bowl, blend meat, beans, Lawry's Lemon Pepper, chili powder, chilies and picante sauce and spoon into baking dish. Bake 45 minutes; sprinkle with Monterey Jack cheese. Let stand 15 minutes before serving.   **Servings: 6**

Alternate Meats: Elk, moose, antelope, caribou, deer

South-of-the-Border Casserole

Present this delicious meal at your next piñata party. Serve with a tossed salad.

2 lb. ground venison
Salt and pepper, sprinkle
1 onion, minced
1 clove garlic, minced
2 cups picante sauce
1 16-oz. can tomato sauce
12 taco shells, broken into bite-sized pieces
2 cups Monterey Jack cheese, shredded
1 cup sharp cheddar cheese, shredded

Preheat oven to 350°. Salt and pepper meat. Brown meat in skillet with onion and garlic and drain on paper towels. Combine picante and tomato sauces in small bowl. In baking dish, layer broken tacos, 1/2 venison mixture, 1/2 cheeses and 1/2 sauce mixture. Repeat layers, ending with sauce. Bake 1 hour or until bubbly. Let stand 15 minutes before serving.

Servings: 6

Alternate Meats: Elk, moose, antelope, caribou, deer

Green Chili Venison Stew

Serve with warmed tortillas, refried beans and a tossed salad.

4 lb. venison steak, cubed	4 large cloves garlic, pressed
1 large can tomato juice	6 large tomatoes, peeled and quartered
2 tsp. salt	2 large onions, diced
1 tsp. pepper	3/4 tsp. cumin
1 4-oz. can diced green chilies, drained	1 tsp. oregano

In large pot, simmer venison cubes with tomato juice, salt and pepper until meat is tender. Add remaining ingredients and simmer 45-60 minutes until flavors are blended.   **Servings: 6-8**

Alternate Meats: Elk, moose, antelope, caribou, deer

"...Warmed tortillas are a must with this stew..."

Mexican Scalloped Corn

Easy to prepare and colorful, this delicious side dish goes well with any barbecued or fried meat.

1 tsp. butter	4 Tbsp. flour
1/2 cup onion, minced	1 1/2 cups Half and Half
1/2 tsp. garlic powder	2 cans Green Giant Mexicorn
1/2 tsp. chili powder	1 egg, beaten
1/2 tsp. dry mustard	1/2 cup dry Italian-style bread crumbs

Preheat oven to 350°. Heat skillet with butter and sauté onion. Add garlic powder, chili powder, dry mustard and flour and stir until bubbly. Gradually add Half and Half and stir until thickened. Pour corn, egg and skillet mixture into baking dish; stir and top with bread crumbs. Bake 30 minutes.   **Servings: 6**

"...Delicious with any barbecued or fried meat..."

Ethnic Recipes...

Squirrel Cantonese

Serve with fried rice and hot tea.

4-6 squirrels, sectioned
3 qts. water
1 Tbsp. baking soda
1/2 cup teriyaki marinade
2 cloves garlic, diced (or)
1/4 tsp. garlic powder
1/4 tsp. Worcestershire sauce
11/2 cups chicken stock or broth
1 tsp. soy sauce

1 tsp. oyster sauce
1/4 tsp. sesame oil
1/4 tsp. white pepper
2 Tbsp. cornstarch
1/2 cup canola or olive oil
1 cup walnuts, halved
1/4 cup white onion, chopped
2 carrots, peeled and sliced
2 Tbsp. ginger root, sliced

In large bowl, soak squirrel pieces 1 hour in 1 qt. water and baking soda. Rinse and place in pressure cooker with 2 qts. water, teriyaki marinade, garlic or garlic powder and Worcestershire sauce. Close lid securely and set regulator. Pressure cook 20 minutes. Let pressure drop and discard liquid. Bone meat and set aside. In large bowl, combine 1 cup stock or broth, soy sauce, oyster sauce, sesame oil and white pepper and set aside. In separate bowl, dissolve cornstarch in 1/2 cup of stock or broth and set aside. Heat oil in wok or large skillet; add walnuts and cook until brown. Remove and set aside. In same cooking vessel, add oil (if necessary) and squirrel pieces; brown meat and drain on paper towels. Stir-fry onion, carrots and ginger root 1/2-1 minute. Return meat and walnuts to pan and stir-fry 1 minute. Add stock and cornstarch mixtures and cook 2 minutes.   **Servings: 6-8**

"...Serve with rice, one of the oldest foods known to man..."

Venison Tortilla Surprise

Save your appetite for this savory dish. Serve with an avocado salad.

2 lb. ground venison
1 onion, diced
1 tsp. cumin
2 cans tomato soup

2 8-oz. cans tomato sauce
1 can Mexican-style stewed tomatoes
24 soft corn tortillas
11/2 lb. cheddar cheese, shredded

Brown meat in skillet with onion and cumin and drain on paper towels. In bowl, combine soup, tomato sauce and stewed tomatoes. In casserole dish, layer tortillas, tomato mixture and meat until gone. Sprinkle generously with cheese and microwave 30 minutes on high, turning after 15 minutes. Let stand 10-15 minutes before serving.   **Servings: 6**

Alternate Meats: Elk, moose, antelope, caribou, deer

Chinese Venison Pepper Steak

Cradle this delicious meal in a bed of rice.

2 lb. venison steak
Lawry's Lemon Pepper, sprinkle
1 tsp. fresh ginger
1/2 cup soy sauce
2 Tbsp. sesame oil
3 cloves garlic, chopped
1 cup onion, sliced
4 cups green pepper, sliced
2-4 Tbsp. cornstarch
1-2 cups chicken broth
1 can water chestnuts
2 tsp. sugar

Slice meat diagonally across grain into thin slices and sprinkle with Lawry's Lemon Pepper and ginger. Top with soy sauce and marinate 1 hour. In skillet with sesame oil, sauté garlic; add meat and brown over high heat. Add onions and green peppers and sauté 3 minutes or until peppers are tender. In jar or bowl, mix cornstarch with chicken broth and add to skillet. Add water chestnuts and sugar and stir until broth thickens.   **Servings: 6**

Alternate Meats: Elk, moose, antelope, caribou, deer, buffalo

---

"...Spice up your menu with these dishes..."

Mexican Rabbit

When you see how good this looks, take it one step further and garnish with tortilla chips.

2 rabbits, cut into serving pieces
4 cans chicken broth
1 can diced green chilies, drained
3 cloves garlic, minced
1 tsp. cumin, ground

1 large onion, chopped
3 cups brown or white rice, uncooked
1/2-1 cup cilantro leaves, chopped
6 tomatoes
Salt and pepper, sprinkle

In large saucepan, combine broth, chilies, garlic, cumin and onion. Bring to boil; add rice and meat. Cover, reduce heat and simmer 1 hour or until meat and rice are done. Add cilantro leaves, tomatoes, salt and pepper. Simmer 5-10 minutes or until tomatoes are just tender.   **Servings: 6**

Ethnic Recipes...

The wok is a popular cooking tool for stir-frying. Mushrooms are being sautéd in light oil.

"...This is where a wok shines..."

Sweet-and-Sour Wild Boar Stir-Fry
Serve this Chinese dish with chopsticks and rice.

1¹/₂ lb. boned wild boar, sliced thin	1 Tbsp. catsup
2 Tbsp. cornstarch	1 egg, beaten
1 Tbsp. cold water	Canola oil
¹/₄ cup white vinegar	2 cloves garlic, chopped
5 Tbsp. sugar	4 green peppers, chopped
2 Tbsp. soy sauce	1 red pepper, chopped
1 Tbsp. teriyaki marinade	1 small can diced pineapple, drained
4 drops sesame oil	¹/₈ cup white wine
2 Tbsp. Worcestershire sauce	

Shape meat with meat hammer to uniform thickness and cut into bite-sized pieces. In small bowl, mix cornstarch with water. In another bowl, mix vinegar, sugar, soy sauce, teriyaki marinade, sesame oil, Worcestershire sauce and catsup. Dip meat into beaten egg and then cornstarch mixture. Heat wok with oil and fry meat; set aside. Stir-fry garlic 15 seconds; add green peppers. Cook until tender. Add red pepper and pineapple; cook 1 minute. Add meat; stir-fry to blend. Add wine and cook down. Stir in sauce mixture and remaining cornstarch mixture.

Servings: 4

Chinese-Style Venison Liver and Onions
Complement this dish with oven potatoes and a tossed salad.

2 lb. venison liver
Cornstarch
2 Tbsp. peanut oil
1 clove garlic, minced
¹/₈ tsp. ginger
1 bunch green onions, sliced
See *Chinese-Style Sauce*

Slice liver into 1-inch long strips; dry on paper towel and coat with cornstarch. Heat skillet with oil and sauté garlic. Add liver and quick fry for 3 minutes. Sprinkle with ginger; add green onions and fry 2 minutes more. Prepare *Chinese-Style Sauce* and add to skillet. Cook 1 minute.

Servings: 6

Alternate Meats: Elk, moose, antelope, caribou, deer

Chinese-Style Sauce
8 Tbsp. soy sauce
3 Tbsp. sherry
3 Tbsp. brown sugar
1 tsp. salt
¹/₄ tsp. pepper
Mix ingredients in small bowl.

Ethnic Recipes...

Stir-Fry Marinade

4 cloves garlic, minced
1 tsp. lemon pepper
2 cups olive oil
3/4 cup balsmic vinegar

Mix all ingredients in small bowl and let stand 6 hours or overnight.

Stir-Fry Vegetables

Toasted almonds are an excellent garnish to this dish.

2 small zucchini, sliced
1 large sweet potato, sliced
12 asparagus spears, sliced
1 green pepper, julienned
6 pineapple slices, cut into chunks

1 Spanish onion, sliced
1 small eggplant, sliced
1 red pepper, julienned
12 large mushrooms, sliced
See *Stir-Fry Marinade*

Marinate all ingredients 1 hour in *Stir-Fry Marinade*. Drain and stir-fry vegetables in wok or skillet over high heat until almost tender. Serve on heated platter with rice. **Servings: 6**

"...When you're in the mood for something different..."

Chinese-Style Vension Steak

Serve with rice and a green salad.

2 lb. venison steak
2 cups peanut oil
1 Tbsp. soy sauce
3 cloves garlic, minced

Cut 1/8-inch slashes across grain of meat on both sides. Soak in dish with peanut oil 2-4 hours. Remove from oil and rub with soy sauce and garlic. Broil until desired doneness. **Servings: 6**

Alternate Meats: Elk, moose, antelope, caribou, deer

"...A very palatable combination..."

Javelina Plus Pork Stir-Fry

*This is a very palatable combination with a Chinese flair.
Serve over rice or noodles with mixed vegetables.*

1 cup soy sauce
1/2 cup teriyaki marinade
3 cups sherry
3 Tbsp. brown sugar
1 Tbsp. sugar, granulated
1 Tbsp. molasses
1/4 cup beef broth

2 tsp. olive oil
2 lb. javelina, boned and sliced
2 lb. pork, sliced
2 cloves garlic, pressed
2 slices ginger
1/2 cup chicken broth

In small bowl, mix soy sauce, teriyaki marinade, sherry, brown and white sugars, molasses and beef broth. Heat skillet or wok with oil and stir-fry meat 2 minutes. Add garlic, ginger and sauce mixture and continue to stir-fry. Add chicken broth and cook 2-4 minutes or until broth looks blended. Reduce to low and simmer 1 hour. Add chicken broth as needed to maintain sauce level. **Servings: 8**

Venison Chop Suey

This is a quick and tasty dinner for those on the run. A bed of rice goes nice.

2 lb. venison steak, cubed
Salt and pepper, sprinkle
1 tsp. garlic powder
2 tsp. sesame oil
1 onion, diced
1 cup carrots, peeled and diced
1 cup red pepper, sliced
1 cup broccoli flowerettes

2 cups celery, diced
1 cup green pepper, sliced
1 cup cabbage, sliced
2 cups fresh bean sprouts
1 cup mushrooms, sliced
1/2 cup water
2 tsp. soy sauce

"...Chopsticks are a must..."

Season meat with salt, pepper and garlic powder and place in pressure cooker heated with oil. Sauté meat and drain on paper towels. Using same cooker, lightly stir-fry vegetables. Return meat to pressure cooker and add water and soy sauce. Close lid securely and set regulator. Pressure cook 10 minutes with regulator rocking gently. Let pressure drop. **Servings: 4-6**

Alternate Meats: Elk, moose, antelope, caribou, deer

Ethnic Recipes...

Stir-Fry Venison with Peas

Serve over rice and garnish with parsley.

2 lb. venison steak
2 Tbsp. sherry
2 Tbsp. soy sauce
1 Tbsp. cornstarch
$1/2$ tsp. salt
2 Tbsp. peanut oil

$1/8$ tsp. ginger, ground
2 10-oz. pkgs. peas, frozen
3 6-oz. pkgs. Chinese pea pods, frozen
1 lb. mushrooms, sliced
1 can water chestnuts, sliced

Cut steak diagonally across grain into 2-inch strips. Place in large bowl with sherry, soy sauce, cornstarch and salt. Marinate 1 hour at room temperature or overnight in refrigerator. Drain meat; saving marinade. Place $1/2$ of meat strips in wok or skillet with peanut oil and ginger. Stir-fry over medium-high heat 3-5 minutes; push meat to one side. Add remaining meat slices; stir-fry 3-5 minutes. Remove all meat. Stir-fry peas and pea pods 3 minutes and remove. Repeat process for mushrooms. Return meat, peas, pea pods and mushrooms to skillet or wok and add water chestnuts and reserved marinade and stir. Reduce heat and simmer 5 minutes.

Servings: 6

Alternate Meats: Elk, moose, antelope, caribou, deer

> ## "...If you have a wok, now is the time to use it..."

> ## "...The spicier the better..."

Spicy-Hot Venison Broccoli

Serve over Chinese noodles or rice with fresh fruit.

$11/2$ lb. venison steak
1 Tbsp. brown sugar
3 Tbsp. soy sauce
$1/2$ tsp. ginger, ground
$1/4$ tsp. Lawry's Garlic Powder with Parsley
$11/2$ tsp. red pepper, crushed
$1/4$ tsp. Lawry's Lemon Pepper
2 tsp. olive oil
4 cups broccoli flowerettes
$3/4$ cup beef broth
2 Tbsp. cornstarch
$1/4$ cup catsup

Slice steak diagonally across grain into thin strips. In medium bowl, marinate meat 1 hour in brown sugar, soy sauce, ginger, Lawry's Garlic Powder with Parsley, red pepper and Lawry's Lemon Pepper. Heat skillet with oil; stir-fry marinated meat until brown and drain on paper towels. In same skillet, combine broccoli and $1/2$ of broth; cover and steam 5 minutes. In small bowl, mix cornstarch with remaining broth and catsup. Return meat to skillet with broccoli and top with cornstarch mixture. Cook, stirring, until mixture thickens and turns clear. **Servings: 4-6**

Alternate Meats: Elk, moose, antelope, caribou, deer

Venison Steak with Chinese Pea Pods

For a change, serve with noodles instead of rice.

1 lb. venison steak
$1/4$ cup soy sauce
1 can beef broth
$1/4$ tsp. ginger, ground
1 bunch green onions, sliced

2 Tbsp. cornstarch
2 Tbsp. water
1 7-oz. pkg. Chinese pea pods, frozen
1 can water chestnuts, sliced

Slice venison diagonally across grain into thin strips. In bowl, combine meat, soy sauce, beef broth, ginger and green onions. Pour into crock pot, cover and cook 6 hours on low. In jar or small bowl, dissolve cornstarch in water and add to crock pot. Cook 10 minutes on high. Add pea pods and water chestnuts and cook 5-10 minutes.

Servings: 4

Alternate Meats: Elk, moose, antelope, caribou, deer

Oriental Salad

This is a colorful side dish for venison roast or ribs.

1 large can mandarin oranges
1 12-oz. can pineapple, crushed
$1/4$ head red cabbage, sliced
1 medium jicama, peeled and julienned
1 bunch radishes, sliced
1 bunch green onions, sliced
1 cup green seedless grapes, sliced

$1/4$ head green cabbage, sliced
1 red pepper, julienned
1 green pepper, julienned
2-oz. fresh bean sprouts
1 red Spanish onion, sliced
1 cup red seedless grapes, sliced
See *Oriental Salad Dressing*

Drain and reserve mandarin orange and pineapple juices for salad dressing. In large bowl, mix all ingredients and toss with *Oriental Salad Dressing*. **Servings: 6-8**

Oriental Salad Dressing

1 cup soy sauce
1 tsp. dry mustard
$1/4$ cup mandarin orange juice
$1/4$ cup pineapple juice

$11/2$ cup red wine vinegar
2 Tbsp. brown sugar
$1/2$ cup sesame oil

Blend all ingredients in mixing bowl. Store in jar; shake before using.

Ethnic Recipes...

Venison Sherry Stir-Fry

Tender meats are key to this recipe. Serve with noodles and a tossed salad.

2 tsp. olive oil
2 lb. venison steak, cubed
White or black pepper, sprinkle
2 cloves garlic, minced
Oregano, pinch
1 lb. mushrooms, halved
1/2 white onion, chopped
1/2 cup sherry

Heat skillet or wok with oil and braise meat cubes. Reduce heat and add pepper, garlic and oregano, stirring constantly. Add mushrooms and onions and cook 1 minute. Add sherry; increase heat and stir-fry until wine incorporates. **Servings: 4**

Alternate Meats: Elk, moose, antelope, caribou, deer

Wild Turkey Chow Mein

This is the hunter's version of chow mein. Serve with fruit.

1 can chicken broth
1/2 cup biscuit mix
2 cups leftover wild turkey, cubed
1 14-oz. can chow mein vegetables, drained
1 can mushroom pieces, drained
1 cup green onions, sliced
Salt and pepper, sprinkle
1 tsp. garlic powder
1 cup chow mein noodles

Preheat oven to 375°. In baking dish, blend chicken broth and biscuit mix. Add all remaining ingredients except noodles. Bake 30-45 minutes. Top with noodles and bake 5-10 minutes. Let stand 10-20 minutes before serving. **Servings: 4**

Venison Sukiyaki

Serve over a bed of rice and accompany with a fruit platter.

2 lb. venison steak
1 Tbsp. olive oil
1 lb. mushrooms, sliced
1 bunch green onions, sliced
6 stalks celery, sliced
1 can bamboo shoots, drained
3 Tbsp. water
1/2 cup soy sauce
1 cup chicken bouillon
Lawry's Lemon Pepper, sprinkle
6 cups spinach leaves, raw

Slice steak diagonally across grain into 2-inch strips. Heat oil in skillet and brown meat. Add all ingredients except spinach. Simmer until vegetables are tender; add spinach and simmer 5 minutes. **Servings: 6**

Alternate Meats: Elk, moose, antelope, caribou, deer

Special Guest Italian Pasta Sauce

A treat when served over pasta and topped with Parmesan cheese.

2 1/2 lb. gameburger
Garlic powder, sprinkle
Pepper, sprinkle
1/2 bunch parsley, chopped
2 Tbsp. Parmesan cheese, grated
2-4 chicken breasts, skinned
2-4 chicken thighs, skinned
2-4 chicken drumsticks, skinned
Olive oil
6-8 sausage links
4 pork chops
2 rabbits, sectioned
1 6-lb., 4-oz. can crushed tomatoes
3 large cans tomato sauce
4-5 cloves garlic, crushed
2/3 tsp. oregano
1 tsp. sweet basil
6 bay leaves
1/2 tsp. black pepper

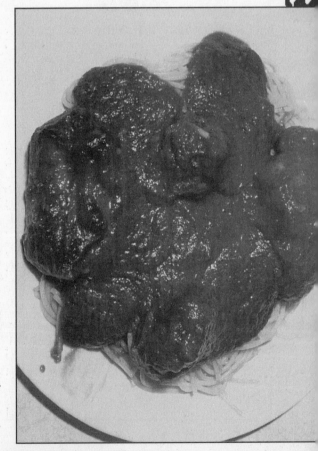

In large bowl, combine gameburger, garlic powder, pepper, parsley and Parmesan cheese. Mix well. Form into small meatballs. Brown meatballs in skillet and set aside. Rub chicken parts with oil and sprinkle with garlic powder. Place on dish with paper towels and microwave on high 3 minutes. Turn chicken and microwave 2 minutes. Fry chicken in skillet with oil and drain on paper towels. Set aside. Pierce sausages with fork and fry in skillet until brown. Place on plate with paper towels and microwave on high 2 minutes; set aside. In skillet, fry pork chops and drain on paper towels. Remove bones and cut into 6-8 squares; set aside. In same skillet, fry rabbit pieces and drain on paper towel. Bone and cut into bite-sized pieces; set aside. In large pot, combine crushed tomatoes and tomato sauce and simmer until bubbly. Add garlic, oregano, sweet basil, bay leaves and 1/2 tsp.black pepper and simmer 1 1/2 hours. Add all meats and stir carefully. Cook 1 1/2 hours, stirring often. Add more spices if desired and check meatballs. Meatballs should be plump and juicy, but not broken. Serve over pasta. **Servings: 8-10**

Alternate Meats: Elk, moose, antelope, caribou, deer

Cooking Tips: When stirring, be careful not to break meatballs.

Reduce moisture in sauce by wiping bottom of lid clean with paper towels after stirring.

This spaghetti sauce has gameburger meatballs to give it extra flavor and texture.

Ethnic Recipes...

Family-Style Italian Spaghetti Sauce
This makes a large quantity of sauce; perfect for freezing for future meals.

2¹/₂-3 lb. gameburger
Garlic powder, sprinkle
1¹/₂ lb. Italian sausage, sliced
1 6-lb., 4-oz. can crushed tomatoes
1 large can tomato sauce
2 cloves garlic, minced

¹/₂ tsp. oregano
1 tsp. sweet basil
4 bay leaves
¹/₄ tsp. black pepper, ground
¹/₂ bunch parsley, chopped

Brown gameburger in skillet and blend with garlic powder. Transfer meat to dish with paper towels and microwave 2 minutes on high. Brown and microwave sausage the same way as gameburger. Set meats aside. In large pot, mix crushed tomatoes with tomato sauce and add garlic, oregano, sweet basil, bay leaves and black pepper. Cook over low heat 1¹/₂ hours, stirring often. Add both meats and parsley. Taste. If desired, add more oregano or garlic. Simmer 1¹/₂ hours over low heat, stirring often. Serve over pasta.   **Servings: 8-10**

Alternate Meats: Elk, moose, antelope, caribou, deer

Cooking Tips: To prevent watery sauce, cook with lid slightly ajar. After stirring sauce, wipe lid clean with paper towel before replacing it on pot.

"...Definitely a 'special-occasion' dish..."

Small Game Spaghetti Sauce
Accent this savory meal with a tossed salad and garlic bread.

4 squirrels or 4 young rabbits, sectioned
Olive oil
Garlic powder, sprinkle
Black pepper, sprinkle
4 large cans crushed tomatoes
2 large cans tomato sauce

4 cloves garlic, pressed
4 bay leaves
¹/₂ tsp. sweet basil
¹/₂ tsp. oregano
¹/₂ bunch parsley, chopped
2 Tbsp. onion, dried

Fry meat in skillet with light oil, garlic powder and pepper. Drain on paper towel and bone. In large cooking pot, combine crushed tomatoes, tomato sauce, garlic, bay leaves, sweet basil, oregano, parsley and onion. Simmer over low heat 1 hour; add meat and simmer 3 hours, stirring often. Serve over pasta.   **Servings: 4-6**

Alternate Meats: Any dark, small game meat, including muskrat.

Cooking Tips: Ensure all bones are removed from meat before adding to sauce.

Spaghetti Venison Pie
The fragrance of this in the oven is enough to get your mouth watering.

2 lb. ground venison
1 tsp. garlic powder
1 tsp. Lawry's Lemon Pepper
4 eggs
2 cups cottage cheese

¹/₄ cup Parmesan cheese, grated
1 lb. spaghetti noodles
1 large jar spaghetti sauce
2 cups mozzarella cheese, shredded

Preheat oven to 350°. In bowl, mix venison, garlic powder and Lawry's Lemon Pepper. In skillet, sauté meat mixture and drain on paper towels. Beat eggs in bowl and mix with cottage and Parmesan cheeses. Boil spaghetti noodles until tender; drain and rinse. Mix pasta with egg mixture and spaghetti sauce. Layer bottom of casserole dish with meat mixture. Top with spaghetti mixture. Bake 45 minutes. Sprinkle with mozzarella cheese and bake 15-20 minutes.   **Servings: 6**

Alternate Meats: Elk, moose, antelope, caribou, deer

"...Oodles of noodles..."

Ethnic Recipes...

Italians aren't the only ones who love pasta, and there are a great variety of noodles out there to choose from.

"...Rabbit Cacciatore is a delicious inspiration to any pasta you choose..."

"...It is true that man cannot live by bread alone, so have fondue..."

Italian Fondue

This calls for cubed bread crumbs and skewers, or fingers, for dipping.

- 2 lb. ground venison
- 1 bunch green onions, chopped
- 1/2 cup green pepper, chopped
- 2 jars Italian pizza sauce
- 1 1/2 lb. Velveeta cheese, cubed
- 1 tsp. oregano, rubbed
- 1 tsp. sweet basil, rubbed

Heat skillet and brown meat. Add onions and green peppers and cook until tender. Drain on paper towel. Combine pizza sauce and cheese cubes in deep dish. Microwave on high 3 minutes; stir and microwave again until cheese is melted. Add meat mixture and spices and blend well.   **Servings: 6-8**

Alternate Meats: Elk, moose, antelope, caribou, deer

Rabbit Cacciatore

Angel hair pasta and garlic bread make this a hearty meal.

- 2 rabbits, cut into serving pieces
- Salt and pepper, sprinkle
- Flour
- 2 Tbsp. olive oil
- 1 onion, minced
- 2 cans tomato paste
- 1 1/2 cups white wine
- 1 can chicken broth
- 2 bay leaves
- 1/4 tsp. thyme
- 1/2 tsp. sweet basil, rubbed
- 1/2 tsp. oregano, rubbed
- 1/8 tsp. marjoram
- 1 lb. mushrooms, sliced

Salt and pepper rabbit pieces and roll in flour. Brown in skillet with oil and drain on papper towels. In same skillet, sauté onion; add remaining ingredients and stir. Return rabbit to skillet and mix with sauce. Cover and simmer 1 hour or until meat is tender.   **Servings: 6**

American Lasagna Rolls

Serve with green salad and garlic bread.

- 2 lb. ground venison
- 1 cup onion, chopped
- 3 cloves garlic, minced
- 2 jars spaghetti sauce
- 1 tsp. basil
- 1/2 tsp. oregano, rubbed
- 2 cups ricotta cheese
- 1/2 cup Parmesan cheese, grated
- 4 Tbsp. parsley, chopped
- 2 cups mozzarella cheese, shredded
- 20-25 lasagna noodles

Preheat oven to 300°. In skillet, brown venison, onion and garlic; drain on paper towel. Return meat to skillet and add spaghetti sauce, basil and oregano and simmer 15 minutes. In bowl, mix ricotta cheese, Parmesan cheese, parsley and mozzarella cheese. Boil lasagna according to package directions; drain and rinse. Spread 2 Tbsp. cheese mixture over each noodle and roll. Place rolls seam-side down in baking dish and top with meat sauce. Bake 1 hour or until mixture is bubbly.   **Servings: 6**

Alternate Meats: Elk, moose, antelope, caribou, deer

Ethnic Recipes...

> ## "...Scallopini, normally made with veal, is excellent with antelope because of its inherent tenderness..."

Scallopini Antelope

Top with chopped parsley and grated Parmesan cheese and serve with pasta and a tomato and onion salad.

2 lb. antelope meat, boned
Flour
Pepper, sprinkle
Garlic salt, sprinkle
Canola oil
Margarine

2 cups sherry
2 chicken bouillon cubes
1/2 cup stock or chicken broth
1 lb. mushrooms, sliced
1/4 tsp. onion powder

Slice boned meat into steak-like pieces. Dredge in flour and season with pepper and garlic salt. Heat skillet with mixture of canola oil and margarine and brown meat. Slowly add wine and cook down. In microwave, melt bouillon cubes in stock. Add to skillet. Stir and simmer 5 minutes. Pour meat and juices into deep dish. In same skillet, melt margarine and sauté mushrooms with onion powder. Return meat and juices to skillet and simmer 5-10 minutes.   **Servings: 4-5**

Alternate Meats: Elk, moose, caribou, deer

Venison Loin Medallions with Italian Sauce

This is a meal with zing. Serve with your favorite pasta.

2 lb. venison loin
Lawry's Lemon Pepper, sprinkle
1 pkg. Lawry's Extra Rich & Thick Spaghetti Sauce Blend
1 16-oz. can tomato sauce
2 cups beef broth

1 tsp. Tabasco sauce
1/2 lb. mushrooms, sliced
1 green pepper, diced
1/4 tsp. celery seed
2 tsp. olive oil

Slice loin into medallions and sprinkle with Lawry's Lemon Pepper. In large saucepan, heat Lawry's Sauce Blend, tomato sauce, beef broth and Tabasco sauce. Heat skillet with oil and sauté mushrooms and green pepper. Add to spaghetti sauce mixture. Stir in celery seed and simmer. In skillet with oil, cook medallions until desired doneness. Top with spaghetti sauce mixture before serving.   **Servings: 6**

Alternate Meats: Elk, moose, antelope, caribou, deer

> ## "...Start with a cup of lime sherbert, to clear the palate..."

Venison Pizza Roll

This is great as an appetizer or a snack that's easy to prepare.

1 lb. ground venison
1/2 cup onion, minced
1 loaf frozen bread dough, thawed
1 jar pizza sauce

1 cup pepperoni, sliced
1 1/2 cups mozzarella cheese, shredded
1 tsp. oregano, rubbed

Preheat oven to 400°. In skillet, sauté venison and onion and drain on paper towels. Roll dough to 1/4-inch thickness. Spread pizza sauce over bread and spoon on sautéed mixture. Top with pepperoni, mozzarella cheese and oregano; roll up dough like jelly roll. Place seam-side down on cookie sheet and bake 45 minutes to 1 hour or until dough is light brown. Cut into 2-inch slices.   **Servings: 2-4**

Alternate Meats: Elk, moose, antelope, caribou, deer

> ## "...A pizza variation you're sure to love..."

Ethnic Recipes...

Crushed tomatoes are essential to most game meat pasta sauces. Tomatoes can be crushed by hand or purchased already crushed.

Lawry's Deep Dish Pizza
Serve with mixed salad.

1 loaf frozen bread dough, thawed
1 lb. ground venison
3 cloves garlic, minced
2 cups mushrooms, sliced
1 tsp. olive oil
2¹/₂ cups Lawry's Extra Rich & Thick
    Spaghetti Sauce Blend
1 tsp. oregano, rubbed
1 tsp. sweet basil, rubbed
2 cups pepperoni, sliced
1 can sliced olives, drained
¹/₂ cup Parmesan cheese, shredded
2 cups mozzarella cheese, shredded
1 cup provolone cheese, shredded

Preheat oven to 400°. Roll out bread dough to fit in cookie sheet. In skillet, brown venison and garlic. Drain on paper towels. In same skillet, sauté mushrooms in oil; remove and drain. Prepare spaghetti sauce mix according to package directions. Spread on dough and top with meat, mushrooms, oregano, basil, pepperoni and olives. Bake 30 minutes. Sprinkle with cheeses and bake until bubbly. **Servings: 6**

Alternate Meats: Elk, moose, antelope, caribou, deer

"...For a change of pace, have your pie for dinner..."

Italian Cheese Pie with Venison Roast
Serve with a tossed salad and garlic bread.

2 frozen pie crusts, thawed
3 eggs
1 cup low-fat mozzarella cheese, shredded
1 cup low-fat provolone cheese, shredded
1 cup ricotta cheese
2 cups leftover venison roast, cubed
4 Tbsp. Parmesan cheese, grated
2 Tbsp. parsley, chopped
¹/₂ tsp. oregano leaves, rubbed

Preheat oven to 400°. Place bottom crust in pie pan. In large mixing bowl, beat eggs and add mozzarella cheese, provolone cheese, ricotta cheese, venison, 3 Tbsp. Parmesan cheese, parsley and oregano leaves. Pour into pie crust and top with second crust; seal and flute. Cut 6 or 8 slits in top crust and sprinkle with 1 Tbsp. Parmesan cheese. Bake 1 hour; let stand 20 minutes before serving. **Servings: 4**

Alternate Meats: Elk, moose, antelope, caribou, deer

Roast Venison Muffin Pizzas
Serve as snacks when those hungry kids come home from school.

1 jar Italian pizza sauce
1 tsp. oregano, rubbed
1 tsp. garlic powder
4 English muffins, split
1 lb. leftover venison roast, sliced
1 cup mozzarella cheese, shredded
¹/₂ cup Parmesan cheese, grated

Preheat oven to broil. In bowl, mix pizza sauce, oregano and garlic powder. Toast muffins and spread sauce on each half. Top with venison slices and sprinkle with cheeses. Place on cookie sheet and broil until cheeses are bubbly. **Servings: 4-8**

Alternate Meats: Elk, moose, antelope, caribou, deer

Ethnic Recipes...

Venison Pizza Pasta Casserole

This will be a family favorite with hot garlic bread and a tossed salad.

2 lb. ground venison	1 pkg. Lawry's Extra Rich &
Salt and pepper, sprinkle	Thick Spaghetti Sauce Blend
1 tsp. garlic powder	1 6-oz. can tomato paste
4-oz. pepperoni, sliced	1 16-oz. can tomato sauce
1 tsp. butter	2 cups beef broth
2 cups mushrooms, sliced	8-oz. mostaccioli pasta
1 small onion, diced	1/4 cup Parmesan cheese, grated
1 green pepper, diced	1 1/2 cups mozzarella cheese, grated

Preheat oven to 350°. In skillet, sauté meat with salt, pepper, garlic powder and pepperoni and drain on paper towels. In same skillet, add butter and sauté mushrooms, onion and green pepper; drain on paper towels. In large cooking pot, combine Lawry's Spaghetti Sauce, tomato paste, tomato sauce and beef broth and simmer 10-15 minutes. Prepare pasta according to package directions; drain. Mix venison, vegetables, sauce, and pasta and pour into large casserole dish. Sprinkle with cheeses and bake 20-30 minutes until cheese is melted and mixture is bubbly.

Servings: 6

Alternate Meats: Elk, moose, antelope, caribou, deer

> **"...A combination of two delicious Italian dishes..."**

American Venison Lasagna

This is American cooking at its best. Serve with a tossed salad and garlic bread.

> **"...American cooking at its best..."**

2 lb. ground venison	1 tsp. oregano, rubbed
3 cloves garlic, minced	1 lb. lasagna noodles
1 onion, diced	1 lb. mozzarella cheese, grated
Salt and pepper, sprinkle	1 large carton cottage cheese
1 small can tomato paste	1/4 cup Parmesan cheese, grated
2 16-oz. cans tomato sauce	

Preheat oven to 350°. In skillet, brown venison, garlic, onion, salt and pepper. Add tomato paste, tomato sauce and oregano; cover and simmer 1 hour, stirring occasionally. Boil lasagna until tender; drain and rinse. In large baking dish, alternate layers of lasagna, mozzarella cheese, cottage cheese, Parmesan cheese and meat sauce. Repeat until all ingredients are used. Bake 30-45 minutes until bubbly. Let stand 20 minutes before serving.

Servings: 6

Alternate Meats: Elk, moose, antelope, caribou, deer

Italian Cheese and Venison Roll

Start with a cucumber salad and finish with lime-orange sherbert.

2 lb. ground venison	1 loaf frozen bread dough, thawed
1 tsp. garlic powder	1 can Italian-style pizza sauce
Salt and pepper, sprinkle	1 tsp. oregano, rubbed
1 small onion, diced	1/4 cup Parmesan cheese, grated
1 green pepper, diced	2 cups mozzarella cheese, shredded

Preheat oven to 425°. Season meat with garlic powder, salt and pepper. In skillet, brown venison with onion and green pepper; drain on paper towel. Roll out bread dough. Spread pizza sauce over dough and top with meat mixture. Sprinkle with oregano and bake 20-30 minutes or until bread is done and sauce is bubbly. Sprinkle with cheeses and bake until bubbly.

Servings: 6

Alternate Meats: Elk, moose, antelope, caribou, deer

> **"...Introduce a Venician night at your house with this dish..."**

Ethnic Recipes...

Popover Venison Pizza

A great Saturday night treat; be sure to save the leftovers.

2 lb. ground venison	2 eggs
1 onion, minced	1 cup milk
1/2 cup green pepper, minced	1 cup flour
2 cloves garlic, minced	1/4 tsp. salt
1 jar Italian pizza sauce	1/4 tsp. garlic powder
1 cup mozzarella cheese, grated	4 Tbsp. Parmesan cheese, grated
1 Tbsp. olive oil	

Preheat oven to 400°. In skillet, sauté meat, onion, green pepper and garlic; drain on paper towels. Return mixture to skillet, add pizza sauce and simmer 10 minutes. Pour into baking dish and top with mozzarella cheese. In small bowl, mix olive oil, eggs, milk, flour, salt and garlic powder. Pour into baking dish and sprinkle with Parmesan cheese. Bake 30-40 minutes or until topping looks wavy.

Servings: 6

Alternate Meats: Elk, moose, antelope, caribou, deer

Antilocapra Italiano

Top with grated Parmesan or romano cheese and serve with your favorite noodles.

3 lb. antelope steaks
2 tsp. olive oil
White or black pepper, sprinkle
Worcestershire sauce, dash
1 tsp. soy sauce
Mozzarella cheese, strips
1 jar spaghetti sauce

Slice steaks with the grain into long strips and fry in skillet with oil. Sprinkle with pepper, Worcestershire sauce and soy sauce. Blot meat with paper towel. Distribute meat slices on individual serving plates, cover with cheese and spaghetti sauce. Cover with waxed paper and microwave each plate 1 minute on 70% power. If cheese is not bubbly, microwave 1 minute on 50% power. **Servings: 6**

Alternate Meats: Elk, moose, caribou, deer

Italian Game Lasagna

This handsome holiday dish is complete with steamed green beans and garlic toast.

2 qts. Family-Style Italian Spaghetti Sauce *(See p. 265)*	Oregano, sprinkle
3/4 lb. lasagna pasta	1 lb. mozzarella cheese, sliced
1 lb. ricotta cheese	1/4 cup Parmesan cheese, grated
	1 bunch parsley, chopped

Preheat oven to 350°. Prepare *Family-Style Spaghetti Sauce* according to recipe. Boil lasagna noodles until tender; drain and rinse. In 11x16 cooking pan, layer the following ingredients: spaghetti sauce, lasagna noodles, ricotta cheese, mozzarella cheese, oregano, Parmesan cheese, parsley. Continue layering until all ingredients are used up, finishing with a layer of sauce. Bake 30 minutes. Let stand 15 minutes before serving. **Servings: 6-7**

Ground venison is called for in many ethnic recipes from pizza rolls to tacos.

Ethnic Recipes...

Wild Turkey Salad Dressing

2 Tbsp. olive oil
2 Tbsp. orange juice
2 Tbsp. lemon juice
2 Tbsp. brown sugar
2 tsp. mustard

Mix ingredients in small bowl and pour over prepared salad.

"...A nice dish to have on a summer's eve, when it's too hot to cook..."

Middle Eastern Wild Turkey Salad
Serve with crackers and iced tea.

1 8-oz. pkg. rice pilaf
2 cups leftover wild turkey, cubed
$1/2$ cup walnuts, chopped
1 large tomato, chopped
$1/2$ cup cucumber, chopped
$1/4$ cup parsley, chopped
See *Wild Turkey Salad Dressing*

Prepare rice pilaf according to package directions. In large bowl, blend pilaf, turkey and walnuts and refrigerate 1-2 hours. Add tomato, cucumber and parsley and toss with salad dressing. Serve on lettuce leaves.   **Servings: 6**

Schweizerschnitzel
Serve this tasty dish with a tossed salad, fruit plate and crusty bread.

12 pieces venison loin
Salt and pepper, sprinkle
6 slices mozzarella cheese
6 slices ham, honey-cured
$1/4$ cup flour
2 eggs, beaten
$1/2$ cup dry Italian-style bread crumbs
2 Tbsp. olive oil

Pound loin thin and season with salt and pepper. Over 6 loins, place 1 slice of cheese and 1 slice of ham. Top with remaining 6 loins and press together. Place flour, eggs and bread crumbs in three separate bowls. Dip meat sandwiches in each bowl, starting with flour. Heat skillet with oil and fry sandwiches quickly to brown each side. Drain on paper towels.   **Servings: 6**

Alternate Meats: Elk, moose, antelope, caribou, deer

"...Great meals — German-style..."

Venison Wiener Schnitzel
Serve over noodles and accompany with a nice German bread.

2 lb. venison steak
Flour
Salt and pepper, sprinkle
1 tsp. paprika
2 Tbsp. olive oil
1 cup onion, sliced
1 lemon, sliced
1 cup sour cream
1 cup water
1 Tbsp. parsley

Cut steak into serving pieces, dredge in flour and season with salt, pepper and paprika. Heat pressure cooker with oil and brown meat on both sides; add onions and sauté lightly. Place lemon slices over meat and add sour cream and water to cooker. Close lid securely and set regulator. Pressure cook 15 minutes with regulator rocking gently. Let pressure drop. Garnish with parsley.   **Servings: 4-6**

Alternate Meats: Elk, moose, antelope, caribou, deer

Moroccan Pot Pie
Save this dish for a Casablanca evening and serve with fresh fruit platter.

2 frozen pie crusts, thawed
1 tsp. olive oil
$1/2$ onion, minced
3 cloves garlic, minced
2 cups hashbrown potatoes, frozen
2 cups leftover venison roast, cubed
$1/4$ cup parsley, chopped
1 tsp. coriander
1 tsp. salt
1 tsp. ginger
1 tsp. cumin
1 Tbsp. flour
1 tsp. paprika
$1/8$ tsp. cayenne pepper
1 cup beef broth
Sesame seeds

Preheat oven to 400°. Place bottom crust in pie pan. Heat skillet with oil and sauté onion and garlic; add hashbrowns and cook 5 minutes. Add meat, parsley, coriander, salt, ginger, cumin, flour, paprika and cayenne pepper. Stir in beef broth and simmer 5 minutes. Spoon mixture into bottom shell. Top with second pie crust. Cut slits in pie crust; seal and flute. Brush top crust with olive oil and sprinkle with sesame seeds. Bake 1 hour. Let stand 15 minutes before serving.   **Servings: 4**

Alternate Meats: Elk, moose, antelope, caribou, deer

Ethnic Recipes...

South Sea Venison and Pineapple with Rice

Serve over rice and garnish with parsley.

2 lb. vension steak, cubed	1 cup celery, diced
1½ tsp. Accent seasoning	1 cucumber, thinly sliced
2 Tbsp. olive oil	2 tomatoes, wedged
1 20-oz. can pineapple chucks with juice	1 green pepper, sliced
2 Tbsp. soy sauce	1 yellow or sweet red pepper, sliced
1-2 Tbsp. vinegar	2 Tbsp. cornstarch
¼ cup brown sugar	2 Tbsp. water

Sprinkle meat cubes with 1 tsp. Accent. Heat skillet with oil; brown meat and drain on paper towels. Return meat to skillet and add pineapple chunks with juice, soy sauce, vinegar and brown sugar. Bring to boil and reduce heat to simmer 15 minutes. Add vegetables; sprinkle with ½ tsp. Accent and simmer 5-10 minutes. In small bowl, mix cornstarch and water into paste. Add to skillet, stirring until mixture thickens and becomes clear.   **Servings: 4-6**

Alternate Meats: Elk, moose, antelope, caribou, deer

"...The fragrant magic of this dish will bring palm trees to their knees..."

"...Especially appealing when the days turn cooler..."

Swedish-Style Venison Steak

Serve over noodles, and don't spare the sauce.

2 lb. venison steaks	½ cup beef bouillon
Salt and pepper, sprinkle	¼ cup sherry
1 tsp. garlic powder	¼ cup flour
2 tsp. olive oil	¼ cup cold water
1 tsp. dill weed	1 cup sour cream
1 onion, sliced	

Season steaks with salt, pepper and garlic powder. In skillet with oil, brown meat and drain on paper towels. Place in crock pot and add dill, onion, bouillon and sherry. Cover and cook on low 6 hours. Remove meat and set aside. In separate bowl, dissolve flour in water. Set control to high and add flour/water to crock pot. Cook until slightly thickened; stir in sour cream. Serve over meat.   **Servings: 6**

Alternate Meats: Elk, moose, antelope, caribou, deer, buffalo

Indian Pan Bread

*The fragrance of this bread is heavenly.
Serve with any game meat recipe.*

4 cups white flour
1 tsp. salt
3 Tbsp. lard
3 cups warm water
1-2 Tbsp. canola or peanut oil

In large bowl, combine flour, salt and lard. Add water and mix by hand to form stiff dough. On lightly floured board, roll dough to ½-inch thickness and slice into 3-inch squares. Punch hole in center of each square to promote even cooking. Place in skillet with oil and fry over medium to medium-high heat.   **Servings: 4-6**

"...The fragrance of this bread is heavenly..."

"...How many beans do you know? Here's another — Creole Beans..."

Creole Beans

This delicious side dish, New Orleans-style, enhances any venison steak or rib dish.

2 pkgs. frozen Italian-style green beans
1 tsp. butter
1 cup celery, diced
Salt, sprinkle
Pepper, sprinkle
2 16-oz. cans Italian-style stewed tomatoes
¼ cup bacon, cooked and crumbled

In large saucepan, cook beans until just tender. Heat skillet with butter and sauté celery; add beans. Stir in remaining ingredients and simmer 20 minutes.   **Servings: 6**

Beer Marinade

Save that last can of beer for this delicious marinade.

1 12-oz. can or bottle of beer
½ cup canola oil
1 onion, sliced
2 cloves garlic, pressed
2 tsp. powdered mustard
¼ tsp. salt
Black pepper, sprinkle

Place beer and canola oil in bowl and stir. Blend in remaining ingredients. Place meat in marinade and refrigerate 4-12 hours. Discard after using once.

Enhanced Wine/Broth Marinade

This is excellent for fried or grilled wild game meats.

10-oz. sherry or port wine
1 can broth
⅛ cup canola oil
2 cloves garlic, pressed
Oregano, pinch
Sweet basil, pinch
Tarragon, pinch
Lime juice, sprinkle
Onion powder, sprinkle
Black ground pepper, sprinkle

Combine all ingredients in a bowl and marinate. Use beef broth for red meats and chicken broth for light meats.

Tomato Marinade

Use with any venison meats or game birds.

1 large can tomato juice
¼ tsp. garlic powder
¼ tsp. oregano, crushed
¼ tsp. sweet basil leaf, crushed
½ onion, chopped
¼ cup Worcestershire sauce

Mix all ingredients in plastic container. Marinate mild meats 12 hours in refrigerator and strong meats 24-48 hours in refrigerator. Do not allow marinade to get warm at any time before cooking meats.

"...Your taste buds give the nod to Beer Marinade with cottontail rabbit meat..."

Cottontail/Squirrel Marinade

This marinade is custom-made for rabbits and squirrels.

1 cup port wine	Paprika, sprinkle
½ cup wine vinegar	½ tsp. dry mustard
2 cloves garlic, pressed	2 stalks celery, quartered
Black ground pepper, sprinkle	1 onion, chopped
Tarragon, pinch	¼ tsp. coriander

Mix wine and vinegar in bowl; add remaining ingredients and stir. Add rabbit or squirrel and marinate 4 hours before cooking. For stronger flavor, refrigerate marinade with meat overnight.

Sauces, Marinades & Gravies...

Microwave Barbecue Sauce

Use for many red game meats, barbecued over coals or gas grill.

1 medium onion, chopped	2 Tbsp. apple cider vinegar
1 stick butter, unsalted	1 Tbsp. Worcestershire sauce
1 clove garlic, minced	1 slice lime
½ cup celery, diced	½ tsp. cumin seed, ground
1 cup water	3 splashes red pepper sauce
1 cup catsup	Salt, sprinkle
1 red pepper, seeded and diced	¼ cup cilantro, minced
¼ cup lime juice	

Place onion, butter and garlic in 2 qt. microwave-safe dish. Cover with microwave-safe wax paper and microwave on high 2 minutes. Stir in celery. Recover with wax paper and and vent so steam can escape. Microwave on high 2 minutes. Add remaining ingredients except cilantro. Cover and microwave on high 3½ minutes. Stir and cook on high for another 3½ minutes. Puree sauce in blender and transfer to bowl. Stir in cilantro.

Servings: 4

Soy Marinade

This marinade can be served as gravy along side of your favorite meat dish.

2 cups soy sauce
¼ cup dry sherry
Oregano, sprinkle
1 sweet basil leaf

Mix all ingredients in bowl. Add meat and marinate 2-6 hours in refrigerator. Use marinade to baste meat while cooking. When meat is done, remove from pan and add ¼ cup of Port wine. Cook down and serve alongside meat.

Cooking Tips: For antelope steaks on the grill, use modified marinade for basting: 1 cup sherry with ¼ cup soy sauce.

"...Soy Marinade is nice to have for basting barbecued meats..."

Sauces, Marinades & Gravies...

White Wine Barbecue Sauce
Serve with grilled red game steaks.

1 cup dry white wine	1 medium onion, diced
1 cup catsup	1 whole lemon, diced
1 cup water	1 clove garlic, diced
1/4 cup Worcestershire sauce	2 Tbsp. margarine

In large saucepan, mix wine with catsup and water. Add Worcestershire sauce and remaining ingredients. Bring to boil; reduce heat and simmer 20 minutes, stirring occassionally. Transfer sauce to roaster and add meat. While meat cooks, baste with sauce. Strain sauce and serve with meat. **Servings: 6**

Microwave Barbecue Sauce
Use for red game meats, barbecued over coals or gas grill.

1 medium onion, chopped	2 Tbsp. apple cider vinegar
4 Tbsp. butter, unsalted	1 Tbsp. Worcestershire sauce
1 clove garlic, minced	1 slice lime
1/2 cup celery, diced	1/2 tsp. cumin, ground
1 cup water	3 splashes red pepper sauce
1 cup catsup	Salt, sprinkle
1 red pepper, seeded and diced	1/4 cup cilantro, minced
1/4 cup lime juice	

Place onion, butter and garlic in 2 qt. microwave-safe dish. Cover with microwave-safe wax paper and microwave on high 2 minutes. Stir in celery. Re-cover with wax paper and vent so steam can escape. Microwave on high 2 minutes. Add remaining ingredients except cilantro. Cover and microwave on high 3 1/2 minutes. Stir and cook on high for another 3 1/2 minutes. Puree sauce in blender and transfer to bowl. Stir in cilantro. **Servings: 4**

"...A quick and easy way to make a wine sauce is by skillet..."

Skillet Wine Sauce with Mushrooms
Enrich the flavor of your fried or roasted meats with this popular gravy.

Olive oil, drop
1/2 cup teriyaki marinade
1/2 stick margarine or butter
2 cups Madeira wine
White pepper, dash
1 lb. mushrooms, chopped
1 bunch bulbless green onions, chopped

In skillet, heat oil until it starts smoking. While stirring, add teriyaki marinade and cook 30 seconds; add margarine or butter, cook 15 seconds; add wine, cook 30 seconds. Mix in white pepper. Add mushrooms and green onions and stir. When wine is assimilated, sauce is ready.

Servings: 6-7

A lot of different ingredients can be used to make a superb-tasting sauce.

This is a fat separator in use. Clear broth leaves the spout, while fat remains in the separator. This is important when preparing many sauces and gravies.

Sauces, Marinades & Gravies

Velouté Sauce

This sauce can be served as is over white game meat, or used as a base for other sauces.

1 cup butter or margarine
1 cup flour
1¼ cups broth or stock
¼ cup cream

In saucepan, melt butter over low heat. While stirring, slowly add flour until mixture is smooth and creamy. Remove from stove; slowly stir in broth or stock. When stock is blended, add cream, stirring slowly until completely blended. Be sure to stir constantly; do not burn.

Servings: 4-6

Cooking Tips: Turn the above into *Almond Velouté Sauce* by blending in ½ cup slivered almonds just before serving.

Hot Velouté Sauce

Serve over big game or upland game roasts.

See *Velouté Sauce*	1 Tbsp. sweet pickles, chopped
½ cup mayonnaise	1 Tbsp. stuffed olives
1 tsp. onion, minced	1 Tbsp. green pepper, chopped
1 Tbsp. lemon juice	1 Tbsp. parsley, chopped

Prepare *Velouté Sauce* and blend in remaining ingredients. Stir over low heat for short time.

Servings: 4-6

Spiked Velouté Sauce

Serve over pheasant, chukar and other game birds.

See *Velouté Sauce*
1 Tbsp. fresh horseradish
1 tsp. mustard

Prepare *Velouté Sauce* and then add horseradish and mustard. Stir until completely blended over low heat for short time.

Servings: 4-6

"...Perk up your Brown Sauce with this variation..."

Bordelaise Sauce

Serve over red game meats.

See *Brown Sauce*
½ tsp. parsley, minced
½ tsp. thyme, minced
½ tsp. bay leaf, minced
½ tsp. onion powder

Prepare *Brown Sauce* and blend in remaining ingredients. Heat through.

Servings: 4-6

Brown Sauce

Serve over any venison or red game roast.

4 Tbsp. butter or margarine
1 slice onion
4 Tbsp. flour
Stock or beef broth
White or black pepper, sprinkle (optional)

In saucepan, melt butter until just brown. Do not burn. Add onion slice and sauté until brown; remove from pan. Slowly add flour and blend until smooth. While stirring, slowly add stock or beef broth. Amount used should be just enough to form a gravy consistency. Add pepper if desired. Bring to boil briefly and remove from heat.

Servings: 4-6

Cooking Tips: To make *Mushroom Brown Sauce*, stir 1 cup sliced mushrooms into onion-flavored butter before adding flour. Brown slowly; add ⅛ tsp. Worcestershire sauce and ⅛ tsp. teriyaki marinade. Continue with the above recipe.

Piquant Brown Sauce

This is recommended for tongue, red game meats, beef and veal.

See *Brown Sauce*	Paprika, sprinkle
½ tsp. onion, minced	2 Tbsp. mild chili sauce or
½ tsp. capers, chopped	1 sweet pickle, chopped
1 Tbsp. red wine	
½ tsp. white sugar	

Prepare *Brown Sauce*. In separate saucepan, simmer onion and capers for 5 minutes. Add red wine, sugar, paprika, chili sauce or sweet pickle. Heat through and stir into *Brown Sauce*.

Servings: 4-6

"...Stir constantly— to leave the stove for even 1 minute is inviting trouble..."

Sauces, Marinades & Gravies...

Sauce can be as simple as this rich broth, which will be ladeled directly over cooked meat.

Orange Sauce I

Delicious with any waterfowl dish.

3 large oranges
Salt, dash
Cayenne pepper, dash
1 Tbsp. mustard
1/4 cup currant jelly

Grate one orange, saving rind in bowl. Mix rind with salt and cayenne pepper. In another bowl, juice two oranges. Stir in mustard and pour over grated rind. Blend in currant jelly. **Servings: 4-6**

Cooking Tips: Instead of juicing two oranges, 2/3 cup concentrated juice with 2 cans of water can be substituted.

Pressure Cooker Barbecue Sauce

Very tasty for barbecuing all red game meats.

1 small onion, minced	2 Tbsp. molasses
1 cup tomato sauce	2 Tbsp. corn syrup
2/3 cup catsup	1 Tbsp. liquid smoke
1/2 cup apple cider vinegar	1 Tbsp. Dijon mustard
1/2 cup brown sugar	6-8 splashes red pepper sauce
4 Tbsp. butter or margarine, unsalted	

Combine all ingredients in pressure cooker. Close lid and set regulator. Pressure cook 20 minutes. Let pressure drop and transfer to bowl for basting.   **Servings: 4**

Orange Sauce II

Save your waterfowl dishes for this savory sauce.

1 cup granulated sugar	3/4 cup boiling water
1/8 tsp. salt	1 tsp. butter or margarine
2 Tbsp. cornstarch	1 tsp. orange rind, grated
1 cup orange juice	1 tsp. lemon rind, grated
1/4 cup lemon juice	

In saucepan, mix sugar, salt and cornstarch. Stir in orange juice, lemon juice and boiling water. Bring to boil over medium heat and boil 1 minute, stirring. Remove from heat and stir in butter or margarine and orange and lemon rinds.

Servings: 4-6

Orange Sauce III

Serve over roasted duck or goose.

1 can frozen orange juice, thawed
1-4 Tbsp. horseradish

In bowl, mix concentrated orange juice with horseradish. For lighter sauce, use only 1 Tbsp. of horseradish.   **Servings: 2-3**

Sauces, Marinades & Gravies

"...This is an old standby recipe that tantalizes the taste buds with a sweet-and-sour flavor..."

Waterfowl Barbecue Sauce

Pour this delicious sweet-and-sour sauce over duck or goose.

4 cups water
2/3 cup brown sugar
1 1/4 cups orange juice
1/8 cup lemon juice

1 3/4 cups catsup
1 1/2 tsp. mustard
1 tsp. molasses

In saucepan, mix water and brown sugar; stir well. Add orange juice, lemon juice, catsup, mustard and molasses. Simmer over low heat 5 minutes. Remove from heat and stir. Return to stove and simmer 10 minutes. Immediately transfer sauce to glass serving bowl.   **Servings: 8**

Homemade Steak Sauce

This is easy to make and is best used as a marinade for game steaks.

2 cups soy sauce
2 Tbsp. sugar
2-oz. bourbon whiskey
1 tsp. white pepper

1 Tbsp. dry mustard
1/2 Tbsp. ginger
1/2 tsp. garlic powder
1 tsp. Tabasco sauce

Combine all ingredients in bowl and mix well. Marinate steaks for 2-4 hours and then use as basting while grilling.   **Servings: 4**

Standard Barbecue Sauce

This is an old standby sauce that is as good as store-bought.

1/2 tsp. salt
1/2 tsp. pepper
1 Tbsp. paprika
1 cup granulated sugar
1/2 cup brown sugar
1 medium onion, chopped

1 cup catsup
1/4 cup butter or margarine
1/3 cup lemon juice
1 Tbsp. Worcestershire sauce
1 Tbsp. soy sauce
1/2 cup hot water

Blend all ingredients in saucepan and bring to boil. Remove from stove before basting meat.   **Servings: 4**

"...Have your wooden spoons ready for this tasty sauce..."

Hollandaise Sauce

A little of this sauce will perk up vegetable dishes and Eggs Benedict made with venison steaks.

2 egg yokes
3 Tbsp. lemon juice
1 stick margarine, cold

In saucepan over low heat, stir egg yolks and lemon juice with wooden spoon. Add 1/2 stick margarine. Stir constantly until well blended. Add remaining margarine. Stir until sauce becomes golden.   **Servings: 4**

Cooking Tips: For dark meat waterfowl, add 1 tsp. orange rind for every 2 cups of *Hollandaise Sauce.*

"...Standard Barbecue Sauce is deep, rich and red..."

Horseradish is an important ingredient in many sauces.

Sauces, Marinades & Gravies...

Favorite Cucumber Dill Sauce

Pour this smooth-tasting sauce over sliced upland game such as turkey.

1 cup salad dressing
½ cup low-fat yogurt, plain
2 Tbsp. lemon juice
2 cucumbers, peeled, seeded and chopped
1 Tbsp. parsley, chopped
2 tsp. dill weed, dry
Salt and pepper, sprinkle

Place all ingredients in bowl and blend well. Cover and refrigerate overnight.   **Servings: 2-4**

Cooking Tips: Sauce can be stored in refrigerator for up to 1 week.

"...One of the easiest ways to perk up your favorite leftover game meat is with this sauce..."

Beurre Rouge Sauce

Spice up your red game roasts and steaks with this "Red Butter" sauce.

6 Tbsp. dry red wine
2 Tbsp. wine vinegar
2 Tbsp. green onion, minced
6 Tbsp. butter, unsalted
Salt and pepper, sprinkle

Place red wine, vinegar and green onion into microwave-safe dish. Microwave, uncovered, on high 7 minutes. Microwave 2 minutes more if liquid has not been reduced to ¼ cup. Cut butter into 6 pieces and whisk, a little at a time, into mixture until well blended. Strain before serving and add salt and pepper.   **Servings: 4**

Stock As Sauce

This tastes great on roasts or fried meats and works well as a marinade for steaks.

1 cup stock or canned broth
½ cube butter or margarine
¼ cup sherry

Heat skillet over high heat and then add stock and butter and stir. Bring to boil; add wine and stir 2 minutes.   **Servings: 4-6**

Cooking Tips: If broth is used, add 2 beef bouillon cubes and 2 sprinkles garlic powder before adding wine.

When preparing sauces or gravies, constant stirring is a must.

"...This sauce is sure to become one of your favorites..."

Apricot, Ginger and Cranberry Sauce

This is tasty with wild turkey, grouse and pheasant.

15 dried apricots, sliced
½ cup cranberry juice
1 12-oz. pkg. frozen or fresh cranberries
½ cup sugar
1 Tbsp. fresh ginger, minced

Place apricots in microwave-safe dish and top with cranberry juice. Cover and microwave on high 2 minutes; let stand 2 minutes. Add cranberries, sugar and ginger. Microwave on high 5 minutes, stirring after 3 minutes. Cranberry skins should pop open. If not, microwave another 2 minutes. Sauce will thicken. Let stand until sauce reaches room temperature; refrigerate 1 hour before serving.   **Servings: 6**

Sauces, Marinades & Gravies

"...Save a little of this for your ice cream or cheese cake..."

Cranberry Sauce

This is a natural for any upland game dish.

1 pkg. fresh cranberries
1 8-oz. can crushed pineapple, with juice
1/2 cup orange juice
1 cup sugar
1/2 tsp. nutmeg

Combine all ingredients in saucepan and bring to boil. Reduce heat to simmer and cook, covered, 20 minutes or until cranberries pop and mixture thickens. **Servings: 4**

Universal Marinade is at work on this meat. It will help tenderize and flavor the meat.

Game Bird Sauce

This is a gem of a sauce that tastes delicious with upland game dishes.

1/2 cup canola oil
1/4 cup lemon juice
1 clove garlic, pressed
1/2 onion, minced
1/2 tsp. celery salt
1/4 tsp. thyme
1/4 tsp. marjoram
1/8 tsp. rosemary
Teriyaki marinade, splash

Mix all ingredients in bowl and use as marinade or sauce. **Servings: 4**

Raspberry Sauce

Tame your wild roast duck, goose or turkey with this tasty sauce.

2 cups frozen raspberries, thawed
3 Tbsp. orange juice
1/2 cup sugar
1-2 Tbsp. cornstarch

Combine all ingredients in saucepan and bring to boil. Reduce heat and simmer until mixture is thickened. **Servings: 2-3**

"...The single best marinade for game meat..."

Universal Marinade

This marinade is excellent with just about every game meat available.

2 cups milk
2 eggs, beaten
1/8 tsp. garlic powder
Paprika, sprinkle
Onion powder, sprinkle
Black pepper, sprinkle
1/4 tsp. sweet basil leaf, ground

Place all ingredients in bowl and beat with fork. Transfer to plastic storage bag or covered container and add game meat. Refrigerate 24 hours, shaking container occasionally to disperse marinade. Discard after using once.

"...You'll be hard pressed to find a meat that does not emerge from *Universal Marinade* tender and tasty..."

Sauces, Marinades & Gravies...

> ## "...Don't be shy about altering this to suit your taste buds..."

Spicy Marinade

This marinade is successful with bear meat and sage hen breast, among others.

½ cup canola oil	¼ tsp. Tabasco sauce
¼ cup catsup	¼ tsp. oregano
2 Tbsp. Worcestershire sauce	1 clove garlic, pressed
1 Tbsp. soy sauce	½ tsp. dry mustard
2 pinches sage	¼ cup red wine vinegar (optional)

Mix all ingredients in bowl. Add meat and marinate in refrigerator for about 4 hours.

Uncooked Oil-Based Marinade

Use this simple recipe for marinating game birds.

1 cup canola oil	1 tsp. sweet basil leaf, ground
1 onion, sliced	2 stalks celery, cut into large pieces
1 cup parsley, chopped	6 peppercorns
2 cloves garlic, pressed	¼ cup white vinegar
4 bay leaves	1 cup white wine

Mix all ingredients in plastic food storage bag or covered container. Add meat and refrigerate 24 hours. Meat can be placed in the container and marinated at the same time the marinade is curing.

Cooked Oil-Based Marinade

This marinade works well with sage grouse breast.

1 cup canola oil	1 tsp. sweet basil leaf, ground
1 onion, sliced	2 stalks celery, cut into large pieces
1 cup parsley, chopped	6 peppercorns
2 cloves garlic, pressed	¼ cup white vinegar
4 bay leaves	1 cup white wine

In Dutch oven or large cooking pot, heat oil and add onions. Add remaining ingredients and stir well. Simmer over low heat ½ hour. Strain marinade and allow to cool before treating meats.

Cooking Tips: Avoid very dry wines as they tend to make this marinade bitter. The wine can be left out of this recipe without harm.

> ## "...Never store marinades in aluminum containers..."

Wine/Broth Marinade

This is an easy marinade to make for venison and game birds.

10-oz. sherry or port wine
1 can broth
Onion powder, sprinkle
Black ground pepper, sprinkle

Mix all ingredients in bowl and add meat to marinate. Use beef broth for red meat and chicken broth for game birds.

> ## "...Canola oil is ideal for marination because it leaves little of its own taste on the meat..."

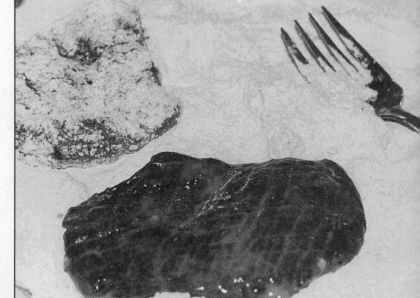

Flour is often used as a coating for marinated meat. Spices such as paprika can be added for flavor.

Sauces, Marinades & Gravies

Beer Marinade

Save that last can of beer for this delicious marinade.

1 12-oz. can or bottle of beer
1/2 cup canola oil
1 onion, sliced
2 cloves garlic, pressed
2 tsp. powdered mustard
1/4 tsp. salt
Black pepper, sprinkle

Combine beer and canola oil in bowl. Blend in remaining ingredients. Place meat in marinade and refrigerate 4-12 hours. Discard after using once.

Enhanced Wine/Broth Marinade

This is excellent for fried or grilled wild game meats.

10-oz. sherry or port wine
1 can broth
1/8 cup canola oil
2 cloves garlic, pressed
Oregano, pinch
Sweet basil, pinch
Paprika, sprinkle
Tarragon, dash
Lime juice, sprinkle
Onion powder, sprinkle
Black ground pepper, sprinkle

Combine all ingredients in bowl and add meat to marinate. Use beef broth for red meats and chicken broth for game birds.

Tomato Marinade

Use with any venison meats or game birds.

1 large can tomato juice
1/4 tsp. garlic powder
1/4 tsp. oregano, crushed
1/4 tsp. sweet basil leaf, crushed
1/2 onion, chopped
1/4 cup Worcestershire sauce

Mix all ingredients in plastic container. Marinate mild meats 12 hours in refrigerator and strong meats 24-48 hours in refrigerator. Do not allow marinade to get warm at any time before cooking meats.

> **"...Your taste buds will give the nod to *Beer Marinade* with cottontail rabbit meat..."**

Cottontail/Squirrel Marinade

This marinade is custom-made for rabbits and squirrels.

1 cup port wine
1/2 cup wine vinegar
2 cloves garlic, pressed
Black ground pepper, sprinkle
Tarragon, pinch
Paprika, sprinkle
1/2 tsp. dry mustard
2 stalks celery, quartered
1 onion, chopped
1/4 tsp. coriander

Mix wine and vinegar in bowl; stir in remaining ingredients. Add rabbit or squirrel and marinate 4 hours before cooking. For stronger flavor, refrigerate marinade with meat overnight.

Easy Wine Marinade

Bear steaks turn out very well with this marinade.

1 cup canola oil
1/2 tsp. dry mustard
4 Tbsp. lemon juice
1 onion, diced
2 cloves garlic, pressed
1/4 tsp. celery salt
1/2 cup sherry or Burgundy wine
Black pepper, sprinkle

Combine all ingredients in mixing bowl, stirring well. Let stand 1/2 hour before adding meat.

Soy Marinade

This marinade can also be served as gravy alongside of your favorite meat dish.

2 cups soy sauce
1/4 cup sherry
Oregano, sprinkle
1 sweet basil leaf

Mix all ingredients in bowl. Add meat and marinate 2-6 hours in refrigerator. Use marinade to baste meat while cooking. When meat is done, remove liquid from pan and place in saucepan with 1/4 cup port wine. Cook down and serve alongside meat.

Cooking Tips: For antelope steaks on the grill, use modified marinade for basting: 1 cup sherry with 1/4 cup soy sauce.

> **"...Soy Marinade is nice to have for basting barbecued meats..."**

Sauces, Marinades & Gravies...

A simple shaker like this works well to mix flour or cornstarch with liquid to form a milk-like thickener.

Teriyaki/Tarragon Marinade

This marinade is delicious with venison steaks.

1 cup teriyaki marinade
Garlic powder, sprinkle
Onion powder, sprinkle
Pepper, sprinkle
1/4 tsp. tarragon

Mix all ingredients in bowl. Add meat and marinate 1-4 hours. When meat is cooking, add marinade to skillet toward end of cooking cycle and blend with meat.

Sam's Marinade for Ducks

This marinade comes in handy when preparing ducks. And it's a snap to make.

1/2 cup soy sauce
Garlic powder, sprinkle
3 drops sesame oil
Onion powder, sprinkle
Lawry's Lemon Pepper, sprinkle
1/4 cup Lawry's Lemon Pepper Marinade

Combine all ingredients in bowl and transfer to large plastic food storage bag. Add duck (whole, sectioned or boned) and marinate in refrigerator 2-4 hours.

> ## "...Stock is a very useful cooking aid in many recipes that you'll use time and time again..."

Stock

Stock serves a great many purposes and can be used in any recipe calling for broth.

4 lb. game meat and bones	1/2 cup soy sauce
8 qts. water	1 tsp. Worcestershire sauce
4 cloves garlic, halved	8 beef bouillon cubes

In large cooking pot, combine meat and bones with water, garlic, soy sauce, Worcestershire sauce and bouillon cubes. Cook until liquid gains color and aroma. Strain and save all juices. Freeze what is not needed for future use.

Cooking Tips: If desired, add 4-6 chopped carrots and 2-4 chopped celery stalks before cooking. Stock can also be prepared in a pressure cooker.

Never use blood-shot meat for stock. Meat used can be a mixture of wild red, waterfowl, upland game or domestic beef.

To involve bone marrow in stock, crack bones lightly with hammer. Wear safety glasses to prevent eye injury.

Waterfowl Stock

This rich stock is an ideal way to use leftover waterfowl parts.

2 lb. duck parts	1/8 tsp. white pepper
2 bouillon cubes	1 tsp. Worcestershire sauce
1 clove garlic, minced	4 Tbsp. soy sauce
3 bay leaves	1 can beef broth
2 qts. water	

Place all ingredients in pressure cooker except beef broth. Close lid securely and set regulator. Pressure cook 30 minutes. Allow pressure to drop. Add 1 cup more water and pressure cook 20-30 minutes. Allow pressure to drop. Add beef broth and bring to boil. Turn heat off and allow stock to cook naturally. Freeze whatever is not needed for future use.

Cooking Tips: This stock can also be prepared in a stock pot for a much longer cooking time.

Mainly Wine Marinade

This marinade can be used before, during and after cooking the meat.

2 cups port, Burgundy, claret or sherry wine
Black pepper, sprinkle
Sweet basil, sprinkle
Oregano, sprinkle
1 bay leaf

Mix all ingredients in bowl. Add meat and marinate 1-2 hours in refrigerator. Add marinade to skillet when cooking meat. Combine with 1-2 pats butter, cook down and serve with meat.

Sauces, Marinades & Gravies

Wine Giblet Gravy

A superb game gravy that's just right for wild turkey, pheasant and grouse.

Game bird giblets, diced
1 Tbsp. margarine
2 carrots, peeled and chopped
1 onion, chopped

¼ cup parsley, chopped
20-oz. stock or 2½ cans chicken broth
¼ cup dry vermouth
2-3 Tbsp. cornstarch

Place raw giblets in skillet with margarine. Cook over low heat until well done. Add carrots and onion and turn heat up to medium. Add parsley and 16-oz. stock or 2 cans broth. Raise heat to high and bring to boil. Pour in vermouth and cook down. Transfer contents to saucepan and thicken with mixture of 4-oz. stock or ½ can broth and cornstarch. Stir constantly. **Servings: 6-8**

"...A little of this goes a long way..."

"...This is a fast and easy way to make a good brown gravy using stock and broth..."

Standard Game Gravy

Serve this delicious gravy over a big game roast and mashed potatoes.

2 cans beef broth
4 cups stock
⅛ cup milk
¼ stick margarine
1 pt. stock or beef broth, cold
4 Tbsp. cornstarch

In saucepan, combine beef broth and 4 cups stock and bring to boil. Add milk and stir well. Cook on low boil 1 minute; add margarine. In shaker, mix cold stock or broth with cornstarch. Shake to mix. Slowly pour into saucepan while stirring. Gravy will thicken. **Servings: 6-8**

Cooking Tips: Use egg beater or whip when thickening sauce to prevent lumps. If gravy is lumpy anyway, strain it.

Pan Gravy

This is delicious when it smothers fried venison steak, mashed potatoes and hot biscuits.

Fried game meat drippings
2 Tbsp. flour
1 cup whole milk

Heat drippings in skillet and slowly stir in flour. Cook until paste forms. Add milk, stirring constantly. Cook until well blended. **Servings: 4-6**

Cooking Tips: The exact amount of milk needed will vary with respect to amount of drippings.

If gravy lacks flavor, add a little powdered beef bouillon, soy sauce, Worcestershire sauce or teriyaki marinade.

Modified Pan Gravy

This is especially good with elk and deer game meat.

Fried game meat drippings
1-2 cups stock or beef broth
2 Tbsp. flour
1 cup whole milk

Heat drippings in skillet. When they begin to smoke, add stock or broth and stir vigorously. Slowly add flour and cook into juices. Add milk, stirring constantly. Cook until well blended.

Servings: 4-6

This degreasing brush will reduce the grease content in stock, broth and other liquids.

Sauces, Marinades & Gravies...

Giblet Gravy

Add this tasty addition to your
Turkey Gravy.

Wild turkey giblets
See *Turkey Gravy*

Place giblets in pressure cooker with 2 qts. water. Close lid and set regulator. Pressure cook 20-30 minutes or until giblets are cooked through. Let pressure drop. Dice meat and add to finished *Turkey Gravy*.   **Servings: 6-8**

Cooking Tips: Use only the soft parts of the giblets for this gravy.

"...This will make an okay meal memorable..."

Turkey Gravy

A "must" for wild turkey feasts.

2 qts. turkey stock, degreased and strained
1/4 cube butter or margarine
1/2 cup whole milk
1/2 can cold chicken broth
2-3 Tbsp. cornstarch

Heat degreased and strained stock in saucepan and bring to boil. Stir in butter and milk; bring to boil again. In shaker, combine chicken broth and cornstarch. Shake until mixed and slowly add to hot stock. Stir constantly until gravy thickens. Add prepared giblets for extra flavor.

Servings: 6-8

Cooking Tips: If strained stock does not measure the recommended amount, add 1 to 2 cans of chicken broth. The amount of stock and broth is determined by the number of guests.

Snappy Gravy

Fried game meat is the winner with this gravy.

Fried game meat drippings
2 Tbsp. granulated sugar
8 gingersnap cookies, crumbled
1 cup stock
2 Tbsp. flour

Add sugar and cookies to drippings in skillet. Cook 10 minutes, stirring to blend. Thicken with stock and flour. Keep stirring until well blended; be sure to cook flour into the gravy.

Servings: 4-6

Cooking Tips: Whole milk may be used to thin gravy if necessary.

Wild Turkey Gravy

Your turkey roasts will melt in your mouth
with this savory gravy.

1-1 1/2 qts. juices from cooked wild turkey
1 can chicken broth
1/4-1/2 stick margarine
2 chicken bouillon cubes
1/2 cup milk
4 Tbsp. cornstarch

Strain cooked turkey juices from roaster and place in large saucepan. Add chicken broth if amount of strained juices is not at recommended measure. Set aside 1 pt. of those juices in separate container and refrigerate. Bring stock in saucepan to low boil; add margarine while stirring. Add bouillon cubes if stock has only a light aroma. Stir in milk. Mix refrigerated liquid with cornstarch and slowly add to saucepan while stirring with egg beater. Sauce will thicken.

Servings: 6-8

"...'Down home' gravy can be made from pan drippings..."

Paprika/Flour Coating

If Pan Gravy is on the menu, coat your fried
meat with this mixture for added flavor.

1 cup flour
Paprika, sprinkle
Celery salt, sprinkle

Mix all ingredients in bowl. Use enough paprika to color flour lightly. Coat meat before cooking.

Upland Bird Gravy

A fine gravy can be made from fried game birds.

Fried game bird drippings
2 Tbsp. flour
1 cup cream
1 cup stock or chicken broth
1 lb. mushrooms, chopped
2-3 Tbsp. onion, diced
1 Tbsp. butter

Sift flour into skillet drippings, stirring constantly. When blended, add cream and cook into gravy. If necessary, thin gravy with stock or broth. In separate pan, sauté mushrooms and onion in butter. Add to gravy and heat through.

Servings: 6

Cooking Tips: Cooked, chopped giblets may also be added to this gravy before serving.

Microwave Apple and Red Cabbage Salad

This savory dish is made in a flash and can be served with waterfowl or venison roasts.

1½ cups apple cider
1 pkg. dry onion soup mix
1 tsp. caraway seeds
Pepper, sprinkle
6 cups red cabbage, sliced
1-2 large apples, chopped coarsley

In microwave dish, blend cider, soup mix, caraway seeds and pepper.

Stir in cabbage and apples. Microwave, uncovered, 10-15 minutes on high, stirring twice. Cover and let stand 10 minutes. **Servings: 6**

Fruit Ambrosia

Sweet nectar from the Gods, this dish will accent your duck roast to a tee.

1 30-oz. can fruit cocktail drained
1 20-oz. can pineapple chunks, drained
1 4-oz. can coconut, shredded
1 cup apple, chopped
1 8-oz. container vanilla low-fat yogurt
½ cup mayonnaise
½ cup golden raisins
½ cup walnuts, chopped

In bowl, mix all ingredients together. Chill 2 hours and serve cold.

Dill Cucumber Slices

This is a tantalizing side dish that goes well with barbecued venison.

5 large cucumbers, peeled and sliced
1 red Spanish onion, sliced
8 Tbsp. apple cider vinegar
2 tsp. brown sugar
1½ cup mayonnaise
½ cup sour cream
1 tsp. Lawry's Lemon Pepper
2 tsp. dill weed, dried

In large mixing bowl, mix cucumbers, onion and vinegar. Cover and let stand 4 hours, stirring ocassionally. Drain and discard liquid. Add remaining ingredients and toss to coat. Cover and refrigerate overnight. **Servings: 6**

Macaroni and Fruit Salad

A fruit salad like this one deserves to be exhibited for its color and texture before it's gobbled up.

2 cups elbow macaroni, cooked
1 can crushed pineapple, drained
1 can mandarin oranges, drained
1 cup seedless green grapes, quartered
1 cup seedless red grapes, quartered
1 cup celery, diced
1 cup carrots, grated
1 apple, diced
1 cup mini-marshmellows
1 cup pecans, chopped
1 cup vanilla non-fat yogurt

Mix all ingredients in large bowl. Add more yogurt if desired and refrigerate 1-2 hours. **Servings: 6**

Side Dish Recipes...

"...There's more elegance to a stuffing made with fruit, like cranberries..."

More Bannock Bread

Delicious for breakfast or dessert, or both.

4 cups flour
1¾ Tbsp. baking powder
1 tsp. salt
2 cups sugar
½ cup shortening
2 cups milk
2 eggs, beaten

In bowl, combine flour, baking powder, salt and sugar. Slowly add shortening and mix with fork. Add milk and eggs and stir into stiff dough. Spread evenly to ½-inch thickness in bottom of skillet. Cook over medium heat or over coals. Keep pan moving and turn bread for even doneness. **Servings: 6-8**

Bannock Pan Bread

Delicious bread for the trail, in camp or in the warmth of your kitchen.

1 cup flour
1 Tbsp. sugar
1 tsp. baking powder
½ tsp. baking salt
Lard or margarine
Water

In medium bowl, combine flour, sugar, baking powder and baking salt. Slowly add lard or margarine until mixture is crumbly dough. Add water slowly until dough becomes stiff. Spread to ½-inch thickness in bottom of skillet. Cook over medium heat or over coals. Keep pan moving and turn bread for even doneness. **Servings: 2**

"...Certain meals seem to demand cornbread..."

Cornbread from Dixie

A stew or soup doesn't seem the same without cornbread.

2 cups flour
2 cups cornmeal
4 tsp. baking powder
2 cups milk
⅔ cup shortening
2 eggs
2 tsp. baking soda
½ cup sugar

Preheat oven to 400°. Grease and flour baking dish with 1 Tbsp. margarine or lard and 1 Tbsp. flour. In large bowl, mix all ingredients, pour into dish and bake 25 minutes or until crust is golden brown. **Servings: 6**

Side Dish Recipes...

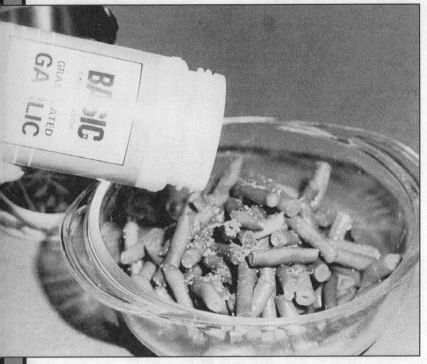

Garlic powder can be used to spice up a great many vegetable side dishes.

Baked Cauliflower with Cheese

Serve with any venison roast.

1 head cauliflower
1 cup Velveeta cheese, cubed
1 cup Half and Half
1 cup Italian-style bread crumbs

Preheat oven to 350°. Steam cauliflower in pan or steamer. Tuck cheese chunks into head and place in baking dish. Top with Half and Half and bread crumbs. Bake 20-30 minutes or until cheese is melted. **Servings: 6**

Mashed Carrots with Cream

This easy-to-prepare dish can be served with any venison or waterfowl meal.

1¹/₂ lb. carrots, peeled
1 Tbsp. butter
¹/₄ cup thick cream
¹/₂ tsp. garlic powder
Salt and pepper, sprinkle

Steam carrots in steamer or pan and mash. Place in serving bowl and add butter, cream and seasonings and stir. **Servings: 6**

"...Those who snub vegies should try this dish..."

Green Bean Casserole

This crunchy and nutritious dish can be served with venison ribs.

2 Tbsp. butter
2 Tbsp. flour
1 tsp. Lawry's Lemon Pepper
¹/₄ cup milk

1¹/₂ cups sour cream
2 16-oz. cans green beans, drained
1 can Durkee French Fried Onion Rings

Preheat oven to 350°. Melt butter in saucepan; stir in flour, lemon pepper and milk and heat until sauce thickens. Add sour cream and green beans and mix. Pour into baking dish and bake 20 minutes; top with onion rings and bake 10 more minutes.

Servings: 6

Zucchini with Green Beans

Fresh from the garden, this summertime combo is a vegetable treat.

1 lb. green beans
¹/₂ lb. zucchini
1 red Spanish onion, sliced

1 tsp. garlic powder
Salt and pepper, sprinkle
8 cooked bacon slices, crumbled

Wash green beans and snip ends. Wash and slice zucchini into large chunks; do not peel. Place beans, onions, garlic powder, salt and pepper in microwave-safe bowl. Cover and microwave on high 10-15 minutes. Beans should not yet be tender. Add zucchini, cover and microwave until zucchini is tender. Top with bacon bits.

Servings: 6

Cooking Tips: If fresh green beans are not available, use uncut frozen or canned green beans.

Glazed Carrots

Serve this tasty dish with Wild Turkey and Biscuit Bake.

8 carrots, peeled
2 Tbsp. molasses
¹/₂ cup margarine
Onion powder, sprinkle

Preheat oven to broil. Cut carrots in half and place in pressure cooker with molasses. Cover carrots with water, close lid securely and pressure cook 3 minutes. Let pressure drop. Drain liquid; place carrots in oven-safe dish. Melt margarine in saucepan and pour over carrots; sprinkle with onion powder. Broil 3 minutes, turn carrots and broil 3 minutes more. **Servings: 2**

Side Dish Recipes...

Marmalade Sweet Potatoes

This is good enough for dessert, but better served with a wild turkey dinner.

4 large sweet potatoes	2 Tbsp. butter, melted
1/4 cup orange juice	1/4 cup brown sugar
1/2 cup orange marmalade	1/4 cup pecans, chopped
2 Tbsp. lemon juice	1 cup mini-marshmellows
1/2 cup pineapple, crushed	

Preheat oven to 350°. Microwave sweet potatoes until tender. Peel potatoes and mash in medium bowl. Add orange juice, orange marmalade, lemon juice, pineapple, butter and brown sugar. Pour into baking dish and bake 20 minutes. Top with pecans and marshmellows and bake 10 more minutes or until marshmellows have melted.   **Servings: 6**

Sweet Potato Balls

Serve with wild turkey or goose roast.

1 29-oz. can sweet potatoes, drained	1/4 tsp. ginger
2 Tbsp. butter, melted	1/2 cup brown sugar
1/4 tsp. cinnamon	1 cup crushed pineapple, drained
1/4 tsp. nutmeg	2 cups cornflakes, crushed
1/4 tsp. cloves	

Preheat oven to 350°. In bowl, mash sweet potatoes and mix in remaining ingredients except cornflakes. Form into balls the size of large walnuts and roll in cornflakes. Place in shallow dish and bake 30 minutes.   **Servings: 6**

> **"...Come autumn, long after the green and leafy vegies are gone, make this underground sweetness appear on your dinner table..."**

Glazed Sweet Potatoes

Add this savory dish to your Buffalo Rump Roast dinner and you won't be sorry.

1 cube butter
1/2 cup maple syrup
1 cup brown sugar
3 Tbsp. molasses
2 29-oz. cans sweet potatoes

In large skillet, melt butter and add all ingredients except sweet potatoes. Cook over medium heat, stirring until ingredients are blended and bubbly. Drain liquid from sweet potatoes and add to skillet. Reduce heat and simmer 20 minutes. Turn potatoes and simmer another 20 minutes.   **Servings: 6**

Fast Scalloped Sweet Potatoes

On a busy day, serve this dish with Fast and Easy Fried Pheasant.

2 29-oz. cans sweet potatoes, drained	1/4 tsp. cloves
4 stalks celery, chopped	1/4 tsp. ginger
4 green onions, chopped	1 can cream of celery soup
1 tsp. nutmeg	2 cups Half and Half
1 tsp. cinnamon	1 cup pecans, chopped

Preheat oven to 350°. Slice sweet potatoes and place in baking dish with celery and onions. Sprinkle with nutmeg, cinnamon, cloves and ginger. Combine soup and Half and Half in small bowl and pour over potatoes. Bake 1 hour, sprinkle with pecans and bake 15 minutes.   **Servings: 6**

Sweet Potatoes with Apple and Cinnamon

This dish along with Stuffed Quail makes a scrumptious meal.

6 sweet potatoes, peeled	1 tsp. salt
6 apples, cored	1 tsp. cinnamon
1 1/2 cups orange juice	1 tsp. nutmeg
1 cup brown sugar	1/4 cup butter, cut into chunks
1/4 cup lemon juice	1 cup pecans, chopped

Slice sweet potatoes and quarter apples. Place in microwave-safe dish. In bowl, mix all remaining ingredients except butter and pecans and pour over apples/sweet potatoes. Distribute pats of butter, cover and microwave on high 15 minutes. Stir and top with pecans; cover and microwave on high 5 minutes or until done. Let stand 5-10 minutes before serving.   **Servings: 6**

> **"...A different way to present the tasty sweet potato..."**

Side Dish Recipes...

Twice-Baked Potatoes

This is a favorite no matter what meat dish you serve.

6 potatoes, large
1/2 cup milk, skim
1 1/2 cups low-fat cottage cheese
1 Tbsp. onion, minced

2 Tbsp. parsley, minced
Salt and pepper, sprinkle
Paprika, sprinkle
1 cup sharp cheddar cheese, shredded

Preheat oven to 375°. Scrub potatoes and cut shallow slits lengthwise around middle. Bake 45 minutes to 1 hour. Cut potatoes in half lengthwise and scoop pulp into bowl. Mash with milk, cottage cheese, onion, parsley, salt and pepper. Spoon mixture into potato skins and garnish with paprika. Place in dish or on cookie sheet and bake 15-20 minutes or until golden. Sprinkle with cheese and bake until cheese is bubbly.   **Servings: 6**

Oven French Fries

This is an easy and delicious side dish for gameburgers or steaks.

8 potatoes, large or medium
1 Tbsp. canola oil
Paprika, sprinkle
Salt, sprinkle

Preheat oven to 450°. Wash potatoes and cut into thick strips lengthwise. Soak strips in cold water; dry on paper towel. Place potatoes in bowl and mix with oil by hand. Place on baking sheet, sprinkle with paprika and salt and bake 30 minutes or until golden brown.   **Servings: 6**

Grated Potato Bake

Try this tasty dish in place of a baked potato. Serve with javelina.

4 large potatoes, grated
2 eggs, beaten
1/4 cup dry Italian bread crumbs
4 green onions, sliced thin

1/4 cup milk
1 tsp. Lawry's Lemon Pepper
1 cup cheddar cheese, grated
8 bacon slices, cooked and crumbled

Preheat oven to 400°. In medium bowl, soak potatoes in cold water. Mix eggs, bread crumbs, green onions, milk and Lawry's Lemon Pepper in large bowl. Drain potatoes and combine with egg mixture; add 1/2 cup cheese and 4 crumbled bacon slices. Pour into casserole dish and bake 30-40 minutes or until bubbly. Top with remaining cheese and bacon and bake 5-10 minutes or until cheese is melted.
Servings: 6

Potato Casserole

There are so many ways to prepare potatoes...here's an easy one.

8 potatoes, large
1 can cream of celery soup
1 cup low-fat yogurt
2 tsp. dry onion, minced
1 cup sharp cheddar cheese, grated
1/2 cup cornflakes, crushed

Preheat oven to 350°. In large pan, boil potatoes until tender. Grate and place in baking dish. In small bowl, mix celery soup, yogurt and dry onion and pour over potatoes. Cover and refrigerate overnight. Bake 20 minutes; top with cheese and cornflakes. Bake another 10 minutes.   **Servings: 6**

Saucy Skillet Potatoes

This is a new way of presenting a potato dish. Serve with Venison Short Ribs *or gameburgers.*

1 tsp. butter
1 cup onion, chopped
1 cup mayonnaise
1/2 cup apple cider vinegar
2 Tbsp. brown sugar

Salt and pepper, sprinkle
1 tsp. garlic powder
6 large potatoes, peeled and sliced
2 Tbsp. parsley, chopped
4 Tbsp. bacon, cooked and crumbled

Melt butter in skillet and sauté onion. Add mayonnaise, vinegar, brown sugar, salt, pepper and garlic powder and stir. In cooking pan, boil potatoes until almost tender. Add to skillet. Cook until potatoes are hot, but not brown. Garnish with parsley and bacon pieces.   **Servings: 4-6**

Green Bean Casserole is always a big hit when hearty eaters get together.

Side Dish Recipes...

Oven-Roasted Potatoes

Simple and good to eat, try this dish with venison steak.

1 pkg. dry onion soup mix
1/4 cup olive oil
6 red potatoes, large

Preheat oven to 375°. In bowl, mix onion soup mix and olive oil. Wash and quarter potatoes and place on cookie sheet. Top with soup mix and bake 1 hour or until potatoes are done.

Servings: 6

Creamed Potatoes

This is a good standby recipe for last-minute meal planners. Serve with venison roast or steak.

4 lb. potatoes, medium
Salt, sprinkle
2 1/2 cups whipping cream, unwhipped

Preheat oven to 300°. Peel and shred potatoes and wash thoroughly in cold water. Layer in casserole dish and sprinkle with salt. Pour over unwhipped cream and bake 2 hours or until potatoes are lightly browned. **Servings: 6**

"...There is nothing like fresh asparagus in the springtime. But frozen or canned, it's just as good..."

Baked Asparagus

This tasty dish complements any venison steak or roast.

2 tsp. butter
2 lb. fresh asparagus spears
1/4 cup onion, diced
1/2 cup celery, diced
1/2 cup dry Italian-style bread crumbs
1/4 cup Parmesan cheese, grated
1/4 tsp. oregano
Salt and pepper, sprinkle

Preheat oven to 350°. Melt butter in baking dish and line with asparagus. In bowl, mix onions, celery, bread crumbs, Parmesan cheese, oregano, salt and pepper and sprinkle over asparagus. Cover and bake 30-45 minutes or until asparagus is tender.

Servings: 6

"...Vegetable dishes are as numerous as the vegetables..."

Summer Vegetable Medley

There's a nursery of tasty vegetables in this dish.

1 cup baby onions
2 cups baby carrots
4 cups baby red potatoes
1 Tbsp. butter
1 can chicken broth
1 tsp. dried dill
Salt and pepper, sprinkle
1 tsp. sugar
1 cup green peas

In large bowl, mix all ingredients except peas. Place in microwave-safe dish, cover and microwave on high 10 minutes or until potatoes are just tender. Add peas, cover and microwave on high 3 minutes. **Servings: 6**

Broccoli with Cheese Sauce

This tasty vegetable dish complements any venison roast dinner.

2 lb. broccoli flowerettes
2 egg whites
1/4 tsp. Lawry's Garlic Salt
1 cup Swiss cheese, shredded
1/2 cup mayonnaise

Preheat oven to broil. Wash and separate broccoli; steam until just tender. Place in baking dish. In bowl, beat egg whites and Lawry's Garlic Salt until stiff peaks form. Fold in cheese and mayonnaise and spoon over broccoli. Broil 6 inches from heat until golden brown.

Servings: 6

"...A colorful medley of vitamins and minerals..."

Curried Vegetables

The subtle taste of curry is just enough to enhance the flavor of the zucchini.

2 cups cauliflowerettes
2 cups broccoli flowerettes
1 green pepper, sliced
1 cup celery, quartered
4 carrots, peeled and sliced
1/4 cup butter
1 onion, wedged
2 cloves garlic, minced
2 tsp. curry powder
Salt and pepper, sprinkle
1 cup water
1 lb. small zucchini, sliced

In bowl, mix all ingredients except zucchini. Place in microwave-safe dish, cover and microwave on high 10 minutes. Stir and add zucchini. Cover and microwave until all vegetables are tender. **Servings: 6**

Side Dish Recipes...

Philadelphia Cream Cheese Cabbage

Serve this tasty dish with wild boar or javelina.

- 6 cups green cabbage, shredded
- ½ cup water
- 1 6-oz. container Philadelphia Cream Cheese
- 2 Tbsp. milk
- 1 tsp. lemon pepper
- 1 tsp. celery seeds

In large saucepan, steam cabbage in water and drain. In small bowl, mix cream cheese and milk and pour over cabbage in saucepan. Add lemon pepper and celery seeds and simmer 10 minutes or until cream cheese is blended into cabbage.

Servings: 6

Ratatouille

This dish is deserving of its lofty title.
Serve with Wild Boar Roast Sherwood Forest.

- 2 red Spanish onions, sliced
- 2 green peppers, sliced
- 2 cloves garlic, minced
- 2 Tbsp. olive oil
- 1 lb. zucchini
- 1 lb. eggplant
- 1 lb. tomatoes
- 1 tsp. sweet basil, rubbed
- Salt and pepper, sprinkle

Place onions, green peppers and garlic in skillet and sauté in oil. Drain on paper towel. Slice zucchini, eggplant and tomatoes into large chunks and place in microwave-safe dish. Add sautéd mixture and sprinkle with sweet basil, salt and pepper. Cover and microwave on high 5 minutes. Stir and microwave on simmer 15 minutes, stirring ocassionally.

Servings: 6

Parsley, Parmesan cheese, hard-boiled eggs, oregano, sweet basil and chopped onions are some of the many ingredients that make up side dishes.

> **"...Side dishes leave a lot of room for creativity..."**

> **"...This dish is guaranteed to get your children eating vegetables..."**

Millet and Vegetable Casserole

Upland game meals and this casserole dish are a perfect match.

- 1 Tbsp. olive oil
- 2 cups millet, uncooked
- 1 onion, minced
- 2 cups fresh mushrooms, peeled and sliced
- 2 carrots, sliced
- 2 cans chicken broth
- 2 cups low-fat yogurt

Preheat oven to 350°. Heat skillet with oil and brown millet. Add onions, mushrooms, carrots and broth. Pour into casserole dish. Cover and bake 1 hour or until liquid is absorbed. Stir to mix vegetables and top with yogurt. **Servings: 6**

Side Dish Recipes...

Enhanced Canned Beans

Turn ordinary canned beans into something special and more flavorful.

½ lb. bacon	2 Tbsp. barbecue sauce
1 large can pork and beans	1 tsp. onion, dried
¼ tsp. mustard	2 Tbsp. molasses
2 Tbsp. catsup	1 Tbsp. brown sugar

Preheat oven to 300°. Slice bacon into ½-inch pieces and fry in skillet until well done. Drain most grease from pan and add pork and beans, mustard, catsup, barbecue sauce, onion, molasses and brown sugar. Stir and heat through. For baked beans presentation, place finished beans in dish and bake uncovered 20-30 minutes.

Servings: 4-6

Cooking Tips: If desired, top finished beans with cheese and microwave until cheese is bubbly.

> **"...This dish will change the image of canned beans forever..."**

> **"...This is an innovative way to present cabbage..."**

Sautéd Cabbage

Serve with Horseradish Venison Roast.

2 Tbsp. butter	1 bunch green onions, sliced
6 cups red cabbage, sliced	Salt and pepper, sprinkle
2 cups celery, diced	2 Tbsp. brown sugar
1 green pepper, diced	

Melt butter in skillet and add all vegetables. Season with salt and pepper and stir-fry over high heat 5-10 minutes. Sprinkle with brown sugar and heat another 2-3 minutes, stirring.

Servings: 6

> **"...This dish got its name because it looks like spaghetti when the pulp is cooked..."**

Spaghetti Squash

This is a very tasty gourd that will enhance any dinner menu.

3-4 lb. spaghetti squash
¼ cup butter, cut into chunks
¼ cup brown sugar

Wash squash and pierce in several places with fork. Wrap in plastic wrap and microwave on high 10 minutes. Turn squash and microwave 10 more minutes. Let stand 5-10 minutes. Cut squash and scoop out seeds and stringy matter; discard. Spoon squash meat into microwave-safe bowl. Fluff and top with butter chunks and brown sugar. Microwave on high 2-3 minutes or until butter is melted.

Servings: 6

Baked Acorn Squash

*In-season squash is best for this dish.
Serve with wild turkey roast.*

3 acorn squash
½ cup maple syrup
1 cup heavy cream

Preheat oven to 350°. Wash squash and cut into halves lengthwise. Remove seeds. Place cut-side down on microwave-safe plate and microwave on low 10 minutes. Place cut-side up on baking sheet; divide syrup and cream evenly among halves. Bake until done.

Servings: 6

> **"...Acorn squash is one of the few American born-and-raised vegetables. Indians of the Northeast grew it and introduced it to the pilgrims..."**

Side Dish Recipes...

"...Here's a dish even Adam and Eve would have enjoyed..."

Stuffed Apples with Almonds and Raisins

You couldn't ask for more from an apple; delicious with wild turkey.

6 baking apples
2 Tbsp. butter
1 tsp. cinnamon, ground
1 tsp. nutmeg, ground

1/2 cup raisins
1 cup almonds, sliced
1 cup brown sugar
1/2 cup water

Preheat oven to 350°. Wash and core apples. In bowl, combine butter, cinnamon, nutmeg, raisins, almonds and brown sugar and stuff into center of apples. Place in shallow baking dish and add water. Bake 30-45 minutes or until apples are done.

Servings: 6

"...Use this salad as an opener for a meal; it's fresh, it's light and it prepares the palate..."

Apricot-Pineapple Salad

This fruity salad is a pleasant surprise with any waterfowl dinner.

1 20-oz. can pineapple chunks, with juice
1 16-oz. can apricot halves, with juice
2 pkgs. gelatin
2 cups boiling water
1/2 cup cold water

1 cup celery, chopped
1 cup carrots, peeled and grated
1 cup pecans, chopped
1 cup sharp cheddar cheese, grated

Separate fruit from juices. Dissolve gelatin in boiling water and add pineapple and apricot juices. Stir and add cold water. Chill in refrigerator until partially set. Add remaining ingredients, stir and chill until completely set.

Servings: 6

Poached Peaches

This is delicious, hot or cold, as a side dish with venison roast.

1 qt. water
6 peaches, ripe
1 cup apple juice
1/2 cup brown sugar

2 tsp. lemon juice
1/2 tsp. nutmeg, ground
1/2 tsp. cinnamon, ground
1/4 tsp. clove, ground

Preheat oven to 325°. In cooking pan, bring water to boil. Dip peaches in boiling water and peel off skin. Slice in half and remove stones. In bowl, mix apple juice, brown sugar, lemon juice and spices. Place peaches cut-side down in baking dish and top with apple juice mixture. Bake 15 minutes, turn peaches over, baste and bake until tender. Serve with juices.

Servings: 6

"...This is a festive dish that creates a special effect with little effort...of course, your guests don't have to know that..."

"...The key ingredient here is easy..."

Chunky Baked Applesauce

This is homemade applesauce without the fuss.

8 large tart apples, cored and chopped
7 large baking apples, cored and chopped
1 cup brown sugar
2 tsp. pumpkin pie spice
2 Tbsp. lemon juice
1 cup cranberry juice

Preheat oven to 300°. Mix all ingredients in large baking dish. Cover and bake 40-50 minutes or until apples are tender. Serve warm.

Servings: 6

Spicy Applesauce

Hot or cold, this side dish is great with casseroles and roasts.

20 apples, peeled and sliced thin
1 cup water
1 cup brown sugar
1 Tbsp. lemon juice
2 tsp. cinnamon
1 tsp. nutmeg
1/2 tsp. cloves

Place all ingredients in crock pot and cook on low 8 hours.

Servings: 6

Side Dish Recipes...

Baked Herbed Tomatoes

Serve this delicious vegetable dish with gameburgers.

6 tomatoes, sliced thick
1 tsp. sweet basil, rubbed
1 tsp. oregano, rubbed
Lawry's Lemon Pepper, sprinkle
1 tsp. olive oil

Preheat oven to 350°. Place tomato slices on baking sheet and sprinkle with basil, oregano and Lawry's Lemon Pepper. Drizzle with olive oil and bake 10-15 minutes or until tomatoes are hot and soft. **Servings: 6**

Tomato Slices with Avocado-Lime Dressing

This is an easy yet elegant way to present tomatoes. Serve with your favorite barbecued meat.

2 ripe avocados
1/2 cup mayonnaise
2 Tbsp. lime juice
1 tsp. Worcestershire sauce
Salt and pepper, sprinkle
6 tomatoes, sliced

Place all ingredients except tomatoes in blender. Set to blend. Place sliced tomatoes on individual plates and top with dressing. **Servings: 6**

The beginning of any bean dish calling for pintos means sorting the beans to remove any rocks and rinsing completely.

> **"...Tomatoes are among the most delicious fruits around..."**

Summer Tomato Relish

Serve over a hotdog or bratwurst for best results.

5-6 large tomatoes, chopped
1 bunch green onions, chopped
2 cucumbers, peeled, seeded and chopped
2 Tbsp. sesame seed oil
2 Tbsp. lemon juice
1 tsp. oregano, rubbed
1 tsp. sweet basil, rubbed

Combine all ingredients, cover and refrigerate overnight. **Servings: 6**

Tomato and Onion Salad

Serve this salad cold with any barbecued meat or atop a slice of French or Italian bread.

1 large can tomatoes, diced
1/2 small onion, chopped
1 tsp. olive oil

Combine tomatoes and onion in bowl and mix well. Add olive oil and stir. If desired, sprinkle with oregano, Lawry's Lemon Pepper or salt. **Servings: 2-3**

> **"...Tomato and onion are a dynamite combo, especially in the summer..."**

Side Dish Recipes...

"...Honey is the oldest sweetner known to man, and it's associated with happiness..."

Honey-Lemon Coleslaw

Chock full of flavor and very easy to make, this is a must with barbecued gameburgers.

4 cups red cabbage, shredded
2 cups green cabbage, shredded
1 tsp. lemon rind, grated
1/4 tsp. ginger, ground
1 cup mayonnaise
4 Tbsp. honey
4 Tbsp. lemon juice
Salt and pepper, sprinkle

In large bowl, mix all ingredients; toss well to coat cabbage. Cover and refrigerate overnight.

Servings: 6

Thanksgiving Salad

The perfect side dish to accompany the wild turkey or pheasant that came home for the holidays.

1 pkg. Knox gelatin
1/2 cup cold water
1 cup sugar
1 cup pineapple, crushed
1 cup carrots, peeled and grated
1 cup cream cheese, softened
1 cup walnuts, chopped
1 cup whipped cream

Dissolve Knox gelatin in cold water. In saucepan, boil sugar and crushed pineapple and mix with gelatin mixture. Cool until thick. Combine carrots and cream cheese in separate bowl; stir in walnuts. Add to pineapple mixture; fold in whipped cream. Pour into serving dish and refrigerate until set.

Servings: 6

Marinated Vegetable Salad

Serve this dish over a bed of lettuce to accompany your venison steak.

2 small zucchini, sliced
1 Spanish onion, sliced thin
1 cup broccoli flowerettes
1 cucumber, sliced
12 cherry tomatoes, halved
2 carrots, peeled and sliced thin
1 cup cauliflowerettes
1 cup radishes, sliced
1/2 cup olive oil
1 cup apple cider vinegar
1/4 cup brown sugar
Salt and pepper, sprinkle

Combine all vegetables in casserole dish. In bowl, mix oil, vinegar, brown sugar, salt and pepper. Pour over vegetables. Cover and refrigerate overnight, stirring ocassionally. Remove from marinade before serving.

Servings: 6

Pineapple Chunks with Carrots

Serve this dish hot off the stove with your venison ribs.

1 lb. carrots, peeled and chopped
1 20-oz. can pineapple chunks, drained
2-3 Tbsp. cornstarch
1/2 cup pineapple juice
1/2 cup orange juice
2 tsp. lemon juice
Salt and pepper, sprinkle
1/2 tsp. garlic powder

Steam carrots in steamer or pan until tender; add pineapple. In bowl, dissolve cornstarch in pineapple, orange and lemon juices and heat in saucepan until thickened and clear. Pour over carrots and pineapple and season with salt, pepper and garlic powder.

Servings: 6

"...M is for marvelous menu entrées that include *Mixed Fruit Chutney*..."

Mixed Fruit Chutney

"M" is not just for meat, it's for a marvelous menu plan that includes this fruity dish.

1 1/4 cups pear, chopped
1 cup peach, chopped
1 cup apple, chopped
1/2 cup maraschino cherries, chopped
1/2 cup lemon vinegar
1/2 tsp. ginger, ground
4 Tbsp. brown sugar
1 onion, chopped
1 jalapeño pepper, seeded and chopped
1 1/2 tsp. Virginia Olson's Savory Seasonings Bake Blend
1/4 tsp. nutmeg, ground

Peel and core fruit before chopping. Mix all ingredients in saucepan. Heat 12-15 minutes until mixture softens. Refrigerate and serve chilled.

Servings: 6

"...Eat this dish without any guilt..."

Low-Fat Coleslaw

Watching your weight? Serve this dish without guilt.

4 cups cabbage, shredded
2 cups carrots, peeled and shredded
1 cup celery, minced
2 green onions, minced
1/4 cup parsley, chopped
3 Tbsp. brown sugar
1 cup low-fat yogurt

Mix all ingredients in serving bowl and refrigerate 2 hours.

Servings: 6

Side Dish Recipes...

Microwave Apple and Red Cabbage Salad

This savory dish can be made in a flash and served with waterfowl or venison roasts.

1¹/₂ cups apple cider
1 pkg. dry onion soup mix
1 tsp. caraway seeds
Pepper, sprinkle
6 cups red cabbage, sliced
1-2 large apples, chopped coarsley

In microwave dish, blend cider, soup mix, caraway seeds and pepper. Stir in cabbage and apples. Microwave, uncovered, 10-15 minutes on high, stirring twice. Cover and let stand 10 minutes.   **Servings: 6**

Fruit Ambrosia

Sweet nectar from the gods, this dish will accent your duck roast to a tee.

1 30-oz. can fruit cocktail, drained
1 20-oz. can pineapple chunks, drained
1 4-oz. can coconut, shredded
1 cup apple, chopped
1 8-oz. container vanilla low-fat yogurt
¹/₂ cup mayonnaise
¹/₂ cup golden raisins
¹/₂ cup walnuts, chopped

Mix all ingredients in large bowl. Cover and chill 2-4 hours.   **Servings: 6**

More Bannock Bread

Delicious for breakfast or dessert, or both.

4 cups flour
1³/₄ Tbsp. baking powder
1 tsp. salt
2 cups sugar
¹/₂ cup shortening
2 cups milk
2 eggs, beaten

In medium bowl, combine flour, baking powder, salt and sugar. Slowly add shortening and mix with fork. Add milk and eggs and stir into stiff dough. Spread evenly to ¹/₂-inch thickness in bottom of skillet. Cook over medium heat or over coals. Keep pan moving and turn bread for even doneness.   **Servings: 6-8**

Dill Cucumber Slices

This is a tantalizing side dish that goes well with barbecued venison.

5 large cucumbers, peeled and sliced
1 red Spanish onion, sliced
8 Tbsp. apple cider vinegar
2 tsp. brown sugar
¹/₂ cup mayonnaise
¹/₂ cup sour cream
1 tsp. Lawry's Lemon Pepper
2 tsp. dill weed, dried

In large mixing bowl, combine cucumbers, onion and vinegar. Cover and let stand 4 hours, stirring ocassionally. Drain and discard liquid. Add remaining ingredients and toss to coat. Cover and refrigerate overnight.   **Servings: 6**

Macaroni and Fruit Salad

A fruit salad like this one deserves to be exhibited for its color and texture before it's gobbled up.

2 cups elbow macaroni, cooked
1 can crushed pineapple, drained
1 can mandarin oranges, drained
1 cup seedless green grapes, quartered
1 cup seedless red grapes, quartered
1 cup celery, diced
1 cup carrots, peeled and grated
1 apple, diced
1 cup mini-marshmellows
1 cup pecans, chopped
1 cup vanilla non-fat yogurt

Mix all ingredients in large bowl. Add more yogurt if desired and refrigerate 1-2 hours.   **Servings: 6**

Bannock Pan Bread

This is a great bread for on the trail, in camp or in the warmth of your kitchen.

1 cup flour
1 Tbsp. sugar
1 tsp. baking powder
¹/₂ tsp. baking salt
Lard or margarine
Water

In medium bowl, combine flour, sugar, baking powder and baking salt. Slowly add lard or margarine until mixture is crumbly dough. Add water slowly until dough becomes stiff. Spread to ¹/₂-inch thickness in bottom of skillet. Cook over medium heat or over coals. Keep pan moving and turn bread for even doneness.

Servings: 2

"...Certain meals seem to demand cornbread..."

Cornbread from Dixie

A stew or soup doesn't seem the same without cornbread.

2 cups flour
2 cups cornmeal
4 tsp. baking powder
2 cups milk
²/₃ cup shortening
2 eggs
2 tsp. baking soda
¹/₂ cup sugar

Preheat oven to 400°. Grease and flour baking dish with 1 Tbsp. margarine or lard and 1 Tbsp. flour. In large bowl, mix all ingredients, pour into dish and bake 25 minutes or until crust is golden brown.   **Servings: 6**

Side Dish Recipes...

"...A good old-fashioned dumpling is a wonderful beginning for soups and stews..."

Cornmeal Dumplings

Here's another cornmeal dish that literally tops off any stew or soup serving.

1 cup yellow cornmeal
1 cup flour
2 tsp. baking powder
1 tsp. baking soda

1/2 tsp. salt
1/4 cup brown sugar
2 eggs
3/4 cup milk

Combine cornmeal, flour, baking powder, baking soda, salt and brown sugar in mixing bowl; add eggs and milk. Mix until blended. Drop by spoonfuls into hot stew or soup, cover and cook 20-25 minutes. Uncover and continue cooking until dumplings are done.   **Servings: 6**

"...Breads help round out any big game meal..."

Twist Bread Over Coals

Your kids will enjoy making their own bread, especially on family camping trips.

2 cups flour
2 tsp. baking powder
1 tsp. sugar
1/8 tsp. salt
Water
2 Tbsp. lard or margarine

Heat coals in grill or pit. In mixing bowl, combine flour, baking powder, sugar, salt and enough water to form stiff dough. Add lard or margarine, mixing well. Use hands to knead mixture. Break off fist-sized piece of dough and roll between hands to form rope. Snake-wrap dough around long skewer, leaving space between dough and skewer for even distribution of heat. Hold over coals and turn often. Slip off skewer when bread is done.   **Servings: 2-4**

Cooking Tips: Skewers can be made out of green twigs. They should be long enough to accomodate bread, and keep hands away from heat. Avoid willow, pine or other woods that may impart undesirable flavor. Bread can be cooked over a grill or open pit.

Use short twists of bread; long twists are hard to cook evenly.

"...Man does *not* live by bread alone, but it's sure nice to have with dinner..."

"...Sourdough Pancakes rev your Sunday mornings up to a great start..."

Sourdough Pancakes

Top these flapjacks with maple syrup, honey, or fruit preserves.

2 cups flour
2 cups warm milk
1 tsp. baking soda
1 Tbsp. bacon fat or oil
2 eggs
1 Tbsp. sugar
Salt, pinch

In mixing bowl, combine flour and warm milk. Stir after adding each of the remaining ingredients. Pour individual servings on lightly oiled griddle and cook. Wait for bubbles to appear before turning.   **Servings: 6-8**

Southern-Style Corn Pones

*In camp as well as at home,
corn pones make an interesting side dish.*

1 cup cornmeal mix
1/2 tsp. salt
1 1/2-2 cups boiling water
1-2 Tbsp. olive oil

In bowl, combine cornmeal mix and salt. Add boiling water to form stiff dough. Pinch off pieces of dough; shape into balls and flatten. In skillet with oil, fry dough pieces on both sides for several minutes over medium heat. Cooking time varies; pones should be cooked through.

Servings: 2-3

Side Dish Recipes...

This scrumptious rice stuffing calls for rice and ground venison. It can be varied in many ways, with different spices and meats.

Wild Rice with Mushrooms and Almonds

Consider this dish the next time you make a javelina or wild boar roast.

- ¹/₂ cube butter
- 1 cup wild rice
- 2 cups white rice
- 6 cups chicken broth
- 1 tsp. olive oil
- ¹/₂ lb. fresh mushrooms, sliced
- ¹/₂ cup almonds, sliced

Place all ingredients except olive oil, mushrooms and almonds in uncovered dish and microwave on high 10 minutes. Fluff mixture, cover and microwave on simmer 30-45 minutes or until rice is tender. Heat skillet with oil and sauté mushrooms. Add to rice; fluff and top with almonds. **Servings: 6**

Pasta Pilaf

This dish can be served with your favorite venison roast.

- 1 cup acini or orzo (macaroni), dry
- 2 qts. boiling water
- 1 Tbsp. butter
- 1 cup mushrooms, sliced
- 4 green onions, sliced
- 2 cloves garlic, minced
- Salt and pepper

Place macaroni in boiling water for 5-8 minutes. Drain in collander, but do not rinse. Melt butter in skillet and sauté mushrooms, green onions and garlic. Add pasta and stir-fry until hot. Season with salt and pepper. **Servings: 2-4**

> **"...Instead of rice, this pilaf dish uses acini or orzo, a small macaroni that's shaped like rice..."**

Old Country Stuffing

This recipe dresses up any wild game dinner.

1 ¹/₂ cups white rice	Worcestershire sauce, dash
¹/₂ cup wild rice	¹/₂ white onion, chopped
1¹/₂ lb. gameburger	4 Tbsp. Parmesan cheese, grated
Turkey giblets	2 pinches oregano
¹/₈ tsp. garlic powder	¹/₄ tsp. sweet basil
6 chicken bouillon cubes	¹/₈ tsp. sage
White pepper, dash	¹/₄ cup celery, dried
¹/₈ tsp. soy sauce	1 bunch parsley, chopped

Mix white and wild rice in bowl; cook according to package directions and set aside. Brown meat in skillet; place on dish with paper towels and microwave on high 1-2 minutes; set aside. In saucepan, cook giblets in 1¹/₂ qts. water with garlic powder, bouillon cubes, white pepper, soy sauce and Worcestershire sauce. Strain liquid; chop giblets and place in large mixing bowl. Add meat, rice, white onion, Parmesan cheese, oregano, sweet basil, sage, celery and parsley and mix well. **Servings: 6-8**

Cooking Tips: If desired, cut 4 hard-boiled eggs into eighths and add to stuffing mix.

> **"...Perked coffee is great in camp, but open-pot is better..."**

Open Pot Camp Coffee

Coffee is always good to have in camp. Here's a way to brew it in an open pot.

- 1 Tbsp. coffee
- 4 cups cold water

Scoop coffee into bottom of pot and pour in water. Bring to boil and boil 1-3 minutes. Remove from heat and let stand 2 minutes. Add 2-ozs. cold water to settle grounds faster. **Servings: 2-4**

Side Dish Recipes...

Cranberry Stuffing

This stuffing has a subtle tart taste that makes it delicious with Smoked Quail or Not Fancy Pheasant.

1/2 cup onion, minced	1 cup pecans, chopped
1/2 cup celery, minced	2 Tbsp. brown sugar
1 apple, minced	1 tsp. poultry seasoning
1/2 cup butter	Salt and pepper, sprinkle
1 cup orange sections, chopped	6-8 cups dry bread crumbs
1 cup raw cranberries, chopped	1/2 cup hot chicken broth

Preheat oven to 350°. In skillet, sauté onions, celery and apples in butter. In large mixing bowl, blend sautéed mixture with remaining ingredients. More hot chicken broth may be required for moisture. Stuff bird or place in baking dish and bake 30-45 minutes until mixture is golden brown. **Servings: 6**

> ## "...There's more elegance to a stuffing made with fruit, like cranberries..."

Easy Mixed Rice

Don't just serve plain rice when this dish is just as easy to make and more flavorful.

- 1 lb. mushrooms, sliced
- 1 Tbsp. butter or margarine
- 2 cups rice
- 2 cans chicken broth
- 1/2 cup celery, diced
- 1/2 cup carrots, peeled and diced
- 2 Tbsp. parsley, minced
- 1/4 cup almonds, sliced

In skillet, sauté mushrooms in butter; place in microwave-safe dish. Add all ingredients. Cover and microwave on high 15 minutes. Stir. Re-cover and microwave on simmer 15 minutes. Fluff before serving. **Servings: 6**

Apple Dressing

This adaptable and delicious dressing mix goes well with any roast or upland game dish.

1/2 cup butter or margarine	1/2 tsp. thyme
6 cups dry bread cubes	1/2 tsp. savory
3 baking apples, cored and chopped	1 tsp. lemon peel, grated
2 green onions, chopped	2 Tbsp. parsley, chopped
1/2 cup ginger ale	1/2 cup pecans, chopped
1/2 cup brown sugar	Salt and pepper, sprinkle

Preheat oven to 350°. In small saucepan, melt butter or margarine and drizzle over bread cubes. In large casserole dish, mix all ingredients with bread cubes. Cover and bake 50 minutes, stirring twice. Check for doneness; center should be set and edges browned. Let stand 10-15 minutes before serving. **Servings: 6**

Cornbread Stuffing

This is just as delicious in a bird as it is as an individual side dish.

1/2 cup butter	Salt and pepper, sprinkle
1/2 cup onion, minced	1/4 tsp. savory
1/2 cup celery, minced	1/4 tsp. thyme
3 cups cornbread, crumbled	1/2 cup hot chicken broth
1 cup soft bread crumbs, white or wheat	1/2 cup pecans, chopped

Preheat oven to 350°. In skillet, melt butter and sauté onion and celery. Pour into mixing bowl and blend with cornbread, soft bread crumbs, salt, pepper, savory and thyme. Pour hot chicken broth over mixture and add pecans. Mix well. Stuff bird or place in baking dish and bake 30 minutes. **Servings: 6**

> ## "...Popeye would have loved Spinach Rice..."

Spinach Rice

Here's a way to dress-up spinach, but not hide its wonderful taste.

- 4 eggs
- 6 cups rice
- 1 Tbsp. Worcestershire sauce
- 1 tsp. onion powder
- 2 cups spinach, chopped
- 1 cup milk
- 2 tsp. salt
- 1 cup cheddar cheese, grated

Preheat oven to 350°. Beat eggs in small bowl; prepare rice according to package directions. In large casserole dish, combine all ingredients. Top with cheese and bake 45 minutes.

Servings: 6

Rice Pilaf with Dry Fruit

Any venison roast will be made more special with this dish.

2 cups rice	1/2 cup dried apricots, chopped
4 cups water	1/4 cup green onions, sliced
1/2 cup dried apples, chopped	1/4 cup almonds, toasted and sliced
1/2 cup dried peaches, chopped	

In microwave dish, combine rice, water, apples, peaches, apricots and green onions. Microwave, uncovered, 10 minutes on high. Stir; cover with plastic wrap and microwave on simmer 15 minutes. Let stand 10 minutes; stir in toasted almonds. **Servings: 6**

Hot Fudge Sundae Cake

Serve this tasty dessert over your favorite ice cream.

1 cup flour	2 Tbsp. salad oil
³/₄ cup white sugar	1 tsp. vanilla
2 Tbsp. cocoa	1 cup pecan or walnuts, chopped
2 tsp. baking powder	1 cup brown sugar
¼ tsp. salt	¼ cup cocoa
½ cup milk	1³/₄ cup hot tap water

Preheat oven to 350°. In ungreased square pan, mix together flour, white sugar, 2 Tbsp. cocoa, baking powder and salt. Add milk, oil and vanilla and fork until smooth. Add nuts and spread mixture evenly in pan. Sprinkle with brown sugar and ¼ cup cocoa. Pour hot water over batter and bake 40 minutes. Let stand 15 minutes. Servings: 6-8

"...This hot fudge sundae is a piece of cake..."

Watergate Cake

Take the blame for this succulant break-in with this delicious dessert.

1 pkg. white cake mix	1 cup club soda
2 pkgs. Instant Pistachio Pudding Mix	½ cup pecan or walnuts, chopped
3 eggs	1½ cups cold milk
1 cup vegetable oil	1 large Cool Whip

Preheat oven to 350°. Blend cake mix, 1 pkg. pudding mix, eggs, vegetable oil, club soda and nuts in bowl; mix 4 minutes. Grease and flour 9*13-inch baking pan and bake 40 minutes. Combine 1 pkg. pudding and cold milk in bowl and mix until thick. Fold in Cool Whip and spread over cake. Servings: 6-8

"...Break-in to this delicious cake and be caught with a smile..."

Before & After...

"...These snow-balls are not for throwing but stuffing in your mouth..."

Snowballs

Your taste buds will be snowed with this tasty excitement.

³/₄ cup ?????	2 cups flour
½ cup butter	1 cup pecan or walnuts, chopped
1 tsp. salt	½ cup powdered sugar
2 Tbsp. vanilla	

Preheat oven to 325°. Mix all ingredients except powdered sugar in bowl. Spoon drop mixture into baking pan and bake 25 minutes. Roll each in powdered sugar. Servings: An igloo worth

"...This is a sweet feast for sore eyes..."

No Bake Cake

This is a fun recipe for your children to help prepare. And so delicious too.

- 8 single Twinkies
- 6-oz. pkg. vanilla pudding
- 12-oz. container extra creamy frozen whipped topping, thawed
- 3 Heath Bars, chilled and crushed

Arrange Twinkies to fill bottom of cake pan. Pour ½ crushed candy over Twinkies. Prepare pudding according to package directions; spread evenly over Twinkies. Cover with whipped topping; sprinkle with remaining candy bars and refrigerate overnight. Servings: 6-8

Banana Split Dessert

No fountain treat can top this tasty dessert.

2 cups graham crackers	3 bananas, cut into bite-sized pieces
6 Tbsp. margarine, melted	1 large can crusted pineapple, drained
1 egg	10-oz. container Cool Whip
1 stick margarine, soften	Pecan or walnuts pieces, sprinkle
2 cups powdered sugar	Marachina cherries, halved
1 tsp. vanilla	

Preheat oven to 350°. Mix graham crackers and melted margarine in small bowl. Spread evenly into 13*9-inch baking pan; pat mixture down and bake 5 minutes. Let cool. Combine egg, soften margarine stick, powdered sugar and vanilla in bowl. Mix until fluffy and spread over graham crust. Lay bananas over mixture and spread with pineapples. Top with Cool Whip and sprinkle with nuts and cherries. Refrigerate overnight. Servings: 6

Before & After...

Venison Taco Dip

Be sure to have tortilla chips on hand for this dip.

1½ lb. ground venison	2 cups taco cheese, shredded
1 pkg. taco seasoning mix	½ head lettuce, chopped
1 can refried beans	2 large tomatoes, diced
1 pt. sour cream	

Preheat oven to 350°. Brown venison in skillet and drain on paper towel. Return meat to skillet and add taco seasoning mix according to package directions. Spread refried beans on bottom of casserole dish and top with venison. Bake 15-20 minutes until hot. Let cool slightly and top with sour cream. Sprinkle with cheese, lettuce and tomatoes. **Servings: 4**

Alternate Meats: Elk, moose, antelope, caribou, deer

Cooking Tips: Recipe may be doubled and baked in a larger casserole dish.

Liver Paté

Serve this at your next party and delight your guests.

⅔ cup chicken fat	2 hard-boiled eggs, chopped
½ lb. onions, chopped	Salt and pepper
1 lb. venison liver, sliced	Green olives, sliced

In skillet, melt chicken fat, stirring constantly. Sauté onions in chicken fat until lightly browned. Add liver and cook until well done. Cool and finely grind skillet mixture in food grinder. In large bowl, mix liver mixture with eggs, salt and pepper. Place mixture in loaf pan and top with ¼-inch layer of melted chicken fat. Refrigerate. Top with green olives and serve with crackers. **Servings: 12-15**

Alternate Meats: Elk, moose, antelope, caribou, deer

"...Sugar and salt make a winning combination..."

"...A must for every party..."

Pheasant Mustard Sauce

Surprise your party guests with this taste treat.

1 cup cream
2 Tbsp. dry mustard
2 egg yolks
½ cup sugar
1 Tbsp. vinegar

Mix ½ cup cream with remaining ingredients in top of double boiler. Heat over boiling water until thick, stirring. And remaining cream until proper consistency is reached. Refrigerate until sauce stiffens. Serve with smoked meat, particularly pheasant.

"...Stuff your friends with this starter..."

Stuffed Mushroom Caps

Before feasting on that big game roast, prepare your palate with this dish.

1½ lb. large mushrooms
¼ lb. ground venison
¼ cup onion, chopped
1 clove garlic, chopped
Seasoned bread crumbs, sprinkle
Cheddar cheese, grated

Set oven to broil. Wash mushrooms and dry with paper towel. Remove stems and chop fine. In skillet, brown venison with onion, garlic and mushroom stems and drain on paper towel. Return to skillet and stir in desired amount of bread crumbs. Spoon mixture into empty mushroom caps and top with cheese. Broil until cheese bubbles. **Servings: 6**

Spiced Nuts

Prepare this sweet-and-salt treat for viewing your next football game.

4 cups pecan halves
1 cup butter
1 box powdered sugar
2 Tbsp. cinnamon, ground
2 Tbsp. nutmeg, ground

In heavy skillet, melt butter and stir in nuts. Cook 20 minutes or until heated through and slightly brown, stirring frequently. Sift sugar, cinnamon and nutmeg together in paper bag. Remove nuts from skillet with slotted spoon and drain on paper towels. Add nuts to bag mixture and shake until generously coated. Pour nuts into colander or sieve and shake gently to remove excess sugar. Spread on paper towels to cool.

Barbecued Dove Snacks

With crackers or cocktail bread, this will help curb your appetite.

16 dove breasts
1 pkg. chicken coating mix

Coat dove breats in coating mix according to package directions. Grill over hot coals until cooked through. Slice and serve on crackers or cocktail bread. **Servings: 4**

Before & After...

There's nothing better than cookies and milk to finish off a game meal.

Captain Crunch Candy

Save your sweet tooth for this delicious dessert.

2 lb. almond bark
4 Tbsp. peanut butter
2 cups Spanish peanuts, salted
6 cups Captain Crunch cereal

Melt almond bark over hot water in double boiler. Turn heat off and stir until cool. Add remaining ingredients. Drop tablespoons of batter onto waxed paper. Set aside or chill 1 hour.

Servings: 2 dozen

Old-Fashioned Oatmeal Cookies

These are good enough for holiday presents.

2$1/2$ cups oatmeal, uncooked	$1/2$ cup shortening
1$1/2$ cups flour	$1/2$ cup butter or margarine
1 cup walnuts, finely chopped	1 cup brown sugar, firmly packed
1 tsp. baking soda	$1/2$ cup sugar
$1/2$ tsp. salt	2 eggs
$1/2$ tsp. cinnamon	1 tsp. vanilla extract

Preheat oven to 375°. Lightly grease 2 cookie sheets. Combine oats, flour, walnuts, baking soda, salt and cinnamon in bowl; set aside. In large mixing bowl, blend shortening, butter and brown sugar until creamy. Beat in eggs and vanilla. Gradually stir in oats mixture until just combined. Drop by tablespoon onto cookie sheets 2-inches apart. Bake 10-12 minutes until golden brown. Cool 5 minutes and transfer to wire racks to cool completely.

Servings: 6$1/2$ dozen

Grandma's Sugar Cookies

You may have to hide the cookie jar unless you want to see these disappear quickly.

2$3/4$ cups flour	1$1/4$ cup sugar
2 tsp. baking powder	2 eggs
$1/2$ tsp. salt	1 tsp. vanilla
$1/2$ cup butter or margarine, softened	1 tsp. lemon peel, grated

Combine flour, baking powder and salt in small bowl; set aside. In separate bowl, mix butter and 1 cup sugar until light and fluffy. Beat in eggs; add vanilla, lemon peel and flour mixture until combined. Divide dough in half. Tightly wrap each half in waxed or plastic paper and refrigerate 4 hours or overnight. Preheat oven to 350°. Grease 2 cookie sheets. On floured surface with floured rolling pin, roll each dough half to $1/4$-inch thickness. Cut out dough with round 2$1/2$-inch cookie cutter. Transfer to cookie sheets and sprinkle with $1/4$ cup sugar. Bake each sheet, separately, 6-8 minutes until edges are golden. Cool on wire racks.

Servings: 5 dozen

"...Flowers are lovely, but why not try this edible centerpiece after dinner..."

"...Have your next date with these delicious cookies..."

Rice Krispie Date Cookies

Complement your venison dinner with this delicious dessert.

1 stick butter or margarine	3 cups Rice Krispies cereal
2 eggs, beaten	1 cup nuts, chopped
1 cup sugar	Powdered sugar, sprinkle
1 cup dates, chopped	

Melt butter in large saucepan. Mix eggs and sugar in small bowl and add to saucepan. Stir constantly, being careful not to cook eggs. Slowly add dates and melt. Remove from heat and cool. Add Rice Krispies and nuts and shape into 2 rolls. Sprinkle with powdered sugar. Wrap in waxed paper and refrigerate. Slice into serving pieces.

Servings: 4 dozen

Before & After...

Serve pumpkin pie with whip cream when entertaining friends.

Yum Yums
This is an after-dinner treat you won't want to miss.

1 12-oz. pkg. chocolate chips
1 12-oz. pkg. butterscotch chips
1 12-oz. can peanuts, salted
1 5-oz. can chow mein noodles

Melt chips one bag at a time in large saucepan or double broiler over low heat. Add peanuts and blend. Add noodles and mix until covered. Drop by teaspoon onto cookie sheet and refrigerate 20 minutes or until hard.   **Servings: 3 dozen**

Strawberry Pie
This is a mouth-watering dessert for any occasion.

1 cup water	3 Tbsp. strawberry gelatin
3 Tbsp. white syrup	2 drops red food coloring
3 Tbsp. cornstarch	1 qt. fresh strawberries
1 cup sugar	1 large container whipped cream

In saucepan over medium heat, combine water, syrup, cornstarch and sugar. Cook until hot. Remove from heat and add gelatin and food coloring. In 9-inch pie shell, place strawberries. Pour pan mixture over top and stand strawberries up on stem end. Refrigerate 1 hour or until jelled. Top with whipped cream.   **Servings: 6**

Chocolate Pudding Pie
This is a festive way to present chocolate pudding.

1 cup flour	18-oz. cream cheese
1 stick margarine	1 large container whipped cream
1 Tbsp. sugar	1 cup powdered sugar
1/2 pecans, chopped	2 pkgs. instant chocolate pudding mix

Preheat oven to 350°. Combine flour, margarine, sugar and pecans in bowl. Spread and press dough mixture evenly on bottom of round baking pan. Bake 15 minutes and let cool. In separate bowl, combine cream cheese, 1 cup whipped cream and powdered sugar; spread evenly over baked dough. Prepare pudding according to package directions and spread over cream cheese mixture. Top with remaining whipped cream and refrigerate 2 hours.   **Servings: 6-8**

Key Lime Pie
You don't have to live in Florida to enjoy this special dessert.

3-4 egg yokes
1 4-oz. container concentrated lime juice
1 can condensed milk
1 graham cracker pie crust, prepared
1 large container whipped cream

Preheat oven to 350°. In bowl, beat eggs, juice and milk until well blended. Pour into pie crust and bake 15 minutes. Let cool and top with whipped cream.   **Servings: 6**

Apple Cheese Tarts
Easy to make, this fruity dessert goes down well after a venison steak.

8-oz. cream cheese	12 pastry tart shells, baked
1 14-oz. can Eagle Brand milk	1 can apple pie filling
1/3 cup lemon juice	Almonds, slivered

Blend cream cheese, Eagle Brand milk and lemon juice in bowl; fill each baked pastry shell. Top with apple filling and sprinkle with almonds.   **Servings: 12**

Before & After...

"...This hot fudge sundae is a piece of cake..."

Hot Fudge Sundae Cake
Serve this tasty dessert with your favorite ice cream.

1 cup flour	2 Tbsp. salad oil
3/4 cup sugar	1 tsp. vanilla
2 Tbsp. cocoa	1 cup pecan or walnuts, chopped
2 tsp. baking powder	1 cup brown sugar
1/4 tsp. salt	1/4 cup cocoa
1/2 cup milk	13/4 cup hot water

Preheat oven to 350°. In ungreased square pan, mix flour, sugar, 2 Tbsp. cocoa, baking powder and salt. Add milk, oil and vanilla and beat with fork until smooth. Add nuts and spread mixture evenly in pan. Sprinkle with brown sugar and 1/4 cup cocoa. Pour hot water over batter and bake 40 minutes. Let stand 15 minutes.

Servings: 10-12

Watergate Cake
Take the blame for this succulant break-in with this delicious dessert.

1 pkg. white cake mix	1 cup club soda
2 pkgs. instant pistachio pudding mix	1/2 cup pecan or walnuts, chopped
3 eggs	11/2 cups cold milk
1 cup vegetable oil	1 large container whipped cream

Preheat oven to 350°. Blend cake mix, 1 pkg. pudding mix, eggs, vegetable oil, club soda and nuts in bowl; mix 4 minutes. Grease and flour 9x13-inch baking pan. Add cake mixture and bake 40 minutes. Combine 1 pkg. pudding and cold milk in bowl and mix until thick. Fold in whipped cream and spread over cake.

Servings: 10-12

"...Break in to this delicious cake and be caught with a smile..."

"...These snow-balls are not for throwing, but stuffing in your mouth..."

Snowballs
Your taste buds will be snowed by this tasty excitement.

3/4 cup spry	2 cups flour
1/2 cup butter	1 cup pecan or walnuts, chopped
1 tsp. salt	1/2 cup powdered sugar
2 Tbsp. vanilla	

Preheat oven to 325°. Mix all ingredients except powdered sugar in bowl. Drop by spoonfuls onto baking sheet and bake 25 minutes. Roll each ball in powdered sugar.

Servings: 2 dozen

"...This is a sweet feast for sore eyes..."

No Bake Cake
This is a fun recipe for your children to help prepare. And so delicious, too.

8 single Twinkies
1 6-oz. pkg. instant vanilla pudding mix
1 12-oz. container extra creamy frozen
   whipped cream, thawed
3 Heath Bars, chilled and crushed

Arrange Twinkies to fill bottom of cake pan. Pour 1/2 crushed candy over Twinkies. Prepare pudding according to package directions; spread evenly over Twinkies. Cover with whipped cream; sprinkle with remaining candy and refrigerate overnight. **Servings: 6-8**

Banana Split Dessert
No fountain treat can top this tasty dessert.

2 cups graham crackers, crushed	3 bananas, sliced
6 Tbsp. margarine, melted	1 large can crushed pineapple, drained
1 egg	1 large container whipped cream
1 stick margarine, softened	Pecan or walnuts pieces, sprinkle
2 cups powdered sugar	Maraschino cherries, halved
1 tsp. vanilla	

Preheat oven to 350°. Mix graham crackers and melted margarine in small bowl. Spread evenly into 13x9-inch baking pan; pat mixture down and bake 5 minutes. Let cool. Combine egg, margarine, powdered sugar and vanilla in bowl. Mix until fluffy and spread over graham cracker crust. Top with bananas and pineapple. Top with whipped cream and sprinkle with nuts and cherries. Refrigerate overnight.

Servings: 10-12

Before & After...

> "...This is a fresh, fruity dessert that sits lightly in the stomach after a heavy meal..."

Champagne Fruit Shrubs

Save your elegant meals for this easy-to-make and delicious dessert.

1 pt. fresh strawberries, sliced
1 container lime sherbert
1 bottle champagne, chilled

Place 1 or 2 scoops of lime sherbert in dessert cup. Sprinkle with strawberry slices and fill cup with champagne. **Servings: 6**

Cooking Tips: For best results, frost dessert cups in freezer before serving.

Twix Bars

Your first bite will guarantee you'll want more.

1 box Keeblers Club Crackers
1 cup graham cracker crumbs
3/4 cup brown sugar
1/2 cup white sugar
1/3 cup milk
1/2 cup margarine
2/3 cup peanut butter
1 cup chocolate chips

Grease 9x13 baking pan and line bottom with Keebler Crackers. In saucepan, combine graham cracker crumbs, brown and white sugars, milk and margarine. Boil 5 minutes, stirring. Pour mixture over Keebler Crackers. In separate saucepan, combine peanut butter with chocolate chips and melt, stirring well. Spread over crackers and refrigerate 1-2 hours. Cut into 1-inch squares. **Servings: 6 dozen**

> "...Be decadent and enjoy the flavor of this special chocolate recipe..."

Tiny Toffee Squares

For an immediate vanishing act, serve these tasty treats.

1 cup margarine
1 cup brown sugar
1 egg
1 tsp. vanilla
2 cups flour, sifted
1/2 tsp. salt
1/2 lb. sweet chocolate, melted
1 pkg. pecans, chopped

Preheat oven to 350°. Mix butter and brown sugar to creamy consistency in small bowl. Add egg and beat thoroughly. Mix in vanilla, sifted flour and salt. Spread batter in ungreased 10x15-inch baking pan and bake 25 minutes. Spread with melted chocolate and top with nuts. Cut into small squares. **Servings: 6 dozen**

Vanilla Tarte

This festive dish can be made ahead of time.

1 cup flour
1/2 cup margarine
1/2 cup pecans
1 large container whipped cream
8-oz. cream cheese
2 small pkgs. instant vanilla pudding mix
3 cups milk

Preheat oven to 375°. Mix flour, margarine and pecans in small bowl. Transfer to 9x12-inch baking pan; bake 15 minutes and let cool. In bowl, combine 1 cup whipped cream and cream cheese. Beat until fluffy. Drop by spoonfuls over pan mixture and spread with knife dipped in hot water. Mix pudding and milk in bowl and add remaining whipped cream. Beat until thickened. Spread over pan mixture and refrigerate overnight. **Servings: 6-8**

Brownie Drops

A blend of chocolate and nuts makes this a special treat.

2 pkgs. German sweet chocolate
1 Tbsp. butter or margarine
2 eggs
3/4 cup sugar
1/4 cup flour
1/4 tsp. baking powder
1/4 tsp. cinnamon
1/8 tsp. salt
1/2 tsp. vanilla
3/4 cup pecans, finely chopped

Preheat oven to 350°. Grease 9x13-inch baking sheet. Melt chocolate and butter over hot water in double boiler. Turn off heat and stir until cool. In bowl, beat eggs until foamy; slowly add sugar and beat until thickened. Blend in chocolate mixture, flour, baking powder, cinnamon and salt. Stir in vanilla and nuts. Drop by teaspoons onto baking sheet and bake 8-10 minutes. **Servings: 4 dozen**

Lemon Bars

These special treats can be made ahead of time and frozen for later occasions.

1 cup butter
2 cups flour, sifted
1/2 cup confectionary sugar, sifted
4 eggs, beaten
2 cups sugar
1/2 tsp. salt
2 tsp. lemon rind, grated
1/3 cup lemon juice
1 tsp. baking powder
1/4 cup flour, sifted

Preheat oven to 350°. Combine butter, 2 cups flour and confectionary sugar in bowl; mix until creamy. Press into ungreased 9x13-inch baking pan and bake 20 minutes. Combine beaten eggs, sugar, salt, lemon rind, lemon juice, baking powder and sifted flour in bowl; mix well. Spread over baked dough. Bake 30 minutes. Let cool and sprinkle with confectionary sugar. **Servings: 4 dozen**

Recipe Index...

Recipe Index...

All recipes have been cross-indexed to make them more accessible to the reader. They have been categorized several ways—by the type of meat and alternate meats listed in each recipe; by the type of dish (ie., stuffing, rice, gravy, etc.); and, in some cases, by the cooking method (ie., microwaved, pressure cooked, etc.). For our purposes, all recipes calling for venison meat can be prepared with elk, moose, antelope, caribou or deer.

Recipe Index...

Recipe Index...

Recipe Index...

Recipe Index...

Recipe Index...

Recipe Index...

Recipe Index...

Recipe Index...

Recipe Index...

Recipe Index...

Recipe Index...

Recipe Index...

Recipe Index...

Recipe Index...